A FABRIC OF DEFEAT

BRYANT SIMON

A Fabric of Defeat

The Politics of
South Carolina Millhands,
1910–1948

The University of North Carolina Press

Chapel Hill and London

The paper in this book meets the guidelines for permanence and
durability of the Committee on Production Guidelines for Book
Longevity of the Council on Library Resources.

Library of Congress Cataloging-in-Publication Data
Simon, Bryant. A fabric of defeat: the politics of South Carolina
millhands, 1910–1948 / Bryant Simon.
p. cm.   Includes bibliographical references and index.
ISBN 0-8078-2401-1 (cloth: alk. paper)
ISBN 0-8078-4704-6 (pbk.: alk. paper)
1. Textile workers—South Carolina—Political activity—History
—20th century. 2. Cotton textile industry—South Carolina
—History—20th century. 3. South Carolina—Politics and
government—1865–1950. 4. United States—Politics and
government—20th century.
HD8039.T42U6682   1998   97-30011
305.9′677′09757—dc21   CIP

Chapter 1 first appeared, in a somewhat different form, as "The
Appeal of Cole Blease of South Carolina: Race, Class, and Sex in
the New South," *Journal of Southern History* 62 (February 1996):
57–86. It is reprinted here by permission of the publisher.

02 01 00 99 98   5 4 3 2 1

CONTENTS

ILLUSTRATIONS

MAPS AND TABLES

Johnny 99, one of Bruce Springsteen's characters, laments, "I got debts no honest man can pay." Like this unemployed New Jersey autoworker, I owe a lot of institutions and a lot of people much more than I can ever pay back. But my debts have not made me, like they did Johnny 99, sad and desperate; I am instead grateful and humble.

The American Historical Association, Franklin and Eleanor Roosevelt Institute, Smithsonian Institution, University of North Carolina, California Institute of Technology and Ahmanson Foundation, and Institute of Southern Studies at the University of South Carolina all provided financial assistance for this project. In the last few years I have received generous support from the Department of History at the University of Georgia as well. Archivists and staff at the University of North Carolina, National Archives, Roosevelt Library, Heard Library, and, especially, South Caroliniana Library and South Carolina Division of Archives and History have been remarkably helpful and often downright indulgent.

Historical texts are, of course, never created in a vacuum or even in a library. They are the products of endless discussion. Fortunately from the moment I started this project, I have had countless opportunities to talk to insightful and generous scholars. Various colleagues and friends have read and commented on rough (sometimes very rough) drafts of chapters or parts of chapters. They have pointed out numerous mistakes and hundreds of overlooked citations and have helped me to clarify and refine my ideas. David Carlton, Josh Cole, Leon Fink, Lacy Ford, Gary Gerstle, Glenda Gilmore, Michael Goldberg, Lee Gutkind, Cindy Hahamovitch, Beth Hale, Martha Hodes, Bill McFeely, Nancy MacLean, and Phillip Stone have all left their mark on this book. Lewis Bateman and Pamela Upton of the University of North Carolina Press have also shaped, and helped to shape up, the manuscript. In addition, Jeffrey Lutzner, John Shanley, Rachel Harle-Shanley, Michael Kline, and Margo Borten Reardon have helped just by being there.

Right after finishing my dissertation at the University of North Carolina, I spent two years at the Division of the Humanities and Social Sciences at the

California Institute of Technology as an Ahmanson Postdoctoral Instructor. Made up of a contentious and creative mixture of economists, social scientists, cultural critics, and historians, the "division" at Caltech was a cauldron of competing ideas. This was an exciting place—the ideal environment in which to reexamine my own thoughts and rework my manuscript. With the help of Lance Davis, Morgan Kousser, Moshe Sulhovsky, Robert Rosenstone, Alice Wexler, and Susan Davis, that is exactly what I did.

I owe enormous debts to several other people. A mere mention would never repay them, but they are friends too gracious, too kind, and too good to ever ask for anything in return. So, really, these next few lines are for me. Doug Flamming read the entire manuscript not once, but twice. I could not ask for a more honest critic or honorable friend. Bill Deverell is also a perceptive reader and a sweet friend. He too has read the entire manuscript, but he read it in a sort of postmodern fashion: a chapter here and there, a line or two over e-mail, a paragraph over the phone, and a section via the fax. No matter what medium, he was always there. And then there is Peter Coclanis—a mentor, friend, and confidante for almost a decade. No one sees the world quite like he does, and just catching a glimpse of his vision has expanded my own view. He and Deborah, Angelo, and Alex know where they stand with me. Finally, I can scarcely think of doing history without the input of Jacquelyn Dowd Hall. She has guided me at every stage of my career, even before it was a career. I can never repay her for her time and caring; all that I can do is to try to give as much to my students as she gave to me.

My biggest debt is to my family: Susan, Bob, Brad, Sharon, Rebecca, and Max Simon. They have supported me for years, paying my rent and providing me with a series of Just Four Wheels vehicles. Mostly, they covered me with warm, thick blankets of love. My parents' quiet nobility showed me how to live, and everyday I chase the shadows of their lives.

And finally, to Ann Marie Reardon: while I spend my days thinking about the past, she shows me the promise of a beautiful future.

A FABRIC OF DEFEAT

Map 1. South Carolina Counties, 1929

Will Thompson was tall and thin, some might have said too thin. Usually he wore a pair of thinning, faded blue overalls that hung from his shoulders like clothes on a hanger, not touching anything until they hit the tops of his beat-up boots. In 1933 Will lived in a mill village in South Carolina's Horse Creek Valley. With his wife Rosamond he shared a four-room, company-owned yellow house resting on brick stilts. They had a nice-sized porch in the front and a big garden in the back. The house next to theirs was also yellow; it too had four rooms, brick stilts, a front porch, and a garden. So did the house next to it and the one across the narrow tree-lined street. All of the houses in the mill village, except for the mill owner's and the superintendent's, were exactly the same. Like Will, most of the people who lived in the identical houses worked from sunup to sundown in the three-story, red-brick textile mill just down the street. And like Will, all of the people in the mill village insisted that they were white.[1]

When Will and his friends from the yellow houses headed to town on Saturday afternoons, white people in starched collars and laced-trimmed dresses stared. It was not that they didn't recognize Will, or "his kind," as they might say. At a glance, seeing his thin frame, pale face, baggy overalls, and lint-filled hair, and hearing his coarse accent and throaty cough, they knew who he was. He was a "no-good, god-forsaken linthead." Will hated the way these uptown people glared at him and said that word "linthead." They seemed to spit it out rather than speak it. Still, he was proud to be a cotton mill worker.[2]

"I'd rather be a God forsaken linthead and live in a yellow company house," Will snarled, than be a farmer or a big man from Augusta, one of "those rich sons-of-bitches who own the mill and ride up and down the Valley in five thousand dollar automobiles." "A loom weaver through and through," that's what he was. He loved the way the mill hummed when everyone was working. The erratic, sometimes violent, rhythms of the village shot through him and energized him. The cacophony of the mill town, the "murmuring mass of humanity on the verge of filling the air with a concerted shout," was for him

A mill house in Graniteville in the mid-1930s.
(South Caroliniana Library, University of South Carolina)

just about the most melodious sound in the world. "It would break his heart," Rosamond told her sister, if Will had "to leave the Valley."

When a lockout closed the factory where he worked, Will reluctantly agreed to take a short trip to the country with Rosamond to visit her family. From the moment he arrived, he felt lost amid the rutty red clay tobacco roads, the cotton fields, and the unpainted, weather-beaten shacks. It was too quiet. The loudest sound was that of the crickets; the nearest neighbor was miles away, and the store—there was only one—was even farther. "The sight of the bare land, cultivated and fallow," it was written of Will, "with never a factory or a mill to be seen made him a little sick to his stomach." Within a day, he had to get back home to the crowded company town in the Horse Creek Valley, to the smokestacks, to the men and women sitting on the porches of their identical, four-room, yellow mill houses. For Will, the noisy streets, the roar of machinery, and the hacking coughs of the men and women sick from the lint-filled air of the factories were not the sounds of death but of the precarious, yet still vibrant life of a millworker.

Will Thompson is an invention of Erskine Caldwell's imagination. He is a fiction but not a fraud. He is a composite of the millhands Caldwell knew in South Carolina.[3] Like many of the more than 300,000 people in the state in 1930 living near the mills of Spartanburg and Columbia, and small towns and

An overview of a mill village in Newberry, ca. 1910.
(South Caroliniana Library, University of South Carolina)

railroad stops from Ninety-Six to Pelzer, the fictional Will Thompson was born in a mill town, baptized in a mill church, and educated for a few years in a mill school. He was a millworker, a permanent industrial laborer, deeply committed to this way of life. Caldwell's Will resembles the contemporary novelist Dorothy Allison's relations, who were mill people from Greenville. Neither villains nor saints, Caldwell's characters and neighbors like Allison's cousins were real people, capable of meanness and tenderness, grace and awkwardness, violence and heroism, rage and nobility. "My people," Allison recently recalled, "were not remarkable. . . . We were ordinary, but even so we were mythical. We were the *they* everyone talks about—the ungrateful poor." [4] The *they* that Allison writes about were not a biologically determined "social type," as sociologist Jeannette Nichols suggested in 1924, but they were a readily identifiable group. [5] South Carolinians recognized mill people on sight as distinct from others. They dressed differently and talked differently and worked in different places and lived in different houses. They were not country folk or city folk, they were mill people. And that is how most mill people saw themselves, not as farmers who temporarily lost their way, but as millhands, members of the largest occupational group of the southern working class.

What follows are stories about Dorothy Allison's family and the Will Thompsons of South Carolina. They are mostly stories about politics. Whereas other scholars have focused on the shop floor and the community lives of southern mill people, on union organizing and cultures of resistance in the region, this

"The mill" in Graniteville, 1935.
(South Caroliniana Library, University of South Carolina)

account examines the politics of mill people from World I to World War II, or between 1910 and 1948.[6] Defining politics broadly, the stories in this volume reveal what the political lives of workers tell us about their private and public lives as well as the larger political culture.

The cotton mill world of South Carolina provides perhaps the clearest vantage point in the region from which to consider working-class politics in the New South. Nowhere else has the textile industry held such a commanding position in the social structure. In 1930 cotton mills accounted for more than two-thirds of the value added to the state's manufacturing output and employed an even larger percentage of industrial workers. Tradition and racism dictated that almost all of these jobs would go to whites. Like other southern states, citizenship in South Carolina was also reserved for whites. But unlike other states in the region, the disfranchisement of African Americans that took place in South Carolina in 1895 did not rob poor white males, including propertyless millworkers, of the right to vote in the all-important Democratic Party primary. By 1914 nearly one out of every seven Palmetto State Democrats lived in a mill village; fifteen years later, one in five voters did so.[7] As a result, textile workers and their families possessed considerable electoral clout in South Carolina.

Introduction

"Let me tell you something a lot of people never realize," a fictional Pittsburgh laborer told his nephew, "If you are making a living in this country you're in politics."[8] The same could be said about South Carolina mill people. They were definitely *in* politics. Policy decisions shaped their lives at work and at home. Workers, in turn, held up placards at campaign rallies, badgered candidates at stump meetings, walked off the job to influence government policy, demanded that management recognize their citizenship rights, signed petitions, wrote letters to politicians, put up pictures of the president, and turned out in droves on election day. They cast their votes for candidates they liked and against those they disliked. Because millworkers represented a quarter of the electorate, politicians sought their support, and, as a result, laborers' ideas echoed through wider discussions about the meaning of public power in the state. Learning about the political "in-ness" of workers, therefore, reveals not only what working people cared about and valued, but also the shifting social and economic climate of the times.

The political participation of South Carolina workers—their multilayered political *in-ness*—challenges narrow conceptions of the meaning of politics. Politics, to some, is the study of politicians. To others, politics begins and ends at the polling station, and political history entails careful examination of electoral behavior and coalitions. As revealing as these aspects of politics are, the actions of elites and voting returns are not the whole of politics, at least not as practiced by South Carolina workers. For these people, politics also involved the implementation and consequences of policy along with the formation and interpretation of law. The rules of the game—voter registration, the structures of political parties, and the composition of government agencies—framed their sense of politics as well.

Working-class politics, in addition, played out on a discursive level. Millhands and manufacturers, townspeople and farmers battled over the meaning of the symbols and phrases that represented and legitimized power relationships. The political activities of South Carolina workers, therefore, extended from the polling station to the workplace to the company store to the kitchen table. They stretched across the breadth of public contests for power, reaching from tense electoral skirmishes for control of the machinery of the state to more subtle, yet still intense, conflicts over the "power to define categories of analysis and social understanding."[9]

Although white Democrats had stripped virtually all African Americans of the right to vote in the 1890s, blacks continued to play a central role in the political imagination of South Carolina laborers. Even when barred from the polls, blacks entered into white politics, sometimes subtly and at other times overtly, influencing every gesture, word, emotion, and idea. Whites, as a result, did not fashion their ideas about power, race, and other matters in isolation. African Americans, if only as the "other," were always present.[10]

The broad range of political engagement demonstrated by South Carolina workers offers a wide perspective on working-class self-expression or identity. Identity reflects how people make sense of the world and of their place in it. It is about how they assign blame and credit for their well-being, label the past and present, define basic rights and government responsibilities, and give meaning to such categories of understanding as race, class, gender, and sexuality. Because identity stems from day-to-day experiences and the interpretations of these experiences, it is never static. As economic, social, and political conditions change, new meanings are constructed and old ways of thinking are transformed. Identity, in other words, is always in flux, perpetually being made and remade. This means that people's ideas about right and wrong, virtue and vice, race and class, gender and sex are constantly changing. Rarely, however, were mill people's shifting notions about politics and society taken seriously, except perhaps by the politicians who sought their votes.

Southern historians typically lump mill people together with other poor white southerners, small farmers, tenants, day laborers, and sharecroppers into the grab-bag category of plain white folks or yeomen.[11] But mill people, the Will Thompsons of the region, lived in a different setting and experienced the world differently from their country or city cousins. As a result, they had a separate identity. In analyzing politics and political ideas, again, scholars generally erase these differences: all poor whites are seen as the same, as virulent white supremacists. Whether described as venal or vicious, white workers and others, according to these accounts, engaged in politics for one purpose only—to keep African Americans out of power and to safeguard the supposed privileges of whiteness. Writing in 1949, V. O. Key, this century's most influential student of southern politics, argued that poor whites were so thoroughly ignorant and brutally racist that they responded more to hollow appeals to white supremacy than to positive economic initiatives and well-intentioned social programs. Key assumed that the only legitimate form of class politics in the New South was biracial politics along the lines of populism—C. Vann Woodward's version of populism to be precise.[12] If white workers had better understood their world, he suggests, they would not have allowed the artificial issue of race to disrupt the natural alliance of southern have-nots—black and white—across the color line.[13]

Without coming out and saying it, Key maintained that the southern working class suffered from a bad case of false consciousness. Infected with the disease of racism, millhands—his argument goes—acted as the pawns of their captors, squandering their votes on an endless parade of do-nothing demagogues, who invariably opposed economic policies that could have freed them from their village prisons of poverty. Wage earners mistakenly put their racial identity ahead of their class identity. This is how the intersection of race, class, and politics in the New South is almost always portrayed, as false consciousness, and only "ignorant," "simple," "uneducated," or "irrational" actors could possibly behave this way.[14]

This book looks at the political identity of the mill people of the New South from a different perspective. It shows that Jim Crow's reign generated political and social identities that were much more nuanced, and even more insidious, than the two-dimensional world depicted by Key and his followers. For one thing, focusing only on racial identity flattens the identity of white southern workers; it says that they were racists, and that is it. No doubt, South Carolina millhands invested a great deal of themselves in the privileges of their "whiteness," which was, after all, their ticket both to mill work and the polling station.[15] Yet mill people had more tangled, multilayered identities. They were not simply racists. They were also men and women, fathers and mothers, children, cousins, aunts, uncles, nieces, and nephews. Many had been farmers before going to work in the mills. They gambled, prayed, drank, sang, knitted, read books and newspapers, canned vegetables, and played baseball. Thousands joined labor unions and a few signed on with the Ku Klux Klan. These different identities and relationships complicated workers' political ideas and outlooks.

The politics of South Carolina millhands were not only about the politicization of "whiteness" and workers choosing their racial identity over their class identity. Rather, they were about "simultaneity," a subtle overlapping of multiple identities and ideas about the state, public power, class, gender, and race.[16] All of these viewpoints got twisted together all of the time so that class identity was experienced and expressed in racial and gendered terms, race was experienced and expressed in class and gendered terms, and so on. Race, therefore, was never the only issue that mattered to South Carolina textile laborers. Throughout the 1920s and 1930s workers, in fact, resisted well-crafted appeals to white supremacy and put their shop floor and economic interests above all else. During this time, white racism remained central to the politics of South Carolina millhands, but it was not always salient in the same way.

As crucial as identity was to the politics of South Carolina millhands, it was not the whole story. Workers' views of the world would change again and again, and their consciousness would shift back and forth along the axes of race, class, and gender, but ultimately their vision of fair play and a just society clashed with other people's visions of fair play and justice. Conflict between groups animated state politics and made it hard for millhands to prevail at the polling station and in the legislature. So, too, did the structures of power. Despite impressive displays of political imagination and resourcefulness, textile workers could not knock down all of the political, economic, and social barriers in their way. In the end, demographics, the rules of the political game, and legislative apportionment stacked the deck against South Carolina millhands, making it hard for them to control the state's political agenda.

The story that follows is told in three acts. Chapter 1 sets the stage. First there is a double murder, and then the action moves around the figure of Coleman Livingston Blease. During the summer of 1914, in a typical scene, millhands skipped work and spent all day outside in the shimmering heat to listen to Blease. Shouting and whispering, joking and haranguing, the perennial candidate railed against compulsory school laws and child labor legislation and vowed to uphold white supremacy. Millhands continued to clap and holler long after Blease had exited stage right.

Blease embodied the politics of male millworkers—men were the only ones who could vote—at the beginning of the story. As first-generation industrial laborers, these men feared that the move from farm to factory threatened to emasculate them, reducing them to the status of dependents, a category in their minds reserved for women, children, and African Americans, not proud white men. Blease promised to uphold their manhood by blocking progressive reforms and bolstering the fortress of white supremacy. Before 1925 millworker politics stressed race and gender concerns ahead of economic issues.

The second act charts workers' retreat away from the politics of Bleasism. Life in the mill villages began to change in 1925. Pinched by falling profits, textile manufacturers escalated the pace of production, laid off thousands, and slashed wages. Workers tagged these changes the "stretchout" and likened them to slavery. In a series of strikes in 1929, textile laborers pressed for their emancipation on the picket line. After losing, many of them turned to electoral politics to redress their grievances. As they did, the bond between Blease and workers began to loosen, and the Great Depression weakened it even further. Then came the New Deal and proof that the government—in this case, the federal government—had a positive role to play in workers' day-to-day lives.

September 1934 marks the climax of the second act. The events of that month showed just how far South Carolina workers had traveled. Rocked by the economic collapse and aroused by Franklin D. Roosevelt's oratory, most millhands shook off the last vestiges of Bleasite antistatism in favor of their own brand of New Deal liberalism for whites only. When the mill owners refused to recognize their self-proclaimed rights as American citizens, 55,000 mill laborers joined the national General Textile Strike. While picket lines lengthened and violence spread, gubernatorial candidates barnstormed across the state. Once again Blease was on the stump, attacking government action and celebrating whiteness. This time, however, millhands did not yell as loud or cheer as long as they had in the past. Most backed Blease's opponent Olin D. Johnston. Addressing striking millhands, Johnston shouted, "I'm one of you." Indeed, he was. Born on a farm, Johnston went into the mills when he was eleven years old and stayed there until his teens. "I understand your problems," he told the crowd. Without mentioning African Americans, he vowed to "end the economic slavery of the masses" and place restraints on business, while promoting welfare programs, labor legislation, and trade unionism. Textile workers swept Johnston to victory over their erstwhile hero Blease. In so doing, they revealed that they had placed their economic interests ahead of other concerns. With one of their own in the governor's mansion, millhands expected a New Deal in the factories and company towns of South Carolina.

The third act tracks the slow death of this vision. Once in office, Johnston tried to tilt government policies in labor's favor. Yet at the close of his four-year term, the balance of power remained angled toward capital. Armed with the ballot and bolstered by an ally in the governor's office, millworkers succeeded in mitigating a few of the harshest aspects of industrial life, but they had trouble remaking the world in their own class-tinged image of the New Deal.

In 1938 the window of opportunity opened by the New Deal and Johnston's victory was slammed shut by Senator "Cotton Ed" Smith, a man *Time* dubbed a "conscientious objector to the Twentieth Century."[17] Shouting the slogans of white supremacy, Smith fended off Johnston's Roosevelt-backed bid to take his U.S. Senate seat. Workers drew a stark lesson from their defeats. Class politics, many concluded, promised more than it could deliver.

The final scene looks ahead to the postwar era. Once again, the political identity of workers changed. Bruised by several rounds of battle with the state's economic elite and frightened by the organizing efforts of African Americans, millhands jettisoned the politics of class that had unified them during the New Deal years in favor of the politics of white supremacy. They emerged as foot soldiers in the army of massive resistance, some five or ten years before the region officially declared war against the courts and the federal government. Still, the activism of the New Deal echoed through South Carolina's political discourse. Even as the rest of the nation drifted to the right during the cold war, South Carolina politicians, aware of the electoral muscle of the millhands, avoided for a time direct attacks on labor.

Then in the 1960s came the highways, the strips malls, the drive-ins, and the two-story suburban homes with carports on culs-de-sac. The four-room yellow houses on brick stilts disappeared and with them went the Will Thompsons of South Carolina, the proud millworkers. Soon after, the mill world slowly faded into memory, into stories.

CHAPTER ONE

The Man for Office
Is Cole Blease

 Like Will Thompson, Joe Childers was a white millworker. A newspaper reporter described him as a "respectable laboring man" with a "good reputation."[1] On the night of March 27, 1912, Childers met Joe Brinson and Frank Whisonant, both African Americans, near the train station in the tiny up-country town of Blacksburg, South Carolina. The meeting proved tragic.

What happened that night among Childers, Brinson, and Whisonant will never be known. Depending on who told the story, Childers either asked Brinson and Whisonant to get him a pint—or a quart—of whiskey or the two African Americans badgered the innocent white man until he finally agreed to buy liquor from them. The three men got drunk. According to Childers, Brinson and Whisonant ordered him to drink all of the whiskey. Fearing for his safety, he drank as much as he could as fast as he could, but he could not drain the bottle. As Childers guzzled the rust-colored rotgut—or maybe it was clear white lightning—Brinson and Whisonant taunted him; when he did not finish, they grew quarrelsome. They forced him into a cemetery and made him take off his clothes. N. W. Hardin, a local attorney, recounted what he heard happened next: "They [Brinson and Whisonant] drew their pistols, cocked them and told Childers to open his mouth, and keep it open, that if he closed it, he would be shot on the spot." Then, in Hardin's version, Brinson made Childers perform oral sex on Whisonant.[2]

Following this consensual or coerced sexual act, or what the press dubbed the "unmentionable act"—the phrase commonly used to talk about the rape or alleged rape of a white woman by an African American man—Childers "escaped." He ran straight to the police. The law officers quickly apprehended Brinson and Whisonant and charged them with selling liquor, highway robbery, carrying a concealed weapon, assault with a deadly weapon, and sodomy. The local magistrate fined the two men twenty dollars each. Some thought that the penalty, which was roughly the equivalent of three weeks' wages for a textile worker, was too lenient. Regardless, Brinson and Whisonant had no money and went to jail.

The next morning E. D. Johnson of Blacksburg got up early and walked to the well in the center of the town square. Johnson discovered that the rope used to pull up the water bucket was missing. Puzzled, he looked around; his eyes eventually stopped at the sturdy stone and brick jail. The front door was knocked down. Johnson peered inside and saw a broken padlock and an open cell. He must have known what had happened. He ran to tell the mayor. It did not take the men long to find the missing rope and the missing prisoners.

"The job," wrote a reporter, "had been done in a most workman-like manner." Brinson and Whisonant's cold, stiff bodies dangled from the rafters of the blacksmith shop located just behind the jail. Bound hand and foot, both victims had been gagged, one with cotton, the other with rope. The killers had not wanted them to scream.

Word of the lynching spread through the area, but the crime did not bring together, in the words of a student of southern vigilantism, Arthur Raper, "plantation owners and white tenants, mill owners and textile workers."[3] Instead, the killings stirred discord. "Law and order," worried the editor of the *Gaffney Ledger*, "has been flaunted" as "passions [have become] inflamed and reason dethroned." "Every good citizen," he was certain, "deplored the crime." The newsman, however, had no sympathy for the dead. "Those were two bad negroes who were lynched in Blacksburg," he conceded. "But," he added, "those who outraged them became worse whites."[4]

No one publicly named the "worse whites."[5] Many people, especially in Blacksburg, speculated that a mob—totaling as many as a dozen or as few as six men—drove into town or rode in on horseback from the mill villages of Gaffney, Cherokee Falls, Hickory Grove, and King's Mountain. Others insisted that the killers were from Blacksburg. Though questions about where the murderers resided lingered, there was little doubt about what they did for a living. "My idea," wrote N. W. Hardin, "is that as Childers was a factory operative, the lynching was done by the operatives of the surrounding mills, trying to take care of their class." If millworkers committed the crime, townspeople were sure where the larger blame for the murders lay. "Some of the d—d fools are already saying," reported Hardin, "this is Bleasism." The *Gaffney Ledger* echoed this view. "If a majority of the people of South Caro-

A lynching in the South Carolina upcountry sometime before World War I. According to John Hammond Moore ("Carnival of Blood: Dueling, Lynching, and Murder in South Carolina, 1880-1920," unpublished manuscript), this picture probably depicts the lynching of Joe Brinson and Frank Whisonant in Blacksburg, March 1912. (Historical Center of York County, York, South Carolina)

lina want Blease and Bleasism," the editor wrote of the lynching, "they will have it in spite of those who desire law and order."[6]

Bleasism was the term used to designate the political uprising of first-generation South Carolina millworkers. This electoral surge took its name from its standard-bearer, Coleman Livingston Blease. "Coley," as his loyal backers called him, had occupied the governor's office for more than a year and was gearing up for his reelection drive when Brinson and Whisonant were killed. Although Blease did not play any role in the murders, commentators who linked him to the disorder in Blacksburg were, at least in part, right. Blease's racially charged, antireform campaigns and his irreverent leadership style inflamed many of the same cultural, economic, and sexual anxieties that ultimately led some working-class white men to lynch African American men.

Despite the homoerotic overtones of the meeting at the railway station, the killers must have decided that Childers was "innocent," that he had been "raped," and that the crime symbolized more than one shocking evening in a cemetery. The imagined rape of the millworker Joe Childers may have represented in microcosm the assaults on white manhood posed by industrialization. Even more than the rape of a white woman, the rape of this white man by another man graphically represented male millworkers' deepest fears of emasculation. That the perpetrators were African Americans magnified the offense. The alleged sexual attack not only erased the color line but also placed an African American man "on top," in a position of power over a white man. A few male textile workers appear to have made a connection between how the "rape" of Childers feminized him and how industrialization stripped them of control over their own labor and that of their families, and thus their manhood. Some southern white wage-earning men apparently felt that industrialization could potentially place them in the position of a woman: vulnerable and dependent, powerless at home and in public.

By murdering Joe Brinson and Frank Whisonant, the killers tried to reassert their manhood.[7] The same fierce determination to uphold white supremacy and patriarchy that led to the Blacksburg lynching propelled Cole Blease's election campaigns. The same sexual and psychological fears that drew the lynch mob to the jail that spring night in 1912 brought many more men to the polls a few months later to vote for Blease. Middle-class South Carolinians—professionals and members of the emerging commercial elite—also connected the lynching in Cherokee County with Blease's political success. They argued that both stemmed from the collapse of "law and order" in the mill villages and together demonstrated the need for reform.[8]

The anxieties that fueled Bleasism and triggered the Blacksburg lynching were not confined to South Carolina or, for that matter, to the American

The Man for Office Is Cole Blease

South. Across the United States and indeed the globe, the reconfiguration of productive landscapes—the shift from fields to factories—jarred gender relations. Industrialization triggered an almost-universal crisis of male identity. In South Carolina, the crisis of masculinity among first-generation millhands aggravated race and gender relations and eventually spilled over into politics, splitting the state along class lines.[9]

South Carolina's turn-of-the-century mill-building crusade and white supremacy campaigns set the stage for the political emergence of Cole Blease. In 1880 there were a dozen mills in South Carolina. Twenty years later the number of textile factories had jumped to 115; in 1920 there were 184. As the mills multiplied, the labor force changed. At first, the mills employed mostly widowed women and children, but as the industry grew and the region's rural economy stagnated, more and more men took jobs in the factories. As early as 1910, two-thirds of all South Carolina millworkers were men, and, because of the state's political makeup, most were eligible to vote.[10]

Industrialization also gave new meaning to South Carolina's traditional geographic divide. A natural fall line, stretching from the North Carolina border in Chesterfield County to the Georgia boundary in Aiken County, cuts across the state, slicing it into two sections commonly known as the upcountry and the low country. A narrow band of sandhills in between is usually referred to as the midlands. More than topography separates these sections.[11] During the antebellum era, small farms and a smattering of plantations dotted the upcountry's rolling red clay hills, while factories in the fields exploiting African slave labor dominated the marshlands and reedy swamps of the low country.[12] These sharply contrasting economic patterns persisted long after the carnage of the Civil War and the drama of Reconstruction. Although the defeat of the Confederacy destroyed the system of slavery, it also accelerated the transformation of the South Carolina upcountry. Because of the area's access to credit and its abundance of fasting-moving streams, mill building—the thrust of New South industrialization—was concentrated above the fall line.

By the time Blease started to campaign for office in 1906, more than 80 percent of South Carolina's textile mills were located in the upcountry, half in Greenville, Spartanburg, and Anderson Counties alone.[13] The modernization of the state's economy produced "unbalanced growth." Growth encouraged more growth, while atrophy bred stagnation. The turn-of-the-century mill-building boom, in other words, benefited the counties of the upcountry, while it skipped over the low country. After this, the state was divided between the relatively modern, industrial, and predominantly white areas of the

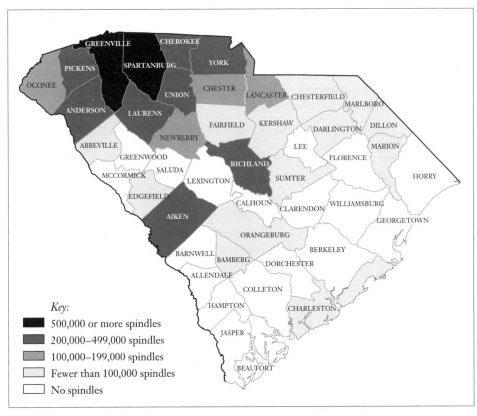

Map 2. Textile Spindleage in South Carolina, by County, 1929
(Adapted from Hall et al., *Like a Family*, xxvi–xxvii)

upcountry and the increasingly stagnant, rural, and overwhelmingly African American sections of the low country.[14]

Meanwhile, unlike what happened in other southern states, South Carolina lawmakers did not cut poor white males, including propertyless upcountry millworkers, out of electoral politics when they put in place the Jim Crow order in the 1890s.[15] But that did not make the state democratic, not even for whites. Besides almost ending black suffrage, the state's 1895 constitution established the basic rules of politics in South Carolina for the next fifty years. Disfranchisement ensured whites a virtual monopoly on state power, but the constitution did not guarantee that all white citizens would be represented equally. For one thing, citizenship was not portable. Voters had to remain in the same place, even the same house, for one year in order to cast a ballot. This provision penalized white millhands, in particular, who in the early twentieth century took advantage of a regional labor shortage by constantly moving around looking for the best deal for themselves and their families. Even when male millhands did stay put, the polls often closed before the end of their shifts, making it impossible for them to vote. The apportionment of the general assembly also diluted democracy in South Carolina. Based, in part, on geography rather than population, it provided rural citizens with a disproportionate amount of political power, especially when compared to up-country millworkers.[16]

While the South Carolina Constitution imposed limits on Palmetto State democracy, it also gave the Democratic Party—the only party that mattered after Reconstruction—the right to determine who could and could not vote in its all-important primary. After a long debate, state Democrats in the 1890s decided to extend the suffrage to all white men over the age of twenty-one, regardless of wealth or education. The constitutional poll tax, moreover, applied only to the rather meaningless general election. As a result of these rules and the racial composition of the textile workforce, the expanding mill population possessed considerable electoral strength. By 1915 nearly one out of every seven Palmetto State Democrats lived in a mill village.[17] Affirming at the same time the ideal of herrenvolk democracy, that is, of white political equality, the state's emerging political culture also provided poor whites with a powerful ideological lever. Despite constitutional checks on democracy, this myth defined citizenship by race and implicitly put forth the idea that all white men were equal. In the years to come, white millworkers repeatedly demanded that elites honor the tenets of herrenvolk democracy by treating them with the respect and dignity that equal citizens deserved.[18]

Although Blease's mentor, the quasi-populist and racist leader of the state's disfranchising forces, Benjamin R. "Pitchfork Ben" Tillman, had little use for industrial laborers—he once referred to them as that "damned factory class"—Cole Blease himself recognized the electoral harvest to be reaped in the textile communities.[19] As soon as Blease turned away from a career in law to one in politics, he focused his attention on the mill hills around his home-town of Newberry. He spent afternoons and evenings in front of company stores and at nearby roadhouses, and he joined the clubs, fraternal organizations, and brotherhoods that textile workers belonged to. Sometime early in this century it was said, and no one disputed it, that Blease knew more mill-hands by name than anyone else in the state.[20] He turned this familiarity into votes. In 1890 he was elected to represent Newberry County in the South Carolina General Assembly. Twice, in 1910 and 1912, Blease triumphed in the governor's race. On a number of other occasions he won enough votes to earn a spot in statewide second primaries or runoff elections. In most of these contests, millhands made up the bulk of his support.[21]

Male textile workers did not just cast their ballots for Blease, they were fiercely devoted to him. When he went up to the mill hills, poking fun at elites, issuing chilling warnings about black rapists, and slamming "Yankee-ridden" unions, overflow crowds greeted him with "tornado[es] of shrieks, yells, and whistles." Mill people named their children after Blease, hung his picture over their mantels, and wrote songs and poems about him. "If you want a good chicken," an upcountry bard was heard to say, "fry him in grease. If you want a good governor get Cole Blease." When a reporter asked a textile worker why he supported Blease, the man snapped, "I know I ain't goin' to vote for no aristocrat." Another millhand once hollered, "Coley, I'd vote fer you even if you was to steal my mule tonight."[22]

Millworkers' allegiance to Cole Blease has long baffled historians. Because he promoted white supremacy, derided national unions, rejected child labor restrictions, and lambasted compulsory school legislation, scholars have accused him of being "a feather-legged demagogue" with "no program for the benefit of the factory workers." Historians have contended that the reform policies Blease opposed would have saved workers from the misery and poverty of the mill village, but they did not care. They preferred a politician who spouted off about race to one who promoted reform. How, historians have wondered, could such perplexing behavior be explained? Ignorance and false consciousness were the answers most often given. Spellbound by Coley's saber-rattling rhetoric, this argument goes, uneducated millhands turned their backs on their natural class interests and a logical alliance with African American laborers and farmers, voting instead with their hateful, racist hearts.[23]

Rather than contextualizing Bleasism, this view measures the electoral behavior of South Carolina workers against an ahistoric ideal of biracial class collaboration and finds it wanting. In addition, it implicitly suggests that working people were too irrational, even too stupid, to understand the world they lived in. Yet examined against the backdrop of the rapid industrialization of the South Carolina upcountry, Bleasism, as David Carlton has shown, looks quite different. From this angle, it represented not working-class false consciousness or foolishness, but the politicization of cultural and social tensions between mill and town—in other words, the rational, albeit sometimes unsavory, response of tradition-bound white southerners to the forces of modernization.[24]

New South entrepreneurs preached a gospel of regional renewal through mill building. Converting people to this creed first required convincing them that industrialization would not lead the region down the road to ruin. Promoters promised "that a combination of the social controls of 'cotton mill paternalism' and the operatives' 'Anglo-Saxon' virtues would spare South Carolina the turmoil and class enmities of northern and British cities."[25] This faith in social harmony, however, quickly faded. Well before the close of South Carolina's mill-building spree, many city and town dwellers concluded that, instead of civilizing rural-born workers, the mill villages actually fostered disorder. Alarmed by reports of whiskey drinking, pool playing, prostitution, cock fighting, and gambling in the mill villages, church and club meetings across the upcountry buzzed with warnings about the cotton mill "problem."

Middle-class South Carolinians blamed poor white parents — not industrialization — for village lawlessness. Accusing mill mothers and fathers of being drunk and lazy, dirty and uneducated, and worse still of inculcating their innocent children with these destructive values, New South boosters feared that their dreams of prosperity and harmony would turn into an endless nightmare of poverty and conflict unless they did something. Through public health programs, child labor restrictions, and compulsory school attendance legislation, would-be reformers sought to "save" the children of millworkers by intervening in their upbringing and teaching them the virtues of law and order. That would take care of the next generation. As for the present, other reformers suggested that suffrage be limited to those white men who had already learned the lessons of discipline and deference, sobriety and thrift. Voting restrictions and interventionist reforms, therefore, became the guiding principles of South Carolina progressivism.[26]

Mill laborers resisted the progressive impulse. Most, for instance, opposed child labor legislation. Why, some questioned, would mill parents want their children to work long hours in a hot lint-filled factory? One answer given, not by workers, but by reformers and later by historians, suggested that laborers were irrational, even mean. They just did not care about their children. But looking at millhands' responses to reform, again, against the backdrop of industrialization, other explanations come to light. Money was part of the reason laborers objected to child labor laws. Because of the southern textile industry's traditionally low wages, cotton mill families could not survive on one or even two paychecks. Often, children's wages kept families out of poverty. Workers also rejected middle-class reforms for ideological reasons.

"Blease's supporters," David Carlton has written, "were spiritual, if not intellectual, heirs of an older America whose citizens viewed all concentrations of power as dangerous, and all government bureaucracies as corrupt and self-interested." Millhands opposed progressive reforms because they viewed them as attacks on traditional notions of independence. Like English Luddites, South Carolina workers were, in Carlton's view, at war with the modern world, and they voted for Blease because he vowed "to wreck the social machinery being created by the middle classes."[27]

To be sure, Carlton's contextualizing of Bleasism makes the politics of first-generation millhands seem less irrational and more understandable. Yet as the Blacksburg lynching indicated, there were still other issues behind workers' support for Cole Blease's antireform agenda. By reexamining Bleasism, this time through the overlapping lenses of sexuality, gender, race, and class, some of these other factors can be seen. Race, it becomes clear, was not the only issue that mattered to first-generation South Carolina textile workers; neither were notions of traditional independence nor the passions of antimodernism.

As the grisly Blacksburg lynching suggests, the attitudes of male workers combined concerns about race, class, and gender. They reflected private fears about declining parental authority as well as public qualms about the actions of elected officials and self-appointed reformers. To male millhands, politics was about power—in other words, about patriarchy and suffrage, economic autonomy and white supremacy. The public and private were closely linked, never really as far apart for workers as they have been for historians.[28] First generation South Carolina industrial workers were certainly committed to independence, as Carlton makes clear, but to most white men this meant more than living unencumbered by the modernizing state. Instead, their concepts of independence mixed together shifting ideas about citizenship, race, economic autonomy, and masculinity.

To the yeomen of the South Carolina upcountry, the ancestors of mill men and Blease backers, independence meant, above all else, political equality. Decades before the Nullification Crisis of 1832, planters and yeomen had reached an accord. They agreed to make slavery the law of the land and to scrap all but the most minimal property qualifications for voting, thereby enfranchising the vast majority of white men. Race and sex, not class, fixed the boundaries of citizenship. At the same time, ideas about suffrage and exclusion took on ideological dimensions that stretched far beyond the public arena of electoral politics. To be independent was to have the right to vote or, in other words, to be white and male. Those who could not vote were deemed to be dependent and unmanly. In antebellum South Carolina, women, children, and African Americans made up the bulk of the state's "dependents," and self-serving white men argued that nature determined the rigid divide between voters and nonvoters, independents and dependents. White men were enfranchised because of their God-given superiority over women, children, and blacks.

The Man for Office Is Cole Blease

Domination in the political realm justified domination of women and children at home and African Americans in all aspects of life. White male notions of independence, therefore, were based not only on the right of all white men to vote but also on patriarchal control over the affairs of the household.[29]

Broad claims about the natural superiority of white men over Africans and women did not, however, eliminate conflict among whites. Poor whites always feared that the state's traditional leaders, wealthy planters and businessmen, would someday attempt to snatch their rights away from them. They voiced this distrust by calling elites "aristocrats." Yeomen defined aristocrats as enemies of democracy—rich white men who might, at any time, try to rob ordinary white people of the ballot and, therefore, their independence.

Slavery also shaped ideas about independence. Living day in and day out near enslaved people of African descent intensified, as Lacy Ford has explained, yeomen's "fear[s] of submission and dependence." Unwilling to be reduced to the racialized and feminized status of dependents, white male South Carolinians clung to the right to vote, or to what one man called "the only true badge of the freeman."[30]

Antebellum notions about independence, masculinity, and suffrage were also enmeshed with ideas about control over the household and the economy. Before the Civil War, again according to Lacy Ford, South Carolina yeomen viewed the world through the prism of "an inherited 'country-republican' ideology." Combined with the vote, they believed that the surest guarantee of personal independence was a political economy based on "widespread ownership of productive property." If yeomen had assets—principally land, draft animals, farm implements, and a house—the aristocrats could not dictate to them, telling them what to do and how to vote. They would, as a result, be virtuous, independent citizens. But divorced from the means of production, white men, whether or not they had the right to vote, could easily be reduced to dependency—that is, placed under the control of others and in the same vulnerable position as women, children, and slaves. Reduced to this status, they would be defenseless against an almost certain aristocratic attack on their social and political privileges. Worst yet, they would no longer be independent men, entitled to dominate at home.[31]

Emancipation threw the intellectual universe of white yeomen into chaos. Shortly afterward, suffrage—that coveted distinction of independence and masculinity—was defined by sex alone. Not only did Reconstruction mark the temporary end of the white monopoly on public power, but it also challenged prevailing ideas about white manhood. In this confusing new environment, some wealthy whites, usually low-country elites, courted the votes of African Americans, implicitly acknowledging the manhood of ex-slaves.[32] Other whites—some rich, some poor—seemed unable to think about suffrage without also thinking about interracial sex.[33] Freedmen, they were convinced, interpreted political equality as a license to assault white women. White men responded with fury, especially after the Republican Party abandoned its Reconstruction policies in 1877. Through intimidation at the polls, ballot box stuffing, and late-night lynchings, South Carolina Democrats attempted to rob African Americans of the right to vote and emasculate them in the process. Yet neither subterfuge nor violence worked, at least not entirely. African American men continued to vote well into the 1890s. Finally, a new, carefully crafted South Carolina constitution, adopted in 1895, all but eliminated black voting in the state. Suffrage was once again defined by race and sex, and most white men over the age of twenty-one were entitled to vote.[34]

Although the new constitution affirmed the political privileges of whiteness and maleness, the economic world of the yeomen was under attack. Beginning in the 1850s, the railroad crept into the South Carolina upcountry, bringing with it the possibilities and pitfalls of a market economy. Growing inequality, widely fluctuating cotton prices, and falling rates of property ownership followed. Nonetheless, poor and middling white farmers held on to their country republican vision of independence, but the changing relationships of production forced some shifts in this ideology.[35]

Whereas the antebellum conception of independence highlighted property and ownership, in the postbellum era ideas about independence rested on control over others and personal autonomy. No matter how much the market economy encroached on their lives, many plain white folks either owned a small parcel of land or worked as free tenants. Either way, they controlled the means of production and worked free from the supervision of others. White husbands and fathers continued to insist that they were the boss and that their wives and children had to follow their commands. While women and children made vital contributions to the household economy, cooking and sewing, picking and hoeing, men placed themselves in charge of growing cotton, the cash crop. In the market-driven world of the New South, money, more than land or anything else, was the nexus of power. By defining their economic activities as those associated with money, men tried to reassert their control over the household in a changing world, even as they lost their land and fell into debt.[36]

As the propertied economic independence of poor whites slowly slipped away, men began to stress with a new sense of urgency the privileges of whiteness and the virtues of patriarchy—of male control over dependent women and children. Plain folks insisted, perhaps more than ever before, that women, African Americans, and wealthy whites recognize the natural superiority of

The Man for Office Is Cole Blease

their gender and their whiteness. Yeomen interpreted any slight as a slap at their manhood, and they responded sometimes violently and at other times politically. White supremacy, personal autonomy, and the control of dependents in public and private—these were the values of independence that poor white men brought with them from the countryside to the cotton mill world of South Carolina at the turn of the century.

Mill village life challenged long-standing male conceptions of independence. Tending looms and operating carding machines stripped men of control of their time and labor. The boss in the rural household now worked to the relentless rhythms of the machines and the angry bark of the foreman. Some even compared the factory regime to slavery. "They are trying to treat the help more like slaves than free people," protested T. V. Blair of Pelzer. S. E. Arthur of Langley added: "We do not have more showing than the negroes in slavery time." Millhands deployed the metaphor of slavery to protest against the nature of mill work and to articulate their fears about their growing dependence on the will of others. Without control over their own labor, male workers must have worried that it now would be difficult for them to impose their authority over others.[37]

Wages, if they had been high enough to support the entire family, might have provided some men with a sense of compensation for their dwindling control.[38] But few mill men earned enough to feed and clothe their families. Under these conditions, children and wives were compelled to take up what southern millhands revealingly labeled "public work"—that is, paid labor. Though fathers often disciplined their children on the shop floor, scolding those who misbehaved and pushing slackers to work harder, they no doubt knew that the real source of authority was the foreman and the mill owner, men who were more powerful than they were.[39] Male millhands familiar with the dynamics of the shop floor also knew that some supervisors used their power over hiring and firing to intimidate female workers sexually, which only heightened the anxieties of fathers and husbands. Yet these men also understood that if they accused the supervisors of harassing their wives and daughters, they risked losing their own jobs, and an unemployed worker was even less of a man than an underpaid one.[40]

The participation of dependents in the paid labor force realigned the balance of power within the family. Feeling enfranchised by their contributions to the household economy, working wives and children periodically challenged their husbands and fathers over the dispensation of their wages. Sons and daughters, in particular, often demanded the right to spend at least a portion of their earnings on whatever they wanted.[41] How they spent their wages was also an issue. Across the urban South in the first decades of the twentieth century, young workers, especially women, shaped a new heterosexual aesthetic. Makeup, bobbed hair, and shorter skirts were evidence of this trend. A refraction of the new city sensibilities quickly reached the mill hills. Some young mill women purchased the latest styles, went out with their friends, male and female, on Saturday nights, and skipped church on Sundays. Much more than their cousins back on the farm, young millworkers expressed themselves as independent, autonomous individuals who were culturally at odds with their parents.[42]

While male millhands worried about their growing dependence and declining authority, it seemed that African Americans were becoming more economically independent and assertive. To be sure, most jobs in textile mills were reserved for whites, but African Americans made strides elsewhere. Between 1890 and 1910, for example, the number of black landowners in South Carolina steadily increased.[43] African Americans also registered other financial gains. Take the case of Allen Green. In 1915 he lived in Walhalla, a town with a few textile mills in upcountry Oconee County. Rumored to be the illegitimate grandson of John C. Calhoun, Green owned livestock, a small truck, and an attractive house just across the tracks from Walhalla's main street. Local white officials praised Green's skills as a firefighter and rewarded him with a slew of municipal jobs, including supervision of a crew of white sanitation and street workers. When Green was accused of sexually assaulting a white woman who worked at a local mill, prominent whites came to his defense. Rather than putting Green on trial, they denounced the white woman as promiscuous.[44]

The doctrine of white supremacy, declared a Bleasite newspaper editor in 1917, "demanded that the LOWEST white man in the social scale is above the negro who stands HIGHEST by the same measurement."[45] Middle-class whites, however, seemed to be turning away from this creed. At the same time that these uptown white men defended the character of African American men like Green, they disparaged working-class white men. Beginning as early as 1890, middle-class South Carolinians attacked male laborers, questioning their worthiness as white men and patriarchs. The press portrayed "mill daddies" as "lazy . . . wife beater[s] . . . and drunkard[s]." A Spartanburg journalist warned about "strong, hearty men . . . with several children, who move to a mill and strut around and form secret societies and talk big while their children support the family." "They say," the reporter added, "some of them spend one tenth of their children's earnings for whiskey." Shifting the burden of labor to their children, "cotton mill drone[s]," as some called mill fathers, sat around all day doing nothing. Occasionally, these no-good scoundrels left their seats in front of the company store and trudged over to the mill, not to tend looms, but to deliver lunch to their hard-working sons and daughters. Before the machines started to whirl again, these "tin-bucket toter[s]" were back, swapping lies and taking their turn at the bottle. Although these ugly portraits of mill fathers twisted the truth, they made a deep impression on reform-minded South Carolinians.[46]

"The character of part of the voting population has changed in recent years," remarked a South Carolina editor soon after the turn of the century, and not for the better, he meant. The group that most alarmed him and other middle-class South Carolinians was the so-called unruly element among the millhands. They wanted to do something before the problem got out of hand. Ever confident, these reformers were certain that they could take care of working-class children but wondered about what could be done with the parents? Initially, a few people quietly spoke of limiting the suffrage rights of the propertyless and illiterate, at least until they could be properly civilized. The emergence of Bleasism added urgency to this talk. For many, Cole Blease's success at the polls—he finished a close second in the 1908 governor's race— confirmed what they had long suspected: that the poor, unthinking multitude was ruled by the baser impulses rather than by reason and civility.[47] Bleasism, charged a Baptist minister, marked the "emergence of the Southern under-world," rising from "whispers on the night corners in mill yards and at the crossroads."[48] The only way to stop Blease and to protect law and order, many argued, was to delete the names of his strongest supporters—undereducated, propertyless white men—from the voting rolls. Limiting suffrage would enable the "best" people of South Carolina to join together to reform the region without having to pander to the enfranchised "unruly element[s]." Reformers predicted that if only the most enlightened members of society were permitted to vote, South Carolina would quickly become a model of efficient modernity. By pushing for voting restrictions, these uptown citizens appeared to call for a wholesale renegotiation of white supremacy, implying that bourgeois values, as well as race, should be the prerequisites for citizenship.[49]

The passions of the unthinking multitude alarmed middle-class women as well as men. The wives and daughters of the state's professional and commercial elite joined with schoolteachers and welfare workers to push for compulsory education, mandatory medical inspections, child labor restrictions, and Prohibition. A few female reformers also advocated woman suffrage. Not many in this small group were radical democrats; instead, they constructed a class-based appeal for the vote. They asked why uneducated white men with little financial stake in the system should be allowed to vote while well-informed white women did not have the franchise. In place of white male democracy, they proposed an oligarchy of the best white people. What many white South Carolina suffragists had in mind was a system of suffrage based on class and race, regardless of sex. From where male textile workers stood, woman suffrage looked like it would recast gender roles, making some white laborers dependent on middle-class white women in public and perhaps even in private.[50]

For first-generation white male workers, assaults on their independence and manhood seemed to be coming from every direction. Each millhand dealt with the confusion of industrialization, low wages, waning parental authority, the growing assertiveness of women, middle-class hostility, and African American progress in his own way. Some workers gave up on the mill and returned to the countryside.[51] Others drank too much, and a few probably deserted their families.[52] A small number took out their frustrations on their wives and children.[53] Violence was not confined to households; during the first two decades of the twentieth century millhands, along with white men and a few women from every part of town, assembled in lynch mobs. They killed African Americans who, they believed, wanted to wipe away the color line and undermine white masculinity.[54] Others spoke out for shorter working hours and higher pay, and a few joined trade unions and went on strike.[55] Many, armed as they were with the vote, turned to politics—or, perhaps more accurately, politicians turned to them. The most famous of these politicians was Cole Blease.

In a nearly biennial ritual between 1906 and 1916, textile workers went to the polls and voted for Cole Blease as a solid bloc.[56] Blease brought male mill-hands out on election day in record numbers because he had honed a political message that expressed their gathering resentments. He spoke to their concerns and frustrations in ways that made sense to them. "The man," W. J. Cash marveled, "was a sort of *antenna* . . . fit to vibrate in perfect unison" with the "exact sentiments" of mill people. He was, noted the Greenville journalist James C. Derieux, laborers' "mouthpiece," articulating their "unexpressed emotions, ambitions, and disgruntlements."[57] Like the Blacksburg lynching, Blease's rhetoric represented a window into millhands' outlooks. The candidate's words both revealed and shaped a complicated and volatile constellation of ideas about race, class, gender, sexuality, and state power.

In Blease's day, South Carolina politics resembled a traveling circus. For six grueling weeks in the middle of the summer, candidates for every public office imaginable endured blistering, sullen heat crisscrossing the state to appear together in each and every county. Usually the catfish man was the

The stump meeting. Gubernatorial candidates talking to a crowd in Walterboro, 1946. (Modern Political Collections, South Caroliniana Library, University of South Carolina)

first to arrive on stump day. Armed with a big paddle and a fifty-gallon iron kettle, he started to make his spicy stew just after the sun rose. He chopped up mounds of celery, onions, and potatoes and cooked them with tomatoes, corn, and butter. Then he threw in pounds of pork and even more catfish. He let it simmer for several hours. By the time the stew was ready, thousands of people, young and old, rich and poor, had showed up to hear the speeches. As they waited for the candidates, they washed the catfish man's steaming soup down with ice-cold lemonade sold by church women. Sometime after noon, it was finally time to talk politics.[58]

The stump was where Blease stood out. Turning politics into vaudeville, he put on the best show in town except perhaps for the annual tent meeting. Strutting across the podium, waving his arms, pointing his finger, shouting and whispering, he played the master of ceremonies, comedian, old friend, and preacher all wrapped into one. He berated, mocked, and belittled his opponents. Low-country planters, middle-class South Carolinians, and re-formers, not factory owners, caught the brunt of Blease's verbal blitzes.

Unimpressed by their sizable bank accounts, college degrees, big words, or claims of selflessness, Blease dismissed the reformers as "intellectuals," "fool theorists," "wise-looking old fossils," and members of the "holier than thou crowd." Grinning and winking, he regularly made light of the rule of law—that cardinal tenet of bourgeois ideology—by admitting to drinking boot-legged whiskey every now and then. Each time that he made this confession, Blease noted, his opponents said that he was a threat to law and order. But, according to the candidate, they were hypocrites. "Why, I saw men up here last summer," Blease said, his voice thick with sarcasm, during his 1913 inaugural address, "hollering, 'Law and Order,' yelling for 'Law and Order,' and 'We must redeem South Carolina.' . . . I saw some of those same people down here at the State Fair drinking liquor and mixing it with coca-cola and betting on horses." "Who," Blease chuckled, "is going to redeem them?" [59]

When Blease was not poking fun at his opponents, he battered them with male bravado. They were, he blazed, unmanly "cowards," "belly crawlers," "pap-suckers," "nigger lovers," "molly-coddles," and "very small m[e]n." [60] Blease was especially dismissive of women reformers and suffragists. He accused them of neglecting their homes and children so they could run around the state " 'doing society,' playing cards for prizes, etc." A supporter complained that female reformers wanted "to give us their dresses for our pants." Blease agreed. He opposed woman suffrage, hinting that the right to vote and enter the public sphere might unsex women. Women, Blease advised, should spend their time aiding "good men" rather then agitating for "drastic reforms." [61]

Blease saved his harshest attacks for the "aristocrats." [62] Tagging his enemies aristocrats, Blease tapped into the tradition of antielitism among South Carolina's poor whites. Before and after the Civil War, "aristocrats" served as a pejorative term for wealthy men who looked down on plain white folks, treating them no better than they did African Americans. These were the same people who tried to restrict the suffrage rights of yeomen and considered entering into an unholy alliance with African Americans to blunt the political power of poor whites. For Blease and his supporters, the meaning of the word had not changed much over the years. "The fight I have tried to make and am making," Coley said of his battle against suffrage restrictions, "is to keep my friends in a position where they will not be oppressed, and to prevent a return to rule of the old aristocracy." [63]

The image of the aristocrat also conjured up gender and class connotations. Like the candidate, Blease's supporters had a clear idea of how an aristocrat looked, sounded, and acted. Aristocrats were effete men—dandies dressed in silk shirts and top hats with soft hands and coifed hair. Unmanly men, aristocrats did not work; instead, they relied on others, typically their fathers, to provide for them. Unlike real men, they lacked self-discipline: they drank,

The Man for Office Is Cole Blease

smoked, gambled, and skipped church. Their thirst for excess extended to sex; they were insatiable and debauched, not that different in the minds of some poor whites from African Americans.

"The best definition I know for aristocracy," Blease said in 1913, "is some fellow who does nothing, lives on his daddy's name and doesn't pay his debts." The aristocrats, he continued, fiddled away their nights watching lewd shows at the theater, screeching with delight at a foul-mouthed Yankee woman and a man dressed as "The Pink Lady." Just below the surface of his attack was the sly accusation that aristocrats subverted traditional gender roles. Because they placed themselves outside the boundaries of manly behavior, he warned, they posed a serious threat to patriarchy and white womanhood. As evidence of their deceit, Blease pointed to their attempts to restrict the citizenship rights of poor whites. Depriving poor white men of their independence and manhood, aristocrats encouraged black men to consider themselves once again the political and social equals of white men. Surely this would lead to a frightening rerun of Reconstruction. No "pure-blooded Caucasian," Blease asserted, would stand by and let this happen.[64]

Blease offered white laborers more than antiaristocratic rhetoric. Understanding their frustrations, he vowed to uphold the privileges of race. Pledging his allegiance to the idea of a white man's democracy, he battled to make sure that all white males over the age of twenty-one could continue to vote in the Democratic primary regardless of their background or income. He also endorsed legislation to bar African Americans from textile mills, despite the fact that by 1910 almost no mills would hire blacks for jobs inside the factories. To make sure that people knew exactly where he stood on the issues of employment and race, as one of his first acts as governor he fired every black notary in the state.[65] Although Blease favored passing new laws to bolster white supremacy, he opposed virtually all other state action.

Blease's fight against laws for compulsory education was a case in point. These measures would have required all children under the age of fourteen, or sixteen, to attend school. Reformers talked glowingly about the social benefits of the classroom for working-class children. Blease scoffed at the humanitarian depiction of these educational statutes, portraying them instead as part of a broad campaign to control mill people's private lives. Nature, he argued, determined that fathers and mothers, not the government, should oversee families. Cotton mill people, he continued, "should be left alone . . . and allowed to manage their own affairs. . . . Compulsory education means disrupting the home, for it dethrones the authority of the parents and would place paid agents in control of the children which would destroy family government." On another occasion he declared of a compulsory school bill, "Of course I am opposed . . . it [the bill] comes . . . from some narrow-minded bigot who has made a failure in raising his own children . . . and now wants to attempt to raise somebody else's." Looking to the Bible to bolster his case, Blease not surprisingly turned out to be a conservative theologian. He told a mill crowd: "The Bible says a great deal about obedience to parents and reverence for parents and believing in that Book and its teachings as I do, I say to the parents, for the sake of their children, our country, and for the future, keep within your own control the rearing and education of your own children." Blease's hostility toward compulsory schooling did not mean that he opposed public education. Indeed, in 1914 he called for higher pay for teachers, more male instructors, improved libraries, longer school terms, and more "books, especially histories, by southern authors for southern children."[66]

Even more than compulsory education, progressive plans to mandate medical inspections of mill children infuriated Blease. Proponents insisted that such examinations would compensate for "the oversight of the child's environment" and would correct deformities that were easily correctable but had been left unattended to by ignorant parents. Blease asserted that such a scheme highlighted the reformers' arrogance and their tendency to treat male textile workers as less than men. "Do you not think," he asked lawmakers, "that every man in this State is able to care and has love enough for his children to care for and protect them? . . . Have all the people and all classes of the people become imbeciles and children that the Legislature at every turn must pass acts creating guardianships? . . . Do you wish to . . . force every poor man to bow down to the whims of all the professions?"[67]

For Blease, sex—that is to say, deviant sexuality—linked the emerging middle class of the New South to the debauched aristocracy. He asked what doctors would do with the information they gathered from their studies of mill children. Would they publicize their findings? If a mill girl suffered from an embarrassing ailment, would they broadcast the news and turn the examination into yet another humiliating ritual for working people? "Do not say," Blease warned, "that every young girl in the State . . . without her consent, must be forced to be examined and her physical condition certified by her physician to some school teacher, to be heralded around as public property." The most dangerous aspect of the law, he insinuated, was that it would make it easier for morally lax men to sexually abuse poor white women. Some "male physicians," a correspondent wrote to Blease in 1914, "boast openly that they can seduce their female patients." One even kept a diary, a supporter told the governor, of his sexual exploits with working-class girls. "If I had a daughter," Blease proclaimed, "I would kill any doctor in South Carolina whom I would be forced to let examine her against her will and mine." On the cam-

The Man for Office Is Cole Blease

paign trail, he promised South Carolina fathers that he would pardon any man convicted of murdering a doctor who "violat[ed] his daughter's modesty." In a final horrific charade of politically opportunistic logic, Blease wondered aloud about doctor's assistants, "third parties," and "negro janitors." Would physicians, he asked, permit the "unmentionable crime" — the virtual rape of a white woman — by allowing voyeuristic black men to watch the medical inspections of mill girls?[68]

Once again, Blease turned the bourgeois conception of the world on its head. Reformers viewed medical examinations as a tool for creating a modern New South. In the minds of the middle classes, doctors were asexual individuals, pillars of the community, and architects of a more orderly universe. Blease laughed at these flattering characterizations. To him, doctors perhaps more than others had the capacity for evil. Under the guise of morality, they undermined morality by defiling innocent working-class women. By vigorously opposing the medical inspection bill, Blease positioned himself as the millworkers' defender of decency, masculine honor, and white womanly virtue.

Blease tied his assaults on elites and reformers and his appeals to white workers together with the threads of race, class, and gender. He accused the reformers of trying to place the "cotton mill men . . . on the same basis as a free negro."[69] Laws that dictated who could vote and who could not and told mill parents when their children had to go to school and when they must stay at home violated the principles of independence, white equality, and patriarchal authority. Only blacks, minors, and women, Blease maintained, should have their behavior so rigidly regulated. To put white men in the same category was to turn the natural order of the world upside down.

"I am no enemy of the negro but I believe in keeping him in his place at all times," Blease often remarked. That place, he told campaign crowds, expounding on his own crude version of the popular mythology of scientific racism, was established by the Almighty to be far below the position of any white man. According to Blease, sexual morality fixed the racial hierarchy. "The negro race has absolutely no standard of morality," he lectured in 1914. "They are in that respect a class by themselves, as marital infidelity seems to be their more favorite pastime." Blease's world was immutable. He opposed spending white tax dollars on black schools. Educating a black person would simply "ruin a good field hand, and make a bad convict."[70] Blease insisted that black immorality was natural and that black men had to be watched at all times. "I tell you that it is not all quiet in South Carolina," he cautioned. In his imagination, "the black ape and baboon" lurked in the shadows waiting for the opportunity to rape a white woman. If this crime did take place, or even if there was a hint of an African American crossing the sexual color line, lynching was the only answer. Not to lynch would only make black men more brazen. To Blease, then, those who joined the lynch mobs were not disorderly or lawless; they were manly and moral. Those who questioned the principles of white equality across class and economic lines and the need for lynching were, like aristocrats and doctors, effete and dangerous, and had to be stopped.[71]

"Whenever the constitution of my state steps between me and the defense of the virtue of the white woman," Blease proclaimed at the national governor's conference in 1912, "then I say to hell with the Constitution!" When it came to defending white women, there was a higher justice than law and order. "The pure-blooded Caucasian will always defend the virtue of our women," Blease declared, "no matter what the cost. . . . If rape is committed, death must follow!" Stumping for office in 1910, Blease promised that he would never send out the militia to stop a lynching. "When mobs are no longer possible liberty will be dead," he proclaimed on another occasion. Sometimes after a lynching Blease publicly celebrated the savage murder with a bizarre death dance. Through his grotesque gyrations, he invited his audience to participate vicariously in the spectacle of vigilante justice.[72]

When white men joined lynch mobs and cheered Blease's ritual dances, they attempted to assert their power not only over African Americans but also over their own homes and families. As Jacquelyn Dowd Hall and Gail Bederman have argued, "by constructing black men as 'natural' rapists and by resolutely and bravely avenging the (alleged) rape of pure white womanhood, Southern white men constructed themselves as ideal men: 'patriarchs, avengers, righteous protectors.'"[73] Blease spoke to the multiple meanings of lynching. In the summer of 1913 a supporter informed the governor of an alleged rape of a white woman in Laurens. "The brute," he explained, was captured and "tried before an honest jury." "It was not a mob," he assured the state's chief executive, "but a crowd of determined men anxious to have justice meted out to one never more deserving of its fruits." "You did like men and defended your neighbors and put their black bodies under ground," Blease congratulated the members of the Laurens County lynch mob, which included "many of the 'cotton mill boys,'" some of whom were apparently angry about the hiring of African Americans for "white" jobs. The governor praised these criminals as well for "their defense of the white womanhood of our state—our mothers and our sisters."[74]

The Blacksburg lynching of Joe Brinson and Frank Whisonant took place fifteen months before the murder in Laurens. Both events demonstrated that sexual tensions, class issues, and vigilante justice were always intertwined in the New South. In each case, millworkers defended their manhood and their whiteness under the cover of darkness. In Blacksburg, some people believed

A Governor Who Lauds Lynching.

Gov. Cole S. Blease,

Who in an address before a conference of statesmen in Richmond, Va., yesterday said he would never call the militia against a mob of lynchers and that he would pardon lynchers in every case in which they did not summarily execute the wrong man.

A Blease campaign poster, probably from 1914, boasting about the governor's stand on white womanhood and lynching. (South Caroliniana Library, University of South Carolina) that local blacks lay in wait to ravage not only white women but also white men like Joe Childers. These same men must have worried about the fate of white womanhood, white manhood, and white supremacy if white men could not even protect themselves from black sexual predators. Male laborers in Blacksburg and Laurens emphatically answered these doubts. They asserted their masculinity by murdering three black men for allegedly sexually humiliating a white man and a white woman and thus all white people. In the anxious world of the industrializing New South, interracial sexual contact of any kind—even a homosexual act—that became public knowledge could easily threaten white independence and white manhood. Although Blease did not dance for, or even condone, every lynching—and he did not comment on events in Blacksburg—he understood why some poor white men executed black men, and these white men repaid him for his understanding with their votes.

Only some whites regarded Blease in this way. In the early twentieth century, white South Carolinians were divided on questions of race, class, gender, and even lynching. These divisions became politicized and eventually fractured the electorate into two rival camps: Bleasites and anti-Bleasites. Blease's message sounded different to each audience. Middle-class residents detected nothing of substance in his critique of society; they heard only the dissonant chords of demagoguery, disorder, and lawlessness. Male millworkers, on the other hand, interpreted Blease's rhetoric and actions as a defense of their manhood against the forces of industrialization and the reform agenda of the progressives. By voicing laborers' discontent and abusing those who demeaned them, Blease provided workers with a way to strike out at their perceived oppressors. Casting their ballots for Cole Blease, textile workers pressed their claims of patriarchal privilege and equality with all white men and asserted in the strongest language available to them that the economic and socially mighty did not control everything. "Even though Coley don't ever do a durn thing for us poor fellows," explained an Aiken laborer, "he does at least promise us somethin', and that's more than any of the others do."[75]

Blease rode to power on the backs of white workers like Joe Childers and the Aiken laborer. Once in office, he did almost nothing to enhance workers' material well-being, but his success at the polls, like the lynching in Blacksburg, exposed the frustrations and aspirations of South Carolina's first generation of male textile laborers. These white men feared that their control over their families was dwindling and that their masculinity was under attack. Blease politicized them along class lines, but his mobilization produced a misogynist, racist, nonradical, and antireform version of class politics. He directed the ire of male workers against the middle classes, not against the mill bosses, and he aroused them to safeguard their manhood by blocking change, not by propos-

ing reforms of their own. Another politician might have urged workers to en-
list in the trade movement or called for child labor legislation linked to mini-
mum wage statutes, but no one in South Carolina, at least not before the Great
Depression, put forth these positions. If there had been such a voice, Cole
Blease's celebrations of white manhood and his harangues against African
Americans, progressive reformers, and aristocrats would have drowned it out.

CHAPTER TWO

Bleasism in Decline,

1924–1930

Another African American was dead. On a Saturday, the first day of summer, June 21, 1930, at approximately 3:00 P.M. in the small town of Santuc in upcountry Union County, twenty-four-year-old Dan Jenkins was murdered. The killers riddled his body with hundreds of bullets.

Union County African Americans did not know much about Dan Jenkins. He had been in the area for only a few months. Born in Beaufort, North Carolina, Jenkins had lived for a while in Batesburg, South Carolina, before moving to Union County to work on a road crew. A day or two before the murder, he lost his job, reportedly for insubordination. It also was rumored that Jenkins was having a sexual relationship with a married white woman. Some said that he occasionally gave her money. Then on June 21, according to African American sources, the sixteen-year-old sister-in-law of Jenkins's lover spotted the two of them together. She knew nothing of the affair. Raised in the South, she was taught that there was no such thing as consensual sex between a black man and a white woman; when she saw her sister-in-law in Jenkins's arms, she saw a black man assaulting a white woman. The teenager dashed off to get her brother, who followed her back to the scene. Caught in the act, Jenkins's lover cried "rape." Like the sixteen-year-old and the married woman, Jenkins had also been raised in the South. Knowing that when a white woman cried "rape," white men acted quickly, he ran for his life. This was the story that circulated in the African American community.

Union County whites told a different story. To them, Jenkins was a "bad nigger." Unlike the happy, shuffling slaves of antebellum mythology, he be-

36

longed to a new generation of young African Americans who refused to smile or tip their hats. Whites barely knew black men like Jenkins, who worked out on the highways and deep in the woods, not close by in the fields or kitchens, and that made them nervous.[1] Prior to June 21, according to whites, Jenkins and the two white women—their names did not appear in print—had never seen each other. That afternoon, the three of them found themselves by chance in a country store at the same time. The women bought some milk and left. Jenkins lingered for a moment and then started to trail the women. When they were halfway home, he leaped from the bushes, drew a revolver, and told them to do exactly what he said or else. He kept the gun trained on them until they reached a secluded spot in the woods. First he attacked the teenager, then he raped the married woman. The younger woman somehow escaped and ran to get her brother, who followed her back to the scene. Jenkins heard him coming, and before the brother saw him, he shot the white man in the leg. Guilty of a monstrous crime and certain of what awaited him, Jenkins started to run and kept on running. His flight proved to local whites that he did it.

No one disputed what happened next. Word of the alleged crime and Jenkins's disappearance spread. Soon everybody in Santuc knew. African Americans braced themselves for the worst. White men formed search parties, one led by the "victim's" relatives, another by the sheriff. They slogged through swamps, crept around cotton fields, and checked along the railroad tracks. Meanwhile, the editor of the local paper, a minister-turned-journalist, notified Governor John G. Richards of the manhunt. Unlike his mentor, Cole Blease, who refused to stop a lynching, the chief executive rushed National Guardsmen to the area with orders to keep the peace. The soldiers got there twenty minutes too late. Sometime around 3:00 P.M., the search party formed by members of the married woman's family captured Jenkins. They, too, had been taught the rules of race in the South. After catching Jenkins, they dragged him back to the site of the alleged crime. Then they brought the supposed victim, who told the crowd of about 150 white men that Jenkins was the man who raped her. Of course, she did not say it that way, she probably just nodded in his direction. Seconds later, the mob started firing. They pumped bullet after bullet into the black man's body. For some this was not nearly enough punishment for the "unmentionable act." "Burn him!" they shrieked.[2]

While the killers debated their next move, the National Guardsmen arrived on the scene. The well-armed officers seized Jenkins's bullet-ridden body before it was thrown into the fire and carried it to a local African American undertaker. They stood guard through the night and the next day, Sunday, when Jenkins was buried in a potter's field.

Two weeks after Jenkins was killed, Cole Blease came to Union County for the biennial stump meeting. Tenants, bankers, secretaries, manufacturers, and thousands of millhands gathered on a grassy hill with few trees and little shade just outside of town to hear the speeches. While a drum and bugle corps played marching tunes, the spectators gulped lemonade and fanned themselves as they waited for the candidates. As usual, Cole Blease was the main attraction. This year the Newberry native was seeking reelection to a second term in the U.S. Senate. Blease began with a quick review of his record: support for cuts in government spending, opposition to Prohibition (earlier in his career he had been bone dry, but who could remember?), and an unshakable commitment to white supremacy and patriarchy. "Negroes," he boasted, "pray for my defeat." Then he turned to the Union County lynching. The Santuc killers, Blease insisted, did the right thing; those who doubted it were not true white men. Repeating a theme he had used in every campaign since 1916, Blease declared: "Whenever the Constitution comes between me and the virtue of the white women of South Carolina, I say to hell with the Constitution." Continuing, his body shaking in a "hysterical death dance," he told the crowd:

> Whenever the negro press and association are to tell me how I am to vote, I ask my God to deprive me of the right to vote. White supremacy and the protection of the virtue of the white women of the South comes first with me. . . . When I was governor of South Carolina you did not hear of me calling out the militia of the State to protect negro assaulters. . . . In my South Carolina campaigns you heard me say, "When you catch the brute that assaults a white woman, wait until the next morning to notify me."[3]

The next person to speak was Blease's opponent, James F. Byrnes. Born in a gritty working-class neighborhood near Charleston's docklands, Byrnes was by 1930 a well-connected, well-heeled lawyer from Spartanburg and a former member of the U.S. Congress. Six years earlier he had lost to Blease in the Senate contest by a razor-thin margin.

"Ladies and gentlemen," Byrnes said in 1930 in a measured professional tone, "I think we've had enough talk about lynching." There was scattered applause. "My speech tonight is about conditions in our factories." "When," he continued, "you destroy the purchasing power of the farmer, you cut down the cotton mill profits and bring curtailment and distress to the mill worker." Loosening international trade restraints, he predicted, would boost the price of raw cotton and create more jobs in the mills. The millworkers clapped. Byrnes sat down. He had said not a word about race or liquor.[4]

Byrnes's focus on economic issues, whether it reflected sound thinking or not, proved to be a successful campaign strategy in 1930. As vote tallies flashed on the big screens set up outside of the state's major daily newspapers on election night, it was clear that Blease's support in the mill precincts was down from six years earlier. At the Woodside Mills, for instance, his share of the vote had dropped from more than 80 percent in 1924 to 66 percent. At the Greenwood Mills his backing fell from 80 percent to 64 percent. These shifts turned out to be crucial; perhaps they even made the difference in this second straight razor-close election. This time Blease lost to Byrnes by only 4,000 votes out of 235,000 cast.[5]

Embedded in these stories from Union County are clues about the changing politics of South Carolina textile workers. On the one hand, they suggest that much remained the same in South Carolina between 1912 and 1930, or between the murders of Joe Brinson and Frank Whisonant and the murder of Dan Jenkins. Race, sex, and private anxieties were still tragically linked. Union County white men killed Jenkins because they believed, or needed to believe, that he had raped a white woman. They posed as heroes—the valiant defenders of virtuous white women. More to the point, their brutal ritual represented yet another thinly veiled attempt by white men to assert their authority over women and African Americans. This was a familiar story in South Carolina.

So too was Blease's agenda. In 1930 he told the crowds in the upcountry what he had always told them: he alone could safeguard white supremacy, which was the central function of government. Matters of money and trade, he said, were best left in private hands. Let white workers negotiate wages and hours directly with their white bosses. Leave the government, especially the federal government, out of the affairs of white men. In the past, this message had played well with millworkers; between 1910 and 1924 they were Blease's most loyal constituents, regularly delivering the Newberry native huge electoral majorities in their neighborhoods. But in 1930 the message of white supremacy was not enough to keep white millworkers solidly in the Blease camp.

What these stories of race and politics tell us, then, is that although race still mattered to white workers, it did not reverberate in the political arena in the same way that it had two decades earlier. Since the turn of the century, race had been central to millworkers' political identity. But gradually, unevenly over time, it lost some of its saliency. The reasons for this transformation can be found in the international cotton market, in the mill villages, in workers' homes, on the shop floor, and on the picket line. In other words, changes in mill people's day-to-day lives between 1912 and 1930 set in motion an ideological shift away from Bleasism toward the aggressive pursuit of state action on their behalf.

World War I marked the beginning, discernible only from a distance, of South Carolina millhands' retreat from Bleasism. Depression stalked the textile industry in 1916, but America's entry into the conflict warded off the threat. War sparked the demand for cotton goods of all kinds. Mill owners racked up immense profits, and stock prices raced upward. In 1916 individual shares of Easley's Alice Mills traded at $93; three years later they sold for $230. Over the same period, the Inman Mills paid an astonishing 400 percent dividend.[6] Textile companies hustled to grab what they could of the windfall. Factories churned around the clock. New mills sprang up across the state, while older plants built additions and crammed more of the most up-to-date looms and spindles into existing space.[7]

With the war's end in November 1918, orders for cloth and yarn slackened. Falling demand cut into profits and dividends, leading to drops in employment and wages. But the textile industry rebounded rather quickly from this downturn. Although it took another twenty years and another global conflict to push demand back up to the lofty heights of the World War I years, southern textile firms did snap out of the immediate postwar slump. Encouraged by the market's resiliency, South Carolina mill men resumed their wartime expansion programs. In 1923, for example, Greenwood County's Grendel Mill doubled in size. The Chiquola Manufacturing Company in Honea Path and the Mills Mill in Greenville also expanded their physical plants.[8]

Northern investment, however, was what really paced the postwar building boom. Battered by southern competition and frustrated by labor unrest, dozens of New England firms went bankrupt in the 1920s; many survivors moved to the Piedmont, lured by promises like the ones made by the Columbia Chamber of Commerce of "Abundant low-priced labor—100% American Anglo-Saxon stock, no foreign element, no textile strikes [and] ample labor available for all enterprises."[9] To northern concerns, this sounded like the ideal union-free, money-making environment. In 1922 Martel Mills, a New York–based corporation, snatched up nine South Carolina plants, mostly in Lexington and Spartanburg Counties. One year later, G. H. Milliken of New York purchased the Ottaray factory in Union and the Goddard brothers of Providence, Rhode Island, bought the Seneca Mill. At the same time, other New England firms took over plants in Pelzer, Tucapau, and Santee.[10] Bolstered by this flow of capital south, the Piedmont by the early 1920s replaced New England as the nation's regional leader in textile production.[11]

Bleasism in Decline

South Carolina boosters like the Columbia Chamber of Commerce told the truth about the race and nationality of southern workers—they were indeed white and native born—but they lied about how many workers were available. As a matter of fact, a persistent labor shortage threatened to turn the southern textile industry's victory over Lowell, Massachusetts, Woonsocket, Rhode Island, and other northern mill centers into defeat. Throughout the early decades of the twentieth century, demand for labor in the Piedmont consistently outstripped supply. Turnover was another persistent problem.[12] Tradition, however, handcuffed the mill owners. Almost from the start of the South Carolina mill-building campaign, factory work was reserved for whites only; blacks were relegated to the dirtiest, lowest-paying jobs outside of the factory.[13] Anytime mill owners tried to break with this tradition, employing African Americans as spinners and weavers, white workers walked off the job. In 1915 tradition became law in South Carolina when the general assembly approved a bill barring African Americans from working in the mills. Moreover, unlike northern mill centers, South Carolina never became, or made itself, a magnet for European immigrants.[14]

Still, South Carolina mill men needed workers. The largest pool of potential white laborers lived on farms within earshot of the mills. By 1910 tens of thousands of first-generation textile workers had already left the farm for the factory. Yet during World War I, the flow of people from the cotton fields to the cotton mills slowed to a trickle. Twenty-cent cotton kept many on the land. An emerging cultural cleavage between the mill towns and the country also kept people away from the factories. Many rural residents looked down on millworkers, whom they regarded as little more than failed farmers. Only weak, lazy, and unmanly men took refuge in the mill villages. Once there, they created a dark world of sin and vice. As long as they could, farm families clung to the moral high ground of their cotton patches. That left the manufacturers with only the millworkers themselves as a source of labor.

During the war mill owners competed with each other as never before for workers. Stories of labor pirating filled newspaper columns. Millhands took advantage of the labor shortage. With jobs available almost for the asking, they moved from mill to mill. They moved after a fight with the foreman; they moved to get closer to family and then farther away; they moved to new villages with bigger houses, better plumbing, and electricity; they moved for higher wages, shorter hours, and reduced workloads; and sometimes they moved just because. A Whitmire worker told an interviewer that he kept "moving money" on hand so that he could leave town on a moment's notice. From 1916 to 1925 the Taylor family relocated sixteen times, stopping in Georgia and North Carolina and in ten South Carolina mill towns in between.[15] All of this movement pushed labor turnover rates to alarming levels. Under these conditions, a mill owner might suddenly find himself without key personnel. Orders might go unfilled. If management wanted to take full advantage of wartime and postwar opportunities for larger profits, they had to reduce turnover rates and assemble an efficient, steady labor force.[16]

During World War I and afterward, firms across the nation turned to welfare capitalism—that is, providing workers with nonwage benefits—to cope with high turnover rates and industrial militancy. As the labor shortage deepened in the Piedmont, South Carolina's mill villages began to sparkle. Manufacturers splashed a fresh coat of paint on workers' houses, planted shade trees along recently paved streets, and built pools, parks, movie theaters, bowling alleys, golf courses, libraries, churches, schools, and YMCAs. They staged glittery holiday festivals and lavish Fourth of July celebrations complete with marching bands, square dances, baseball games, and food for everyone.[17] Welfare capitalism entailed more than oak trees and fried chicken; it aimed to construct a new context for industrial relations. The goal was to tie workers as individuals to the firm and keep them from leaving for another job, while also demonstrating to reformers that the corporation, rather than the government, could and should provide for the well-being of its employees. With these ends in mind, manufacturers advertised that community and individual uplift, not profits, were their principal objectives. Labor, they said, was not a cog in the machine but a partner, albeit a junior one, entitled to fair treatment. By linking workers and managers together, business leaders hoped to forge an industrial universe built on loyalty, stability, and profitability, instead of one wracked by strife, uncertainty, and bankruptcy.[18]

For workers, income mattered more than gifts from management. During the war, the earnings of millhands soared.[19] This is not to say that textile workers were well compensated; indeed, they remained among the nation's lowest-paid industrial workers. Nonetheless, between 1916 and 1918 real wages rose swiftly and substantially. One study suggests that the earnings of South Carolina millworkers tripled during this period. Management's inducements did not stop at hourly wage hikes or increased piece rates. Even before the war, absentee rates, like turnover rates, threatened to cut into profit margins, and southern manufacturers decided to act. One mill official offered his employees a 5 percent bonus as a reward for full-time, steady work. Soon a neighboring mill, seeking to stabilize its labor force, raised the bonus to 10 percent, then to 15 percent, and so on. By the end of the war, some firms paid bonuses as high as 50 percent of weekly wages.[20]

When orders for textiles started to lag right after the war, earnings dropped as well. Millhands, however, fought back against management's postwar retrenchment plans. In the Horse Creek Valley and Rock Hill, they went on strike in 1919—joining Pittsburgh steelworkers, Chicago meatpackers, New Jersey textile workers, and millions of others.[21] Although the South Carolinians failed to hold wages at their wartime peak, all was not lost. After World War I, textile workers' wages remained well above prewar levels. Throughout the early 1920s, millhands earned twice as much as they had in 1915.[22]

Fatter paychecks transformed mill life, both public and private. The biggest winners were adult males. Pay hikes for older men outstripped all other groups. Many gained higher wages through promotions. With factories expanding and new plants opening all the time, mill owners needed additional second hands, overseers, and other shop floor supervisors. Usually they hired from within. Men who resisted the moving bug and stayed sober could expect to advance up the occupational and earnings ladder. The experience of Lora Wright's father was typical. Starting out in his teens as a doffer, he moved on to become a weaver, then a loom fixer, and finally a secondhand, a position just below foreman. With incomes on the rise, family life changed: husbands proudly assumed the part of the breadwinner; married women left the factories, working instead at home, sometimes quilting or canning and selling the surplus; and children, while still working, remained in school longer and entered the paid labor force later.[23]

Higher wages also eased southern workers' entry into the nation's emerging consumer economy. They marveled at the new radios and gathered around them at home and at the store to listen to baseball games, soap operas, and *Amos 'n' Andy*. Mill people watched Vallentino at the movie house on Saturday and kept track of star-crossed lovers and rugged cowboys in weekly serials appearing on crinkly paged five-and-dime magazines. Imitating the styles displayed on screen, in mail-order catalogs, and in uptown store windows, they bought, often for the first time, store-made clothes—bright linen dresses and shiny synthetic suits. When they could, workers bypassed the mill store in favor of chain stores like the A&P and the Piggly Wiggly and purchased name brands they had seen advertised in the newspaper. Perhaps most important, thousands of millhands bought, sometimes with the help of credit, their first car, usually a dented secondhand black Ford Model T. Now they could cruise into town to shop or head out to the honky-tonk or over to the ball park.[24]

The consumer economy, and the new culture of consumption that it created, transformed the meaning of success in the mill towns. "Making it" in the older agrarian society had meant autonomy, land ownership, and independent proprietorship.[25] Achievement in the postwar world was increasingly measured in terms of cars, clothes, and canned goods. For men, it meant fulfilling the role of the breadwinner, bringing home enough money so that their wives and children did not have to engage in "public" work and having enough left over to pay for a baseball game or play a hand or two of cards outside the local store. The new emphasis on fulfillment through consumption reshaped the political outlook of male millworkers. They spoke less frequently in a Bleasite idiom, accenting the privileges of whiteness and masculinity, and more about unions, hours, machine loads, wages, and purchasing power. Although concerns about race and patriarchy never disappeared, as indicated by the 1930 lynching in Union County, higher income and greater mobility made these issues less salient.

The good times on mill hills, however, did not last.[26] Three painful years before the stock market crash of 1929, the effects of factory expansion and the influx of northern capital were beginning to be felt. Too many mills were competing with one another for everyone to prosper. Even in the best of times, this would have precipitated a crisis of overproduction, but beginning in the late 1920s demand for American textiles tailed off. Export opportunities, shrinking since the war's end, evaporated as countries such as India and Japan, once large importers of cotton goods, developed their own indigenous textile industries to supply domestic markets. Tariff barriers erected after the war by the probusiness Republican Congress also put limits on the market. Fashions changed as well. During the Jazz Age, designers hiked up hem lines and popularized synthetics.[27]

The downturn of the late 1920s exposed the textile industry's structural weaknesses. Cotton manufacturing ranked among the most competitive industries in the world. Low capital requirements made entry into the textile market relatively cheap and easy. Unlike steel, auto, rubber, and electrical parts and appliances, textiles never underwent the consolidation process that paved the way for a few vertically and horizontally integrated firms to dominate the industry. The automobile industry is a counterexample. Where there were once dozens of car manufacturers, by the mid-twenties many of the characteristics associated with the later period of the big three had already begun to take shape. First, the industry started to consolidate. Second, concentration encouraged stability as a handful of companies set informal production quotas and essentially agreed on pricing. By contrast, more than a thousand factories produced cotton goods after World War I. The three largest companies probably never accounted for more than 5 percent of total output.[28] Moreover, only a handful of southern firms made highly specialized or brand-name goods, and even fewer marketed their own wares. Most South Carolina plants produced low-value-added, partially finished gray goods—that is, woven yet neither dyed nor bleached cloth—which were sold by New York City's Worth Street commission houses.[29] Cutthroat competition ruled this unregulated and undifferentiated market. The only way for a company to stop its profits from sliding was to increase production or undersell its rivals. This strategy might bolster an individual company, but it brought "collective damnation" down on the industry.[30]

Boxed in by the structure of the industry and backed into a corner by flat demand and overproduction, mill men in the 1920s faced some difficult decisions—decisions that would eventually alter the thrust of worker politics. One way to revive profits was to reduce competition. Government regulation of production, however, remained near the bottom of the political agenda of South Carolina mill men and Republican leaders in Washington. Efforts by manufacturers to reach voluntary "gentlemen's agreements" to cut output repeatedly gained the handshakes of mill owners, but each time the deals promptly fell apart.[31] Another solution was to cut costs. Far ahead of equipment, transportation, or raw materials, wages topped the list of expenditures in the textile industry. Although by 1925 wages had dropped by a third from their wartime peak, they remained well above prewar levels. The reason for this was quite simple. The strikes of 1919 proved that workers would not give back wage gains without a tough fight. Rather than risk another outburst of working-class militancy, southern mill owners decided to leave wages alone. Manufacturers tried to clip costs elsewhere.[32]

Welfare capitalism was the first casualty of management's retrenchment strategy. After 1925 fewer houses were wired with electricity, village beautification plans were cut, and church construction tapered off, though less expensive programs, such as basketball teams, father-son banquets, and gardening classes, continued. Still, the savings were not enough to solve the industry's structural problems. Unable to limit production and unwilling to slash wages, mill owners were left with one option. Firms could survive only by underselling their rivals. To do this, manufacturers had to find a way to make their employees produce more, thereby reducing the overall cost of the finished product.

"If you have not already doubled up your processes per operative these men can show you how to do it," advertised an industrial engineering firm in a textile trade publication in 1925.[33] Promises like these grabbed the attention of southern mill owners. Desperate to gain an advantage over their competitors, manufacturers hired scores of industrial engineers. Preaching a gospel of scientific management, bands of the efficiency experts descended on the Piedmont in the late 1920s.[34] After conducting countless time-motion studies, the white-coated engineers compiled their data. Behind closed doors, they presented mill officials with the results of their findings along with a pile of recommendations, diagrams, and order forms for new equipment. After scanning these materials and gazing at the price tag, some managers simply decided to speed up their workers by revving up existing equipment or starting a night shift. Others, swayed by the engineers' impressive tone of scientific authority and their assurances of productivity gains, purchased items like the Veeder-Root counter, a watchdog in the weave room they were told, and rearranged the shop floor, pushing older machines closer together and introducing new and faster equipment.[35]

Across South Carolina, the weave room was the initial target of companies' scientific management strategies. Once staffed by both men and women, weaving over the years increasingly became men's work. As it did, weavers emerged, next to card room workers and loom fixers, as the highest paid operatives in the mill.[36] The new factory regime dissected their jobs. Under what efficiency experts touted as the multiple-loom system, tasks such as cleaning the frames and filling batteries were transferred to employees who earned about half as much as weavers. Individually motorized looms replaced older centralized belt-driven machines. As a result, work stoppages became less frequent, and when they did occur, they affected only a single loom, not a dozen or more.[37] With new machines also came a new set of supervisors. College-educated bosses, unattached to the communities in which they worked, succeeded overseers who had risen through the ranks. They watched over the shop floor, trying to get laborers to perform their tasks with the same ceaselessness as the machines.[38]

Even before the introduction of the new industrial order, mill work was hard. The noise was deafening. Often, it was hotter than the hottest summer day in the factory and the air was thick with deadly lint, but still the pace of labor was relatively relaxed. Charles Putnam was a somewhat typical mill-hand. In 1926 this veteran weaver from Spartanburg's Saxon Mills oversaw twenty-eight looms. "Now . . . [that] . . . was a fair job," he determined. During a shutdown or a break, Putnam would stroll around the plant, talking to friends and family, gossiping, discussing politics, conducting business with an insurance agent, and swigging an ice-cold Coca-Cola. Most days he and a friend "doubled up"—that is, one of them performed two jobs at a frantic clip for a brief time while the other rested or smoked a cigarette.[39]

All of this changed in the fall of 1927, when a team of industrial engineers showed up at the Saxon Mills. Dressed in stiff white coats and armed with stopwatches, calibrators, and clipboards, the industrial engineers—mill people called them "minute men"—shadowed workers around the factory. Step right or left, they were there. They timed every move, noting how long it took to tie a knot, eat lunch, go to the bathroom, and drink a glass of water.

After the minute men left, Putnam's workload tripled. He found himself

Bleasism in Decline

tending machines "by the acre." Terrified of falling behind, he almost never left his station, not even to go to the bathroom. As the multiple-loom system sent his workload soaring, the quality of Putnam's labor deteriorated and the number of inspections increased. The new shop floor boss, who was not from Saxon like the previous boss, pored over the cloth checking for defects. He docked Putnam's pay for every flaw he found. At the end of his nine-hour shift, the weaver's cramped hands ached and his swollen feet throbbed. "Too tired to play ball," he complained, "used to play two or three hours nearly every afternoon." The extra burden did not mean a bigger paycheck. In fact, in 1930 Putnam made just about half of what he had earned ten years earlier and a little less than before his workload tripled. Still, he felt lucky to have a job. A third of his coworkers in the weave room lost their positions, and others were put on short time or were categorized as spare hands. Worst of all, a few longtime weavers were reassigned, some as doffers—a boy's job. Putnam's story was the story of millhands across South Carolina.

"Stretchout" was the term that Putnam and other mill people used to describe the cumulative changes of the postwar era. Millhands associated the stretchout with stopwatches, industrial engineers, new supervisors, the frenzied pace of production, rising workloads, falling wages, and the waning of welfare capitalism. Stretchout also conveyed how workers felt when they walked away from their jobs trembling all over and feeling so drained that they could "hardly get rested for the next day." Finally, the term captured workers' sense of betrayal, their feeling that management had reneged on an unspoken agreement to pay them a fair wage for a fair day's work.[40]

Workers compared the stretchout to slavery. Labor conditions are "worse than miserable," declared one millhand, "they are no less than slavery." "The most damnable system ever put on free people" was how another worker saw the stretchout. "The stretch-out system is worse than Roman slavery. If our government had surrendered their arms to the Kaiser of Germany in 1918," wrote a Greenville resident, "our textile people would be better off." "I ask you," wrote another laborer pointing to the Old Testament, "to read of the Pharaoh's treatment of the Israelites to get a comparison." "The cotton mills," he and others insisted, "are not as different as . . . people think." Yet another thundered against the stretchout: "[It is] . . . the true device of the devil. It is enslaving our workers[,] making nervous wrecks of them and bringing their youthfulness to an end."[41]

Language—like the language of slavery—is always a code that must be taken apart to be understood. Words themselves provide clues about meaning, but definitions change over time and place with shifts in the linguistic, political, economic, and social context. This was true of millhands' use of the word slavery. When first-generation male workers—Bleasites—compared factory life to slavery, they were talking about race. Slavery referred directly to African Americans. To be dependent was to be powerless, to be less than a white man, to be a slave to the will of others. Speaking of slavery in this way, new recruits to the factory world voiced their uneasiness with industrialization in general, not necessarily with specific conditions in the mills. To their children —the millhands of the 1920s—the meaning of slavery changed. Certainly, in a society with an ugly past of racial slavery and a brutal present of racial oppression, the word slavery could not be uttered without racial overtones. Nonetheless, for millhands in the postwar period, slavery became more of a descriptive term referring to class issues rather than to gender or racial concerns.

Since the advent of industrial capitalism, workers in both Europe and America have invoked slavery, or wage slavery, as a metaphor for cruel and callous treatment at the hands of their bosses. When South Carolina laborers spoke of slavery, they, too, were fabricating a metaphor. Yet second-generation millhands did not employ the term because they literally perceived themselves as slaves, but rather to express their outrage over the deterioration of their working conditions and material well-being. Rarely, if ever, did white South Carolina millworkers after World War I liken themselves to African Americans held in bondage.[42] Instead, they mentioned slavery either in the abstract or in an allusion to the ancient civilizations of Egypt and Rome. Ironically, the more textile workers spoke of slavery, the less they stressed the staples of Bleasism—the privileges of white supremacy and male authority— and the more they zeroed in on shop floor and economic issues. The focus of their ire shifted as well. Prior to the stretchout workers took aim at middle-class reformers and wealthy aristocrats, but as they faced increased workloads and thinner paychecks they concentrated their resentment on mill managers and minute men. In the end, the metaphor of slavery served as a call to arms, uniting mill people in the fight against the architects of the new industrial order.[43]

In equating the stretchout with slavery, millhands said something about how they saw the world. Using the most powerful language available to them to talk about work, they indicated that class issues stood at the top of their list of grievances. This does not mean that male millhands did not bristle every time someone called them a "linthead," or that they did not worry about the commitment of others to white democracy, or that they did not fret about the actions of their wives and children, but now they concentrated their public energies on getting lighter workloads and higher wages. At the same time, recasting the metaphor of slavery to highlight mutual anguish blunted some of the misogynistic edges of Bleasism and working-class identity. Though patriarchal overtones lingered, the metaphor of slavery pointed to an ominous new social evil that did not discriminate between men and women, husbands and wives, parents and children. Violating the principle of fairness, it oppressed workers and nonworkers alike. As such, the language of slavery enlisted women, both as wage earners and as family members, in the class struggle in ways that the rhetoric of Bleasism never could.

This system of "slavery," moreover, was put in place at the very moment that the Piedmont's long-standing labor shortage disappeared. Several factors contributed to the swelling of the regional pool of workers. Falling demand for textiles and increased workloads meant fewer jobs. But it was really the actions of rural people that altered the supply of labor. Like their brothers and cousins in the factories, farmers thrived during the war years, but peace triggered a downturn in prices paid for cotton, tobacco, and livestock. This was the start of twenty years of depression in the countryside.[44] To make matters worse, the boll weevil invaded South Carolina. The inoffensive-looking grayish-brown critter quickly became the state's largest consumer of cotton; in 1921 it chewed up a third of the crop. "We never would have left the farm if Mr. Boll Weevil hadn't come when he did. Why he just eat us out of everything," a Winnsboro millhand lamented in 1939.[45]

Rural people left the countryside only after much soul-searching. For many, to move to the mill village was to admit defeat. Obviously, few did this easily. Ideas about morality made still others hesitant to relocate. Rural people continued in the 1920s to see the villages as dangerous places where criminals, hucksters, and prostitutes thrived. Even the purest, most innocent souls could find themselves debauched and debased there. North Carolina country people told their relatives as they left the farm for the factory that "they might as well be going to a whore house as the mill."[46] Such admonishments, however, were not enough to keep people on the land. During the 1920s thousands of farmers and tenants pinched by financial necessity gave up their rural lives to make new homes for themselves and their families in the cotton mill world. Many more who remained on the land close to a factory began to view the mill as a much-needed source of cash. Although they did not like the work, they grudgingly tended looms when hard times demanded that they do so. Increased road construction and car ownership narrowed the distance between farm and factory.[47] Each morning thousands of people hopped into their tin lizzies for the short ride to the mill. Rural commuters usually did not work all the time. Instead, they joined the ranks of spare hands, extra operatives retained by management to work when the mills had a backlog of orders. By 1926 some firms had substitutes for every position in their plants. This also gave them a pool of potential strikebreakers.[48]

The labor surplus of the late 1920s proved decisive. With mills not hiring, workers had to stay put; they could not bolt to the mill across town or in the next county to protest perceived injustices. As a result, turnover rates in the mills fell after 1925. While the glut of wage earners limited workers' choices, it multiplied management's options. With plenty of eager hands lined up outside the gates each morning, owners did not worry about losing workers if they tampered with shop floor traditions. They cranked up the machines to full blast. Those who could not keep up were let go. The decline in turnover rates, however, represented a double-edged sword. A constantly moving workforce militated against collective action. Laborers simply did not stay in one place long enough to form strong ties in the community. But those who did remain in the same mill village year after year were better able to answer management's challenge on the shop floor with a well-coordinated walkout. That is exactly what happened: longtime workers went on strike in the late 1920s while strikebreakers—victims of the collapse of cotton prices—waited outside the mill gates to take their jobs.[49]

At first, small groups led the fight against the stretchout on the shop floor, but by the late 1920s loosely organized resistance gave way to an unprecedented round of community-based collective action. In the spring of 1929, strikes engulfed the southern textile belt. National attention was riveted on three flash points of conflict: Elizabethton, Tennessee, and Gastonia and Marion, North Carolina. The uprising at Gastonia's Loray Mills attracted the most headlines. Reporters wrote of squalid conditions, the murder of a sheriff and a balladeer, and mostly of the strike's Communist Party leadership.[50] That spring South Carolina stirred as well. In 1929 Palmetto textile employees staged fourteen strikes that involved nearly 12,000 people or one-sixth of the state's full-time millhands.[51] Nearly everyone, even the editor of the probusiness *Southern Textile Bulletin*, recognized that the stretchout had caused the unrest. "I'm inclined to think that the recent strikes have resulted from the stopwatches of the efficiency experts," David Clark concluded.[52] A legislative committee of the South Carolina House of Representatives headed by a leading trade unionist determined that mill managers provoked the strikes by "putting more work on the employees than they can do."[53]

Lifelong millhands, the children of Bleasites, stepped forward to lead the revolt against the stretchout.[54] Like the mythical Will Thompson, strikers were typically born in a mill village, baptized in a mill church, and educated in a mill school. Unlike their parents or recent recruits to the cotton mill world, who compared the factory to the countryside, the industrial world served as their frame of reference. The stretchout violated what might be called these permanent workers' moral economy of work, or sense of right and wrong. "Its killing [us] faster than the World War did," one worker declared. "We were running entirely too many looms," protested another weaver.[55] So he and others went on strike to force the mill owners to respect their view of a fair day's work.

Strikers in 1929 insisted that the owners slow down the pace of work. Speaking through their demands, they suggested that prior to the stretchout, a fair and just system had prevailed in the mills. At rallies, on the picket lines, and in private conferences, they repeatedly asked management to go back to the older way of doing things, to return to a past—that was, of course, part myth, part reality—of harmonious industrial relations.[56] Three times, for instance, in a brief address before a rally in Pelzer, a strike leader called for the reinstatement of the "old" system.[57] Spartanburg weavers insisted on the "restoration of conditions that existed before the new system."[58] Extending the metaphor of slavery, millworkers pressed for the *abolition* of the onerous new work regime and an end to falling wages. "That is what we are striking for[,] the abolition of the stretch-out," a Greenville strike committee informed its employer. "Contrary to the custom in most union strikes," an observer noted of the unrest in South Carolina, "they had only one demand and that was the abolition of the stretch-out."[59]

While strikers in North Carolina and Tennessee marched against the new industrial order under union banners (a bright red one in Gastonia), Palmetto State laborers headed down a different path. "No, we don't want no organizers from outside," announced strikers from Greenville's Brandon Mills. "We're doing this ourselves." A group of Pelzer workers asked a United Textile Workers of America (UTW) organizer to leave their community as well. "Two folks come down here from that bunch an' we told 'em how much we appreciated their good feelin' an' gave 'em a drink of Coca Cola, an' put 'em on the street car."[60]

Rejecting the UTW was not what it seemed. South Carolina strikers did not shy away from the union because, as some have suggested, they lacked class consciousness; rather, their actions reflected a carefully considered strategic choice. The promise of white unity, central to the ethos of white supremacy and encouraged by the discourse of welfare capitalism, shaped their decision. Drawing on the ideas of industrial partnership and white egalitarianism, workers gambled that they could deal directly with white mill owners. They petitioned the manufacturers, the same individuals who professed to be selfless benefactors of the white community, to treat them not like slaves, but with the dignity and respect that all white men and women deserved. As children of the South, workers also understood the antipathy of their employers, as well as the professional classes, toward trade unions.[61] Mill owners, ministers, and newspaper editors usually blamed labor unrest on external forces: NAACP fronts from Chicago, communists from Moscow, Jewish anarchists from New York, or agents of New England manufacturers. Rarely did these leading citizens acknowledge the underlying grievances that sparked trade unionism. By shunning the national labor organization, workers tried to steer the public discourse away from incendiary charges of outside influences toward the internal source of the strikes, the stretchout.[62]

The attitudes of UTW leaders also influenced workers' actions. Founded in 1902, the United Textile Workers limped along through its first thirty years of existence. Built on a shaky foundation of unsteady locals in New England and Pennsylvania, the union had made only brief forays into the South, and none had been very successful. Despite the fact that the Piedmont led the nation in textile production in 1929, the UTW had no more than a handful of southern locals, few, if any, southern organizers or southern representatives on its executive board. Union leaders spoke a language of business unionism that was alien to South Carolina workers. Trumpeting efficiency, they assured mill managers of increased productivity in exchange for union recognition. The UTW even hired its own industrial engineer, who traveled south to show manufacturers how to enhance profitability without antagonizing their wage earners. South Carolina millhands had no interest in "humanizing" the stretchout; they wanted it abolished, period.[63]

South Carolina strikers won some initial victories against the stretchout in 1929. The protest wave started in Ware Shoals in March. Residents of the "Shoal" did not wait for the stretchout to be introduced before walking off the job. When weavers learned that minute men were in town to conduct time-motion studies, they cut off the power and sprinted over to the hotel where the industrial engineers were staying. Luckily for the scientific managers, they heard the weavers coming and slipped out the back door and hopped on a train before the workers could catch them.[64] The owner of the tiny American Spinning Company of Greenville averted a strike at his plant when he announced "that the efficiency system [has] been abandoned." Workers at Issaqueena Mills in Central were on strike for less than twenty-four hours when the managers agreed to lower the number of looms assigned to individual weavers from forty-eight to twenty-four, labor's notion of a reasonable limit.[65]

Elsewhere in South Carolina, especially at the state's larger mills, managers did not give in so easily. After six weeks on the picket line, Brandon Mills employees returned to work under a vague agreement that they had rejected earlier. Weavers who ran forty-eight looms before the walkout were assigned

Bleasism in Decline

forty afterward, and those who oversaw ninety-six looms prior to the strike "were to take up reductions of the numbers of looms one at a time with overseers after returning to work."[66] Between 1927 and 1929 Union's Buffalo Mills extended the number of looms assigned to each weaver from thirty-two to one hundred. Workers protested, but officials refused to "abolish the stretch-out," informing strikers that they could either "return to work or get out." When their employees did not rush back to the plant, mill authorities lowered the weavers' workload to seventy-two looms.[67] Wage earners at the Woodruff Plant in rural Spartanburg County and the Anderson Cotton Mills wrested comparable concessions from their bosses. At Whitmire's Aragon-Baldwin Mills, company representatives spurned strikers but offered "individual" weavers help with their workloads and a small raise. Officials at Greenville's Mills Mill did not end the stretchout regime, but they did institute a nominal wage increase, which strikers rejected at first but later accepted.[68]

Despite these partial victories, workers quickly discovered that the old way of doing things had not been restored, that the stretchout had not been abolished. A few months after the strike wave ebbed, many found themselves once again running more machines for the same pay, if not less. Managers were not swayed by the nonunion course taken by Palmetto State laborers or by their subtle appeals to white unity. Manufacturers saw the strikes, in the words of the president of Brandon Mills, as "a challenge to the right of the mill owners to operate their plants as they saw fit." "It is the province of the management and the mill," he insisted, "to adopt the policies and system of work that are to prevail in the mill.... Upon this we stand!"[69]

Having failed to abolish the stretchout on the picket line or through direct negotiations with their bosses, some workers shifted tactics. They signed up with the union. At about the same time, the United Textile Workers changed its approach as well. Jarred into action by the spring strike wave in the Piedmont, the UTW sent a handful of organizers to the South.[70] The results of the organizing campaign, while not extraordinary, were still impressive. In 1928 the textile union did not have a single local at any of South Carolina's more than two hundred mills. Two years later three locals operated in Greenville and Columbia, two in Union, and one in Anderson, Bath, Chester, Rock Hill, Graniteville, Ware Shoals, Whitmire, and Woodruff. Between 1929 and 1931, 17,000 South Carolina textile workers, or approximately one out of every five millhands in the state, belonged to the UTW.[71]

From the start of its organizing efforts, the UTW was attacked relentlessly on the race question. Newspaper editors warned textile workers that the American Federation of Labor (AFL) "recognizes no color line." "Are the cotton mill workers of South Carolina," asked another editor, "willing to . . . be placed on equal footin' with negro labor union members, and . . . contribute their earnings toward the maintenance of negro car porters while negroes are on strike?" Yes, some answered. Apparently by 1929 workers' fears of industrial slavery overrode any worries about the survival of white supremacy.[72]

The strongest of the state's fledgling textile unions sprang up in Ware Shoals, where the strike wave began in 1929.[73] The earlier walkout at the "Shoals"—the one that started when the workers ran the industrial engineers out of town—lasted only three days. Assuaged by management's assurances that piece rates would be adjusted to meet the added demands of the multiple-loom system, millhands returned to work. Within days, weavers found themselves operating additional looms at lower rates. Local activists responded by going door-to-door and methodically building a local union movement. By the spring of 1929, seven hundred Ware Shoals employees had signed UTW membership cards. On June 2 mill officials staged a showdown with the fledging union by sacking the leaders of the local, R. E. Campbell and O. H. Barnwell. The dismissals triggered the second Ware Shoals strike of the year.[74]

Only 140 of Ware Shoals's 1,700 permanent employees reported to work on the first day of the strike. Strikers demanded the reinstatement of Campbell and Barnwell, the establishment of a company arbitration board, and union recognition. Mill officials refused to talk to the UTW strike committee, although they did announce that they would listen to the grievances of "loyal" individual employees. On June 10, one week into the strike, Governor John G. Richards, a steadfast Bleasite and self-described friend of the workingman, appointed a mediation board headed by James C. Self, the president of two Greenwood County mills, to look into the strike.[75] Neither the UTW nor the mill people of Ware Shoals had a voice on the panel. Without hearing from a single trade unionist, the board signed an "agreement" with management in which the company promised to take back "without discrimination" all workers not associated with "illegal activity."[76]

Adamant about avoiding a "replay of the troubles they had in Gastonia," Governor Richards sent ninety-one National Guardsmen, twelve constables, and two machine gunners to Ware Shoals. On June 20 the plant reopened under the protection of armed guards. The troops ushered strikebreakers, mostly newcomers to the village or young men from the countryside, in and out of the plant at the start and close of each shift.[77] Hundreds of union members crowded behind the soldiers, yelling "scab, scab" at the women and men who crossed the picket line, but their nasty taunts could not shut down the mill.[78] Meanwhile, relief supplies were running low. Some strikers drifted back

Bleasism in Decline

to work, and others wandered off to mill towns down the road or across the state line. Finally on July 25, the union called off the protest. "The presence of the troops was very instrumental in breaking the morale of the strikers," a local union leader argued, adding that the government forces "fitted into the scheme of the management to defeat labor organization among their employees."[79] Over the next several months the Ware Shoals management evicted UTW members from the mill village, blacklisted strike leaders, and hired rural residents to fill their places.[80]

The Ware Shoals union did not survive the year. Other UTW locals endured, but they too were doomed by the potent combination of managerial repression and the deepening depression. By 1931 only four union locals remained active in the state. Twelve months later there were two. As the union movement collapsed, mill masters slashed piece rates, increased workloads, and laid off thousands. In the long days after the strikes and the union building campaigns, workers repeatedly complained that management stretched out the stretchout. To be sure, through collective action, workers took some of the sting out of the multiple-loom system and the speedup, but they did not win their independence from the stretchout. Even so, the mill people of South Carolina would not be resigned to a life of slavery.

Following the strikes, the UTW's collapse, and the partisan mobilization of the state's military might in Ware Shoals, South Carolina workers shifted gears in their fight against the stretchout, focusing their energies on a political solution. Although millworkers had been active in politics before the 1929 strikes, afterward they embraced a new political agenda and mobilized themselves, rather than being mobilized by someone else, like Cole Blease. In August 1929 the UTW-dominated Greenville Trades and Labor Council signaled the new direction of millworker politics. "We must employ our most effective means," read a council resolution, "by combining ourselves in political unity and strive diligently to place in office candidates whom we know to act with equality and justice." Ware Shoals's W. H. Riddle called on the general assembly to "make conditions . . . better in the cotton mills."[81]

Only the government, people like Riddle came to believe, was strong enough to provide the needed counterweight to the mill managers. The government, moreover, looked like the most powerful lever available to millhands who were armed with the ballot yet unorganized on the shop floor. If textile workers marshaled their electoral might not simply to check state intervention and preserve white supremacy, but to send to Columbia men who would, in Riddle's words, fight for the "many, not the few," they could convert the state government from an agent of their oppressors into a great emancipator.

As millhands tentatively began to advocate state action on their own behalf, Cole Blease found himself increasingly out of step with his core constituency.

Senator Blease remained silent throughout most of the 1929 strike wave in South Carolina. Finally with troops garrisoned at Ware Shoals, he returned home from Washington. Speaking to Anderson workers, he "heartily" endorsed "any legal organization of cotton mill people." But in hushed tones, Blease warned them to watch out for "Yankee trash running around here stirring up devilment . . . [and] . . . preaching lawlessness, communism, or IWWism." These men, he continued, loathed the South's traditions. Tossing out the race card, he charged that trade unionists were willing to "place white and blacks on the same equality." Blease, however, was not worried; he trusted the sound judgment of South Carolina's "pure white Anglo-Saxon" labor force and management. "You should organize yourselves among yourselves," he counseled. "You can get consideration at the hands of the manufacturers without having to send North to get a committee to go in and talk with the officials." The senator must not have been following the news reports, or maybe he forgot that millhands had already tried this strategy and it had failed.[82]

Near the end of his Anderson address, Blease bragged, "During the whole forty years of my career, I have been a friend of the laboring people." "You haven't proved it," someone shot back. Blease muffled the heckler with a racially charged personal attack—something about his affection for African Americans—but working-class disquiet with the senator did not go away so easily.[83] Following the Anderson rally, a growing number of millhands questioned Coley's devotion to their cause. The AFL and the South Carolina Federation of Labor rebuked him and demanded an explanation for his anti-union outburst at Anderson, which they never received. Some even whispered that Blease was now in the pocket of the mill owners. From Aiken to Gaffney, laborers chafed at his refusal to help them fight the stretchout. A Graniteville weaver and formerly fervent Bleasite lambasted Coley for voting against the Wheeler bill, a measure to conduct a federal investigation of the stretchout and other conditions in the textile industry. Stung by the senator's indifference to his pain, a Union County worker captured the views of many mill hill residents when he announced, "To hell with Blease politically."[84]

Blease's apparent indifference toward workers' suffering cost him at the polls. He would never win another statewide campaign, nor would he again command the support of millhands as an electoral bloc. Still, Coley would linger as a candidate and Bleasism would survive as a political ideology, picking up some unlikely recruits along the way.[85]

While Blease's support on the mill hills slipped, a new electoral hero of the masses emerged. He was not James F. Byrnes, the man who defeated Blease in 1930, but the millhand-turned-politician, Olin D. Johnston. Johnston's early life was the life of thousands of South Carolina millhands. Born just before the turn of the century, he was reared on the countryside. Frustrated by fluctuating cotton prices, his family abandoned its rented farm a decade later and moved to the Honea Path mill village. When he was eleven years old, Johnston went to work for the Chiquola Manufacturing Company as a sweeper. He quickly learned to tie a weaver's knot and took charge of his own side of the looms. War pulled him out of the factory and placed him on the battlefields of France. Returning to South Carolina a decorated veteran, he put himself through college and law school, tending looms at night. As an attorney he stayed close to his working-class roots, taking on negligence cases for injured laborers and defending wage earners evicted from their homes. In 1926 Spartanburg County voters—many of whom were residents of the area's twenty or more mill villages—sent Johnston to the state house of representatives. There he aggressively advocated workers' interests. During the 1929 legislative session, for instance, he orchestrated the passage of a sewage bill that required mill owners to install modern sewers in their villages or pay a fine. This was the first piece of labor legislation enacted in South Carolina in almost a decade.[86]

In 1930 Johnston ran for governor. Speaking before mass rallies, he voiced the new political direction of the millhands. He almost never mentioned race. It was not, he explained when asked, that he questioned white supremacy. What true South Carolinian would? Rather, he argued that the issue had already been resolved—white men were in control and would remain in control—now it was time to recast the political discourse. He declared that by 1930 South Carolina had become "an industrial state instead of an agricultural state." Government policy, he maintained, should reflect this transformation. He pressed for the adoption of a workers' compensation law and promoted the creation of a separate department of labor to consider workers' grievances. (At the time, the South Carolina Department of Agriculture handled working-class concerns.) He backed hour and wage regulations, urged millhands to enlist in trade unions, and condemned the mobilization of the state militia to break strikes. All of these measures, Johnston predicted, would foster his prime objective—to end "the economic slavery of the masses."[87]

When the polls closed on election night, a Johnston victory appeared to be at hand. But just as millhands began to celebrate, the Charleston vote came in. Johnston's opponent, Ibra C. Blackwood, a Spartanburg attorney with close ties to the mill owners and rural elite, was pushed over the top by the astonishing boost he received from Charleston. In that city he won 80 percent of the vote, whereas across the rest of the state he outpolled Johnston by only four-tenths of 1 percent of the vote. When Johnston backers asked to inspect the Charleston ballots, they were told that they had mysteriously burned. Some cried foul.[88] Convinced that victory had been snatched from their hands, many millhands recognized how close they had come to placing one of their own in the governor's mansion. They had seen the future of their political hopes and dreams and his name was Olin Dewitt Talmadge Johnston, not Coleman Livingston Blease. His message was government action on behalf of the economically weak, not obstruction and white supremacy. Still, workers would have to endure the Great Depression and the New Deal before their new favorite son would become their governor.

CHAPTER THREE

Searching for Answers to the Great Depression

 Blumer Hendrix lived in Prosperity, South Carolina. After her husband lost his job, the family had no money for food, clothes, or a weekly church offering. Adding to their trials, Hendrix had just had a baby. She named him after Olin Johnston. In exchange for this tribute, she told the millhand-turned-politician, "I am expecting a big present." She addressed her letter, "Dear Olion Johnston."[1]

Soon after G. L. Ridger and his son were fired by the Marlboro Cotton Mills, their backs started to ache. Later, after their mouths began to throb, they broke out in a deep red rash on their hands, feet, and faces. Following a bad case of diarrhea, Ridger went to see a doctor, who asked about the family diet, only to learn that they subsisted on fatback, cornmeal, and molasses, two, sometimes three, times a day. The physician told Ridger that he had pellagra, a classic hard-times disease, and instructed him to eat fresh meat, green vegetables, and eggs. The unemployed millworker said he had no money for these items. There was nothing the doctor could do.[2]

W. H. Riddle lost his job at the Ware Shoals Manufacturing Company after the 1929 strikes. For months he searched for work, wearing out his only pair of shoes before he found a new job. Struggling to support his family of five, he exhausted his savings and tapped every available source of credit. By winter, he reported that there was "no relief in sight." Despite having "always been honest hard working and law abidin'," Riddle lamented, "[m]y family is almost on starvation." Desperate, he determined that "It would be a fine time for me to blow my brains out if I knew my wife could collect my insurance."[3]

Edgar Gaddis of Calhoun Falls wrote Olin Johnston that he was in love with the "sweetest girl in the world." But jobless, homeless, and penniless, he decided against marriage. Gaddis was heartbroken.[4]

These are snapshots of life on the mill hills of South Carolina during the Great Depression. They are pictures of disorder and dislocation caused by unemployment and falling wages. They reveal pain, suffering, and misery. Hard times and uncertainty, however, were not new to millhands. Despite the wage gains of the early 1920s, white working-class families were well acquainted with long layoffs, low pay, illness, and crippling industrial accidents.

Women, in particular, were accustomed to making "endless little economies," wasting nothing that could be used, borrowing from the grocer to pay the insurance agent. With the onslaught of the depression, wives, sisters, and daughters redoubled their efforts. They scrimped and saved, bought less food, and made what they did buy last longer. They cut back on fuel, planted the rows of vegetables in their mill gardens closer together, canned more produce, and sewed and repaired tattered coats and pants. Kin doubled up to reduce their rent. Housewives, who had left the paid labor force during World War I, took in washing and boarders and scrubbed the floors of uptown businesses. When these family strategies proved ineffective, long-standing community traditions of reciprocity and mutuality served mill people as buffers against destitution. Families pressed by tragedy or trying circumstances could usually count on their neighbors to take up a "pounding" of food and clothing to help them through their difficult days.[5]

Focusing on working people's imaginative personal, family, and community efforts to cope with the Great Depression reveals only a portion of their stories.[6] Mill people also fashioned inventive political solutions to deal with the era's disorders. Building on the conclusions drawn from the antistretchout struggles, namely, that the government could serve as a powerful ally in conflicts with employers, workers and their families concentrated their political energies on state action. As the depression deepened, millhands moved beyond vague assertions of government responsibility for protecting the weak against the strong and constructed their own detailed legislative agenda to address the problems of unemployment and low wages. What these proposals demonstrated was that South Carolina mill people were walking in lockstep with laborers around the country. Anticipating some New Deal reforms, the nation's working class in the years leading up to Franklin Roosevelt's 1932 election committed itself to creating an industrial order whose priorities were set by social needs rather than market imperatives.[7] As white mill people fought to restructure the state, race—in the case of Chicago and Woonsocket, Rhode

Island, workers, ethnicity—drifted to the margins of their public identity, although it never completely disappeared.[8]

Millworkers, however, were not the only group in South Carolina trying to influence policy during the depression. Farmers and businessmen also tried to steer the course of government action, often away from labor legislation. White discord, not white unity, once again accented political debate in South Carolina.

On Black Tuesday, October 29, 1929, the day of the stock market crash—the symbolic start of the Great Depression—an already unsteady economy, badly weakened by underconsumption and an unequal distribution of wealth, toppled. Over the next twelve years, and especially over the next three, the nation's economic engine ground down to a painfully low gear of joblessness and suffering. Statistics tell part of the story. Between 1929 and 1932 manufacturing output dropped by 48 percent, and steel plants operated at only 12 percent of capacity. Decreased output translated into mass unemployment. In 1932 one out of every four Americans was without work. Seventy percent of the nation's coal miners were idle. Joblessness reached 50 percent in Cleveland, 60 percent in Akron, and a staggering 90 percent in Gary. Breadlines filled with grizzled men snaked through city blocks, and children thin from hunger sifted through garbage cans. Skilled machinists sold pencils on street corners next to corporate lawyers hawking apples.[9]

Hard times came to South Carolina mill towns after Black Tuesday, but the story there was not exactly the same as the national story. Few textile workers heard the crash on Wall Street; instead, many were still talking about the big football showdown between Clemson and the University of South Carolina at the state fair grounds in Columbia. (Clemson won 21–14.)[10] Soup kitchens were rare, and not many beleaguered professionals sold fruit on mill village street corners. In 1932 output in the textile industry stood at 75 percent of that in 1929. Unemployment, although high, never soared to the ghastly heights that it reached in the North. Part of the reason for this was structural. No matter how little they had, people had to wear clothes, so although the textile industry felt the sting of the depression, it did not feel it as sharply as the makers of cars, electrical appliances, and other consumer durable goods. In addition, the southern textile industry and cotton economy had been in the doldrums for at least three years at the time of Clemson's 1929 victory. Millhands and their country cousins did not, therefore, have to fall as far to hit rock bottom as did Detroit auto workers or Pittsburgh electrical workers. Still slowly, insidiously, the Great Depression crept up on the mill hills, making its impact felt everywhere: at work, at the store, and at home.[11]

Unemployment was the most conspicuous mark of hard times. Prior to the slowdown in sales and the emergence of the labor surplus in the mid-1920s, unemployment in the mill villages had been virtually nonexistent. Between 1927 and 1930, however, an estimated 13,000 workers, or 17 percent of South Carolina's mill labor force, lost their jobs. During the next several years, ten mills shut down altogether, while dozens of others either eliminated the night shift or sacked whole sections of workers.[12] A closer look at Columbia shows some finer details of the unemployment situation. Before the crash, the capital was home to six textile mills employing approximately 1,500 workers. In 1930 the Palmetto Mill closed permanently, leaving 200 laborers out of work. Pacific, Columbia, and Glencoe Mills cut their payrolls as well. A social worker based in the city's mill districts reported an elevenfold jump in joblessness in 1932.[13]

Unemployment, as extensive as it was, represented only part of the problem. Even more vexing was underemployment. After World War I, textile laborers typically worked eight- to ten-hour days, Monday through Friday, and five hours on Saturday morning. As orders started to lag, managers scaled back production. Throughout the late-1920s and early-1930s, most mills operated on abbreviated schedules, perhaps three or four days a week, although when they did open they cranked up the machines to full blast. During the summer of 1930, plants in Greenville, Greenwood, and Ninety-Six shut down for extended "holidays." Many millhands also found themselves underemployed on the job itself. Depression-era narratives are filled with stories of longtime wage earners being reassigned to less skilled, lower-paying jobs, of second hands tending looms and weavers sweeping floors.[14]

Because South Carolina millhands always worked without a union contract, which would have provided a codified system of seniority, layoffs, cutbacks, and demotions were capricious at best and often downright vindictive. Some mill owners divided what work there was as fairly as possible; each family in the village got the same number of shifts per week. Overseers in other factories discharged those they did not like and kept on those they did, regardless of the employee's needs or the quality of his or her labor. Families that had counted on two, three, and even four salaries were left with one person or sometimes nobody with a job. Meanwhile, kin and friends of the overseer might still have several workers on the payroll.[15]

Incomes fell right along with employment opportunities. With fewer people at work, families earned less. Not only were less people employed, the earnings of those with jobs dropped as well. Reduced hours translated into pay cuts. Making matters worse, hourly wages, stuck above prewar levels throughout the 1920s, began to fall in 1929, reaching their postwar nadir in 1932. By this time, despite increases in productivity and output, the average millworker earned half of what she or he had made in 1920. Falling incomes meant that millhands had to make do with less. At the same time, workers' expectations of better days were dashed; families could no longer participate as they had in the consumer economy, and husbands found it harder to hold onto the breadwinner role.[16]

Erratic work schedules and falling wages left a quarter of the state's population, and 14 percent of the mill families, in need of relief. But the economic crisis rocked a state—indeed, a region and a country—with the most rudimentary welfare system in the industrial world. In South Carolina, there was no unemployment insurance, no workers' compensation, no social security, and no jobs programs. Federal efforts, notably the Hoover administration's Reconstruction Finance Corporation, benefited only a fraction of those in need. Across the country, the burden of relief fell to state and local agencies and charities.[17]

In South Carolina, that meant that the destitute usually had to rely on "primitive," sometimes degrading, forms of relief. Upcountry municipal officials, for instance, launched voluntary campaigns urging home owners to "Give a Fellow a Job" by hiring an unemployed worker to install a laundry chute, paint a spare bedroom, or dig a drainage ditch.[18] Estimating that 1,400 Union County residents needed help, Mrs. J. B. Bradley envisioned setting up "a Community Garden . . . to aid the jobless, and at the same time teach them about nature and the dignity of work." The hard-line conservative editor of the *Charleston News and Courier*, William Watts Ball, championed an Arcadian "back-to-the-farm" program. With erstwhile mill people happily planting cotton and vegetables, Ball forecast an end to mass unemployment and the threat of industrial rebellion.[19] Chester's D. Euta Calvin recommended a special day of prayer to rejuvenate the economy, and the upbeat editor of an upcountry newspaper urged people to "work more, worry less."[20] Even Ku Klux Klansmen, decked out in the order's customary white robes and pointy headgear, solicited assistance for the victims of the depression, at least the white Protestant ones.[21] The Red Cross and church organizations also pitched in, distributing flour, clothes, medicine, and other items to destitute farmers and workers.[22] None of these efforts, however, were enough to end the widespread suffering.[23]

The failure of public, personal, and family schemes to deal with the depression reinforced in the minds of many the need for prompt, decisive state action. "I am writing you to see what you can or will do about the unemployment [situation] in Anderson," M. E. Underwood began a letter to Governor Richards. Then, in an edgy tone, he wrote: "Don't tell me you can't do anything for I know you can." "I never did think that I wanted to be an anarchist," Y. P. Harrison confessed, "but sum times hit [*sic*] looks like they run things around here to suit their values and the law abidin' citizens is shut out." [24] Though many shared Underwood and Harrison's frustrations, few became anarchists. Most began to think like Lexington's H. A. Hendrix. "Public work," he complained, "is running on short time and [the] mills are shutting down each day. . . . We Democratic voters of the State of South Carolina think that our Governor should help us poor laboring class of people." [25] For scores of millhands, in the wake of the 1929 strikes, broadening the authority of the state over the economy appeared to be the surest way to end the Great Depression.

"We are cotton mill people," J. M. Fletcher of Ware Shoals proudly informed Governor John G. Richards in 1930. On the back of a letter-size, bright-colored print of Jean-François Millet's *The Gleaners*, the painting depicting a trio of bent-backed peasants toiling in a hay field under gray skies, he sketched his own portrait of a beleaguered community. "Their [*sic*] is hundreds of men walking the roads looking for work with wife and kids at home suffering," Fletcher wrote. "The stretch-out is what is wrong." Given the failure of industrial action or trade unionism to moderate the grueling work regime, the Ware Shoals resident proposed state intervention. "Please," he requested, "help to pass the thirty loom law, they will have work to do and their kids wont [*sic*] suffer any longer." [26]

Toward the end of his letter, Fletcher changed his tone. There were no more pleases and no more pleas for help. Instead, he held up the power of the ballot, asserting that politicians who asked millworkers for their vote owed them something in return. "If it had not been for us," he told Richards, "you would not be Govner [*sic*] and I think we have a right to ask you as well as you had to ask us and proble [*sic*] you will want another office and by our help you will get one and if you help to pass the thirty loom law it will not only help us but it will help you." [27]

Although largely unknown, Fletcher's voice was the voice of the moment on the mill hills. Displaying a flare for the dramatic—few letters arrived at the governor's office on the back of prints of French paintings—he pushed his way into the political process, demanding to be heard as a citizen of South Carolina. What he did not say, moreover, was as significant as what he did say. Fletcher did not mention African Americans. He did not pin the rise in unemployment or the diminished status of the breadwinner on people of color, nor did he accuse immigrants, as some of the leaders of South Carolina craft unions did, with setting off the Great Depression.[28] Fletcher said nothing about middle-class reformers, the frequent target of Blease's vicious blasts. Rather, he blamed the painful dislocations in the mill world on the stretchout and the mill owners. Anticipating the New Deal, he pressed for government action—at this point, at the state level only—to curb corporate power, spread employment, and spark recovery.

Echoing Fletcher's analysis, South Carolina workers argued that the stretchout, by "taking three mens jobs and putting it on one," touched off the depression.[29] "The 'Stretch-out System' is the cause of the whole trouble," asserted one wage earner. "We wouldn't have the depression if it were not for it." A group of Greenville workers stated: "We believe that the establishment of an inconsistent economic policy . . . which permits . . . the payment of interest and dividends by corporations irrespective of the number of producers employed . . . to be responsible for the displacement of workers by labor saving machinery . . . [and] . . . the present unbalanced conditions."[30]

Most millhands agreed with Fletcher and the Greenville workers not just about the problem, but also about the solution. Legislation to limit the number of looms that an employer could legally assign to an individual weaver, like the thirty-loom law advocated by Fletcher, was the most popular answer to the Great Depression on the mill hills. A potent streak of radicalism undergirded these antistretchout proposals. Calling for government regulation of workloads, millhands launched a grassroots attack on private property, or what the owner of the Brandon Mills proclaimed as the "sacred right [of manufacturers] to operate their plants as they saw fit" regardless of the consequences.[31] Devastated by the depression, workers espoused a different morality. They argued that the stretchout demonstrated that the mill owners were too irresponsible to warrant the right of unilateral control over production. In place of the old system, millhands pressed for state intervention to ensure that work was distributed in the interests of the many, rather than the profits of a few.

Laborers' campaigns for shorter hours went hand in glove with their fight for reduced workloads. Despite extensive underemployment and unemployment, mill owners regularly defied a toothless state law passed ten years earlier establishing sixty hours as the maximum workweek. Some operated their factories on the basis of twelve- to fourteen-hour shifts, occasionally without even the customary fifteen-minute break. "I want to explain to you about [*sic*] the Kershaw Cotton Mill is not abiding by the Labor Law," A. P. Dewitt told the governor, "they hold the night hands in 12 hours every night."[32] "Thousands [are] out of work," grumbled a group of millhands, "and we who have work have too much."[33] Instead of two stints a day, Paul Clark suggested that "they could have 3 shifts at 8 hours each and the jobless would have jobs." Not only would the check on hours create openings in the mills, but, according to Clark, it would be a "blessing in Christ's name."[34]

Long hours, low pay, demotions, and unemployment rekindled white working-class fears of emasculation. Men, who — along with women — worried that the depression and the stretchout might bring back the dreaded double shift of wage work followed by home work, endorsed plans to allocate jobs to breadwinners first. Prohibiting women from public work emerged as a popular scheme in South Carolina and nationwide for combating joblessness.[35] Firing women, this argument contended, would create jobs for unemployed men and quickly bring an end to the depression. It was that easy. Many zeroed in on married women in particular.[36] "Why are mill owners of this state allowed to work married women?" asked a Clinton man.[37] An Anderson woman pressed for the passage of a statute banishing married women from cotton mills. "There are men living [near] me that really needs work," she disclosed, "but they don't work at public work now. . . . [I]f every women was cut off public work I am sure times would be better, it would end this awful depression."[38] More than misogyny (although it was certainly prevalent) fueled attacks on women in the workforce. These schemes were part of a broader attempt by millhands, which included loom limit laws and maximum-hour measures, to enlist the government in the struggle to end the depression. A fair economic system, many believed, would distribute jobs equally among those who needed them most — in this case, relatively well-paid male breadwinners. Plans to limit women's access to employment, therefore, were part of the larger campaign to impose order and stability on the industrial world, at least on male terms.[39]

The battle to subdue the Great Depression led mill people to endorse several other legislative initiatives. Some demanded passage of a law making it illegal for textile firms to dock an employee's pay for defects in the cloth. Proposals requiring textile manufacturers to give employees thirty days' notice before any production curtailment, work stoppage, or plant shutdown also won the backing of laborers. So, too, did a measure requiring a moratorium on rental charges on mill homes until the depression waned. Mill people also wanted lawmakers to make it easier to organize and fight against the stretchout by passing legislation to bar antiunion discrimination. Following the lead of the state's craft unions, some textile laborers, in addition, joined the fight for workers' compensation.[40]

Unwilling to remain on the sidelines during the economic downturn and let others determine their fate, workers joined J. M. Fletcher and pushed themselves onto the state's main political stages. "If the legislative body doesn't abolish the stretch-out in the next session," warned an angry millhand, "the textile people will remember it in our next campaign."[41] Millworkers made

Table 3.1. Population of Spartanburg County, Selected Years, 1900–1940

Year	Total Population
1900	65,560
1910	83,465
1920	94,265
1930	116,323
1940	127,733

Sources: Derived from U.S. Bureau of the Census, *Twelfth Census, 1900, Population*, liii; *Thirteenth Census, 1910, Population: Report by States*, 659–67; *Fourteenth Census, 1920, Population: General Report*, 1360; *Fifteenth Census, Unemployment*, 784–87; and *Sixteenth Census, 1940, Population*, 375.

good on their threats. Consider the political contests in 1932 in Spartanburg County. The state's largest textile center in 1930, Spartanburg had thirty-nine cotton mills, employing between 12,000 and 15,000 people. (See Tables 3.1 and 3.2.) As early as 1927, Marjorie Potwin, a welfare worker at the local Spartan Mills, estimated that a third of all Spartanburg voters came from the villages. This figure may have been even higher, but the percentage of eligible voters enrolled or registered to vote in the mill precincts seemed to lag behind the countywide average. Mill women in particular, Potwin reported, stayed out of politics. Nonetheless, the candidate who won the mill vote—textile workers, as Potwin noted, tended to vote as a bloc—stood on the verge of victory.

In 1932, as in previous years, candidates for every imaginable office stopped by the mill villages in search of votes. Addressing crowds of textile people, sometimes numbering in the thousands, electoral hopefuls laid out their views on labor laws and industrial recovery. All of them, whether running for coroner or sheriff or state senator, mentioned millhands and their plight. Some delivered vague endorsements of "legislation for the mill worker" and "just and fair labor laws," whereas most others pledged their allegiance to a portion of the millworkers' legislative program. Several backed statutes to prevent antiunion discrimination and evictions during strikes. Many candidates advocated the eight-hour day, workers' compensation, and the establishment of a separate state department of labor. Most workers, however, made the anti-stretchout bill their electoral litmus test, and there was no skirting the issue. If a candidate did not volunteer his position on the matter, workers badgered him until he told them where he stood. Spartanburg mill village residents applauded backers of the loom limit law during the campaign and cast their ballots for them on election day. Those who opposed it were jeered at the stump meeting and shunned at the polls.[42]

Table 3.2. Population of Mill Village in Spartanburg County, 1925 and 1937

Year	No. of Workers	No. of Mill Village Residents	% of County Population
1925	11,740	27,040	25.68
1937	15,795	32,000*	25.74

Sources: Seventeenth Annual Report of the Commissioner of Agriculture, Commerce, and Industries of the State of South Carolina—Labor Division (Columbia, 1925), 32–35, South Caroliniana Library, Columbia. Percentage estimates are derived from extrapolations based on even growth population between census years. See also Potwin, *Cotton Mill People*, 59.

*Approximate number.

Either out of sympathy with the millhands' legislative agenda or fearful of their electoral wrath, Spartanburg politicians, and their counterparts across the upcountry, took up labor's cause not just on the stump, but in Columbia as well. Between 1929 and 1933 South Carolina lawmakers—all from mill districts—introduced thirty or more pieces of labor legislation in the general assembly. One popular measure proposed a study of the "injurious" health effects of the stretchout system. Supporters planned to use the evidence marshaled from this investigation to sharpen their attacks on the new work regime.[43] Others proposed bills to bar antiunion discrimination and docking, suspend rental charges until the end of the depression, discourage plant closings, and provide injured workers with automatic compensation. Each year during this period lawmakers also introduced on the floor of the general assembly loom limit bills and maximum-hour statutes.[44]

Almost as important as the legislation itself was the way legislators talked about the measures. Lawmakers repeatedly echoed the language and analysis of millhands. In 1933, for example, with a thirty-six-loom bill on the floor of the house and mill people crammed into the galleries, member after member from the upcountry rose to speak. Proponents compared the stretchout to "Roman slavery." Passage of the plan, another upcountry lawmaker predicted, would end "industrial slavery." An Anderson representative alleged that increased workloads crippled many operatives, even killing a few. Other house members pointed to the strikes of 1929 and forecast tumultuous social unrest if the measure was defeated. "Unless something is done . . . a cotton mill [will] be blown up," prophesied one legislator. Another accused the mill owners of "inviting Communism." Workers, meanwhile, sat on the edges of their seats listening to the debate, applauding the bill's advocates and hissing at its detractors.[45]

Despite the aggressive efforts of millworkers and some of their representatives, the bicameral general assembly did not pass a single antistretchout bill. In 1929, 1930, and 1931 these measures were killed either in committee or on the floor of the house. In both 1932 and 1933 the thirty-six-loom limit won approval in the house but was crushed in the senate. Hours legislation met a similar fate. Support from upcountry lawmakers, fed by grassroots agitation, gained momentum and an eight-hour measure finally made it through the house, only to be defeated in the senate.[46] The legislative program of millhands was rejected, in part, because the workers failed to establish a permanent political organization, but the apportionment of the general assembly represented perhaps an even more daunting hurdle.

Although the state's political structures promoted nearly universal white male suffrage, ensuring propertyless whites a voice in politics, it did not bring white democracy to South Carolina. Above all, it failed to guarantee that all white citizens would be represented equally, that the vote of one white man would be as valuable as the vote of another white man. For starters, the state constitution gave the popularly elected governor little authority. Except for the power to exercise the veto, the chief executive could do little more than commute a few prison sentences and appoint some supporters to serve on the constabulary and the highway patrol. Control over the budget, taxation, appropriations, and most appointments lay in the hands of the general assembly, and this body was hardly democratic.

The constitution of 1895 put in place a federal-style system of legislative apportionment. Under this arrangement, the house of representatives had 124 members, allotted in proportion to the population of each county, white and black alike, despite the fact that African Americans could not vote and certainly would not be represented. In addition, each county, regardless of size, was allocated one seat in the senate. Mirroring the U.S. Congress, a bill had to have the support of a majority in both houses in order to become law, meaning that one chamber could check the initiatives of the other. Aside from law enforcement, the constitution also made no provisions for local or county government. By tradition, county legislative delegations handled affairs for their home districts ranging from judicial appointments to road building to budgetary matters. Tradition also made the senator the head, or, according to one observer, the "little dictator," of his county delegation. The constitution and tradition thus combined to make the senate the nexus of political power in South Carolina.[47]

During the first decade of the twentieth century, the number of people required to elect a senator was about the same across the state whether it was in the low country, upcountry, or midlands.[48] All of this changed in the wake of the state's mill-building campaign. Because of financial and geographic advantages, the textile plants were concentrated above the fall line. Industrialization, in turn, sparked urbanization and population growth. At the same time, the once wealthy and still agriculturally based low country stagnated. Yet apportionment in the state senate remained a geographic constant: each county still had one representative. This meant that voters in the urban, industrial, white-majority sections of the state, more often than not textile districts, were increasingly underrepresented in the legislature.

Between 1895 and 1920 the general assembly created eleven new counties, giving South Carolina a total of forty-six counties. Though the new districts were spread evenly across the state, most of those established in the low country were exceedingly small and all had significant African American, disfranchised majorities. The redrawing of county lines combined with the economic progress of the upcountry drove up the value of the vote in the lowlands. In 1900 there was one state senator for every 2,718 eligible voters (white men over the age of twenty-one) in the low country and one for every 3,686 in the upcountry. Twenty years later, the ratio of eligible voters to each senator increased in the low country to 3,058 to 1, whereas in the upcountry it stood at 5,925 to 1. By 1930 twice as many citizens were needed to elect a senator in the upcountry as in the low country. The situation was even worse in counties where more than 15 percent of the residents lived in the mill villages. In these areas, there was one senator for every 24,555 eligible voters. In the most disparate case, Jasper County, located near the coast and carved out in 1912, had only 1,466 eligible voters in 1930, whereas Greenville, home to dozens of mills, had 45,746.[49] Yet each county had one senator, and there were more nonindustrial locales like Jasper than there were textile centers like Greenville. The malapportionment of the South Carolina General Assembly allowed politicians from rural, low-country, black-majority counties to dominate the state's political system to a degree vastly out of proportion to their numerical strength, and, as it turned out, these politicians typically opposed labor's political agenda.

Edgar A. Brown epitomized low-country, conservative domination of South Carolina politics. Trained as a lawyer, Brown was elected to the senate by the white citizens of the low-country, black-majority county of Barnwell in 1928; he remained in the senate until 1972. Throughout Brown's forty-four-year tenure, Barnwell never had more than 7,000 eligible voters. In fact, if all of his votes spanning his eleven electoral triumphs were tallied up, they would have amounted to barely enough to win a single senate race in Charleston or

Greenville County in 1930. Despite his narrow electoral base, Brown was not shy about grabbing hold of power. Linking up with other low-country conservatives, he got himself appointed to the crucial senate finance committee and was eventually elected president pro tem of the senate. His influence over state politics consistently outstripped that of the popularly elected, but relatively powerless, governor. A journalist dubbed him the "Bishop of Barnwell," and V. O. Key called him "the prime minister" of the state. Ruling with ruthless indifference to the problems of poverty, Brown made sure that the few remained on top of the many. Although he lived in one of South Carolina's least industrialized areas, he believed that the business of politics was to keep wages and taxes low in order to attract capital and corporations to the state. Labor legislation was not part of the plan, and Brown and his senate allies regularly blocked workers' initiatives, killing them either in committee or on the senate floor.[50]

The structure of South Carolina politics provides yet another clue to the fate of labor legislation. Several times between 1931 and 1933 key parts of the millworkers' program, including a few antistretchout bills, passed in the house of representatives only to die in the senate. From the perspective of workers, the house victories demonstrated the popularity of these plans. Undoubtedly some representatives favored loom limits and hours restrictions, but others voted for labor legislation because they knew that the senate, dominated by low-country conservatives like Brown (along with a few upcountry lawmakers bankrolled by mill owners), would kill any prolabor measure. Even when textile workers did appear to be inching ahead, they were in fact going nowhere.

Raw numbers further limited the political potency of millhands. Although workers had an impact on elections, they could not dictate legislation. Although a powerful bloc in state politics, millhands and their families still represented only 20 percent of the electorate. But politics is always a matter of arithmetic, and politicians can add and subtract as fast as anyone. When the candidates in both local and state elections left the mill hills to campaign along "tobacco roads" in the early 1930s, they scarcely mentioned labor legislation. Instead, they talked about fiscal retrenchment, budget cuts, property taxes, and cotton prices, the issues that mattered most to rural people, the majority of voters in the state.

Olin D. Johnston was wrong when he told campaign crowds in 1930 that South Carolina was an industrial state. Fifty years of mill building and investment did not change the fact that 70 percent of its residents—and probably a slightly smaller proportion of voters—lived in rural areas.[51] Most South Carolinians, then, depended on land, not mills, for their livelihood. Of course, a few owned elegant white-columned mansions and huge plantations stretching over several thousand acres, but the majority, black and white alike, lived in simple wood-framed homes without electricity or plumbing on small plots that they either owned or rented. Even those who did not farm for a living—the banker, grocer, insurance agent, carpenter, teacher, and fertilizer salesman—still depended on the land.

For most rural South Carolinians, King Cotton still reigned in 1930. Seminar papers and agricultural outreach programs calling for a retreat from monocrop agriculture registered with only a few. The price of cotton, therefore, remained the single most important economic fact of life. When cotton sold for ten cents or more a pound, people could, as Erskine Caldwell once explained, "not only eat well, but also be able to buy some new clothes and a few pieces of new furniture." If it dipped below eight cents, people lived on short rations. If it went lower, starvation loomed.[52]

By the start of 1933 the price of cotton, which had been declining for seven years, hit rock bottom. Fetching just six cents a pound, cotton sold for less than it cost to plant. Between 1929 and 1933, income from cotton in the South dropped by 71 percent and yearly per capita farm incomes fell from $372 to $203.[53] Foreclosures and bankruptcies became commonplace as the rural economy ground to a standstill. Farmers stopped going to the cotton gin, paying off debts, and visiting the doctor; they bought just the bare necessities, and even those were out of reach for some.

Like white textile workers, rural white citizens did not just endure the Great Depression; relying on creative family and community strategies of survival, they jumped into the political arena. Again like millhands, they eschewed explicitly racial solutions to the collapse, although a biracial alliance of white and black farmers, along the lines of the Arkansas-based Southern Tenant Farmers Union, never formed in the state. In fact, such an alliance apparently was never discussed publicly. Yet again like mill people, the vast majority of rural whites concentrated on promoting legislative solutions to their economic problems. Here, however, is where white workers and most farmers parted ways. Though some rural South Carolinians wanted to mobilize the machinery of the state to impose order over the economy, most saw the government as the problem, not the solution. They wanted to scale back the functions of the state rather than enlarge them.[54]

Fairfield County state senator Ashton Williams—J. M. Fletcher's counterpart—spoke for the countryside. "The present problem of unemployment was the result of . . . an unsound tax policy," Williams argued. "Our only hope for a return to prosperity is to lower taxes." This was his simple cure for the state's complicated economic ills. If lawmakers slashed government "expenditures and extravagance," they could cut taxes. Reduced levies would give consumers more money and result in increased spending. Expanded purchasing power, in turn, would resuscitate the state's moribund economy. According to Williams, South Carolinians needed to cast their votes for men like him, that is, candidates pledged to a program of "economy in government." [55] The "economists," as people who agreed with Williams came to be called, saw the depression as a question of money. Plenty of goods were in the stores, they contended, the problem was that people did not have the cash to buy them. They proposed slashing taxes for property owners in order to aid farmers, spark consumption, and revive the economy.

The push for economy in South Carolina rose in response to the expansive programs of business progressives.[56] Although certainly not the only reformers in the state between 1919 and 1929, business progressives, with their agenda for turning the government into an engine of modernization and economic growth, held sway. Like the apostles of the New South before and after them, they preached that every white person from the mill owner to the millworker to the cotton broker to the tenant farmer would benefit from higher industrial profits and increased investment. Making money, they argued, first required spending public money on roads and schools. Funds for public education would pay double in dividends of more productive workers, more imaginative entrepreneurs, and more efficient housewives. Echoing the almost evangelical oratory of nineteenth-century railroad boosters, highway backers promised that each mile of paved roads would bring the state closer to economic salvation by opening markets for farmers and reducing transportation costs for manufacturers.

Schools came first. Passage of the landmark school measure in 1924, known as the 6-0-1 law, transformed educational funding in South Carolina. The statute had an immediate impact: spending per white pupil tripled, the school term increased by 25 percent, and the teacher-student ratio fell by a quarter.[57] Then, the modernizers, led especially by lawmakers from the underdeveloped low country, turned to roads. Between 1925 and 1940 the number of miles of paved roads in South Carolina increased from 228 to 6,537.[58] State officials utilized an array of funding mechanisms to underwrite the road-building frenzy, from local option to "pay-as-you-go" to a controversial multimillion-dollar bond issue passed in 1929. In addition to schools and roads, lawmakers established twenty-two new state boards, bureaus, agencies, and departments after World War I. The also authorized substantial salary increases for many state employees. As a result, government expenditures zoomed in South Carolina from $6.036 million in 1919 to $23.302 million in 1929.[59]

Mounting expenditures required larger revenues. Trying to meet the demand between 1922 and 1929, legislators enacted thirty new taxes, including—for the first time in the state's history—inheritance, income, and corporation taxes. But fearful of scaring off potential investors, they kept the latter three levies low. The bulk of new revenues came from a slew of consumption-based, or what lawmakers labeled "luxury" taxes. Though representatives balked at imposing taxes on furs, jewelry, golf clubs, and silk stockings, they did assess such working-class comforts as Coca-Cola, cigarettes, snuff, and mill village baseball games. They also placed levies on billiards tables, gasoline, automobile sales, vehicle registration, and movie tickets.[60]

Property owners, mostly farmers, had always shouldered a disproportionate share of the tax burden in South Carolina, and they still did in 1929. Nine years earlier, property taxes, based on the presumed market value of real estate, had accounted for almost 90 percent of the state's income, a higher proportion than anywhere else in the country. Ten years later, following the so-called tax reforms of the preceding decade, this figure dropped to 25 percent, but total receipts from property taxes remained roughly the same, although over this same period the value of farm acreage fell by 45 percent and the price paid for the state's agricultural products plunged by 68 percent. For the majority of property owners, in fact, taxes had not declined but had gone up; now they endured a mounting double burden, paying levies on land as well as for licenses, soft drinks, and sporting events.[61] A federal government study concluded that "the real weight [of the farmers' tax burden] has been doubled by falling prices." Tax delinquency was rampant and cost a growing number of South Carolinians their homes and their land. In 1929 about one out of every four rural households evaded taxes, not so much because of the unwillingness to settle, but because of the inability to pay. With income falling and tax bills mounting so quickly, many began to question what services they received from the government in return for their hard-earned money.[62]

"Those of us," declared a "Hard Pressed Taxpayer" in 1933, "who for so many weary years have been struggling under increasing tax burdens know there should be some relief."[63] Echoing Senator Williams's assessment of the situation, he pushed for deep tax cuts through the elimination of all "unnecessary" public offices, the slashing of government employees' salaries, and strict limits on state expenditures. Economy in government was this taxpayer's and many others' answer to the riddle of the depression.

In the early years of the Great Depression, the economy campaign quickly won a legion of followers in South Carolina. Its popularity stemmed from the compelling simplicity of its message; it offered beleaguered rural families a remedy to their suffering, provided identifiable scapegoats as enemies, and put forth a seductive vision of a just society. In the economists' ideal world, rural people, unfettered by government intervention, worked hard, earning enough to pay for food, clothing, and fuel with a little left over for extras. But this was not the reality of life in the countryside in 1930. Rather than blaming the collapse of cotton prices on tariff barriers, wild fluctuations in international markets, or overproduction, the economists attacked the villainous "tax spender"—the phrase used for most members of the general assembly. While these selfish men boarded in Columbia's finest hotels, voting themselves fat pay hikes, the masses of South Carolinians scrapped and clawed for basic necessities.[64] Political mobilization was the economists' answer to the state's economic problems. They proposed voting the tax spenders out of office and replacing them with candidates committed to fiscal retrenchment, lower property taxes, and less government. After these reforms were put in place, rural consumers would have more money to spend, pushing up demand and ultimately the price of agricultural goods and manufactured products. Then, the Great Depression would be a thing of the past.

Rarely is a well-crafted message enough on its own to make it politically salient. Transforming ideas into action depends on the emergence of a set of leaders and an organizational framework with the capacity to turn broad, yet inchoate, support for change into an effective political force. The Farmers and Taxpayers League (FTL) became that vehicle for the economists. Formed at a gathering of two hundred farmers, agriculturists, educators, and politicians in Columbia in April 1930, the FTL started out sounding more like a prelude to New Deal farm policy than a blistering denunciation of the tax spenders. The league's original manifesto demanded economy in government, along with protection from foreclosure, extended credit for farmers, and federal price supports. Throughout its first year of existence, the FTL remained on the political fringes. But beginning in 1931, it emerged as the loudest, most strident voice in the state, one that politicians ignored at their electoral peril. This shift coincided with the ascent of Niels Christensen and John Kolb Breedin to the organization's helm and, more important, with the league's tight, even myopic, focus on austerity and drastic tax reform.[65]

At the start of the 1931 session of the general assembly, FTL partisans marched on Columbia to present representatives and the newly elected governor, Ibra C. Blackwood, with a list of demands.[66] They insisted on cutbacks in appropriations to "the lowest limit possible," consolidation of all bureaus and departments, and a total freeze on hiring until "farmers and others reach an American standard of living." Education, the league contended, was the state's "greatest source of extravagance." The organization pressed for the restructuring of the 6-0-1 law, so it would include mandatory increases in teacher workloads, state school funding based on average daily attendance over seven months rather than initial enrollment figures, and an end to tuition-free learning at the University of South Carolina. At the top of FTL's wish list, however, was the repeal of the property tax, which was, according to Niels Christensen, "the worst tax known in the civilized world." In its place, the FTL advocated a controversial sales tax. The reforms, a league spokesman said, would bring an end to "bureaucracy as the controlling force of our Government" and the restoration of "democracy" to South Carolina.[67]

Almost overnight, the FTL built a broad-based, cross-class coalition that promoted economy in government in South Carolina. Upcountry white farmers and low-country planters, desperate for relief from the property tax, made up the core of the league's constituency. Mill owners enlisted in the fight for economy as well. Complaining that even the state's moderate corporate tax rate was too high, they supported the antitax campaign but played an essentially behind-the-scenes role.[68] Textile laborers also jumped on the economy bandwagon. Greenville millworker and house candidate Nigel League, for instance, campaigned in 1930 on a platform of lower taxes, budget cutting, an eight-hour day, and the "betterment of my people."[69] Although not particularly concerned about property taxes, few millhands doubted the need for retrenchment or curbing the wasteful extravagance of state officials.

Sympathetic to the principle of economy, wage earners nonetheless rejected key planks of the FTL platform. As proponents of public schools, though leery about compulsory attendance statutes, workers opposed, for instance, the league's attack on government-supported education. Increased salaries for teachers and the introduction of a free textbook program, in fact, topped labor's list of demands. Workers disagreed not just with the specifics of the league's program, but with its analysis of the situation as well. Whereas most FTL supporters blamed the economic cataclysm on the prodigious spending of corrupt lawmakers, textile workers chastised selfish mill owners and narrowed-minded minute men. Wage earners and tax revolters also split on the question of what would cure the region's economic ills. Whereas economists believed that less government would bring about recovery, millhands placed their faith in government action. In the end, labor's agenda for change lacked the far-reaching appeal of the economists' vision. As a result, unlike the tax cutters, millhands failed to build the political bridges needed to link them to other electoral blocs.[70]

Fusing together property owners and workers, industrialists and planters, the FTL dominated the public debate over the solution to the depression before the New Deal. Almost every politician paid lip service to the credo of economy. In the very first line of his annual message in 1932, Governor Blackwood announced, "The people of our state are burdened by taxes."[71] The height of the league's power came the next year during the 1933 legislative session. An unusually large number of political neophytes, many of them league supporters, had triumphed in the previous summer's campaigns.[72] Vowing to undertake a crusade for economy, they arrived in Columbia eager to get started. Sitting through a 128-day marathon session, the longest since Reconstruction, dampened their enthusiasm somewhat but did not stop them from pushing through the legislature the lowest general appropriations bill in eleven years. The final plan hacked the state budget by a third. Property taxes were reduced, luxury taxes retained, and corporate taxes left low. The representatives eliminated several agencies, consolidated a few more, and sliced teachers' salaries to such a degree that some lawmakers worried that educators might turn to mill work to make more money.[73]

The 1933 legislative session marked the zenith of the FTL's power in South Carolina. Even before adjournment, the league's support for a sales tax stirred discontent and threatened to break up the coalition of fiscal conservatives. While representatives debated the measure, more than three thousand merchants and laborers marched through downtown Columbia, protesting that the regressive levy would be a "burden on men [like] . . . millhands . . . less able to pay." An elected official also charged that "some South Carolina corporations are behind a sales tax to take the tax off their property." Hearing the angry voices outside the windows of their chambers, lawmakers killed the sales tax. Nevertheless, the league continued to back the unpopular proposal.[74]

At the same time, the FTL faced a credibility crisis. A growing number of lawmakers accused the league of conflict of interest. Widely circulated reports charged that Christensen and Breedin accepted hefty contributions from mill owners and in turn acted on behalf of the corporations rather than oppressed farmers and embattled taxpayers. Sensing that the once-dominant league was wounded, opponents, beginning in 1933 and increasingly in 1934, leveled stinging attacks on its leaders and finances.[75]

Although the assaults eroded the FTL's political legitimacy, it might have survived as a dominant political force had it not been for the election of Franklin D. Roosevelt and the advent of the New Deal. FDR's programs introduced at a lightening pace during the first one hundred days of his administration preempted the league's program. More important, they shifted the terms of the debate in the state. During the next five years, the language of class conflict muffled harangues against government action. Workers and managers pushed farmers and economists off the political center stage as they wrestled over the government's role in industrial relations, the state's relationship to the federal government, and the meaning of New Deal symbols and rhetoric.

CHAPTER FOUR

We the People of the U.S.A.

New Deal Americanism on the Mill Hills

By the fall of 1934 most mill people had removed the portraits
of Cole Blease hanging over the mantels of their company-
owned houses and replaced them with pictures of Franklin D.
Roosevelt (FDR), the Democratic president.[1]

Laura Stringfield and W. P. Stringfield signed their letter
to the leading New Dealer and New York senator, Robert F. Wagner, "an
American citizen."[2]

"We want to organize and support the NRa [sic]," explained a group of
Pelzer trade unionists, "do our part and stand by our President." "Roosevelt
Our Greatest Leader" read a hand-painted placard at a union rally outside of
Columbia. A Horse Creek Valley striker declared: "The National Government called us out." "You ought to respect the flag, get out of the way, you
ought to respect the flag," Greenville unionists yelled at strikebreakers as they
tried to cross a picket line. At the funeral of seven Honea Path strikers shot
in the back by the hired guns of management, union leader George Googe
raised a bullet-ridden American flag.[3]

"We the people of the USA," wrote twenty-one-year-old Lillian Davis to
Franklin Roosevelt, "are all assembled under the same stars and stripes, and
are doing our part in this vicinity to live up to one of the nation's greatest
acts: the National Recovery Act."[4]

These are voices and images from South Carolina mill villages during
the New Deal era. Occasionally, pictures and sound bites like these from
working-class communities across the country show up in the historical record, but only occasionally. When they do appear, they are usually pointed to

79

as illustrations of larger trends, anecdotes to a master narrative of the New Deal. But they are more than examples, they are evidence of other New Deal stories. They are the "stuff" of the New Deal from below; they are clues to South Carolina millworkers' interpretations of the New Deal and the nation.[5]

For South Carolina workers to become New Deal supporters they had to re-interpret history. In the early 1930s whites southerners read history books and watched films that presented a singular version of Reconstruction. In this view, the postbellum years were a "tragic era" of fraud, corruption, racial chaos, and sexual disorder. Carpetbaggers and scalawags were cast in the role of the bad guys. Led by these moral degenerates, nefarious Republicans forced the prostrate South to let ignorant African Americans vote. Clutching the ballot, they imperiled the noble world of white southerners. South Carolina was supposedly the most afflicted place in the region. Facts hardly mattered. Although freed people did indeed take an active part in postbellum South Carolina politics and there were a few black sheriffs as well as some black legislators, Republicans never dominated state politics. During one session, however, the party did gain a majority in one house of the legislature. In the unreconstructed Reconstruction narratives, this scene of African Americans in power in the South Carolina General Assembly stands out above all others.

Based more on racist fantasies than evidence, scholars, filmmakers, and cartoonists depicted this moment as a "season of scandal" and a "golden age of stealing in South Carolina."[6] According to another hyperbolic account, African American lawmakers appointed trial judges who could not read, bilked the state treasury out of millions, and used public funds for clothes, furniture, food, and "forty kinds of liquor."[7] "It is," wrote yet another historian, "barbarism overwhelming civilization by physical force. It is the slave rioting in the halls of his master, and putting that master under his feet." Striking a similar theme, a Thomas Nast cartoon pictured coal-black, thick-lipped, heavyset, drunken South Carolina lawmakers defying Lady Liberty's pleas for peace.[8] Seventy years after Reconstruction, the governor of South Carolina continued to evoke the horrors of that moment to rally the troops to the banner of white supremacy. Corrupt, immoral African American legislators, he claimed, "left a stench in the nostrils of the people of South Carolina that will exist for generations to come."[9]

References to bodies, smells, and sex were always part of Reconstruction mythology. Stories about African Americans raiding the legislature almost always included a passage or two about black men lurking in the shadows, waiting for white women. "Southern whites," wrote Claude Bowers, "literally

We the People of the U.S.A.

were put to torture" by hateful Yankees, who inflamed the "negro egotism" and inspired "lustful assaults" on white womanhood. "The rapist," another scholar added, "is a product of the Reconstruction period."[10] But this was not the end of the story. The Confederacy may have lost the war, yet it did not lose its fighting spirit, its sense of honor, or its heroism. Just when things grew dire, valiant white Democrats donned red shirts and redeemed South Carolina. Armed with rifles and clubs, they threw the unholy Republican alliance of blacks, carpetbaggers, and scalawags out of power. For many white scholars, the lesson of Reconstruction was clear: white supremacy must be maintained. The only way to prevent a return to the thievery, humiliation, and lust of the postbellum years was to preserve states' rights and limit federal power.

This is how Reconstruction was portrayed in the white South.[11] Well into the twentieth century, it continued to shape people's thinking. Federal action of any sort was easily branded a "second invasion of the carpetbaggers." No one had to say what would happen next: a return to Reconstruction would unleash the filthy passions of African American men. Vulnerable white women would again be sexually victimized. Buried between the lines of these Reconstruction narratives about lust and thievery, whiteness and blackness, was a coded message. For white southerners, Reconstruction represented disorder of any kind, not just racial upheaval. Whenever the status quo was challenged, some white person invariably raised the specter of Reconstruction, warning that change would produce chaos. In the end, this discourse hindered reform, especially federal initiatives. Just before the start of the New Deal, the highly regarded southern historian, Francis Butler Simkins, remarked that the "tragic era" view of Reconstruction froze the "mind of the white South in unalterable opposition to outside pressures for social change."[12]

Speedups, strikes, layoffs, wage cuts, the mobilization of the National Guard, and legislative setbacks, however, opened the minds of many South Carolina millhands. Slowly and unevenly from the late 1920s through the early 1930s, workers moved away from the racially, sexually charged politics of Bleasism toward government intervention in the economy on their own behalf. They saw the partisan mobilization of the state machinery as the surest way to restore the prosperity of the twenties and to force mill owners to improve shop floor conditions. Yet until the New Deal, South Carolina millhands looked only as far as the state capital for solutions.

By the time Roosevelt came to power in March 1933, the Great Depression had reached its lowest point. People were tormented by hunger and uncertainty. Indeed, they were so desperate that they were willing to consider new ideas, new policies, and a New Deal. Without explicitly challenging the white South's interpretation of Reconstruction, workers began to see the federal government less as an alien force and more as a powerful protector of freedom and economic rights. As the New Deal tentatively crept to the left of the political spectrum, their faith in the federal government steadily grew. By the close of the decade, millhands pushed for the centralization of authority in Washington, even if it came at the expense of states' rights.

Workers' support for the centralization of power—the antithesis of the mythology of Reconstruction—was smoothed over by their personification of the nation-state. For South Carolina millworkers, the government was Roosevelt and Roosevelt was the government.[13] Piecing together snippets from pictures, radio broadcasts, newsreels, rumors, and FDR's carefully crafted public persona, millhands constructed their own image of the New Deal presidency. Roosevelt's confident smile gave them confidence. When they listened to his fireside chats and heard him explain complicated government programs in straightforward terms like their favorite teacher or preacher, workers felt connected to the president. Roosevelt strengthened the tie with his use of inclusive language. "My friends," he began his addresses, seeming to speak directly to each person in the audience. Often in the middle of a talk, he would stop and ask listeners to write to him at the White House about their troubles and triumphs. No president, at least none that South Carolina laborers could recall, had ever solicited their opinions.[14] Here was evidence that the president cared about their personal problems. "He has made us feel close to him," one worker wrote. Following a tour of Piedmont mill villages, another observer noted: "People down here all seem to think they know the President personally! . . . They feel he is talking to each one of them." "Roosevelt himself has suffered, fought and conquered," wrote one South Carolina woman, apparently thinking about the president's battle with polio, "and has the keenest understanding of the suffering of others."[15] A South Carolina weaver showered FDR with the highest praise, telling him that he was "the first man in the White House to understand that my boss is a son of a bitch."[16]

Despite the mesmerizing appeal of Roosevelt's winning smile and soothing voice, it took more than these qualities to persuade South Carolina workers to put aside their Reconstruction-inspired fears of federalism and join his New Deal. But labor laws, relief programs, and recovery measures would demonstrate that the administration was committed to ending the depression, that the president was a strong ally in the long-standing fight of working people to transform their daily lives, to end their ceaseless toil for low pay under dirty, risky conditions. With the government's help, one millhand told the novelist Sherwood Anderson, "we might be able to make the South into something gorgeous."[17]

Workers credited the president for the New Deal, and they drew important conclusions based on this association. Roosevelt's actions and choreographed gestures showed wage earners that a determined and partisan federal government could end "industrial slavery." At the same time, he said little about race. Fearful of scaring off southern lawmakers, FDR left white supremacy alone, concentrating on economic issues. His tactical decision about race allowed white millhands to back federal action, confident that it would do nothing to undercut the privileges of whiteness.

FDR's adroit political packaging eased South Carolina millhands' entrance into the national community. Never before had these white workers felt so attached to America. "He's the first President who made us feel that we really are part of the United States," declared a Palmetto State laborer. According to a veteran weaver, he "is the only President we ever had that thought the Constitution belonged to the pore man too." As far as this machine tender could tell, until FDR entered the White House the law favored the wealthy. "Yessir, it took Roosevelt to read in the Constitution and find out them folks way back yonder that made it was talkin' about the pore man right along with the rich man. I am a Roosevelt man." [18]

As Roosevelt men and women, South Carolina workers identified their interests with the nation and the federal government. In waving the American flag and signing their letters "an American citizen," they announced that they now saw themselves as American citizens first and foremost. In the early 1930s U.S. citizenship, or what Gary Gerstle has called Americanism, had multiple meanings. For some it conjured up patriotic glories of military conquest and national superiority. For others, race, gender, and ethnicity defined the nation in exclusive terms. America was male, white, and Protestant. Women and African Americans were shuttled off to the sidelines of citizenship. Immigrants could join the nation only by flattening their foreign accents and shedding their Old World religious and cultural practices. Industrialists put forth yet another vision of Americanism. Anchored in constitutional safeguards for private property, factory owners trumpeted the creeds of individualism and unfettered economic competition. Theirs was a land of vigorous, sustained capitalist growth. [19]

South Carolina millworkers fashioned an alternative, progressive, although still racist, brand of Americanism. Rooted in the Declaration of Independence, the Bill of Rights, and the glories of consumption, their Americanism highlighted the notion of "life, liberty, and the pursuit of happiness" for all white people. As U.S. citizens, white millhands claimed not only the right to vote but also economic rights to a job set at a reasonable pace that paid a fair wage. They also demanded the right to join a union free from the interference of "autocratic" mill owners. This vision of America imagined a powerful federal government ready and willing to step in and uphold the rights of patriotic citizens against any attack on their freedoms.[20] When it came to political economy, workers wanted an America where the system of capitalism was reconfigured but not destroyed. They pressed the government to build a safety net beneath them without putting a ceiling over their heads. Someday, they or their children might make it out of the mills, and then they wanted nothing to get in the way of their progress.[21]

As South Carolina millhands began to speak the language of New Deal Americanism, they described themselves less as besieged white South Carolinians. This shift in self-representation altered the tone of their demands. Starting in 1933, these workers insisted that the manufacturers recognize their newly declared political and economic rights as U.S. citizens. The more South Carolina workers asserted themselves in the vernacular of New Deal Americanism, the more they highlighted their economic concerns over their racial anxieties, and the more they did this, the faster their fears of the federal government dissolved.

The New Deal's first sign of federal action to assist the working class came in the summer of 1933 with the National Industrial Recovery Act (NIRA). During the 1932 presidential campaign, FDR had blamed the economic collapse on "self seekers" and spotlighted the plight of the "forgotten man." His rhetoric ignited workers' expectations for change. Roosevelt's inaugural address heightened their anticipation of a better future. On that crisp March day in 1933, the president pledged to run the "money changers" out of Washington.[22] Most working people welcomed FDR's remarks, but still they wanted proof that a New Deal was on the way.

Wage earners' concerns, however, did not head the president's agenda throughout most of his legendary first hundred days in office. Right after moving into the White House, Roosevelt addressed the nation's banking crisis, then he lifted Prohibition, after which he took a stab at solving the agricultural quandary. By May he still had not tackled the problem of industrial atrophy. Trying to goad the president into action, Senator Hugo Black of Alabama introduced a bill barring interstate commerce of goods produced in plants where employees worked more than thirty hours a week. Black predicted that his plan would create millions of new jobs and "eliminate the vexing problem of technological unemployment." Seeing the bill as a panacea, William Green, president of the American Federation of Labor (AFL), threatened a national general strike if Congress did not adopt the measure. Hearing the footsteps of labor, the Senate passed the bill. Convinced that Black's proposal was ill-conceived, fiscally dangerous, and even unconstitutional, Roosevelt and his advisers hustled to find an alternative. They proposed the NIRA.[23]

Signed into law on June 16, 1933, ninety-nine days after FDR took office, the NIRA was a "crazy patchwork quilt of . . . ideas" that "had a little for everyone."[24] The legislation suspended antitrust statutes, allowing business leaders to fix prices and regulate output in their industries. In exchange for industrial self-rule, manufacturers' groups had to agree to abide by a "code of fair competition." Every code of fair competition had to include Section 7(a).

Perhaps the most controversial and potentially explosive part of the plan, Section 7(a) appeared to guarantee workers the right to "organize unions of their own choosing." Each code also had to set minimum-wage and maximum-hour guidelines. Finally, the NIRA authorized the formation of the National Recovery Administration (NRA) to oversee the rebuilding of the nation's economy.[25]

Normally plainspoken—some would say bland—AFL president Green gushed over the NIRA's labor planks, heralding them as a "Magna Carta" for workers. John L. Lewis, the head of the United Mine Workers and sometimes AFL rival, compared the NIRA to the Emancipation Proclamation.[26] Prose could not quite capture textile trade unionist Thorton Oakley's enthusiasm for the law, so he wrote a poem to the NRA:

Now swells the glad voice of the nation,
    Now breaks the bright dawn of a new day
Black hopelessness yields to elation
    Exultant thy cry, NRA!
Ride on! To the stars throw thy pinions,
    With light of truth blaze thou the way,
The call reaches all man's dominions,
    Proclaim a new age, NRA![27]

President Roosevelt, however, never intended to declare a new age or deliver workers from industrial slavery. When he signed the NIRA into law, he had more prosaic and more narrowly political concerns on his mind.

Mill owners saw the law differently as well. Battered by endless rounds of punishing competition, many textile manufacturers, especially the larger ones, considered the NRA their last chance for financial salvation. For years prior to the New Deal, overproduction and price cutting had sapped the industry's vitality. Schemes put forth by the Cotton Textile Institute (CTI), a coalition of northern and southern manufacturers formed in 1926 to jump-start business by fixing prices and restricting output, had not worked.[28] In the summer of 1933, desperate CTI officials rushed to Washington to gain the federal government's backing to help to stabilize the industry. Once in the nation's capital, they overwhelmed ineffectual citizen's groups and the national textile union—the United Textile Workers of America (UTW)—and essentially drafted the textile industry's code of fair competition all by themselves.[29]

Hailed by New Deal officials as a "patriotic thing," the textile code, as it came to be called, was "code #1"—the nation's first code of fair competition under the NRA. Like all the NRA codes that followed it, the textile code loosened antitrust constraints for management, while vaguely spelling out labor's right to organize. It mandated a maximum workweek of forty hours and, taking into account the customary regional wage differential, it set up a minimum pay scale of $12 per week in the South and $13 in the North. But "learners," a loosely defined category, could be paid far less. Seeking to limit output, the code also outlawed the night shift. In addition, it barred the use of child labor. Finally, Section 15 of the textile code addressed machine loads and the implementation of newer and faster equipment.[30]

At first, industry representatives stifled discussions about technology and work assignments, but South Carolina's U.S. senator James F. Byrnes, ever eager to capture the mill vote at home, pressed for and got an investigation of the stretchout. During the first week of July 1933, Byrnes and a few NRA officials traveled to his hometown of Spartanburg to conduct hearings into the matter. Following several days of moving testimony from laborers physically and mentally drained by running more and more machines, Byrnes returned to Washington. Pointing to these powerful stories, he strong-armed the CTI into writing into the textile code a section covering workloads. That was all he got. Watered down through compromise and clever wording, Section 15, as this portion of the code came to be called, suggested that employers could not increase their employees' workloads or introduce new machinery without government approval.[31]

The manufacturers' slight concession on workloads was more than offset by their staggering victory on the question of enforcement. In effect, the voice of the mill owners, the Cotton Textile Institute, became the code authority responsible for overseeing the law and investigating all violations. As the code's watchman, the manufacturers' group had almost unlimited power to adjust machine loads, production levels, and wage rates.[32]

In July 1933, however, the CTI's strategic triumph did not seem all that significant to workers. Most laborers thought that the textile code represented the start of a new era. How else could South Carolina workers interpret a law that overnight handed them, and legitimized, almost everything they had been fighting for on the shop floor, on the picket line, and in state politics

We the People of the U.S.A.

for eight or so years? As textile workers saw it, the code guaranteed them a decent, albeit modest, paycheck; protected their right to join a union; and, with Section 15, ended the stretchout. It also offered them a firm yardstick with which to gauge the owners' actions. In the past, millhands had complained that they worked too long for too little; after July 1933, they argued that if their bosses forced them to work more than forty hours a week or paid them less than twelve dollars, they would be violating the law, or even worse, Roosevelt's will.[33]

Family life would also improve as a result of the code. Freed from the rigors of a sixty-or-more-hour workweek, women and men looked forward to a new life at home. "The men want to fish, play baseball, do odd jobs around the house," a reporter heard. "Most mothers say they want to spend more time 'tending their children.' "[34] Hardened by years of disappointment, some still could not help thinking that the code was a sham; according to one laborer, "there's a trick to it."[35] But in the summer of 1933 most workers put aside their misgivings and took to the streets to celebrate.

"A new era has dawned," shouted a South Carolina millhand after hearing about the textile code. Just after dusk on July 17, a thousand people from Greenwood and the surrounding areas gathered on the edge of town. For the next four hours, they snaked through the streets of the city dancing and singing. Long past midnight, the party ended with millhands "making merry" in front of the Greenwood Cotton Mill. Several days later, Spartanburg millhands marched through the streets of their hometown. Another celebration took place in Greenville later in the week.[36]

"The industrial recovery act," a Horse Creek Valley man declared, "is our industrial declaration of independence." Mixing patriotic metaphors, others saw the code as a new industrial bill of rights. John Peele, a popular UTW official from Greenville, talked about the code in another nationalist, class-tinged idiom. "For years and years," he proclaimed, "those who toil in industry have dreamed of Democracy. For those who have been able to amass wealth there has been Democracy. For those who produce the wealth there has been Industrial Slavery." With the enactment of the NIRA, he concluded, "Labor is upon the threshold of industrial freedom."[37]

The NRA rhetoric of the president and New Dealers strengthened the link between working people and the federal government. From where laborers stood, the speeches coming from national leaders provided evidence that Washington was on their side, ready and willing to guarantee their newly won freedoms. "It is," declared NRA chief General Hugh "Ironpants" Johnson in the summer of 1933, "the purpose of the National Recovery Act to put people back to work promptly."[38] Paying laborers a fair wage for forty hours of work now amounted to a patriotic duty. "As a nation," Secretary of Labor Frances Perkins stated in 1933, "we are recognizing that programs long thought of as merely labor reforms, such as shorter hours, higher wages are really essential factors for recovery." In another speech Perkins observed, "If . . . the wages of mill workers in the South should be raised to the point where workers could buy shoes, that would be a social revolution."[39]

With the formation of the NRA, the Roosevelt administration declared war on the industrial depression.[40] "We Do Our Part" became the New Deal's battle cry. The president compared the blue eagle—the NRA's symbol—to "bright badges" worn by soldiers "in the gloom of a night attack . . . to be sure that comrades do not fire on comrades." "Those who cooperate in this program," he added, "must know each other at a glance." Meanwhile, the NRA chief held what seemed like an endless series of flag-waving parades to rally the nation to recovery, calling on Americans to sacrifice equally in the war against the depression. Over the radio and in person, Johnson voiced disdain for the selfish few who defied the blue eagle. "[M]ay God have mercy on the man or group of men," he cautioned, "who attempt to trifle with this bird."[41]

Millhands were convinced that the president and his lieutenants waged this war against the depression on their behalf. They were, after all, the "real" victims of the economic collapse. General Johnson's fiery rhetoric was a warning to mill owners to respect the New Deal rights of labor or face dire consequences. For millhands, no aspect of the New Deal was more compelling than the idea that the president and the machinery of the national government were squarely behind them in their struggle for better conditions. They believed that the mill owners, far more than structural flaws in the economy or the ruinous effects of overproduction, stood between them and a return to the prosperity of the 1920s. Now the president was ready to force the manufacturers to slow down the machines to a humane pace and to pay decent wages. Who better, workers thought, to have on your side? The president was, after all, more powerful than all of the supervisors, foremen, and mill owners combined. At least that was what they thought in 1933.

Faith in a better future can sustain people through a dark day. But hope can also distort things. Deeply religious, often evangelical, millhands understood faith almost without thinking about it. During the 1930s South Carolina workers put their faith in Franklin Roosevelt. In their eyes, he could not, would not fail them. He was "a god-sent man," "a modern day Moses," determined to lead them "out of the Egypt of depression to the promised land of prosperity."[42] The problem was that FDR, though eager to have labor's vote, did not see himself as a working-class savior. Faith, however, was hard to

We the People of the U.S.A.

shake. When the stretchout did not end and industrial democracy remained a distant dream, millworkers still believed in Roosevelt. In the end, faith seemed to stamp out any critical appraisal of the president, the New Deal, and the nation-state. In the yellow, four-room company houses on the mill hills of South Carolina, ordinary people were, for a time, blinded by faith.[43]

CHAPTER FIVE

Mr. Roosevelt Ain't Going to Stand for This

New Deal Battles, 1933–1934

 "A new day has dawned," declared William Anderson, an industry spokesperson, about the implementation of the textile code. These were the same words that millhands had used to describe the promise of the code, and Anderson was not alone. Palmetto State mill owners also broadcast their support for the code in letters to the editor, full-page newspaper advertisements, and town hall meetings.[1] In Greenville, industrialists joined workers at a mock funeral to bury "Old Man Depression" and celebrate the enactment of the national industrial recovery statute. Manufacturers everywhere put large blue eagle banners—the symbol of the National Recovery Administration (NRA)—over mill gates and stapled copies of the code next to the time clocks in their factories.[2]

On the surface, mill owners and millhands appeared to be in agreement. Both hailed the textile code of fair competition, but in fact a battle was brewing. For textile manufacturers, the code meant recovery and recovery meant only one thing: a revival of profits. The proof would be in the numbers: supply and demand, productivity and dividends. Recovery would also mean labor peace. What it did not mean to the mill owners was exactly what it meant to workers: an expansion of citizenship rights, industrial democracy, emancipation from the stretchout, shorter hours, and a return to the relatively high wages of the 1920s. These two visions of the New Deal placed millworkers and mill owners on a collision course.

Between the spring and summer of 1933, a brief spurt in textile industry profits papered over the ideological gap that separated workers and management. Owners, anticipating rising costs due to the textile code's higher wage standards set to take effect in August, as well as a new processing tax on raw cotton, increased production in order to stockpile surpluses of cheaply made goods. Sales climbed and employment rose. By the end of the summer, textile manufacturers had hired 100,000 additional workers nationwide. During the same period, employment in South Carolina's mills rose from a ten-year low of 67,004 to an all-time high of 80,154.[3]

Recovery proved short-lived. By the fall of 1933 the scourge of overproduction once again battered the textile industry, generating the familiar litany of cut-throat competition, vicious price cutting, and warehouses crammed with unsold goods. Disingenuous mill men blamed the new code for their long-standing problems. Far from reviving profits, industry representatives complained, the code doubled fixed costs while pushing down prices. Something had to be done. What the owners did, according to NRA chief General Hugh Johnson, was "chisel" away at the code. They increased workloads, eliminated jobs, pinched pennies, and stretched out the stretchout further than before. No one was spared from this new assault. Everyone worked harder than ever.[4]

"Mr. Roosevelt," one woman announced, "aint going to stand for this."[5] South Carolina workers believed that the president, and by implication the federal government, would not tolerate "code chiseling." They flooded FDR's and Johnson's offices with reports of the mill owners' actions. Scrawled on coarse, thick-lined gray dime-store store paper, workers' letters told agonizing stories of unemployment and layoffs. Mixed with the bitterness, millhands demonstrated what they saw as their duty as members of New Deal America. Just as they needed the president's political muscle against the mill owners, they felt certain that he needed their information. Without their updates, how would he know what was going on? Referring to themselves as "citizens of the United States" and "members of the NRA," these laborers claimed to be "doing their part" to ensure recovery by informing FDR of code violations. "I am taking it into my hands to write you a letter and tell you how the mills are working against you," one wage earner began a typical letter. Wrapping themselves in the flag, workers created an image of themselves as representatives of recovery and defenders of the president and the nation against greedy textile manufacturers.[6]

The most stirring letters came from spinners.[7] Almost exclusively women, spinners earned the lowest wages of all adult millhands, and they had the most to gain from the textile code's wage provisions. Seeking to hold wages below the legal minimum of twelve dollars per week, manufacturers launched a guerrilla war against the spinners. Some mills reclassified veteran employees as learners, and others simply paid spinners as little as they could get away with.[8] Managers and second hands pushed the women to the breaking point. "Faster and faster and then FASTER" was how one spinner characterized the postcode regime in her section of the mill. Not even the most highly skilled laborer could keep up with this frenzied pace. "I've been a mill worker for the past eleven years, have been considered one of the best spinners," explained a Lancaster employee, "but the load has almost got the best of me for the machinery has been speeded to the highest notch . . . till we can't hardly bear any more." Each eight-hour shift left her clothes soaked with perspiration. She had no time to wash up before lunch, even though her greasy hands left dark black spots on her sandwiches. Mrs. A. T. Watt of South Greenwood observed, "The operatives run like race horses all day and they can't get production." For those who tried to work at this rate, the toll was tremendous. "When I came out of the mill down here last Friday evening," wrote a spinner, "I felt like I was nearer dead than living."[9]

Spinners, weavers, and doffers alike found the postcode regime crueler than anything they had encountered previously. Though many continued to invoke the menacing metaphor of slavery to describe their working conditions, more increasingly also spoke of death. A Langley man fused these two images together, telling the president he feared that he would "slave to death" under the intensified stretchout. "They are killing the women," a spinner wailed. "We are working to death here," added another. "Instead of taking any work off us they put more on[;] they are killing their hands every day," wrote still another beleaguered spinner. "I think this should be seen into wright [*sic*] away."[10]

Despite the ambiguous language of Section 15 of the textile code—that portion of the law that dealt with machine assignments—mill laborers were emphatic that deadly workloads defied the NRA. Putting words into FDR's mouth, Roy Adams of Anderson announced, "President Roosevelt said in his speech on the textile code that the mills were not allowed to speed up machinery." Nevertheless, the owners did just that. After management raised spinners' workloads for the second time in two months, a Honea Path trade unionist complained bitterly of code violations. "This mill is installing new machinery," protested a Greenwood worker, "they are oppressing us in so many ways that is [*sic*] unlawful and contrary to the N.R.A." The "honest" spinners from the nearby Watts Mills told Hugh Johnson: "We are all for the NRA. . . . If the mill authorities would only comply with the NRA code. They display the code emblem in every room, but since July 17th our machine load has again been raised."[11]

Increased workloads, millhands informed the president, caused unemployment, and ending unemployment, they thought, was the central aim of the New Deal. "You said you wanted everybody back to work," stated a Rock Hill man. "I thought they was to put more people to work," wrote Spartanburg's Clyde Rodgers, "but there are more peoples out of jobs." "The reason so many people are out of jobs," T. M. Copeland of Greenville told FDR, "is because the mill owners have put two and three mens jobs on one man." "Since you have put on the code," another operative explained to a New Deal official, "they have cut out the old machinery and have put in the improved machinery and have laid off about one third of the help."[12]

Millhands also wanted Roosevelt to put an end to violations of Section 7(a). As in other parts of the country, the NRA's endorsement of collective bargaining sparked a trade union revival in the textile belt. In 1932 the membership list of the United Textile Workers of America (UTW) barely topped the 20,000 mark out of 700,000 textile workers nationwide. Two years later, the UTW boasted a following of 300,000. This burst of activity took place without a coordinated drive for unionization.[13] Workers, for all practical purposes, organized themselves at the grass roots. South Carolina followed the national trend. Only a handful of locals operated in the state before 1932, yet by the spring of 1934 a UTW chapter existed in 75 percent of the mill towns. Over half of all millworkers in South Carolina joined the national textile union. At no time before or since has a larger percentage of the state's mill laborers considered themselves to be trade unionists.[14]

Trade unionists in the Palmetto State turned the rhetoric of the New Deal into a language of prolabor nationalism. Stretching the truth, union organizers proclaimed: "The President wants you to join the union."[15] "To refuse to join the UTW meant a worker was a slacker who violates the spirit of the law," broadcast Rev. Paul W. Fuller of the Horse Creek Valley. For their part, workers interpreted the petitions of FDR and Hugh Johnson for national support for the NRA as calls for unionization. "I complied with your request to organize," explained a UTW member from Greenwood. An Appleton trade unionist wrote, "The workers went ahead and organized as you had give [sic] us orders to." Many millhands defined union membership as an emblem of their commitment to the New Deal: "We want to organize and support the NRa [sic] do our part and stand by our President." For others, the question of whether or not to join the UTW revolved around the balance of power in the mill towns. In the past, signing up with the union had been a risky proposition, but with the advent of the NRA, workers trusted that Roosevelt stood with them and would not let the owners get away with their usual antiunion tactics. Workers also became members of the UTW in the fall of

1933 because they were confident of victory. "We've been in the union three times now," three members of a Graniteville family explained, "and the first two failed because we did not have the backing of the President."[16]

Skirting around Section 7(a), mill owners fought the UTW's rise. They depicted union organizers as radical outsiders, who gobbled up dues to finance lavish New York lifestyles. Others characterized the union as a satanic force. "About the 11 [sic] day of December," recalled a Saxon Mills employee, an overseer "come [sic] to me about the Union. He told me not to join the Union[,] that it was wrong for the Bible said not to stir up strife among men[,] that is what the Union will do." Horse Creek Valley mill managers tried to bribe area workers with "a big fish supper" if they spurned the UTW.[17]

The owners also disputed the union's prolabor interpretation of the NRA. Roosevelt, they argued, did not "order" millhands to join the UTW. "There is nothing," insisted John Law, chief officer of two South Carolina mills, "in the National Recovery Act, and under the Constitution of the United States . . . that will compel the humblest employee in the industry to join this or that union." Though conceding that the NRA protected a worker's right to organize, owners maintained that the statute did not spell out the exact shape that these organizations had to take. Some industrialists judged that the best way to meet the UTW's challenge, without overtly obstructing the law, was to set up company unions, or what they called "goodwill associations."[18]

Employers' antiunion activities did not stop with fish dinners or company unions. Some tried to intimidate workers through surveillance. Learning from an informant the time and place of a UTW rally, company representatives would stand at the entrance of the meeting and jot down the names of all those in attendance. The next day a manager might approach a UTW supporter asking her why she was "mixed up with that lot." If he did not like the answer, he might repeat the question again and again until she pledged to leave the union. Local activists also found themselves under the constant eye of overseers. The first mistake they made became grounds for dismissal. "They are doing everything they can think about to down the union," reported a UTW member from Cateechee, "fire men or women if they just look cross-eyed."[19] In June 1933 Laura McGhee, an employee of the Graniteville Manufacturing Company for more than a decade, joined the UTW along with her father and brother. They became active in the local, going so far as to hold a union meeting at their home. Soon after the get-together, mill managers raised McGhee's production quota. They continued to add a few machines to her workload each day until she could not keep the pace. She was immediately discharged. The overseer told her, "You don't do enough work to make the $12 week minimum."[20] Elsewhere, mill managers did not even

Mr. Roosevelt Ain't Going to Stand for This

pretend to uphold the law. They simply fired union members. Naomi Duke had worked at the Bath Mills for eighteen years before she joined the UTW in 1933. "[F]rom that time on," she told Eleanor Roosevelt, "the union people have been fired until there are more than 100 families out of work." A weave room boss from a nearby mill held a pistol to the head of another UTW member and whispered in his ear, "If you are here at daylight you will be strung up." Rather than hang him, he fired him, replacing him, perhaps, with a new recruit from the countryside.[21]

Mill owners had traditionally regarded rural residents as a more tractable, though less productive, source of labor. Before the code, few manufacturers were willing to make this trade-off, except, of course, during a strike. But with experienced millhands flocking to the UTW, clamoring for new rights and privileges, the owners began to reconsider hiring rural laborers. "Farmers of this section," wrote a Gaffney worker in 1933, "can come to town and ask for a job in the mill and nine out of ten gets jobs." Often these newcomers were classified as learners and paid less than the code minimum. "I have never seen this mill this way before," fumed Minnie Stowe of Greenville, "taking jobs from the employees on the hill and giving them to people living in the country. . . . We have nothing to look for but the mill, that is not right, they don't go by the law, they go by their own rule."[22]

Of course, the textile code never mentioned a word about farmers or hiring policies, but this omission hardly mattered to millhands. To them, the New Deal represented a social contract handed to them personally by the president, providing them as citizens with rights that the hiring of rural residents violated. As Americans, they believed that they had the right to a job, a decent wage, work at a reasonable pace, and the option to join a union without being harassed. By the fall of 1933, most millhands knew that they had not secured these rights. Yet few found fault with the code or the president. Instead, they charged the owners with trampling their rights and focused their political energies on stricter enforcement of the New Deal.

"Many of us are wondering," a UTW leader asked a government official in December 1933, "when those in authority are going to begin enforcing the Codes." Rather than wait for a reply, workers offered their own ideas about enforcement. An Appalache Mill employee pushed for clandestine investigations of textile factories. Others demanded harsh punishments for lawbreakers. Stiff penalties, it was reasoned, would frighten mill officials into line. "We believe," a group of Gaffney laborers stated, that "if some of the mills were pulled for these violations then others would come to know they would be dealt with severely." "Very few have gotten the wages provided and never will," maintained a Laurens spinner, "unless these big headed men are put in

Mr. Roosevelt Ain't Going to Stand for This

95

prison." A "Little Woman" from Greenville's Watts Mills railed against the mill owners: "Oh how they love Hoover these old slimy serpents crawling spitting their Poison fighting your Program and the Government—don't let them fool you with their slimy tongue." "President Roosevelt," she advised, "use the big stick."[23]

Not a single mill owner spent time in jail or felt FDR's wrath, leading one disillusioned South Carolina millhand to ask, "what backing we have by our federal government?"[24] Still, most kept the faith. Despite the renewal of the stretchout and other setbacks, millhands clung to the belief that FDR remained on their side, ready and willing to help them carve out a better life. Now, if only they could find a way to get his attention.

Throughout the fall of 1933 millhands continued to write to the president, compiling a long list of code violations and suggestions for tighter enforcement of the law. Roosevelt probably never read many, if any, of the thousands of letters sent to him by South Carolina textile workers. Shuffled through a maze of government bureaus, most of the correspondence ended up at the offices of the Code Authority, the agency charged with enforcing the textile code. Because most code investigators had apprenticed as mill managers or CTI officials, the Code Authority showed little concern for workers. Most representatives did not think that millhands were smart enough to understand the intricacies of the code, and they ignored laborers' grievances, even when they were well documented. A federal study of compliance with the cotton textile code concluded that "[i]nvestigators were not at all inclined to punish members of industry for . . . violations unless it was forced upon them."[25]

Typically, when the Code Authority received a letter from a millhand spelling out a code violation, it sent the complainant a form letter with a copy of the code attached. Investigations into code violations amounted to little more than a short telephone call or a hasty visit to the accused employer. For example, after Appleton Mills laborers charged company officials with disregarding Section 7(a), investigator R. F. Howell wrote, "Management assures me that every one in a supervisory capacity at this plant understands the provisions of the code." Case closed. Between August 1933 and August 1934 the Code Authority received 3,920 complaints from around the country. It conducted only ninety-six probes, and resolved only one case, an hours-and-wages dispute, in labor's favor.[26]

Angered by continued code infractions and the Code Authority's indifference, some workers decided to take matters into their own hands. Beginning in the fall of 1933, strikes broke out across the Piedmont. Workers walked

Mr. Roosevelt Ain't Going to Stand for This

off the job to protest low wages, harsh conditions, and antiunion harassment, but these were not typical industrial disputes. The NRA politicized industrial relations in the mills, and workers took to the streets to gain a voice in administering the law. Resembling the Civil Rights campaigns of the early 1960s, at least in terms of the targeted audience, workers staged dramatic public demonstrations to grab the attention of federal officials in Washington. From the picket line they tried to speak directly to the president, telling him what they could not get the Code Authority to believe: that they, the best citizens, were taking up his fight against the treasonous mill owners. Once Roosevelt knew what was happening, workers felt certain, he would jump into the fray to uphold their rights as citizens of New Deal America.[27]

The New Deal political protests began in October 1933 in the Horse Creek Valley. Situated just across the Savannah River from Augusta, and sandwiched between Edgefield and Barnwell Counties in Aiken County, the valley anchors the South Carolina upcountry. Located there was the Graniteville Manufacturing Company, William Gregg's celebrated antebellum experiment with industrialization. After a shaky start, Gregg's plant turned a hefty profit. His success, along with an abundance of swift-moving streams, lured other investors to the valley. By the turn of the century, textile plants dotted the banks of the Horse Creek. At least one mill operated in Vaucluse, Bath, Clearwater, North Augusta, Warrenville, Gloverville, and Langley, towns along the water within a few miles of the old Graniteville factory. By 1930 there were more than 3,000 millworkers in the valley who produced goods valued annually at $8 million.[28]

Not only did the valley's industrial heritage date back to the antebellum era, but it also had a long history of industrial militancy. In 1876, while federal troops buttressing the Reconstruction government remained garrisoned in the Palmetto State, "the first major strike in southern textiles" erupted in Graniteville.[29] Ten years later, the Knights of Labor established a beachhead in the valley. At the turn of the century, area millhands flocked into the fledgling National Union of Textile Workers and in the spring of 1902, the union launched a valleywide general strike.[30] Industrial unrest again rocked the district after World War I as laborers battled mill managers' postwar retrenchment plans.[31] Again in 1929 and 1932, these same South Carolina millhands went on strike, protesting against the speedup and the stretchout.[32]

During the NRA era, Horse Creek Valley workers once again stood at the cutting edge of industrial protest. Led by Paul W. Fuller, a Methodist-Episcopal minister, graduate of Brookwood Labor College, and director of the Education Department of the American Federation Labor (AFL), valley millhands revived the local labor movement. Preaching his own brand of the social gospel, Fuller called on millhands to create God's Kingdom on Earth by joining the union and fighting for a New Deal in this world, rather than waiting for the promises of the next world. In 1933 workers paid tribute to Fuller and their faith in his theology by building a labor temple outside of Langley that served as both union hall and church.[33] While millhands prayed and organized, local owners increased workloads, laid off hundreds, and slashed wages. They also sacked UTW members, apparently replacing them with rural laborers. Complaining that managers infringed on their rights as American citizens and boasting that God and Roosevelt were on their side, three-quarters of the valley's four thousand laborers went on strike on October 21.[34]

"This strike is not the same kind of strike as we have had," Fuller broadcast the first morning of the protest. "We are striking to have Roosevelt and his program incorporated in the operation of the mills." "The National Government called us out," reported Era Duncan. According to a Bath weaver, valley laborers struck "to make the mills live up to the NRA code." "All that we want," explained another millhand, "is for the mills to observe President Roosevelt's NRA textile code, which they drafted themselves." The Leopard family of Warrenville told the president: "In your speeches and in the code you gave us the right to organize. We did and our members were treated so hard we went out on strike." Not only was the rhetoric of the protest political, but so too were its aims. Workers sought to publicize the intransigence of the mill owners to force the federal government to intervene in local affairs.[35]

Jolts of violence electrified the strike. Even by the valley's expansive standards—this was, after all, an area reputed to have the highest unsolved murder rate in the country—the walkout generated an alarming level of acrimony.[36] Fights and shouting matches between trade unionists and company loyalists raged through the first morning of the strike. By afternoon, one man had been stabbed, another pistol-whipped, and a security guard badly beaten. Several days later a UTW member smashed a man over the head with a brick as he crossed the picket line, and another trade unionist shot his strikebreaking brother-in-law in the leg when he refused to stay away from work.[37]

The combat in the valley crested on October 28, the day that mill managers advertised that they would reopen the factories. Just after 7:00 A.M., a truck packed with replacement workers from the countryside came lumbering toward the Bath mill. Over a thousand union women and men, some drunk, others edgy, and many eager for a fight, waited. UTW supporters called strikebreakers "apple knockers." "Those are cotton pickers," one man hollered. "We," he proudly proclaimed, "are cotton mill workers." As the strikebreakers jumped out of the truck and darted toward the factory, the picket line collapsed around them. All hell broke loose. Fists flew, rocks whizzed back and forth, and screams and shouts filled the air. Trying to break up the melee, company officials lobbed tear gas canisters toward the picket line and aimed fire hoses at the fleeing crowd. Police officers chased after the throng. When they finally caught up with it, they arrested twenty-two men and four women, charging them with crimes ranging from "assault and battery with intent to kill, simple assault, disturbing the peace, and drunk and disorderly conduct." Not a single nonstriker was arrested.[38]

"This is not a strike," Governor Ibra C. Blackwood declared the next morning, "This is an interference. . . . The laws of the United States and South Carolina guarantee [the nonstrikers] the right to work." To uphold these legal principles, he authorized the Aiken County sheriff to deputize a platoon of special officers. He also rushed a dozen highway patrolmen and a machine gun unit of the South Carolina National Guard to the Horse Creek Valley with instructions "to keep the mills running." Following the mobilization of the state's military might, the strike's center stage shifted from the picket lines to the untested turf of the textile code's labor relations boards.[39]

Carefully assembled to convey the impression of impartiality, the Cotton Textile National Industrial Relations Board—better known as the Bruere Board—had a tripartite structure. Robert Bruere, a New York economist and editor of *Survey* magazine, headed the tribunal and represented the government; Bennett E. Geer, the president of Furman College, a Baptist school in Greenville, and a stockholder in several textile firms, spoke for industry; and George Berry, a Tennessee native and the leader of the craft-based Pressmen's Union, stood for labor. Initially, the Bruere Board had been put together by NRA chief Hugh Johnson to examine the stretchout at South Carolina senator James Byrnes's urging. The board's vaguely worded report, which was heralded in manufacturing circles, did have one explicit passage. It recommended the formation of a labor relations board, separate from the other national labor relations boards, to oversee the textile code, and General Johnson appointed the members of the Bruere Board to serve on it.[40]

If "Blackwood represents the mill owners," as a valley strike leader alleged, then he expected the Bruere Board to speak up for labor. Sharing this view, UTW members cheered the announcement that the New Deal agency would investigate the strike. Trade unionists felt certain that any organization that wore the NRA's blue eagle, as the Bruere Board did, would immediately recognize that they were Roosevelt's foot soldiers and the mill masters his enemies. After examining the underlying causes of the dispute and discovering workers' patriotic contributions to the war against the depression, valley unionists believed that the council would hammer out a strike settlement in line with their interpretation of the code.[41]

On Wednesday, November 1, 1933, two of the three members of the Bruere Board arrived in the Horse Creek Valley.[42] Less than forty-eight hours later, the board issued its first report. Without addressing wages, machine loads, or union recognition, it urged strikers to return to work on Monday. The board asked management to reinstate laborers "without discrimination accept [*sic*] for acts of sabotage or violence." The Willis Board—the Bruere Board's South Carolina counterpart—would oversee reemployment disputes.[43]

Arriving for work on Monday morning, UTW members found the mill gates bolted shut. Second hands and overseers, backed by highway patrolmen and National Guardsmen armed with picker sticks and rifles, blocked the entrances. "Not a single man on strike has been re-employed," Fuller fumed.[44] Angry union members dashed off word of the lockout to the Willis Board. On November 10, the three-member Palmetto State panel, in its first official decision, reissued the Bruere Board's recommendation that all "non-violent" workers be rehired without discrimination. Still, valley mill owners ignored the ruling.[45]

Responding to UTW protests on December 2, the Bruere Board returned to the valley, this time at full strength. The board once again asked mill officials to extend to strikers "preference in employment before any other new employees are taken on, and to rehire them as rapidly as they present themselves and work is available, without discrimination as to rehiring." The Willis Board was again assigned to handle any grievances that arose.[46] Because it did not command the mills to rehire the strikers at once, but only "as rapidly as . . . work is available," the decision represented a defeat for the union. Anticipating the ruling by several weeks, manufacturers had already started to recruit replacement workers from the countryside "by the truckload." One UTW member testified that the mills hired three hundred rural spare hands to avoid taking back strikers. Langley's Viola Smith bitterly complained that while she starved, the mill flew the blue eagle and hired "scabs . . . from far and near." "Something must be done," she wrote, or else there would be more "trouble" in the valley.[47]

Evictions sealed the fate of Horse Creek Valley strikers. In one case, the superintendent of the Bath Mills ousted an employee of twenty-five years for marching in a union parade. Another family was thrown out of its home after one member attended a meeting at the local labor temple. When a Roosevelt administration official asked Blackwood in early 1934 to do something to halt the evictions, the governor did not even bother to respond. Instead, his secretary wrote NRA leaders a terse defense of the mill men. They had, he explained, already been "very indulgent" on the matter. Evictions gained added force through blacklisting. "They happen to have our names where ever we go," a UTW activist complained, "They no [*sic*] you are from the valley."[48]

By New Years Day 1934, the strike was over. There was no dramatic climax. The factories reopened slowly without fanfare or violence. Staffed by crews of loyal hands, new recruits from the depression-ridden countryside, and ex-unionists who had signed yellow-dog contracts, the mills were again operating at full capacity. Under the blue eagle banner, the owners ran their plants as they saw fit. Strikers, meanwhile, were out of work and without relief. In the end, these Horse Creek Valley trade unionists and New Deal Americans could not make the "mill owners live up to the code."[49]

The South is often depicted as different from the rest of the United States. One of the things that marked the region was its distinct pattern of industrial relations. Until recently, the South consistently had the lowest rates of unionization in the country. In 1989 almost a quarter of all American manufacturing workers belonged to a union, and nearly half of all New York laborers were trade unionists. Among southern states, only in Alabama and Tennessee did more than 12 percent of the workforce join a union. In the Carolinas, less than one in twenty wage earners was organized. The conclusion typically drawn from this evidence is that southern workers do not like unions—never did, never will. The proof is in the numbers.[50]

Various explanations have been offered for the failure of trade unionism in the South. Some have attributed it to white racism. Refusing to join integrated unions, this argument goes, white southern workers gave up a voice in determining seniority, the pace of production, and wage rates in order to uphold white supremacy. Others have suggested that southern lawmakers were more willing than politicians elsewhere to use the power of the state to crush unions. Still others have contended that white southern laborers lacked class consciousness, that they were committed individualists who refused "to bend their stiff red necks to the yoke of organization."[51]

However persuasive, these analyses do not explain what happened to the Horse Creek Valley in 1933. Without question, valley laborers, like other southern millhands, insisted that the workforce remain white. They would not work with African Americans, let alone form a union with their black neighbors. But this was not an immediate issue in the valley in 1933. The factories there were all white, and so were the UTW locals and the strikebreakers. Horse Creek Valley millhands, moreover, exhibited what many scholars would call class consciousness: they identified their fate with the fate of the other workers and the New Deal. They joined the national union and stuck together, maintaining a solid picket line for three months. In the end, neither solidarity nor class consciousness was enough to force the mill owners to give in to their demands. Valley unionists lost the battle, but not because they lacked solidarity or effective leadership or because they did not have the ideological resources needed to wage a successful strike. More complex factors contributed to their defeat.

Industrial unionism in America has generally thrived in industries quite different from textiles. Unions have tended to grow in oligopolistic, less competitive sectors of the economy such as automobiles, rubber, steel, and aeronautics. Because of the enormous fixed capital costs required to compete in these high-value-added industries, labor costs represent a relatively small portion of total expenditures. With only a handful of gigantic vertically and/or horizontally integrated firms dominating large, lucrative markets, companies can almost unilaterally determine pricing. Essentially, executives in these industries can pass limited wage hikes on to consumers without worrying about a sharp drop in their market share and thus their profits. Additionally, they typically produce goods in an interlocking manufacturing framework, making them vulnerable to a "well-positioned strike." A walkout in one division could halt production across the entire system overnight. Together, these structural factors have encouraged the nation's largest businesses to press for industrial peace and allowed them to tolerate, although certainly not welcome, a union presence in their factories.

Textile manufacturers operate in a much different economic environment. In 1930 more than a thousand firms churned out endless spools of yarn and miles of cloth, while demand shot up and down with the whims of fashion. Firms were forced to sell their wares in a fiercely competitive, elastic market. One company's gain translated into another's loss, and everyone battled just to stay afloat. Meanwhile, labor costs made up a large portion of total costs. In order to remain profitable, managers had to either hold down wages or increase productivity. The slightest rise in overall costs would increase the price of the final product, and in the competitive jungle of the textile industry, there was always a company ready to undersell a firm that had given its workers a raise or eased up on the stretchout. In addition, when orders ran low, as they did throughout most of the New Deal era, mill officials could easily afford a strike. A work stoppage might, in fact, save them money. Whatever it did, it did not impede other divisions of the firm, because if a manufacturer owned more than one factory, each continued to operate more or less independently of the other. All of these factors fueled the antiunionism of Horse Creek Valley mill owners. To recognize the UTW and uphold workers' view of the

New Deal would cost money and power, and these men were not prepared to relinquish either without a knock-down-drag-out fight.[52]

Industrial structures certainly help to make sense of the failure of the 1933 strike in the Horse Creek Valley, but they do not explain everything. Workers in Appalachian coal mines, northeastern garment factories, and a few New England textile mills, each intensely competitive industries, did manage to win strikes and form strong, durable unions in the twentieth century.[53] To win a strike in these industries, workers had to gain the backing of almost everyone in the plant or mill. But such support alone did not guarantee victory. Trade unionists also had to keep strikebreakers at bay, and this was a complicated proposition. Alliances with the larger community, political traditions and connections, state repression, the absence of financially strapped families living close by, imaginative union leaders, ties to tightly knit ethnic neighborhoods, and the difficulty of picking up the skills of a job, in various combinations, allowed some miners, millhands, and needle workers to establish impermeable picket lines. Although Horse Creek Valley unionists demonstrated an impressive degree of solidarity in 1933, they could not hold back strikebreakers.

In large part, replacement workers made it into valley factories because Governor Blackwood mobilized the state's military might to bust the strike. Still, questions remain: once the troops were activated, who were the women and men who rushed past the picket lines, and why were they willing to break the strike?

Typically strikebreakers are "others," or outsiders to the community. Often in the first half of the twentieth century, especially above the Mason-Dixon line, they were African Americans or recent immigrants. But in the Horse Creek Valley, strikebreakers were indistinguishable from strikers. Both groups were almost exclusively white, native-born Protestants. Rather than splitting along ethnic or racial lines, unionists and loyalists in the valley were divided by day-to-day experience and their sense of identity.[54]

Despite the tradition of trade unionism in the Horse Creek Valley, a cross section of local millhands rejected the UTW. More than a few strikebreakers were probably either related to or close friends of second hands and overseers. When hard times hit, they managed to hang onto their jobs, and so did their family members. A union would replace this system of favoritism with a contract, spelling out specific rules governing seniority, hiring, and firing. Workers who were favored by the bosses had much to lose from joining a union, and thus they stayed away from the UTW.[55]

Mill village residents had other motives for eschewing the union. The same devotion to Americanism that led many to drape the flag around the UTW made others susceptible to xenophobic charges leveled at the national union. Some millhands refused to associate with an allegedly red-tainted foreign organization. Antiunion forces attacked Reverend Fuller and the UTW on the religious front. Whereas valley labor leaders linked union membership to Christian duty, mill ministers and traveling evangelists preached an altogether different gospel. Organized labor, they professed, was the instrument of the Devil. Believers in this gospel did not want to gamble away salvation in the next world for a chance at higher wages and shorter hours in this one.[56] Other, fiercely individualistic mill village residents also renounced the UTW. Such men and women would not be dictated to by anyone, not a company boss and not a union representative.[57]

Nevertheless, according to newspaper accounts and workers' comments, most strikebreakers lived outside of the villages, generally it seems in the countryside. Valley strikers, by contrast, were concentrated in the villages. Observers described local unionists as "life-livers" and "old citizens of this place."[58] Place of residence alone, however, did not fix loyalty during the protest, but identity, or what some at the time called "class," might have. Few people in the upcountry in 1933 used the word "class" in a Marxist sense to refer to relationships to the means of production. Class, instead, designated occupational and cultural groups. People who did similar work, lived in similar communities, and shared common values were members of a class.[59] With this definition in mind, upcountry residents regarded millworkers and farmers as two distinct classes. For example, S. Hay Wilburn, a candidate for the state house of representatives in 1930, pledged to "stand for the interests of the farmers and mill people, because these two *classes* [emphasis added] are the making of Union County and when you have laws that discriminate against the rights of the these two classes you hurt all people."[60] This same class divide that Wilburn hoped to heal in Union County split the Horse Creek Valley in 1933. Rural residents crossed the picket lines of committed industrial laborers and doomed their strike.

To identify oneself as "rural" in 1933 did not preclude working in a mill. Throughout the first half of the twentieth century, people driven by economic imperatives moved back and forth from farm to factory. Bad harvests, rock-bottom prices, the boll weevil, and New Deal agricultural programs all contributed to the migration of rural residents to the industrial world. But whether they lived in the village or commuted from the countryside, tended looms for several years or several months, these "rural" people regarded their stints in the mill as a brief interlude in an otherwise rural existence. Even if they did not become proficient spinners or weavers, they still learned how to run the equipment and this education would prove invaluable if these part-

Mr. Roosevelt Ain't Going to Stand for This

timers ever decided to serve as strikebreakers. The red brick of the mill, the screech of the morning whistle, and the crashing sound of the looms represented to country people a vital source of cash to hold off creditors, pay taxes, buy farm equipment, or purchase more property, not a way of life. Their lives were rooted in the land.[61]

Proud textile workers made up the other "class" of people in the valley. By the 1930s these people were probably second- or even third-generation cotton mill workers, born in a mill village, baptized in a mill church, educated in a mill school, and married to another millworker. Rooted in the mill community, few could imagine themselves living on the land, planting, plowing, and picking rows of cotton. Unlike rural folk, they did not struggle to get away from the shop floor and the rule of the clock but battled to control industrial time and the pace of work. The factory was their existence; their lives flowed from it and back into it.[62]

Different cultural values and lifestyles magnified the distance between the mill and the countryside. Rural people continued in the 1930s to view the mill world with a mixture of fear and loathing. At the time of the Horse Creek Valley strike, farmers still believed that they stood a rung or two above millworkers on the social ladder. They looked at male laborers and saw failed farmers—individuals too lazy to earn a living on the land. Having veered off track, the "fallen" created a wild, sinister, and depraved world in the mill village. From the vantage point of the country, textile laborers lived in a stifling environment; day after day they frantically raced up and down long rows of noisy, cold machines. Rural folk could not fathom how or why mill families crammed into those tiny company-owned houses, one right next to the other, on noisy, narrow streets. Disorder, many believed, reigned in the close quarters of the village. Gender roles were confused and inverted; sluggish men sat on their front porches babbling about politics and spitting tobacco, while their "Amazon" wives and emaciated children trudged off to work and their delinquent teenagers terrorized neighbors. An alluring, yet threatening, sexuality hung in the lint-filled air. Women and men danced close together and made love in the back seats of cars. Whiskey flowed freely. Violence lurked in the shadows. Dreading trouble, or maybe fearing their own dark side, most farmers were reluctant to visit a mill village. When financial concerns dictated, some went to work in the mill, but as soon as their shift ended, they jumped into their used cars and raced back to the farm. They did not want to risk staying in the mill village, at least not after the sun set.[63]

Textile workers, on the other hand, viewed the rural world with a mixture of scorn and nostalgia. For some, the farm symbolized a sweet past. Others thought that farmers were stubborn, even foolish. They could not understand why a man would stand out in the scorching sun day after day, only to find himself further in debt at the end of the year.[64] For others, especially younger workers, the country was "lonely and dead." They wanted to live near the city, the movie houses, and stocked store shelves.[65] Sure, millhands admitted, the factory was hot and noisy, the foreman was mean and crude, and the work was hard and boring, but they had Saturday night. Men with their hair slicked back and women "dressed up fit to kill" roamed village streets, white lightning flowed from roadhouses and back porches, fiddle music blared, and now and then a slot machine spit out a nickel. For those who shied away from the rougher edges of the roadhouses and pool halls, there were baseball games, marching bands and orchestras, swimming pools, libraries, the YMCA, and friends and family to visit. Even Sunday mornings were more exciting in the mill villages: there was more than one church, the services were louder and more vibrant, and the preacher showed up every week, not just once a month.[66]

Erskine Caldwell, Georgia-born and South Carolina–reared, probed the "class" tensions that divided poor whites in the Horse Creek Valley and surrounding areas.[67] Jeeter Lester, the pellagra-ridden protagonist in *Tobacco Road*, would not leave the farm for a "durn cotton mill." Even though his children fled the country for the mill villages in search of "stylish clothes," Jeeter was determined to remain "where he was at all costs." "God," he speculated, "put me on the land to start with, I ain't leaving it."[68] "Maybe God made two kinds of us, after all," observed Ty Ty Walden, a major character in *God's Little Acre*, Caldwell's follow-up to *Tobacco Road*, "a man to work this ground and a man to work the machinery."

When the mill and farm worlds collide in *God's Little Acre*, nothing binds them, not even ties of kinship. Walden's son-in-law is Will Thompson, a Horse Creek Valley weaver. When a strike shuts down the plant where he works, he reluctantly agrees to accompany his wife, Rosamond, to visit her parents in rural Georgia. As soon as Will is left alone with his two brothers-in-law, Buck and Shaw, sparks fly. "Aw go to hell, you Valley linthead," Shaw shouts at Will. "You damn linthead," Buck adds. "Come on both of you sons-of-bitches," Will fires back, "I'll take you both on at the same time. I wasn't raised to be scared of no countryman." Just as they are about to come to blows, Ty Ty intercedes. Shaw explains: "Every time that son-of-a-bitch comes over here he invites a beating. Its just the way he talks and acts. He acts like he's better than we are, or something. He acts like he's better because he works in a cotton mill. He's always calling Buck and me countrymen." Buck agrees with his brother. Will Thompson, he says, is a no-good "linthead." That fact alone is what makes him different; and that is why Buck and his brother hate him. "He ought to stay with his own kind," Buck tells Ty Ty, "We don't want to mix with him."[69]

Men like Jeeter and Ty Ty were never going to work in a loud, hot mill, yet for every one of them, there might be a Shaw or a Buck, who, pinched by economic necessity, might cross Will Thompson's picket line in search of a quick fix of cash. For them, the walk through a gauntlet of screaming, angry strikers was made necessary by dismal financial prospects, but the cultural chasm and simmering animosities that separated workers and farmers made this move easier. It is not nearly as hard to tread on someone you loathe as it is someone you respect.

On several occasions, this was exactly what happened in the Horse Creek Valley. Determined to break a strike, mill owners recruited impoverished rural laborers as strikebreakers.[70] W. J. Cash, that shrewd observer of the folkways of the Piedmont, noticed the same "class" divide in North Carolina that Erskine Caldwell saw in South Carolina. He also recognized how that divide shaped industrial conflict in the region. "The very common whites of the rural areas, the tenant farmers and sharecroppers," Cash wrote, "whom . . . you might reasonably expect to have been on the side of the strikers, generally showed a rabid dislike for them and their cause." Once the mill owners had orders to fill and found enough people willing to work, they started up the machines. Predictably, the sound of someone else making the equipment in *their* factory hum demoralized militant trade unionists like Will Thompson and Paul Fuller. After the power was back on, strike leaders were inevitably evicted from company housing and forced out of town. And, in the case of the 1933 walkout in the Horse Creek Valley, the federal government did nothing for these "new born Americans."[71]

Rather than an isolated episode of defeat, the Horse Creek Valley walkout turned out to be a dress rehearsal for a series of strikes that followed in South Carolina. During the winter of 1933-34 millhands in Bennettsville and Greenville and several other mills walked off the job to make the owners "live up to the code." They learned the same harsh lessons about government power, industrial structures, and strikebreakers that had been drummed into the heads of Horse Creek Valley unionists. In December 1933 UTW members at the well-organized Musgrove Mill in Gaffney protested management's dismissal of four of their leaders. The owner of the factory, H. C. Hamrick, agreed to reinstate the workers but balked at their request for back pay. With no orders to fill, and unwilling to give in to the union's wage demands, he shut down the plant. UTW members turned to the Bruere Board for help; they waited seven months for an answer. Finally, they were told that Hamrick had not discriminated against UTW members but had simply made an oversight either through "a lack of fact or judgment." Pelzer trade unionists waited two months for the board to review their complaints of antiunion discrimination and five months for a vague endorsement of their right to organize. By this time, the recruitment of rural workers and managerial repression had taken its toll and broken the union.[72]

By Christmas 1933 the summer street celebrations staged to mark the implementation of the textile code seemed like a distant dream. Having their expectations raised by the NRA then dashed so quickly, workers were furious that conditions in the mills and in the villages were worse than before. They were outraged by what they saw as the arrogance of the mill owners, who repeatedly defied the textile code and went unpunished. "Now who is the most powerful," Clint DeVore of the Horse Creek Valley asked FDR in 1933, "the mills or the people?" Workers feared that their employers thought that they were outside of the reach of the New Deal.[73] Laborers at the Victor Monhagan Mills informed Roosevelt that their bosses brazenly "DARE the US GOVERNMENT." Palmetto State millhands were angry, moreover, that the Bruere Board "sat idly by" as the "the textile barons of the South . . . are laughing up their sleeves at President Roosevelt."[74] They were infuriated by Governor Blackwood, a man one wage earner complained, who "can't find money to feed the hungry, but he can send an armed guard to a place where there is a labor controversy, but not disorder, to intimidate workers."[75] Textile laborers, lastly, resented the "apple knockers" who broke their strikes and took their places in the mills. By the time that spring rolled across the Piedmont, the mill hills of South Carolina were tinder boxes of discontent. One spark and they might explode.

Despite mounting frustrations, millhands still clung to their faith in the president. Most of them continued to see him as a powerful God-sent man, who would deliver them to the promised land of industrial democracy. But they also recognized that something would have to change. Somehow they had to get Roosevelt's attention, make him more aware than their letters and isolated strikes did of what his enemies, the mill owners, were up to.

CHAPTER SIX

The General Textile Strike, September 1934

On May 23, 1934, the Bruere Board, the administrative arm of the textile code, made public a decision that set the stage for the largest labor uprising in South Carolina since the Stono Slave Rebellion. Without consulting the United Textile Workers of America (UTW), the board authorized a scheme, approved by National Recovery Administration (NRA) chief General Hugh Johnson, to ease the textile industry's latest crisis of overproduction. Seeking to restrict output, the plan called for a 25 percent cut in hours. In and of itself, the curtailment was not a problem. The problem was that it was accompanied by a corresponding drop in pay. For many millhands, this went too far: it was time to stand up for their rights as citizens of New Deal America.[1]

Millworkers from Greenville to Graniteville sent President Roosevelt letters, petitions, and resolutions opposing the Bruere Board's May ruling. They implored him to step in and stop the wage cut. Others tried more direct ways of getting FDR's attention.[2] Toward the end of May, trade unionists in Cowpens, Greenwood, Ware Shoals, Anderson, Belton, and Lonsdale went on strike. Before the end of the month most of them had returned to work after mill men agreed to limit the proposed pay cut.[3] Not all of the May protests ended so quickly or so quietly, however. At Orr Mills in Anderson overseers attacked strikers with picker sticks, leaving twenty workers with cuts, bruises, and bumps on the head.[4] Several Greenwood County mills did not reopen until July, and when they did, it was under the state militia's protection.[5]

Rankled by the Bruere Board's promanagement stance, encouraged by grassroots agitation, and ready to flex its newly developed organizational muscles, the UTW also tried to get the president's attention. National leaders threatened a general strike if the May curtailment went into effect. On June 2 bravado turned to conciliation as union president Thomas McMahon withdrew the strike order in exchange for a vague offer from New Deal officials to place a UTW representative on the Bruere Board and the promise of yet another government study of the industry. All the same, the wage cut went through.[6]

Southern workers could hardly believe it. Having risked so much to join the union, they were incensed by the national leadership's capitulation. Despite stern warnings from the UTW president not to strike, many union members decided to fight even if they had to do it on their own. On July 16, 1934, workers at a handful of northern Alabama mills walked off their jobs. Two days later, another 20,000 Cotton State textile laborers joined them on the picket line.[7] The protest spread east, and several North Carolina locals joined the strike movement. On August 16, two thousand Columbus, Georgia, millhands shut down a handful of plants in their area. A week later, wage earners at the Lonsdale Mill in Seneca, South Carolina, went on strike as well.[8]

Sprinting to catch up with its membership, UTW leaders convened a special convention in New York City in the middle of August. Too poor to ride the train, many southerners hitchhiked north for the meeting. Fifty times they introduced motions for a general strike. "Amen," shouted "Walking Charlie" McAbee of Inman, South Carolina, each time. An Alabama trade unionist, his head wrapped in blood-stained bandages, electrified the crowd when he rose to speak in favor of one resolution. "I have been wounded in the head and shot in the leg," he said in a low, dramatic voice, "but I am ready to die for the union and I call upon you to do the same."[9] With only ten dissenting votes, UTW delegates backed his motion for a national general strike to begin on September 1, 1934. One skeptic, a UTW member from Newberry, South Carolina, claimed, "The people from the southern states don't want a strike at the present time, and our treasury won't stand for it." "A burly man" from a nearby mill town disagreed. The overwhelming majority of South Carolina workers, he contended, "favored action." Copying the Alabama strikers' list of demands, the delegates insisted on a twelve-dollar minimum wage for a thirty-hour workweek, union recognition, and abolishment of the stretchout. Two weeks later, the South Carolina Federation of Textile Workers unanimously endorsed the strike platform.[10]

Throughout the fortnight between the New York convention and the scheduled start of the strike, UTW leaders hustled to find a settlement and avoid a walkout. They tried to lure the manufacturers to the bargaining table, but the owners would not take the bait. Mostly, they looked to Roosevelt. Several days before the strike deadline, union president McMahon pointed to FDR as the "only man in God's green earth who can stop the strike." At the local level, workers also petitioned for federal intervention. "Only you can save us," Piedmont's Neal Bass wrote to Secretary of Labor Frances Perkins. Guy Bradley pressed Roosevelt to "call a cotton industry holiday like you did for the banks and give Mr. George Sloan [head of the Cotton Textile Institute (CTI)] so many days to make a settlement with the labor leaders . . . if he does not . . . see that we get a settlement and force the companies to abide by the law." Bradley's plea, as well as the others', went unanswered. The president and Perkins did nothing, said nothing.[11]

With the scheduled start of the national strike—midnight, September 1— only a day away, millworkers around the country gathered to listen to Francis Gorman's radio address. Gorman, rather than UTW president McMahon, emerged as the leader of the strike. Born in a mill town in northern England in 1890, Gorman grew up around trade unionists who regularly gathered at his father's pub. When the bar business went sour in 1903, the family emigrated to the United States, settling near a Providence, Rhode Island, textile mill. Like the rest of the children in the neighborhood, young Gorman went to work. It did not take him long to learn to operate his own looms or to join the union. Soon he became a UTW organizer and rose quickly through the ranks. By the time of the textile strike, the jittery, thin, forty-four-year-old Gorman was the vice president of the United Textile Workers. Aggressive, innovative, and full of bluster, Gorman created an image of the strike, however distorted, as a fine-tuned, well-coordinated national offensive. Unfazed by Roosevelt's apparent indifference, he assured his listeners the night before the walkout, "We have a friend in the White House." Sparked by "abuses no longer bearable," he said, the strike was "fully justified under the law and the New Deal." "Victory," Gorman told workers, was possible only "through solidarity." "We can NOT fail this time or they will drive us into slavery," he wrote to union locals.[12]

On September 2, carloads of South Carolinians drove to Charlotte, North Carolina, for a strike rally. The spirit of revivalism abounded. "I fervently believe," O. D. Lisk told the faithful, "God is with us . . . he will not desert us in this just struggle for ourselves and our families." "Amen!" answered the crowd. R. R. Lawrence spoke next. Pounding out his address in a preacher's cadence, he shouted: "The hour has arrived when the fight must go forward. We fight for the Lord and for our families. Many sacrifices will be required of us in this fight. I know you are ready to make them." With the crowd swaying, Lawrence concluded his sermon with a familiar Old Testament analogy: "The first strike on record was the strike in which Moses led the children of

Israel out of slavery from Egypt. They, too, struck against intolerable conditions, and it took them forty years to win that strike, which had the sanction of God, as I am sure our strike has also. But it won't take us forty years to win our strike. It will be won in less than forty days, if everybody will do his part." South Carolina strike director John Peele was even more optimistic, predicting victory in ten short days.[13]

The troops were primed for battle. The UTW local in Chester wired the national headquarters: "ATTA BOY COME ON WE ARE READY." Worried about government intervention, J. A. Frier of the South Carolina Federation of Textile Workers warned eager millhands to "[a]void boisterousness and violence." "Be sober," he cautioned. "Give no excuse for calling in troops to coerce the workers back to their jobs."[14]

Textile workers answered the general strike call in numbers that startled the owners, New Deal and state officials, and even UTW leaders. Mills shut down, according to one account, "so rapidly that tabulators almost lost count." The Associated Press estimated the strikers' ranks at 200,000 on September 4, 325,000 the next day, and 400,000 by the end of the first week.[15] The strike spread just as quickly across South Carolina, although here too it was difficult to determine the exact size of the protest. Predictably, the UTW and the mill men wrangled over the depth of support for the walkout; the union inflated its figures, and the manufacturers downplayed the magnitude of the revolt. Reports of the number of strikers, moreover, varied from newspaper to newspaper. The press could not even agree on the number of men and women "normally" employed in the state's mills. At the start of the strike, the Associated Press estimated that 67,000 people worked in South Carolina's textile factories, and two weeks later it put the number at 85,000. Furthermore, in some places it was impossible to distinguish between walkouts and lockouts.[16] Even taking into account these discrepancies, it appears that by the end of the first week of September, more than two-thirds of South Carolina's two hundred textile mills were shut down and almost 43,000 workers were either on strike or out of work.[17]

Palmetto State strikers raised the American flag as their symbol; it flapped over every picket line and at the front of every union parade. Strikers portrayed themselves as defenders of the nation and the New Deal pitted against the enemies of America and its president.[18] "We are the best citizens," a UTW member said of his neighbors on the picket line. Next to flags held high, workers marched under banners bearing the slogans: "Roosevelt Our Greatest Leader," "We Are Backing Roosevelt 100 Percent," "New Deal," "The Strike Is On—Dont Scab—Its Now or Never," and "Union Stands for equal rights for All."[19]

The imagery of the strike fit the moment. From the start, this was a political protest. Just as they did in the Horse Creek Valley in 1933, strikers wanted Roosevelt to step in and make the manufacturers abide by the workers' vision of the law. "[The] strike threat was intended . . . to bring pressure for action by the government," Gorman reflected in 1956, ". . . this was the union's chief hope and expectancy in calling the strike." Again like the Civil Rights demonstrations that swept across the South twenty-five years later, UTW sympathizers sought to precipitate a crisis that would draw the attention of federal authorities to the conditions in the southern cotton mill world. Under the glare of publicity, strikers would reveal themselves as "new born Americans" committed to the New Deal and willing to suffer the hardships of a walkout for national progress. At the same time, they wanted to spotlight the employers' refusal to "live up to the code" and recognize workers' rights. Once management had been stripped of the mask of patriotism, millhands expected FDR—in order words, the federal government—to rush to the textile towns and take over the factories. Some meant this quite literally. If the president could not provide them with a "new set of bosses," one group of workers asked, could he come down and run the mills himself?[20]

Union shock troops, better known as "flying squadrons," fanned the strike fires. "With the speed and force of a mechanized army," UTW members equipped with pistols, rifles, and clubs swarmed across the Piedmont. They stopped at the mills that were still operating and tried to persuade laborers who were still working to join the protest. If the millhands did not promptly walk off the job, the squadrons sometimes forced the issue, storming plants, knocking down doors, and cutting off power. Of course, everywhere they went they waved the American flag. Made up of five women and one man, the lead battalion of a Spartanburg flying squadron invaded a factory, waving the Stars and Stripes and exhorting nonstrikers "to respect the flag." Another yelled: "Come over on to this side . . . the President is with us—help him out."[21] During the first days of the protest, the flying squadrons mushroomed everywhere they went. One grew to include 655 strikers in 105 cars and trucks. Another swelled to 2,000 workers; when it reached Columbia, the participants staged an impromptu flag-waving parade around the state capital.[22]

Women stood on the front lines of the strike army. They sped from mill to mill in flying squadrons, walked the picket lines, and raised the flag. Female UTW members taunted company loyalists, telling them to show their manhood by joining the protest. At the Powell Knitting Mills, women grabbed the hair of male strikebreakers and slapped them in the face. What kind of man, the strikers seemed to ask, would cross a picket line? Behind the scenes, guiding relief efforts and making do with less, women shielded their families from starvation.[23] Women's strike roles should come as no surprise. As mothers, wives, and daughters, low-paid workers, and managers of family consumption, women had a great deal to gain from the textile code, especially from the minimum-wage statute. Operating in a tight labor market, women, moreover, faced countless episodes of sexual harassment. Some male supervisors let female employees know that they could keep their jobs only in exchange for sexual favors or tolerance of lewd gestures and vulgar talk. A union, some women thought, would protect them from unscrupulous overseers.[24] Finally, UTW supporters spoke the essentially inclusive idiom of New Deal Americanism. Stressing citizenship and equality of sacrifice, trade unionists beckoned women as workers and members of the community to enlist in the struggle to make the mill men "live up to the code."

The protest proved more effective in some communities than in others. In Spartanburg County almost every mill was idle; 13,000 out of 14,000 local laborers were on strike.[25] Ninety-six percent of the workers at mills in Abbeville and Calhoun Falls voted in favor of the shutdown. Support was so solid in Columbia that UTW members did not have to picket.[26] Millworkers in Chester, Gaffney, Pelzer, Rock Hill, Union, and York also stood firmly behind the union. But flying squadrons could not crack some of the state's most hardened antiunion fortresses. Strikers made only shallow inroads into those communities most recently rocked by labor unrest, where discrimination, the recruitment of rural laborers, evictions, and blacklistings robbed workers of a core of indigenous activists. In the historically militant Horse Creek Valley, the factories operated at half of their normal capacity throughout the strike. And the UTW managed to shut down only one of the seven heavily fortified factories of the Springs chain in Lancaster County.[27]

"Please help us. . . . The Woodside Cotton Mill has downed your flag," a member of a flying squadron wrote to FDR after a failed attempt to close the Greenville factory.[28] A center of unrest in 1929, 1932, and again in the spring and summer of 1934, during the general strike, the mills in and around Greenville proved to be almost as solidly antiunion as neighboring Spartanburg was prounion. More than one-third of all of the state's nonstrikers, in fact, resided in Greenville County. Prior to the walkout, local mill owners mapped out meticulous battle plans for the fight to come. "Dunean mill," union leader John Peele explained, "has two deputy sheriffs[;] these men attend every meeting which is held . . . by labor organizers, and keep a carefull [sic] watch on these men. . . . Already three employees have been discharged for talking organization among the employees." A member of the local Ku Klux Klan, a chapter reportedly made up of second hands and supervisors, informed Peele "that the matter of organization of the workers has been men-

National Guardsmen prying open a picket line of company loyalists
in Greenville, 1934. Note the American flag in the upper right corner.
(UPI/Corbis-Bettmann)

tioned in the meetings and they are not going to allow the employees of this
mill to organize." In preparation for the strike, Greenville managers further
strengthened their defenses by arming loyal workers with pistols and picker
sticks. When the UTW finally did call out its followers, Governor Ibra C.
Blackwood provided Greenville manufacturers with extra soldiers. The combination of private and public might and the specter of eviction of local activists that would inevitably follow a union defeat, as had previously occurred in
the area, allowed the owners to keep their machines running throughout the
general strike. Without indigenous leaders to show the way, Greenville's repressive atmosphere, in the end, made local workers "afraid to strike." [29]

Rural mills stood as yet another obstacle in the union's path. Workers in
these more remote areas tended to split half for the strike and half against
it. Honea Path, in Anderson County, was one of these places. The Chiquola
Manufacturing Company dominated the community; in fact, the mill superintendent doubled as the mayor. The general strike divided the small town
in two. During the opening days of the protest, union members showered
strikebreakers, who reportedly came from "the farms and nearby towns," with
abuse. "Scab, scab," they screamed at them in a menacing tone. "Ain't no damn

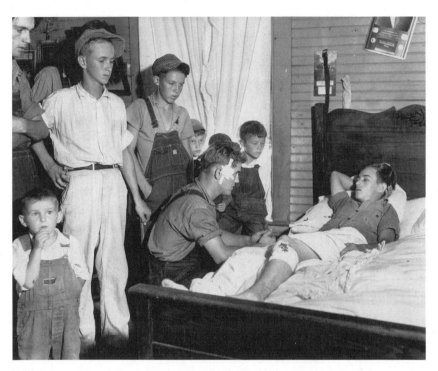

Honea Path millhands comforting a neighbor and member
of the UTW wounded in picket-line violence, September 1934.
(UPI/Corbis-Bettmann)

son of a bitch gonna keep me out of that mill," growled a loyal employee.
After three days of shouting matches and fistfights, Honea Path was said to be
"near the breaking point." When word leaked that a flying squadron planned
a raid on the town, Anderson County sheriff W. A. Clamp deputized dozens
of loyal workers and overseers.[30]

Before daybreak on September 6, 1934, a flying squadron left Belton for the
twenty-mile ride to Honea Path. Singing gospel hymns and waving a gigantic American flag, local strike supporters waited for them in front of the mill.
Inside the factory longtime lawmen, newly deputized officers, and the mayor
readied their defenses. The blast of the morning whistle signaled the start
of the battle. Strikers and the flying squadron lurched forward to block the
mill gate. Strikebreakers surged to the entrance. One man was smashed over
the head with a club, another was stopped in his tracks by a stiff right hook,
and still another was jabbed with a picker stick. Suddenly, a lone pistol shot
cracked. Next came a furious flash of fire. People scurried in all directions
as bullets kicked up dust at their feet. The shooting lasted for three min-

The General Textile Strike

utes. Then everything was quiet. Only the cries of the fallen and the sobs of family and friends broke the silence. Six strikers lay dead and more than a dozen wounded. Most had been pierced in the back, apparently cut down as they fled.[31]

The Chiquola Manufacturing Company would not allow any mill churches to hold funeral services for the strikers. None, it turned out, was big enough. On September 9, ten thousand people gathered on a grassy bank on the outskirts of town to pay tribute to the slain millhands. The memorial opened with a short prayer followed by a soulful version of "In the Sweet By and By." Local union organizer Furman Rodgers described the shootings as cold-blooded murder, prophesying that Governor Blackwood and the mayor would "feel the brand of Cain." Next to speak was Reverend James Myers, industrial secretary of the New York–based Federal Council of Churches. "They died for the rights of the hard-working man . . . [and] . . . to make industry Christian," Myers said. "The movement for improved industrial conditions dates back to Jesus's conception that we are children of God and entitled to better things. . . . Had the principles of democracy been recognized by the mill employers these men need not have died." Shouts of "Amen" and "Praise the Lord" punctuated Myers's address. "We are Americans and we think we know what constitutes Americanism," strike leader Gorman wrote in a letter read by a local laborer, "Americanism does not mean shooting workers in the back and that is what has been done by the hirelings of the employers." As the crowd cheered, George Googe, the AFL's southern director, climbed onto the stage. Saying nothing, he held up the bullet-riddled flag carried by strikers on the morning of the killings. As people drifted away singing "Thou Art Gone," some mumbled "Remember Honea Path, Remember Honea Path."[32]

It was hard to forget Honea Path. Yet not everyone carried the same memory. "It is impossible to negotiate with anarchism," textile executive A. G. Furman concluded after the killings. Pharmacists, lawyers, and shopkeepers concurred: the rebellion had to be quelled before it tore apart the fabric of society. Middle-class South Carolinians sent telegrams and letters to Governor Blackwood begging him to do the "humane" thing and declare martial law "to restore law and order," "protect . . . life and liberty," and "stem the floodtide of passion aroused by trained labor agitators."[33]

The governor did not need this advice; he was already on the side of the owners and the professional classes. Even before the Honea Path killings, Blackwood talked of war and encouraged mill companies to stockpile weapons and assemble private armies. He deputized overseers in his office and appointed hundreds of other loyal operatives to the post of constable without pay "for the textile strike."[34] He made sure that the owners were loaded with

Children playing with National Guardsmen at the
Woodside Mills in Greenville during the General Textile Strike.
(UPI/Corbis-Bettmann)

army grenades and tear gas.[35] He also mobilized South Carolina's military might. Throughout the first week of the protest, he rushed troops—National Guard units and the Highway Patrol—to strike hot spots. There was little doubt about which side the soldiers were on. "In the event that anyone attempts to incite riot or insurrection by speech or otherwise," Blackwood counseled one sheriff, "you are authorized to arrest such persons and if necessary call the military authorities to your aid."[36] In Ninety-Six, guardsmen built an ominous-looking machine gun nest above the mill and aimed the weapons at the picket line. When a rumor spread through the village that the automatic weapon was a fake, the commanding officer instructed his men to demonstrate its authenticity by blasting apart a tree in front of the factory. Up the road in Greenville, the captain of a "hard-boiled company" equipped with tear gas, rifles, and bayonets told reporters that his unit had been ordered "to go wherever the flying squadron goes and stop it each time." "My men," he added, "have instructions to shoot to kill if any effort is made to rush the mill." Troop movements and the arms buildup were justified, Blackwood

The General Textile Strike

explained, because South Carolina was "suffering a ruthless and insolent invasion" by groups bent on "illegal and destructive enterprises."[37]

The Honea Path murders only reinforced Blackwood's view of the strike as a "lawless" wave of "mob rule." Hours after the shootings, the governor told a stunned press corps that UTW members had threatened his life, but he vowed not to back down. He ordered the remainder of the state's National Guard units to positions across the strike zone and demanded the dispersal of all "groups engaged in unlawful obstruction, combination, and assemblage," meaning, of course, the flying squadrons. On September 9 Blackwood declared that a "state of insurrection" existed in South Carolina. To stop the chaos, he imposed "partial martial law," directing the troops to ensure that everyone who wanted to work would be able to do so.[38] Under military protection, three mills, including the Chiquola Manufacturing Company, reopened the Monday after the shootings.[39]

Blackwood's actions coupled with the events in Honea Path and elsewhere rattled strikers.[40] Once again, UTW members called on Roosevelt, their friend and ally, to rush federal troops to South Carolina to act as a counterweight against Blackwood and, in the words of one millhand, to "protect strikers and their Constitutional rights." "With human lives hanging in the balance," union leader J. A. Frier suggested, "the mills should close for a week in order to allow people to regain their composure and secure . . . an adjustment of the existing disagreement." The White House did not respond.[41]

Terrified of more bloodshed and wounded by public criticism, UTW leaders in South Carolina disbanded the flying squadrons on September 11. Defying predictions, the dispersal of the union's shock troops did not lead to the immediate crumpling of the strike lines. Throughout the second week of the protest, despite mounting government repression and editorial attacks, the strike front remained intact.[42]

On September 17, meanwhile, southern mill men surveyed the industrial landscape and agreed to launch a "gigantic effort . . . to break through the strike lines and start the movement back to the mills." Two days later, an army of 3,200 militiamen and several thousand more deputies assembled in South Carolina. They pried open only two small mills in the state. The next day a few more factories opened. Although more plants—backed by the state's military muscle and staffed by strike defectors, rural laborers, longtime spare hands, and "soda jerkers"—started up each day, the floodgates had not been opened.[43] For the most part, Palmetto State trade unionists repelled the counteroffensive, and many, like Columbia's H. F. La Cons, remained confident that the strike would continue "until we win or starve to death."[44]

Starvation loomed first on the horizon. Day after day, UTW supporters subsisted on beans and cornmeal, but by the third week of the protest, even these merger stocks were running low. On September 14 hundreds of strikers carrying banners that read "We Are Hungry" converged on an upcountry relief office. "Give us some bread and meat," pleaded a trade unionist, "and we'll get out in the country and get some beans."[45] Hobbled by a puny treasury, the UTW could do little to help. Other AFL affiliates chipped in, but not enough. From the start of the walkout, trade unionists had banked on the federal government to bail them out. "The President," wrote a North Carolina man, "said we could strike . . . and that the government would pay us $6.00 per week as long as we are out on strike."[46] In theory, he was right. New Deal relief programs promised assistance to unemployed workers whether they were laid off or on strike. Yet like so many New Deal formulas, local control acted against national aims. In Aiken County, the president of the Graniteville Manufacturing Company chaired the county relief board. "The relief workers get their orders from him," explained UTW member Mrs. J. W. Hallman. "They think they will be able to starve us out and force us to do there [sic] bidding. And there wont be any thing to the N.R.A. in the South." Similar stories were told across the strike zone. Federal officials, uneasy about underwriting the strike, did nothing, allowing the law to go unheeded and hungry workers to go without food.[47]

At UTW headquarters in Washington, news of the declaration of martial law in South Carolina, the employer counteroffensive, and the relief crisis created the impression among union leaders that the strike was falling apart at the grass roots. They searched for a face-saving way out of the conflict.[48] On September 20, they got their chance when the textile mediation board, appointed fifteen days earlier by President Roosevelt and chaired by former New Hampshire governor John G. Winant, issued its report. The tribunal proposed that the Bruere Board be replaced by a new textile labor relations board staffed by "neutral" members, that the Federal Trade Commission study the capacity of the industry to raise wages, and that an ad hoc panel investigate the stretchout. The report offered nothing to striking workers or their union. Nonetheless, Roosevelt, who viewed industrial unrest as a nuisance and an obstacle to recovery, asked the UTW to call off the strike on the basis of the Winant Board's recommendations.[49] On September 22 Gorman, maintaining that "force and hunger" were driving millhands across the picket line, bowed to FDR's request. He ordered UTW members back to work, telling them that they had scored an "overwhelming victory."[50]

"The strike is dead," headlined the UTW's monthly magazine. "There will be adjustments of wages and hours. The union will grow stronger. The textile workers at last are free." "On foot, in trucks, and automobiles," the *New York Times* reported on September 24, "strikers paraded all night through mill towns and villages singing hymns of joy and celebrating the news that tomorrow the whistles will blow again."[51] But few mill whistles blew the next morning. Where they did sound, strikers learned that they had been replaced and if they wanted their jobs back, they had to sign yellow-dog contracts. Ku Klux Klansmen harassed unionists. L. L. Smith, the head of the UTW local in Greer, woke up one night to find a cross burning on his lawn. Some plants did not reopen until New Year's Day, leaving thousands of laborers unemployed, penniless at Christmas, and terrified of the coming winter. Rubbing salt into strikers' wounds, mill managers reminded workers that they had lost, that they had gained nothing that they had demanded—not a reduction in hours, more pay, or an end to the stretchout. Wherever millhands asked for old jobs back on the basis of FDR's recommendations, they heard the same refrain from manufacturers: "The President of the United States does not run this mill, I do."[52]

"Many of us did not understand fully the role of the Government in the struggle between labor and industry," wrote national strike coordinator Francis Gorman after the protest. "Many of us," he continued, "did not understand what we do now: that the Government protects the strong, not the weak, and that it operates under pressure and yields to that group which is strong enough to assert itself over the other. If nobody learned anything but this from the strike it was worth the lesson." South Carolina workers drew a similar lesson from the strike. They, too, learned that the government "protected the strong against the weak." But here is where Gorman and most South Carolina millworkers parted ways.[53]

For Gorman, the strike revealed the bankruptcy of the New Deal. Laborers had risked their jobs to defend the president's policies. Yet he did not lift a hand to help them. Roosevelt's strike performance convinced Gorman that it was time for American workers to cut a new path: to leave the party of Roosevelt and start an independent labor party. Unlike Gorman, South Carolina millhands never thought of leaving the party of their fathers, the white Democratic Party. Instead, workers blamed the strike failure on the repressive policies of the manufacturers, on the Bruere Board, on Blackwood, who one worker tagged the "sorriest white man I have ever heard of," and on the actions of "yellow scabs," strikebreakers, and spare hands, in other words, on everybody but the president.[54]

Nothing—not the fact that FDR failed to answer their letters or to punish the mill owners—rocked their faith in the president. Over the next four years South Carolina millhands expressed their continued commitment to the New

Deal. They supported FDR's reelection in 1936, defended his controversial plan to "pack" the courts, endorsed his program for consolidating authority in the hands of the chief executive, and backed his widely criticized attempt to purge conservatives from the Democratic Party. In state and local elections, millhands voted for candidates who pledged their allegiance to all kinds of little New Deals. And on the shop floor, they continued to press for their economic rights as citizens of New Deal America.

Without really looking for it, Martha Gellhorn spotted evidence of South Carolina millhands' enduring faith in Roosevelt and the federal government on a trip to the state in November 1934. The St. Louis–born, Byrn Mawr College–educated novelist went to the Piedmont to investigate local conditions for the White House. In the wake of the 1934 strike wave that passed over not just the mill hills but also the coal mines and entire cities like San Francisco, some of Roosevelt's key advisers worried that the nation's workers were on the verge of revolution. Gellhorn assured them that as far as South Carolina was concerned, there was no need to worry. As she wandered from mill town to mill town, one image stood out. "Every house I visited—mill worker or unemployed," Gellhorn noted with surprise, "had a picture of the President. These ranged from newspaper clippings (in the destitute homes) to large colored prints, framed in gilt cardboard." "The portrait," she added, "holds the place of honor over the mantel; I can compare this to the Italian peasant's Madonna." [55]

CHAPTER SEVEN

The Enthronement
of Textile Labor

The 1934 Governor's Race

 In August 1934 David Coker puzzled over the lesser of two evils. His candidate for governor, Wyndham Manning, had been knocked out of the race in the first primary. Now Coker faced the choice of "voting for a communist on the one hand or a man without a moral sense on the other."[1] Backing the "man without a moral sense," Cole Blease, meant supporting someone whom he had spent decades trying to destroy. Many of his associates in walnut-paneled boardrooms, dark-toned hotel lobbies, and white-columned country clubs were, by their own admission, endorsing Blease for narrow, self-serving economic reasons.[2] Coker did not know if he could follow their lead. But could he vote for the "communist," Olin Johnston? This would be a hard pill for the midlands industrialist and agriculturist to swallow. Johnston was sure to push for labor legislation, foment unrest, and cut a different path of economic development. Coker did not know what to do, but he had to do something; the long-term prosperity of South Carolina was at stake in the 1934 election.

Millworkers also thought that the future was up for grabs, and they too faced a dilemma. Should they vote for the "immoral" candidate or the "communist"? Should they vote for their past or their future, for Blease or Johnston?

The election season that so befuddled millhands and David Coker was also the strike season in South Carolina. Eight men entered the race, which began in July, but only three—Blease, Johnston, and Manning—had any chance of winning. As thousands gathered in counties across the state to eat, drink, and listen to the candidates, millhands debated with family members and friends at home, at work, and in front of the company store whether to join the national walkout. The first primary took place on August 28, 1934, only days before the scheduled start of the general strike. While voters slogged through thick layers of summer heat and humidity, mill owners fortified their defenses and workers made plans to form picket lines. No one received a majority in the initial contest and that meant a second primary. Over the next two weeks, the run-off candidates, Blease and Johnston, dashed around the vote-rich upcountry looking for support and dodging flying squadrons and National Guardsmen. The runoff was held on September 14, 1934, one week after the Honea Path massacre and right in the middle of a full-blown labor revolt. The general strike made labor and related questions about gender and economic development the key issues in the 1934 governor's campaign.[3] As the would-be governors positioned themselves on the strike, talking about the New Deal, labor legislation, military force, picket-line violence, and public spending, they staged a public forum on the relationship between class and citizenship.

For millworkers, the general strike unleashed threats of violence, joblessness, and hunger. These were tense, nerve-wracking days. But they were also thrilling. Members of the United Textile Workers of America (UTW) must have felt the surge of power that came from challenging the bosses and asserting control over their lives. After years of struggling "for a bare existence," Bennettsville's A. F. Brigman proudly announced, "thank God we're bold enough now to come in the open and fight back." Being part of something bigger than their four-room, yellow, company-owned houses, even bigger than their own communities, something as big as the entire nation, must also have been exhilarating.[4]

Raw power and nervous energy—these were not the feelings pulsing through middle- and upper-class South Carolina homes, especially in the strike-torn areas of the upcountry and midlands. Amid the marching of National Guardsmen and militant workers, many thought they heard the shrill sounds of class warfare. Mob rule and anarchy, executives and lawyers said, were replacing law and order. "Everybody is feverish, restless, and worried," reported a Greenwood man. A fortress mentality set in. People barricaded themselves inside their homes, businesses closed, schools shut down, and golf tournaments and baseball playoff games were canceled. On September 8 the *Spartanburg Herald* observed, "In one short week industry in the Piedmont has been paralyzed . . . the flow of money has ceased, merchants

The Enthronement of Textile Labor

find their stores robbed of customers, transportation is ruined and all business is disturbed." The General Textile Strike, warned another upcountry man, represented "the gravest emergency which has confronted our people since Reconstruction Days."[5]

Drawing a parallel to Reconstruction, this man tapped into a widespread fear that New Deal encouragement of working-class militancy would eventually trigger a crisis that threatened more than just personal safety and sporting events. Brick by brick the entire social order seemed, to some, to be falling apart. Labor conflict, according to middle-class observers, turned gender roles, for instance, upside down. "Belligerent wives" from Greenville supposedly defied the authority of their husbands by joining the protest. Somehow by stepping into the public light of picket lines and flying squadrons, according to a *Charlotte Observer* reporter, women metamorphosed. Female trade unionists stopped being housewives and mothers and became "muscular and stockingless, Amazon battalions." Even women who stayed on the job were depicted as being out of control. "You can strike all you want to but I've got to do something to feed the kids," one woman reportedly shouted at her husband as she shoved him aside on her way into the factory. "Work on, dern you," he yelled back in frustration, "I'll go cook." Men also lost their way during the strike. Fighting broke out in Honea Path, declared the editors of the *Abbeville Press and Banner*, only after ruffians and unionists began "manhandling women workers." What kind of men, the *Textile Bulletin* asked, were "willing to put their children through the suffering that a strike will bring, while self-appointed leaders live off the fat of the land?"—certainly not worthy white patriarchs.[6]

Fears of gender disorder and a renewal of Reconstruction spilled over into the 1934 governor's race. Noting that it was force that ended Republican rule, business leaders and conservatives judged the candidates by whether or not they would "use the militia as Governor Blackwood is using it."[7] In the first primary, an admirer of the governor's industrial policy—Sumter farmer and businessman Wyndham Manning—won the backing of manufacturers and others frightened by the strike. A generation earlier Manning's father, Richard, had defeated Cole Blease in a race for the governor's office. Once in power, the elder Manning, speaking the language of business progressivism, returned the reigns of government to the state's traditional elite: planters, bankers, and manufacturers. Many hoped that his son could repeat this performance, this time by knocking off both Blease and Johnston and putting an end to the scourge of working-class rebellion.[8]

Although the younger Manning praised Roosevelt personally and saluted New Deal agricultural programs, he voiced concern over the rancor stirred by the administration's labor policies. He called for a less contentious tone in industrial relations, paid tribute to textile manufacturers and their contributions to the state, and affirmed the rights of nonstrikers. Distancing himself from the national protest, Manning trivialized the causes of the strike. "[O]utrages," he claimed without mentioning code chiseling, wage cuts, or the stretchout, were "being perpetuated . . . by small groups of striking operatives under the domination of labor organizers." Manning also promised to beef up law enforcement. In the charged atmosphere of the General Textile Strike, this pledge reassured business leaders and boosters that more troops would be available to stop future labor revolts.[9]

If Manning lost, his supporters cautioned, the plagues of radicalism, labor strife, and gender disorder would overrun the state. "You and I have got to live in South Carolina," the conservative editor of the *Charleston News and Courier* alerted his readers. "It won't be safe for us to live in it, or for our children, unless we shall have a governor of sterling and stainless character. This character the people recognize in Manning."[10] But no amount of praise from well-heeled backers could make up for the fact that Manning was a listless stump speaker—a significant liability in South Carolina, where the theater of politics mattered as much as its substance.[11] Still, his backers remained upbeat. Convinced that the traditional mill candidates, Blease and Johnston, would split the vote in the textile precincts, they calculated that their candidate could scoop up enough of the remaining votes to slip into the runoff, where they anticipated that his prospects for victory were brighter. Their calculations were wrong. Johnston and Blease, in that order, whipped Manning in the first primary.[12] Mourning this defeat, a Manning booster worried that "the conservative element in the state is dwindling in number and in influence, that the people of culture and refinement are occupying a less consequential position, and that the safety of themselves and their property may be less secure than it has been heretofore."[13]

With Manning out, the race was between Blease and Johnston, two favorite sons of the millhands running for governor just as the General Textile Strike gripped the state. Sensing something significant in the pairing, the *New York Times* considered the options in the second primary to be a "good indication" of the "enthronement of labor, particularly textile labor in South Carolina."[14] From the packed streets of Manhattan, the two candidates looked the same; both were labor candidates in a traditionally agricultural state. But from strike-torn South Carolina, Johnston and Blease looked quite different, especially when it came to the central issues of labor and class. One was a liberal New Dealer and the other was an antistatist obstructionist.[15]

Some called Olin Johnston "Olinsky Bolshevik Johnston" or that "Red,

The Enthronement of Textile Labor

"Weekly Newsmap of South Carolina," September 1934. This cartoon depicts
what was going on in South Carolina as the General Textile Strike raged and Olin
Johnston battled Cole Blease in the second primary for the governor's office.
(*Greenville News*, September 10, 1934)

Radical, Communist."[16] In the fall of 1934 no one in South Carolina actually
thought that Johnston was a bomb thrower or a member of a clandestine revo-
lutionary cell or even an ardent supporter of the Soviet Union. Rather, the incendiary communist label reflected the alarm of some people, especially business leaders and upcountry professionals. Tagging Johnston a "red" was like
ringing a warning bell indicating that this man is dangerous. Beware, the label
said, he is "the leader of the textile workers who favor the strike." It said, moreover, that he was "inclined to pseudo-proletarianism." His election would
mean higher taxes, increased wages, endless strikes, and little, if any, military support to put down labor rebellions. "The souls of these gentlemen, all
of them leading industrialists and financiers," one political commentator observed, "are oppressed with a singular terror of this young fellow Johnston."[17]

Always a crafty, chameleonlike politician, Blease reinvented himself in the
second primary to court the Manning vote. On the stump, he still issued chill-

ing warnings about the sexuality of African American men and railed against government action. Adding to these old standards, he now spoke about Johnston's radicalism, antagonism toward private property, and encouragement of social unrest. When it came to labor issues, Blease sounded like a factory owner. Blaming the general strike on the "hidden hand" of "outsiders," he spoke in favor of local organizations over "foreign-controlled national unions" and endorsed the mobilization of military force against "violent" strikers. One campaign advertisement blazed: "NEITHER RADICALISM NOR COMMUNISM HAS TAINTED THE CAREER OF BLEASE: Vote For Blease and Safety for Lives, Homes and Business." Another boasted: "Flying squadrons of disorderly invaders from out of the state do not flaunt the banners of Blease." [18]

In the fall of 1934, some felt that the old "Prince of Darkness," Cole Blease, was not nearly as scary as he had seemed in the past, at least not next to Olin Johnston. Lifelong anti-Bleasites and recent Manningites found themselves, suddenly and for the most part unhappily, in the perennial candidate's electoral camp. They backed Coley, not so much because they believed him or liked his platform, but because they feared that Johnston meant what he said; that, if elected, he would introduce a little New Deal to the state and support labor legislation and other progressive measures. "Well, I am for Blease 100% and will do what I can to help save the state from unionized labor," a Greenville businessman explained. "It was the election of men like Johnston in New England that caused the number of spindles in that section to drop from 22 million to 7 million." One textile executive told a reporter that he supported Blease because "Coley will keep the hands quiet." The "Big Men," Charleston newspaper editor W. W. Ball theorized, feared Johnston and "went to Blease because they thought that Blease would lie to his old followers and that Johnston wouldn't." [19] "It seems a strange thing to admit," confessed an upcountry commercial leader, "but I'm going to vote against Johnston because I believe he is the sincerer of the two." [20]

While Blease welcomed the applause of women and men who had opposed him in the past, his traditional electoral base, dwindling since 1930, crumpled. Clearly the sixty-six-year-old politician had lost some of his stump magic. The antenna in his head that tuned into the thoughts of ordinary people, which W. J. Cash had marveled at, seemed to have lost some of its range.[21] His well-rehearsed sermons about the sanctity of white supremacy and his familiar warnings about African American predators no longer enthralled working-class crowds. Even his gags about effete aristocrats did not leave them slapping their knees or doubled over laughing.[22]

Workers clapped instead for Johnston. Picture Olin D. in front of a crowd of millhands gathered on the outskirts of town. It is twilight; the day shift is over and the picket line is down. Someone from the mill village introduces Johnston. "Welcome the next Governor of the great state of South Carolina. A man of the people. Olin D. Johnston." There is loud applause. Six feet four inches tall and over two hundred pounds, Johnston takes a few long strides up to the podium. Then he shoves his gray coat sleeves over his white shirt and runs his hands through his greased-back, jet-black hair and begins to talk about his life. He tells them he is just like them: he was born in a tenant shack, and when he was young his family moved to a mill village—in his case, the one surrounding the Chiquola Manufacturing Company, the scene of the Honea Path shoot-out. "I understand your problems," he tells them. To make sure they know exactly where he stands, he says that they have "a true friend in Olin Johnston." If they help elect him, he to make their lives better. Pledging his allegiance to what sounds like workers' version of New Deal Americanism, Johnston praises FDR; promotes trade unionism; champions an antistretch-out bill, a workers' compensation act, and a minimum-wage and maximum-hour law; opposes the mobilization of military force against strikers; vows to lift the tax on mill baseball games; and swears to use the government to "get something for the masses instead of the few."[23] As millhands head home to catch some sleep before the morning whistle blows, Johnston's campaign aides hand out a flyer that reads, "Vote for Olin Johnston: Help Us Win the Strike and Control Industry."[24] With this one short line, Johnston vows to push workers over the top in their battle to defend the New Deal against re-calcitrant mill owners. At the same time, he affirms the faith of both striking and nonstriking workers in the power of the government, in the idea that the state can make a difference on the shop floor and at home.

Johnston's backing on the mill hills could take him only so far, and he knew it. In 1930 he had run on a prolabor platform, racked up big majorities in the mill precincts, and lost the contest.[25] Four years later he walked a tightrope, appealing to textile workers while trying to reach out to other constituents. His task was made harder, but not impossible, by the walkout. Following the Honea Path shootings, he chided then Governor Blackwood for sending out the militia but also tried to allay middle-class fear of his alleged "radicalism" by speaking at length about the virtues of industrial harmony, his enduring respect for private property, and his advocacy of law and order. When asked about his political philosophy, Johnston answered, "I shall cooperate with President Roosevelt." "Is that," he added a bit testily, "radical?"[26]

Sensing the volatility of the moment, Johnston also carefully staged his appeals to laborers. Only at night and only on the outskirts of town away from the leery gaze of reporters and business leaders did he dare in 1934 to talk directly to millworkers, delivering his prolabor message of government activism and working-class empowerment. At the countywide stump meetings, where women and men, farmers and factory owners, lawyers and doctors, millhands and ministers drank and ate, he barely mentioned the millhands or the issues behind the strike; instead, he highlighted his support for the New Deal and spoke in vague terms about his lifelong commitment to a "square deal for labor and capital."[27]

What Johnston did discuss when he tried to broaden his electoral coalition was his past and the highway department. Just as he courted millhands with his autobiography, he told another version for these big stump audiences, one that downplayed his proletarian identity and emphasized a Horatio Alger–like tale. The son of a poor farmer, he put himself through high school, college, and law school working nights in textile factories. He underscored that he never drank alcohol. A World War I veteran, he recalled in a somber voice the many nights he lay awake in a dank, dark trench in France blanketed from his fears only by his faith in God. At this point, he would stop talking and hold up a dirty brown pocket Bible that he said he had kept with him at all times during the war. He returned to South Carolina, the story went, a decorated soldier, ran for office on a platform of lower taxes and better schools, and won a seat in the state house of representatives on his first try. His was a glorious life. It was, he insisted, the fulfillment of the promise of America, of South Carolina, and of the New Deal. Nevertheless, Johnston warned, something sinister threatened democracy and everyone's chances for social advancement. It came not from strikers or the UTW's Francis Gorman, but from the South Carolina Highway Department and its power-hungry leader, Ben Sawyer.[28]

Given the strike-inflamed context of the 1934 election, the highway department might seem like an unusual villain. Yet the issue had resonance with working people, farmers, and the antitax crowd, and Johnston used it to steer the political discourse away from labor militancy without wiping away class concerns. However, Johnston did not, by himself, turn Ben Sawyer and the highway department into political lightning rods in South Carolina. They had been hotly debated long before the 1934 governor's race.

Prior to World War I, each county in the state had built and paid for its own roads. Road building, as a result, was the stuff of local politics, and to the victor went the spoils.[29] The more prosperous industrialized districts of the upcountry and Charleston benefited the most from the state's locally controlled system of financing. Using their broader tax bases, these counties funded a wide range of road-building projects. New roads, in turn, fostered economic growth, whereas no roads meant economic atrophy. For boosters, especially in the low country, the lessons were clear. They saw long stretches

The Enthronement of Textile Labor

of smooth black tar roads, just like their nineteenth-century predecessors had looked at miles of railroad track as a ticket to economic renewal and prosperity. Recognizing that commercial capital and local initiatives could not get the job done in their sections of the state, black belt leaders mobilized their legislative power. Although less than a quarter of South Carolina whites lived below the fall line, at least half of the state's forty-six senators came from the low country—the region in desperate need of roads. Armed with this legislative muscle, low-country lawmakers and representatives from other underdeveloped areas of the state took the lead in trying to convert the government into a vehicle for economic growth, most notably through extensive road building.[30]

Throughout the 1920s debates over roads, and related questions about local power versus state control, rippled through South Carolina politics. During the 1925 session of the general assembly, low-country senators proposed a $25 million bond to underwrite a modest road-building campaign. The house of representatives, splitting largely along sectional lines, rejected the measure in favor of a more fiscally conservative pay-as-you-go plan. Under this program, roads would be financed through regressive taxes on gasoline, vehicle registration, and automobile licenses. Yet the responsibility to build and maintain roads was transferred from individual counties to the state. The newly formed South Carolina Highway Department decided where new roads and bridges would go and who would clear the ground, pave the streets, and supply the dirt and gravel. Overnight, the road authority became the single most powerful government agency in South Carolina and the head of the highway commission became the most powerful nonelected official in the state.[31]

The road builders were not through, however. In 1929 low-country lawmakers, led by senate kingpins Edgar A. Brown of Barnwell and R. M. Jeffries of Colleton, proposed a $65 million build-now-pay-later road program to be funded by bonds.[32] This was a staggering sum of money for a state mired in depression. It represented one-sixth of the total assessed value of all property in South Carolina and seven and a half times the previous year's entire state budget. Nevertheless, the senate, which was dominated by the low-country black belt counties, passed the bill by a margin of 30 to 9. A much tougher contest loomed in the more representative house, where upcountry legislators had a greater say.

Olin Johnston, then a Spartanburg representative, spearheaded the house opposition to the road measure. He said that it was too expensive, that it penalized the upcountry for financing its own development, that it gave too much power to a few unelected men, and that it would shift too much of the burden of road building on to the little guy. Proponents of the bill met Johnston and his upcountry allies on each front. The debate went back and forth until both sides were deadlocked. Then the weather, some said God, intervened.[33]

While house members fought over the road measure, spring showers soaked South Carolina. Traffic north of Columbia was brought to a standstill when rising waters swept away seventy-five feet of the Broad River Bridge. Elsewhere thousands of irate motorists—and voters—were literally stuck in the mud. On March 12, 1929, despite the unanimous opposition of representatives from the textile centers of Anderson, Greenville, and Spartanburg, including Olin Johnston, the house approved the megabond bill already passed by the senate.[34] Opponents of the measure did not give up. They pressed their case as far as the U.S. Supreme Court, but they lost. The only forum left was the campaign trail.

During his 1930 bid for governor, Johnston spoke for the workingman and against the road plan. Not only was the build-now-pay-later scheme fiscally risky, he declared, but it was also, along with the expanding power of the highway department, a threat to democracy. By driving such an expensive measure through the general assembly without hearing from the voters, Johnston said, his adversaries showed their contempt for the rights of the people and the principles of democracy. At the same time, he gave the enemy a sinister human face. Masterminding the retreat from democracy in South Carolina was the head of the highway department, Ben Sawyer. Johnston's Sawyer looked and acted like Blease's aristocrats and Roosevelt's money changers. An enemy of the people, he wore stiff collars and tailored suits and spent his weekends on a luxurious yacht, bought and paid for by construction companies and bridge makers. Lording over the highway department, Sawyer did the dirty work of wealthy men who loathed the people and regarded the state government as a private enterprise, not as Johnston did as a tool to end "the economic slavery of the masses."[35]

Johnston lost to Ibra Blackwood in 1930, but defeat did not blunt his attack on the highway department. Over the next four years he crisscrossed the state warning crowds big and small about Ben Sawyer. Johnston even linked his narrow electoral defeat—he lost by 995 votes—to the highway crowd. "The smoke from the burning ballots of Charleston," he told campaign audiences in 1934, "is still noxious to the fair-thinking people of South Carolina." Although he never named the arsonists, he made certain that everyone understood the aim of their treachery—to deny the majority of the people the right to run the state. The Spartanburg native also hinted that these ballot burners knew the way to Sawyer's offices, at least through the back alleys.[36]

In the 1934 gubernatorial campaign Johnston again attacked Ben Sawyer and the highway department. Pointing out that the department had become the state's largest and most powerful agency—its yearly expenditures almost equaled that of the entire state budget—and that it was controlled by a cadre of low-country men who secured their posts through appointment rather than election, he charged that the road bureau had matured into an "unruly boy who has outgrown parental restraint and discipline." Run by "Ben Sawyer the dictator" and a "ring" of corrupt associates, this "political octopus" stood in the way of bringing a New Deal to South Carolina. If elected, Johnston pledged as his first order of business to crush this illegitimate concentration of power, rescuing the *people* of South Carolina from tyranny.[37]

Taking up the banner of the people and reaching out to the economy crowd, Johnston blamed South Carolina's fiscal problems on the reckless and outlandish spending of Sawyer and his "cronies" in the highway department. This "organized minority," he protested, squandered the hard-earned tax dollars of the poor for "selfish purposes." If elected, Johnston pledged to fire Sawyer, slash the highway department's budget, and give something back to the people.[38] "South Carolina," a Johnston campaign advertisement read, taking a swipe at the highway department, "needs a Governor who cannot be controlled by a clique of politicians and public pap-suckers, [but] one who has the courage of his convictions and will remember the People, Johnston is the man."[39]

Few political images are more commonly evoked, yet more elusive, than the idea of the people. Vagueness was, in part, its source of resonance. By rousing the people—that is, the white people—Johnston tried to broaden his appeal without rubbing away the class-tinged, radical edge of his message. The "people" were all of those women and men—striking textile workers and loyal millhands, day laborers and tenants, small farmers and struggling merchants—who felt powerless before the forces of the depression, the modern economy, and, indeed, the highway department. Johnston told them, like Roosevelt did, that if they put aside their differences and voted for him, a man of the people, they could make the government work for them, rather than in the interests of mill men, planters, and road contractors.[40]

After weeks of reading campaign fliers, listening to speeches, and debating the issues over supper, voters went to the polls on September 12, 1934, to choose between Johnston and Blease. More than 43,000 workers remained either locked out or on strike that day.[41] In Johnston's hometown of Honea Path, the Chiquola Mill was running again, while machine gunners guarded factories in Blease's native Newberry. Rifle-toting National Guardsmen and flag-waving pickets faced off against each other at mill gates from Spartan-burg to Graniteville, but voters, many of whom had refused to step foot outside since the start of the strike, made it to the polls that day. In fact, turnout in 1934 was up 19 percent from four years earlier.[42]

As night fell and the pickets and the troops relaxed, word leaked out that Johnston would be the next governor of South Carolina. By the next morning everyone knew that the former mill boy had won, taking more than 56 percent of the votes cast. He did well across the state—in midland communities, black belt towns, and upcountry farmlands as well as the mill villages.

Textile workers provided Johnston with a sturdy foundation of electoral support. The former weaver trounced Blease on the mill hills, winning, for instance, over 87 percent of the vote in the Abbeville Cotton Mill Village and 91 percent in the Isaqueena Mill precinct.[43] In the textile sections of Aiken, Cherokee, Greenwood, Pickens, Spartanburg, York, and Union Counties, Johnston garnered nearly 70 percent of the ballots cast.[44] Blease barely beat Johnston in the mill districts of his home county, which for years had been his most dependable polling stations.[45] Overall, Johnston did better in communities on strike than those still working, but the differences were not great. In the mill precincts of Greenville, where the strike front was weakest, he won nearly 60 percent of the vote.[46] By checking the box next to Johnston's name, textile workers broadcast their final break with Bleasism, a rupture nearly ten years in the making. Throwing off their earlier racially charged, patriarchal, antistatist loyalties, wage earners lined up behind a candidate committed to bringing South Carolina's government in line with the New Deal and the larger principle of positive state action.

Millhands were not the only group to shift their political allegiances in 1934. Going into the race, Johnston knew that to win he had to pick up some support in the low country. In his failed run for the governor's office in 1930, he had stumbled in the counties below the fall line. His industrial, upcountry roots combined with his aggressive stand on the highway plan had alienated voters in these areas. Johnston's "dry" stance did not help much in typically "wet" Charleston, either. Four years later, however, armed with endorsements from Charleston's two major papers, Johnston's campaign performed much better in the low country, winning slim majorities in the region and in Charleston County.[47]

S. C. Wiggins of Beaufort was typical of Johnston's low-country supporters.[48] Without much enthusiasm, he wrote, "I will vote for Johnston though he is not altogether to my notion." What Wiggins and many of his neighbors could not do was vote for Blease, no matter how "radical" his opponent seemed. Conceding that Johnston had not been "too scrupulous in his

The Enthronement of Textile Labor

assaults upon industry and business," that his offensive against the highway department had "been more passionate than convincing," and that his economic views "are not clearly defined," the *Charleston Evening Post* nonetheless pointed out that he was also not Blease. That was all that really mattered. "He has never shown favor to criminals," the paper's editors continued, "He has never consigned the Constitution to Hell."[49] Besides, Johnston's identification with the United Textile Workers seemed much less frightening several hundred miles away from the picket lines. "In short," Charleston editor W. W. Ball wrote after the election, "Johnston got the votes of the anti-Bleasites who had no axe to grind and who were not under the domination of the Big Business Crowd."[50]

Johnston also won the backing of citizens on both sides of the fall line who placed bourgeois respectability above all else. His lawyerly demeanor contrasted sharply with Blease's outlandish, even clownish, public image. Always clean-shaven, dressed in a gray flannel suit with a pressed white shirt, Johnston did not look like a wild-eyed radical. The former millhand's journey from a tenant shack to the statehouse, moreover, embodied middle-class notions of uplift and social mobility, affirming faith in the just nature of the system. Then came the character issue. Next to Blease, Johnston resembled a choirboy. Whereas Blease joked about taking a drink of whiskey every now and then and years earlier had openly campaigned against U.S. entry into World War I, Johnston was a devout Baptist, a teetotaler, and a decorated war veteran. "Practically everything I know about Johnston personally is reassuring," wrote a well-connected Columbia lawyer, "His habits are good, his life is clean." Another Columbia resident added: "I'm voting for Olin D. Johnston. . . . He's an honest young man, a Christian and you'll find he will not associate with men of smeared reputations."[51]

Johnston's attack on the highway department dovetailed, moreover, with his attempt to reach out to the shrinking, but still formidable, economy crowd. Lifting what sounded like a line or two from a Farmers and Taxpayers League pamphlet, his 1934 platform called for "strict economy" and the "elimination of waste, graft, extravagance, and corrupt practices."[52] Nonetheless, Johnston did not share the economist's vision of limited government.[53] Instead, he planned to divert funds from the highway department's slimmed-down budget into a modest social welfare program featuring workers' compensation, teacher pay hikes, free textbooks, and increased aid for county schools. Taking a page from Georgia governor Eugene Talmadge's campaign book, Johnston also promised to cut the fee for automobile tags from seven dollars to three dollars.[54] For many voters, especially those in the countryside, where cash was always in short supply and a car or a truck had become a necessity not a luxury, the three-dollar tag conveyed Johnston's public commitment to "all the people," not just the millhands.

Johnston also promised farmers that he would cut the property tax. In his earlier run for governor, he had done poorly in rural precincts. Given the festering tensions between workers and country people, Johnston's ties to the mill villages made him suspect to some rural voters. Comments like the one he had made in 1930, declaring that South Carolina had changed from an agricultural state to an industrial one, merely exacerbated these concerns. Four years later Johnston was more responsive to farmers' grievances and aspirations. His strategy appears to have worked. One careful poll watcher reported that Johnston received almost half of the farm vote, still the biggest bloc in the state.[55]

Despite the broad backing of anti-Bleasites and teetotalers, economists and farmers, low-country editors and professors that carried Johnston to victory in 1934, South Carolina's textile workers hailed his triumph as their own. The governor-elect was, after all, one of them. For a moment their faith in political action was redeemed. Millhands believed, in the words of one observer, that with Johnston as governor "they can run the mills." They thought that they had won at the polling station at least part of what they were fighting for on the picket line during the general strike—to make South Carolina part of New Deal America. Beginning on election night and continuing the next day, laborers celebrated the victory of "South Carolina's Roosevelt." Johnston's achievement, one man hoped, "means a New Deal in South Carolina." Another compared Johnston to Pitchfork Ben Tillman and predicted that he would wrest the government from the hands of "so-called blue bloods" and "the favored few and deliver it back to all the people." Yet another observer claimed that Johnston's victory meant an end to the state's "mint julep era." Once again, South Carolina workers waited for the dawn of a new day— this time they looked for it to rise over Columbia and Washington at the same time.[56]

The Enthronement of Textile Labor

When Votes Don't Add Up

Olin D. Johnston and the Workers'
Compensation Act, 1935–1937

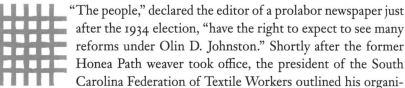 "The people," declared the editor of a prolabor newspaper just after the 1934 election, "have the right to expect to see many reforms under Olin D. Johnston." Shortly after the former Honea Path weaver took office, the president of the South Carolina Federation of Textile Workers outlined his organization's expectations for change. "We trust," he wrote the new governor, "that you will reward us for what we have done for you." A thirty-five-year veteran of the mills complained to Johnston, "We haven't much 'say so' in the way things are run," but now he was looking forward to "some legislation to be passed that will help the mill people to make a living wage."[1] Having "united in mass action at the ballot box" on his behalf, one group of laborers insisted that Johnston commit himself to "the salvation of Democracy by proper regard to the question of the greatest good for the greatest number." Mrs. C. Forster Smith of Newberry wrote, "Sir, I hope and trust you are going to give us a new deal."[2]

Thousands of South Carolina millworkers traveled to Columbia, many for the first time, on January 16, 1935, to celebrate Johnston's inauguration and remind him who had elected him. Dressed in their Sunday best, dark suits and print dresses, mill people arrived early in the morning. Hundreds stopped by the governor's mansion to greet him in person. By noon they had clustered around a podium set up near the capitol. The icy drizzle did not dampen their enthusiasm. For hours they chanted, "Hurrah for Johnston! Hurrah for

Johnston!" When Johnston arrived for the swearing-in ceremony, the crowd cheered wildly, then grew silent as he recited the oath of office on the same water-bloated Bible that he had carried with him through war-torn France and the previous summer's bruising campaign. The applause rose again as Johnston belted out his address. Pledging to "see South Carolina unsurpassed in the Union for the consideration shown her working people," the new governor signaled to laborers and their families that their expectations for class-based government action under his leadership were not misplaced.[3]

During his first year in office, Johnston tried to keep the public debate focused on class issues. He spoke out in favor of a long list of labor reforms, supported workers' right to strike, and extolled mill people's contributions to the state. Following along the lines of New Deal liberalism, he promoted the needs of labor and the people ahead of the interests of big business and the rural elite. His backers warned him to anticipate resistance. "The anti-Johnston men, autocrats, Bleasites, mill executives, and their associates, et al.," Claude Graves of Greenville alerted the governor, "are opposed to any move you make regardless of merit." "Your case," he wrote, drawing a parallel between Johnston and Roosevelt, "is similar to that of the President, and you may expect a continued fight, against you as long as you stand by labor, and the poor man, which of course, you will do." Graves was right. Behind the scenes, mill owners and low-country conservatives, fearful that Johnston would shepherd "radical" legislation through the general assembly, began to mobilize almost as soon as he assumed power, pressuring lawmakers to see things their way.[4]

During the Johnston years, South Carolina millhands traced a story different from the one usually told about southern workers. Typically race is identified as the main purpose of working-class politics, but Johnston and his supporters concentrated on class issues, while trying to keep the volatile language of white supremacy in the background. However, neither the governor nor his backers were racial liberals. They chuckled at minstrel shows at church fund-raisers and said the word "nigger" as easily as they talked about the relentless summer heat. No one advocating the noble, tender liberalism of an Atticus Finch, the hero of Harper Lee's classic novel *To Kill a Mockingbird*, emerged on the mill hills, and no one spoke out in favor of a biracial coalition of the state's have-nots. Perhaps the racial exclusivity of the movement of the millhands doomed their legislative offensive, leaving it from the start without a sturdy base from which to challenge the rich and powerful. But this was not the whole story. Millhands' adherence to the doctrine of white supremacy did not stop them from pursuing their class interests. In fact, it was the class interests of other white southerners who prevented these white laborers from fulfilling their class-based political agenda.

"It seems," Lyman's J. D. Derby explained to Governor Johnston in 1935, "that the cotton mill heads have kept the working people down under their feet so long untill [*sic*] it seems that it is more then they can stand to have to recognizing them in any respect." The manufacturers, he continued, "have never given the working people a chance. . . . On the other hand their motto is hold them down." Breaking up this wall of power would require that "[t]here . . . be laws enacted to protect the working class of people."[5] Things looked good, for a time, for millhands.

"Textile Workers Have Political Power Enough to Kill [the] Stretch-Out," headlined an upcountry weekly at the start of the 1935 legislative session.[6] Pointing to the election of Johnston and a handful of other prolabor lawmakers, the paper forecast that the general assembly would finally approve a loom-limit law. For a time, it appeared that this prediction would come true. Just after the opening session of the general assembly, H. C. Godfrey, of Spartanburg, a minister, a millhand, and leader of the South Carolina Federation of Textile Workers, introduced a thirty-six-loom-limit bill in the house. The governor backed the measure. "I am thoroughly in sympathy with the working people," he explained to a supporter of the plan, "when I worked in the mill, I ran twenty-six looms, . . . now . . . mill workers are being forced to run over 100 looms. I would like very much to see this situation remedied in the interest of our working people."[7] Bolstered by the governor's endorsement, the Godfrey bill passed in the house of representatives by an overwhelming 94 to 6 margin. Some lawmakers probably voted for it anticipating that the senate would reject the plan, and they were right. Unfazed by the house and the governor's endorsement or by the boisterous band of mill people above them in the gallery, the senators killed the proposal after only a brief discussion.[8] Labor's other legislative initiatives in 1935, twenty-nine bills in all, including measures to fix minimum-wage and maximum-hour levels, bar antiunion discrimination, prohibit eviction during strikes, and establish a separate state department of labor, except for one, met similar fates; they either drowned in committee or sank on the senate floor.[9]

Only South Carolina's first-ever workers' compensation act passed both houses of the general assembly. Although this measure proved to be the exception to the rule, the process leading to its approval revealed the limits of working-class political power in South Carolina. Though labor had its supporters in the legislature, it never obtained a majority. That meant, if it wanted to get a bill passed, it would have to compromise, and compromise always meant concession.

When Johnston took office in January 1935, South Carolina was one of only four states in the country without a workers' compensation law.[10] Arkansas, Florida, and Mississippi were the others.[11] The principle of employers' liability covered workers' claims for compensation. Under this formula, employers were required to hire competent operatives, keep an eye on the equipment, maintain a safe workplace, and issue warnings about dangerous conditions. In the event of injury or death, operatives or their surviving families had the right to sue and collect damages from a negligent employer; in other words, they received compensation only if they reached a settlement with management or could prove in court that oversight on the employer's part contributed to the accident.

Three common-law defenses further bolstered the employers' position. First, the concept of employers' liability assumed that an employee understood all the risks of the job, both stated and unstated. If a laborer knew of dangerous conditions and continued to work, she, not the employer, was to blame. Second, the fellow servant rule asserted that if a laborer was injured as a result of the negligence of a coworker, the employee, not the employer, was liable. The principle that undergirded this section of the law was that a worker should acquaint himself with the bad habits of his peers and exercise a "salutary influence upon them." This meant, for instance, that if someone worked next to a heavy drinker, he either had to cure his coworker's alcoholism or quit. Third, the rule of contributory negligence absolved the employer of culpability if the injured party was in any way at fault.[12]

Under the rules of employers' liability, an injured laborer did not automatically receive compensation for lost time, pain, or suffering, and sometimes an operative who was hurt or maimed on the job received no compensation at all. For instance, C. C. Johnson, a Union County millhand, lost part of his hand in a machine in 1912. Turned away by his former employer and unable to work, he had no choice but to beg Governor Blease for money.[13] Some factory owners did compensate injured laborers. Usually in exchange for signing a waver promising not to sue, the employer agreed to cover all or some hospital costs, lost wages, and other accident-related expenses. T. H. Watson, for example, negotiated a lifetime employment contract with the Pelzer Manufacturing Company after he broke his leg at work.[14] Following World War I, many millhands also began to carry their own personal accident insurance. Still, before 1935 there was no safety net for most South Carolina workers.

The only way to recoup lost wages or damages was to sue for negligence and that meant hiring a lawyer.

The quality of legal representation varied. "Ambulance chasing lawyers" as well as more reputable attorneys like the young Olin Johnston specialized in defending injured workers. In courtrooms, these jurists usually faced better funded and more experienced defense lawyers familiar with the many loopholes of the common law associated with employers' liability.[15] Moreover, no attorney—no matter how clever or cunning—could speed a case through the state's Byzantine judicial system or guarantee a large, or even equitable, settlement. Occasionally after months of litigation, an injured or maimed laborer received a substantial settlement, a large portion of which was paid to his attorney; more often the worker received little or nothing.

M. D. Lee, an employee of the Ware Shoals Manufacturing Company, was one of the lucky ones, at least in terms of compensation. A mill explosion in 1934 burned him from the waist up. For six months, Lee could not work. The company paid his medical and hospital bills but refused to reimburse him for lost wages, and he decided to sue. Convinced that Lee's employer had been negligent, a jury awarded him a $3,000 settlement, or roughly the equivalent of the average salary of a South Carolina millhand over a four-year period.[16] Another worker, "Mr. Z.," was less fortunate. For two decades he had worked for an upcountry paving company. When a ditch caved in on him, he suffered serious injury. His employer rushed him to the hospital, and while he lay flat on his back, the company tricked him into signing an agreement that settled all future claims against it for a mere $140. Not long after the accident, the firm moved to another state. Unable to work, Mr. Z. was dependent on charity.[17]

Because of the capricious nature of employers' liability, workers' compensation had long stood at the top of organized labor's legislative agenda. At its annual meeting in 1915, the South Carolina Federation of Labor (SCFL) endorsed "a form of workman's compensation law for giving workers some form of protection while employed or engaged at work for a corporation." Stressing efficiency over workers' rights, a cadre of progressive reformers proposed their own version of the measure, predicting that their plan would regularize costs, reduce corporate legal bills, and create an easily controlled agency to administer the law. A few mill owners agreed with this logic. Nonetheless, the majority of business leaders and boosters, fearing that the cost of workers' compensation would cut into profits and discourage new industries from entering the state, lobbied against the proposal. Bleasite lawmakers, whose antistatism often dovetailed with the interests of manufacturers, also opposed the measure. Lawyers, many of whom had become rich off the law, joined the anticompensation forces.[18]

After World War I, support for workers' compensation steadily grew. Each year at its annual convention, the SCFL issued a call for just and fair restitution for injured operatives. As millhands drifted away from Bleasism, many joined the campaign for workers' compensation. By 1930 textile workers pressed candidates for the general assembly to support a compensation law. "There can be no argument against a fair and equitable workman's compensation law," insisted one lawmaker, claiming to speak for labor. Workers, he said, demanded a law that honored the "value of human life."[19]

In the late 1920s several leading newspaper editors joined the push for workers' compensation. Each day for two straight weeks in December 1929, *The State*, under W. E. Gonzales's stewardship, featured detailed editorials advocating such a step. In these columns Gonzales trumpeted the modernity of the measure, took a few swipes at "shyster lawyers," and highlighted family issues, arguing that workers' compensation would enable mothers to stay at home and care for their children in the event of the breadwinner's death or injury. Nervously looking back on the previous spring's strikes, the editor also argued that the implementation of a workers' compensation law would lessen the friction between labor and capital and reduce the chances for a resurgence of working-class unrest. Yet the thrust of the Columbia newspaper's crusade for workers' compensation centered on the idea that the law was good for business. Troubled by the flagging health of the state's economy, Gonzales searched for ways to jump-start commerce. Citing studies from other states, he argued that a workers' compensation law would reduce accidents and absenteeism on the job. He also predicted that it would eliminate the threat of the "big verdict," permitting employers to cut down on legal fees and calculate insurance costs in advance. A modern and rationalized legal code, Gonzales concluded, would lure new industries to the state, bringing with them new opportunities and an end to the depression. For many, this was the clincher. Given the grim economy, the promise of increased employment and investment converted many to the cause of workers' compensation.[20]

Business leaders and boosters across the state embraced the pro-growth conception of workers' compensation. In 1930 the Columbia and Charleston Chambers of Commerce passed resolutions in favor of the measure. Retailers and merchants also endorsed it, as well as many of the state's largest textile manufacturers. In 1932 the presidents of Monarch Mills, Brandon Corporation, Glenwood Mills, and Arcadia Mills broadcast their support for a workers' compensation law. Prominent low-country residents also got behind its passage, for the same reason that they supported the multimillion-dollar highway bond issue—they wanted to turn the state government into an engine of economic growth powerful enough to pull their own communities out of their depression doldrums.[21] "Outsiders," Charleston's H. C. Pace speculated, "will not voluntarily become associated with the uncertainty of the liability system now in use in South Carolina." Whereas sixty new plants started up in 1934 in the three states surrounding South Carolina, Pace pointed out, not a single new factory had opened in the Palmetto State. "We have much unemployment. We are not creating new jobs. We need new industries." He concluded, "Until we have a fair and just workman's compensation law, we have little hope of attracting new industries."[22]

The proselytizing campaigns of Pace, the press, and others between 1929 and 1934 converted scores of pro-growth, reformed-minded citizens to the cause of workers' compensation. Olivia C. Fuller, general secretary of the YWCA of Charleston, John H. LoFitte, post commander of the American Legion of Columbia, Niels Christensen, head of the Farmers and Taxpayers League, and Wil Lou Gray, a leading advocate of adult education for laborers, all favored the idea. A blue-ribbon panel that included a low-country lawmaker, a representative of the American Federation of Labor (AFL), a mill owner, and a university professor also spoke out for workers' compensation. "Neglect of such legislation," the committee concluded in 1932, "may be judged a symbol of sluggishness and keep forward looking industry from setting up in our state." Despite the emerging public consensus on the need for a workers' compensation law, there remained nagging differences among millhands, skilled laborers, manufacturers, business leaders, and planters about what kind of a law the state needed.[23]

Members of the South Carolina General Assembly, meanwhile, lagged behind public opinion. Throughout the second half of the 1920s a handful of reformers and prolabor lawmakers, such as Olin Johnston, pushed for a compensation law, but they did not get very far. In 1930 the momentum behind the measure picked up when Senator R. M. Jeffries, an influential, conservative lawmaker from the black belt county of Colleton, introduced a workers' compensation bill in the upper house. Though many of the state's textile manufacturers theoretically supported the idea of automatic compensation, some still groaned about the cost, even of Jeffries's cut-rate plan. Lawyers fearful of lost revenue also lobbied against the bill. Lack of support from these two key camps killed the Jeffries proposal. The next year Union County representative E. R. Aycock brought the same bill before the house, only to watch it die in committee. During the 1932 session Jeffries, not wanting to see his workers' compensation bill go down to defeat for a third time, rewrote the legislation to mollify business interests.[24] Labor leaders were furious. "We are unanimously opposed to this bill," SCFL chief Earle R. Britton fumed; it is "entirely out of line with the instructions of our last convention." Industry spokesmen, at the same time, continued to complain about the program's cost. Division and doubt once again wiped out the workers' compensation initiative.[25]

During a meeting of southern labor officials in Atlanta the next year, U.S. secretary of labor Frances Perkins cornered J. Roy Jones, the head of the South Carolina Department of Agriculture, Commerce, and Industry, and urged him to bring his state's labor laws in line with the rest of the nation. As a first step, she suggested that he set up a committee to draft an acceptable workers' compensation bill. Jones did not act right away. Waiting almost a year, he finally, in December 1934, appointed a seven-member commission made up of labor leaders, textile manufacturers, reformers, and low-country boosters. After weeks of wrangling, the group agreed on a compromise workers' compensation program that resembled that of other southern states. Officials from Perkins's federal labor department praised the draft bill, judging it "an exceptionally good one as to scope and benefits."[26]

During his inaugural address the next month, Olin Johnston promised that if the general assembly passed a workers' compensation bill, he would sign it. A few days later sixty-four members of the house of representatives introduced the Jones committee's draft measure on the floor for consideration. In April the lower chamber overwhelmingly approved the bill and sent it to the senate, the proverbial burial ground of labor legislation.[27] Johnston lobbied senators to pass the house blueprint without change, but they did not listen. Over the next six weeks the senators tinkered with one section of the bill, then another. By the time they finished, they had tacked fifty amendments onto it, and it hardly looked like the original house plan. On May 24, 1935, the senate approved this version of the compensation act and sent it to the governor.[28]

Thirty-seven pages long, the bill that reached Johnston's desk was both incredibly precise and deceptively vague.[29] Buried between the small print and the legalistic language was a compensation plan riddled with exemptions and loopholes.[30] Since the days of Dickens's "dark satanic mills," textile workers knew that something in the thick layers of lint in the factories slowly choked some of them to death, but the statute before the governor said nothing about this or any other occupational disease.[31] The measure did not require firms with less than fifteen laborers to provide compensation. It also excused timber concerns, rock quarries, steam laundries, and sand mines—low-country industries that almost exclusively employed African Americans. Moreover, it mandated compensation payments well under the national average and slightly below regional standards.[32] The total amount to be paid to a permanently disabled worker was capped at $5,000. In cases of partial or temporary

When Votes Don't Add Up

disability, employers would be required to provide half of an employee's average weekly wage up to $2,500, with a minimum of $5 and a maximum of $18 per week. Restitution was to begin two weeks after the injury occurred. Periods of time during which compensation had to be paid were listed in almost gruesome detail: 30 weeks for the loss of a big toe and 10 weeks for any other toe, 125 weeks for the loss of a foot and an additional 50 weeks for the loss of a leg. Finally, the bill gave the governor the power to appoint, with senate approval, a five-member Industrial Commission to administer the law and serve as judge and jury in all contested compensation cases.[33]

Now it was up to Johnston to decide whether or not to sign the bill into law. As the governor studied the matter, South Carolinians weighed in with their opinions. Professionals, for the most part, promoted the measure. "My opinion is that in signing this bill you will be doing not only the humanitarian thing," wrote an upcountry educator, "but also the most politic." The head of Wofford College, Johnston's alma mater, also favored passage. "We believe," stated the chair of the legislative committee of the South Carolina Federation of Business and Professional Women's Clubs, "that a workman's compensation law in our state will be conducive to bringing much needed business." Industry leaders backed the measure as well. They, too, saw it as a potential boost to commerce. The president of the Industrial Cotton Mills of Rock Hill told Johnston, "I really believe that the lack of a compensation law in South Carolina has been the means of depriving us of some very large manufacturing enterprises during the last year or two."[34]

Clinging to the notion that a workers' compensation statute would fuel economic growth, low-country residents, especially Charlestonians, also urged Johnston to approve the bill. "It will . . . be the means of stimulating industrial development . . . surely needed in South Carolina at this time," predicted the president of the city's Lions Club. The chief officer of the Charleston Hotel Incorporated, the superintendent of the city's branch of the American Tobacco Company, and the owner of the Planters, Fertilizer, and Phosphate Company all echoed this view. "If you do not accomplish any other good during your administration," Charleston's Dr. C. B. Boette counseled Johnston, "the signing of this bill alone will be an outstanding event of your administration, as from now on, industry will begin to come to this state." The Charleston Central Labor Union informed the governor, "Our body passed a resolution . . . to solicit . . . your signing of the workers' compensation act."[35]

Mill folks, the backbone of Johnston's constituency, were divided on the merits of the senate bill. Despite its many uncertainties, a few judged the system of employers' liability to be better than state-sanctioned workers' compensation. R. W. Gossett, a Spartanburg trade unionist, scoffed at the senate plan. "It not only deprives him of his right for a trial by a jury," he complained, "but allows the corporations and insurance companies to state the amount that he should receive." Another opponent depicted the proposal before the governor as a "nonsuit bill" crafted by insurance companies to deny poor folks the chance to strike it rich through the courts.[36] Most of the measure's detractors, however, endorsed workers' compensation in principle but objected to the specifics of the senate program. Anderson millworker W. H. Hayes favored "a proper bill" but considered the "present bill unfair to workers." Others grumbled about the payment scale. Although the senators may have thought that half pay was better than nothing, most textile workers knew that half of their already meager wages spelled hunger for themselves and their families. Reminding Johnston of his past vocation, Clarence Brown of Spartanburg wrote: "You had quite a bit of experience in handling suits for the mill boys, and . . . I doubt if you have settled many if any cases as set out in the schedule of the workmen's compensation law. The mill boys here are expecting you to take care of them, so do it by vetoing this bill." "This bill is an abominable camouflage," thundered H. C. Godfrey of the South Carolina Federation of Textile Workers, "this is just a bluff at compensation—it is being put over on the people of the state to keep as real compensation for lost fingers, arms, legs, and feet." Others worried that it benefited business at the expense of wage earners. "Knowing that you came from the ranks of labor," wrote a group of trade unionists, "we . . . ask you to use your full veto power to prevent this . . . law, we believe it will only serve to help big business and cause . . . greater suffering to the working man."[37]

The workers' compensation plan did not stir opposition on every South Carolina mill hill. United Textile Workers of America (UTW) locals from Clinton, Glendale, and Newberry wired telegrams of unanimous support to the governor.[38] Others were more guarded. "Just a few lines to let you know that all of the people are wanting you to sign the Workman's Compensation Bill," one millhand wrote to Johnston. "We realize that it is not a perfect bill. But it beats what we have got. An [sic] we can have amendments put to it later." This seemed to be the way the governor was leaning.[39]

On July 17, 1935, almost two months after the senate approved the workers' compensation measure, Johnston signed the bill into law. At a lavish ceremony to mark the occasion, he announced his nominees to the Industrial Commission, the panel charged with administering the statute. Choosing these men had not been easy for the governor. Following senate approval of the bill, he was deluged with mail. Residents from all over the state and every trade group and occupational association hounded him for an appointment to the commission. Those not looking for a post for themselves recommended a friend or colleague. When he whittled down his list, the Industrial Commission consisted of two business leaders, two labor spokesmen, and an insurance man. Industry representatives, who had feared that Johnston would stack the board with "radicals," applauded his restraint. More than anything, the governor's caution reflected the reality of power in South Carolina. If he had chosen only labor leaders, probusiness senators would certainly have rejected them. As it turned out, all of Johnston's nominees won approval without dissent.[40]

Compromise and concession enabled the workers' compensation law to get through both houses of the South Carolina General Assembly, but these were not the themes that Johnston stressed at the signing ceremony staged to mark the law's passage. Although conceding that the law was not a "perfect piece of legislation," he assured working people that they would "receive full justice in every instance." Surrounded by trade union leaders, rather than businessmen, reformers, or other members of the proworkers' compensation coalition, he promised laborers "fair play and fair dealing from the Industrial Commission." While touting the pro-growth aspects of the new statute, predicting that it would attract new industries to the state, the governor again highlighted the theme of labor, hinting that working-class South Carolinians would benefit the most from the new job opportunities created by the law. In one last symbolic gesture, he presented John Nates, a UTW official and the newly elected head of the South Carolina Federation of Labor, with the pen he had used to sign the bill into law.[41] "This is a great day for labor in South Carolina," a trade unionist beamed.[42]

Desperate for a first-term legislative victory, especially one that helped labor, Johnston oversold the workers' compensation bill. By downplaying the limits of the law, he eliminated many of millhands' doubts about the measure. At the same time, he raised their expectations for a "new deal." Because the plan had been signed into law on their behalf, textile workers expected it to function in their interests; in others words, to take care of them when they were injured. When things did not turn out as anticipated, workers let Johnston know what was wrong and how to fix it. Millhands and others were convinced that he would listen, indeed some thought that he had to listen; after all, they reasoned, it was their votes that had elected him.

Among those who told their story to the governor was Paul Murdaugh. After suffering a leg injury while working for the Robert Lee Construction Company, Murdaugh filed a claim for compensation and won an award of "temporary total disability." He was also reimbursed for hospital expenses and received $500 for "permanent body dis-figurement on account of the alleged 1¼" shortening of his left leg." Nevertheless, he disputed the decision and petitioned for full disability. According to the Industrial Commission's investigation, "Murdaugh's leg was from ½ to 1″ short before the accident reduced it—thus the accident reduced his leg by only 10%, which does not constitute a permanent disability." Nor did the injury render the "appearance of the claimant obnoxious or repulsive in the eyes of his fellow man." Complaining that he had been treated with disrespect and that he was left with a bad limp, Murdaugh appealed to Johnston for help. The governor never replied. There was nothing that he could do except to wish him the very best.[43]

Mrs. G. S. Price of Calhoun Falls was injured on the job at the Iva Cotton Mills. The company, she charged, took "my womanhood away from me." How, she did not say, although she did mention that she might have to be "sterilized." Price appealed her case to the Industrial Commission but "was defeated," in her words, "on account of falsehoods sworn by the eye witnesses to save their jobs. Well, they saved their jobs, I lost mine and my compensation." Price was furious. "I'm not through talking about it . . . because I'm not through suffering," she told Johnston. "Because you don't enforce justice with it, your workman's compensation isnt [sic] worth a flip." Price did not blame the governor, whom she judged to be a "just and honest" man, for the law's shortcomings. Instead, she reasoned, the "big mistake" occurred when he "signed [the law] out of your hands to the authority of some one that wasn't quite as interested in the working folks as you were."[44]

A. B. Styles was also infuriated by his treatment under the workers' compensation law. A veteran weaver, Styles was hurt on New Year's Day 1937 at the Franklin Mills in Greer. He received compensation and spent several months regaining his strength. Eager to return to work and earn his full salary, Styles applied to get his old job back, only to discover that the company had permanently replaced him during his absence. "I would like very much to no [sic] the man that got up such a law," he wrote to Johnston, "I would like to punch him on the nose." He told the chief executive to amend the measure so it would operate in the interest of labor, not business.[45]

Even before Johnston heard from Styles, he announced his intention to "change this law so it will . . . protect the interests of working people." In 1936 he urged the general assembly to scrap most of the exemptions, raise the scale of payments, and attach a "reasonable occupational diseases clause" to the statute. Lawmakers did not move on his recommendations until 1937.[46] After much debate, they voted to increase payments and cut the waiting period between the time when an accident occurred and compensation began. In addition, they gave the Industrial Commission the authority to issue subpoenas and compel employers in special cases to make lump-sum payments.[47]

The amendments, however, failed to convince some millhands that the law, even in its new form, would operate in their best interests. New industries and new jobs never poured into the state; working on a relief job was just about the only new employment opportunity in South Carolina in 1937. Compensation payments, despite the raise provided by the amendments, still added up to poverty wages. Laborers were particularly aggravated by the decisions of the Industrial Commission. All too often, the commissioners hounded wage earners about the veracity of their ailments and misfortunes, while allowing employers to slip through loopholes. This was not the "fair play and fair dealing" Johnston had promised the day he signed the bill into law.[48]

By 1937 some mill people were so frustrated with the workers' compensation law that they wanted it repealed. Campaigning in the Olympia Mill Village, house candidate C. J. Cole pledged, if elected, to fight to amend the statute and won the cheers of the working-class crowd. The SCFL also demanded changes in the law.[49] Yet some called for more drastic action. "The sentiment of textile labor in Spartanburg County," reported Furman Garrett of Lyman, "is in favor of repeal."[50] Chances for just compensation, a few concluded, were better under the risky old system of employers' liability. One millhand wrote, "I hope labor has enough friends in the legislature to repeal this act, which is the most iniquitous and unjust law ever written on our books, since the carpetbaggers passed a law to give slaves the right to vote and hold office." Picking up on the comparison to Reconstruction, the South Carolina House of Representatives in 1938, led by upcountry lawmakers claiming to speak for millhands, voted to scratch the workers' compensation act from the state's law books. If it remained in place, these same legislators insisted that textile laborers be excluded from its provisions or at least have the option of rejecting its coverage. The senate upheld the measure and left millhands under the umbrella of compensation, suggesting that what had originated as a prolabor reform had been transformed into a tool of probusiness conservatives and low-country boosters.[51]

For Johnston, dangerous political signals accompanied wage earners' frustrations with the workers' compensation act. Laborers began to waver in their allegiance to the mill boy governor and in their faith in government activism. "You haven't backed any thing you said in your campaign," a Graniteville textile operative challenged the chief executive, "you said you was for labor." Surveying the political landscape around his hometown of Greer, Marvin Reese—a magistrate and Johnston lieutenant—uncovered similar misgivings. "Outside of the bosses," he reported, "I must say that . . . [the workers' compensation bill] . . . is hated by practically 100 percent. . . . This law will hurt you in this section of the State."[52]

In the end, millhands did not abandon Johnston so easily, but their loyalty had been strained. More important, South Carolina laborers learned a hard lesson from the administration of the workers' compensation law: their votes were not enough. In 1934 the workers had carried one of their own to the highest position in the state. Once in office, Johnston exhibited a willingness to fight for laws that would provide the "greatest good for the greatest number," yet at the end of his four-year term, the balance of state power remained in the hands of a few. Armed with the ballot, white workers had the strength to pressure legislators into mitigating some of the harshest aspects of industrial life, but alone they lacked the political muscle to enforce their interpretation of the laws. This was a reality that South Carolina workers would revisit over and over again during the 1930s.

CHAPTER NINE

Fighting for the Right
to Strike, 1935–1936

Ware Shoals, 1929, Horse Creek Valley, 1933, and Rock Hill, 1934: a familiar pattern unfolded in each of these places. Millhands aided by cagey leaders established sturdy United Textile Workers of America (UTW) locals; three-quarters or more of the workforce joined the union. Management lashed out, and laborers responded with a strike. Millhands threw dense picket lines up around the factories, held nightly rallies to boost morale, and did what they could to feed themselves. Immediately after the protest started, the mill managers dashed off word of the unrest to the governor—Richards or Blackwood, it did not matter. Citing constitutional obligations to maintain the peace, defend private property, and safeguard the right to work, the chief executive rushed troops—rifle-toting highway patrolmen or machine gun-carrying National Guardsmen—to the scene with orders to keep the machines running. Fortified by military might, mill owners recruited replacement workers from the ranks of nonstrikers, spare hands, and nearby rural residents. Once the spindles and looms were operating again, they began to systematically crush the union, discriminating against activists, evicting strike leaders, and sending out blacklist notices. This was the well-worn script for industrial relations in South Carolina when Olin Johnston took office in January 1935.

At the same time that millhands sought to shape the workers' compensation law, some tried to rebuild the labor movement and secure the right to strike. But before Johnston's inauguration the future of South Carolina textile trade unionism looked bleak. Two months after the national walkout ended in defeat, Martha Gellhorn—the woman who noticed the pictures of President Roosevelt hanging over the mantels of many mill houses—visited Anderson, Columbia, Greenville, Greenwood, Newberry, Rock Hill, Spartanburg, and Whitmire. She was stunned by what she saw. Management discriminated against trade unionists at every turn. The stretchout extended workers to the breaking point. Thousands of women and men were without jobs.[1] "As for relief," Gellhorn told Harry Hopkins, the head of the Works Progress Administration, "the authorities tell me that it is below subsistence level . . . clothing is short . . . [and] . . . there is much pellagra." Everywhere she turned she spotted desperate people, bent-backed women, painfully thin, hollow-eyed teenagers, and embittered, angry men. Families without coal, having only newspaper for insulation, shivered through the night and subsisted day after day on fatback, flour, and cornmeal. These scenes reminded Gellhorn of "something out of Dickens."[2]

Hunger, joblessness, and unemployment—for many these were the haunting legacies of the General Textile Strike. In the wake of the political protest, thousands of South Carolina millhands fled from the house of labor and never returned. Not surprisingly, scores of wage earners felt an "extreme sense of disillusionment with both the government and with the union." Memories of the defeat left some leery of organized labor for years, even decades, to come. Many opted for the "securities of job and home" over the "air and promises" of trade unionism.[3] Across the state after the general strike, UTW meetings grew smaller and dues collections diminished. In Greenwood County and the Horse Creek Valley, UTW strongholds in the past, workers bolted from organized labor's ranks. Once-formidable locals in Columbia and Spartanburg faded into obscurity. In other towns, workers had no choice but to abandon the union. Efforts to revive battered locals incurred the wrath of management, newspaper editors, and the Ku Klux Klan.[4]

Defeat and disillusionment, however, did not extinguish the spirit of trade unionism on every South Carolina mill hill after the general strike. A committed remnant of UTW members clung to the labor movement, and they were soon joined by a core of new recruits to the creed of unionism. Testifying to some people's enduring faith in organized labor, Ethel Rucker, the widow of a slain Honea Path striker, named her son Francis Gorman Rucker after the UTW leader.[5] In the winter of 1934–35 UTW locals survived or regrouped in Clifton, Columbia, Gaffney, Inman, Pelzer, Spartanburg, Tucapau, Union, and a few places in between.[6] Poststrike unionists continued where their predecessors had left off; that is, they tried to bring workers together to gain some leverage against their employers and force them to improve conditions, raise wages, and slow down the pace of production. "Fighting for our living, the education of our children, the opportunity to do a fair day's work at a fair price under the law, and the opportunity to secure a few of the blessings of life"—this is how the "Members of Organized Labor" described the mission of trade unionism in 1935. Prounion workers also recognized that before they could build a strong labor movement, they had to have "the right to make our own fight to use every lawful means to win without the interference of outside parties." In other words, they needed the right to strike.[7]

Educated by defeat, workers, beginning in 1935, pressed for the passage of laws to make it illegal for companies to hire outsiders ahead of unemployed mill village residents; to prohibit the use of military supplies, like tear gas, during a strike without the consent of the secretary of war; and to bar sheriffs from deputizing men paid by textile companies during industrial disputes. Above all, many understood that if they wanted unions to be a force on the shop floor and beyond, they needed a prolabor, or at the very least a neutral, politician in the governor's chair.[8]

With Johnston's election, labor had their man in power. The former Honea Path weaver injected a distinctly different tone into the public discourse surrounding industrial relations in the state. Gone were lectures on the menace of wicked communist organizers and the sacred rights of nonstrikers. In their place came diatribes against selfish manufacturers and speeches about laborers' "irrevocable" right to organize. "The children of Israel," Johnston preached to a group of workers soon after his inauguration, "organized in Egypt and there has been organization ever since." "Even the Governors are organized," he added, "and we met once a year. The manufacturers are organized for dividends and you have a right to organize for humanity." Johnston also affirmed, at least implicitly, labor's right to strike. Unlike his predecessors, he recognized the picket line as a legitimate means of protest. During the 1934 campaign he repeatedly chided former governor Blackwood for calling out the troops against general strikers and pledged to use the highway patrol to monitor traffic, not to break up solid picket lines. In addition, Johnston confessed, not shyly but with a measure of pride, to having participated himself as a teenager in a brief and successful strike. Still, the newly elected governor implored millhands to follow a cautious course of arbitration and conciliation. "A strike at this time, I fear," Johnston warned a group of Gaffney workers on the verge of a walkout during the summer of 1935, "would jeopardize . . . getting Labor Legislation passed during this term." The Cherokee County millhands bowed to his request and stayed on the job. As it turned out, only a single piece of labor legislation—the workers' compensation bill—made it all the way through the general assembly that year; six months later, the Gaffney workers found themselves on strike.[9]

Not all South Carolina millhands heeded the governor's call for patience. During Johnston's first year in office, eight major walkouts involving more than 5,000 textile workers rocked the state. Like previous labor disputes, the 1935 strikes were violent and bloody, and they left scores of workers without jobs, dozens of families homeless, and a number of communities reeling in disarray. One journalist described the strikes of that year as "some of the sharpest in South Carolina history."[10] Laborers struck against the stretchout, antiunion discrimination, and the formation of company unions. Perhaps most important, these strikes laid bare the limits of Governor Johnston's power as well as the structural obstacles to working-class mobilization in South Carolina. Once again, millhands' faith in government action was tested.

Clinton was the site of the first strike of the year. Workers at the Clinton Mills and the Lydia Mills walked off the job even before Johnston's inauguration.[11] During the General Textile Strike, the UTW closed both of these Laurens County factories. When the national union called off the protest, management took everyone back who applied for a job without question. Over the next several weeks, however, it began to sack UTW leaders.[12] The local responded with another strike. At the same time, it filed charges against the company with the Textile Labor Relations Board (TLRB), the Bruere Board's replacement established after the general strike in keeping with the Roosevelt-appointed Winant Board's suggestions. On December 7, 1934, the TLRB ruled in the UTW's favor and gave W. J. Bailey, owner of the Clinton Mills, one month to rehire the strikers or risk losing his privilege to fly the blue eagle over his factory. To some textile workers, the Clinton decision signaled a sharp break from the "do-nothing" policies of the defunct Bruere Board. Theodore McCroskey of East Rockingham, North Carolina, hailed the judgment as the beginning of the end of the "oppression, Depression, and Domination" of textile workers "by capital."[13] As a show of good faith, the local UTW called off its strike, but Bailey did not take back the trade unionists. In January the TLRB delivered on its threat and yanked the once-coveted symbol of the New Deal from above the Clinton Mills. Yet as winter loomed, Bailey's factories stayed open and many trade unionists remained out of work.[14]

Not long after the blue eagle's flight, Bailey established a company union, the Clinton Friendship Association. Overseers and second hands dominated the organization. While wages dropped, unemployment jumped, and job assignments got tougher, members of the bogus company union busied themselves passing resolutions that repudiated the TLRB, lambasted the Wagner Act, and pledged support for "President Bailey's fight against the Government."[15] On the shop floor, company representatives pressured UTW members like Jessie Wooten to sign up with the Friendship Association. Wooten had joined the national textile union in June 1934 and continued to pay dues after the general strike. Then hard times struck her family when her mother became ill. The spinning room overseer of the Clinton Mills learned of Wooten's misfortune. He approached her several times, saying that if she resigned from the UTW and enlisted with the Friendship Association, he would settle the family's medical bills. Eventually, she turned in her union card but her mother's medical debt went unpaid.[16]

In August, following the passage of the Wagner Act, Bailey, who had blasted the historic labor measure earlier that summer, announced that in accordance with the law he had signed an exclusive, closed shop agreement with the Friendship Association. All workers were invited to join, yet those who declined forfeited their right to a job at his mills. One hundred and twenty UTW members spurned the offer. Most were fired. They took their cases before the newly formed National Labor Relations Board (NLRB), which judged the Friendship Association to be an illegal company union and ordered the mill owner to rehire them. Bailey simply disregarded the ruling. And just to make sure that no one forgot where the real source of power rested in Clinton, he fired two more workers and doubled rental charges on the sixty union families left in the villages. When they fell into arrears, he evicted them. Federal authorities did nothing.[17]

"The people are being driven and coerced," F. A. Gedeist told Governor Johnston. "If one cotton mill President, a couple of lawyers, and a state Senator can defy all laws and run a County to suit themselves then," he protested, "this County should be cut off, and made a Free and Independent Territory, known as Bailey domain."[18] Johnston was also alarmed by the mill owner's conduct. He wrote to Secretary of Labor Frances Perkins alerting her to the evictions and the violations of the Wagner Act. Yet his hands were tied. As governor, he did not have the constitutional authority to make the Clinton Mills comply with the national labor board's decisions. Unlike his predecessors, however, he did what he could to soften the blows. Responding to pleas for aid, Johnston rushed military tents to Clinton for evicted families to sleep in until they found new homes. He also persuaded the Federal Surplus Commodities Commission to ship foodstuffs to hungry workers. Although Johnston's efforts did not tip the balance of power in the union's favor, they did display his willingness to intervene in an industrial dispute on labor's behalf. How far he would go was yet to be seen.[19]

Soon after the Clinton strike began, Johnston faced another test at the Tucapau Mills located ten miles west of Spartanburg. As in Clinton, the UTW in Tucapau had weathered the storm of September 1934. In January 1935 the local textile union shut the mill down again to stop management from adding "more work" without a "proportionate increase in pay." The strike lasted less than a day. At the urging of federal labor officials, workers and management agreed to allow the Work Assignment Board, a branch of the TLRB, to investigate conditions and judge what constituted a fair workload. Both sides vowed to abide by the board's recommendations. "There was little or no overloading," the Work Assignment Board concluded after studying the Tucapau situation for several days. Mill officials, it turned out, tricked the three-member panel. Just before the investigators arrived, managers rolled back the stretchout. Then as soon as the examiners' train pulled out of the station, the mill men revved up the machines again.[20] Meanwhile, the company continued to harass local trade unionists. Dozens of UTW members were replaced by the sons and daughters of farmers and tenants. At the end of April, mill managers sacked two local union leaders for allegedly sabotaging a reel of cloth with a lead pencil. The Tucapau UTW responded with its second strike in two months. It turned out to be a long fight.[21]

With no orders to fill on account of a spring lull, Tucapau mill president Alan McNab seemed content to keep the factory closed. However, when business picked up McNab intended to operate his plant unhindered by the UTW. Following the lead of Clinton Mills managers, once the strike began he established the Tucapau Good Will Association.[22]

The UTW responded to McNab's actions with defiant rhetoric. One member of the Tucapau local promised that workers would hold out until "moss growed on the plant." "If they want to talk to us in six months, we'll talk to them," he proclaimed, "If they want to talk to us in 1937, we'll talk to them. If they want to talk to us in 1950, we'll talk to them, but we're not going back until we get a written contract." The textile union delivered more than tough talk. It also set up a well-stocked relief center. As the strike dragged on, however, the food went quickly and the union turned to Johnston for help. The governor arranged for the opening of a commissary to disperse federal foodstuffs and sent in the Red Cross to distribute clothing and medical supplies to needy children. With his assistance, workers avoided starvation and the Tucapau strike lines held steady longer than they might have under, say, former governor Blackwood.[23]

Toward the end of spring, company officials announced that they planned to restart the mill in June. Applications for jobs in the factory, they let it be known, would be accepted from all but twelve UTW members whom they charged with sabotage and violence. Few of the potential replacement workers made it to the personnel office to apply for jobs on the appointed day. Six hundred union supporters blocked the entrance to the building and showered prospective strikebreakers with "bottles, bricks, and bats." Away from the mill gate, UTW members dragged a company loyalist from his car and then smashed his windows. When word of the confrontation reached Johnston in Columbia, he rushed to Tucapau to address striking workers gathered at a nearby baseball field. Only his personal intervention, reporters claimed, prevented further bloodshed. Unlike other chief executives in South Carolina and across the nation, Johnston did not tell unionists to hurry back to work on management's terms nor did he threaten to mobilize the National Guard against them. Instead, he volunteered to serve as an arbitrator between the union and management.[24]

After quickly obtaining the UTW's backing for mediation, Johnston headed to McNab's office to get him to agree to talk with the union. Although the mill president postponed reopening the factory, he balked at direct negotiations with the UTW. He wanted from Johnston what South Carolina mill men in similar situations had come to expect from their governor—the mobilization of the state's military muscle to break strikes. "The right to strike," the mill president lectured Johnston, "is a recognized one . . . but far more laudable is the right to work." Based on his reading of the South Carolina Constitution, McNab instructed the governor "to provide the necessary protection to employees who want to work."[25] Johnston refused to be intimidated or told what to do. Rather than calling out the troops, he admonished McNab for refusing to enter into a dialogue with the union. "[P]rotection would be provided for all factions involved," Johnston retorted, "if and when the mill faction is disposed to cooperate in the peaceable settlement of the labor controversy."[26] Public rebukes of manufacturers such as this one were not the norm in South Carolina. The UTW recognized Johnston's break with the past. "He has set a new milestone in industrial relations in the South," proclaimed the editors of the UTW's monthly newsletter, "a milestone that recognizes industrial workers as human beings with rights equal to those of the men who are fortified with money and power."[27]

Over the next three weeks, Johnston repeatedly and publicly blamed the Tucapau management for the failure to reach a settlement in the strike. Privately, he continued to search for a resolution, but talks stalled over the question of what to do with the twelve workers accused by management of sabotage and violence. McNab made it clear that he would not take them back, and the United Textile Workers refused to abandon its members. At this point, Johnston stepped in and resolved the deadlock by finding state jobs for the men. Finally, the UTW accepted a package of terms that promised to return workloads to their prestrike levels. On July 17, nineteen weeks after the strike began, all but the twelve men now employed by the state returned to their mill jobs.[28]

One month later the Tucapau management violated the terms of the strike-ending agreement by raising workers' machine loads. It also signed an exclusive collective bargaining agreement with the Good Will Association, hired additional rural laborers, and badgered UTW members to join the company union or leave town. A few union diehards stayed on in Tucapau to carry on the struggle, but this was more than the mill managers would tolerate. They wanted every last UTW member out of the village.

Magistrate R. D. Hicks of Inman served the eviction notices on the Tucapau trade unionists who had been thrown out of the mill village. This seemed strange to Governor Johnston. Why, he wondered, had these cases been heard in Hicks's Inman courtroom, twelve miles across rutty dirt roads from the factory, and not in the magistrate's office in Tucapau or in Spartanburg, which was only ten miles away? Why, he asked, had mill officials from the Starex Mills and Spartan Mills also traveled this path? Johnston also wanted to know why Hicks blocked textile workers from serving on juries that deliberated eviction cases. The answers were rather obvious. For years, mill officials had handpicked malleable magistrates to adjudicate the law in their districts, and previous governors and state senators had rubber-stamped their selections. In an effort to end this practice, Johnston discharged the Inman magistrate for being "grossly negligent in failing to administer the law" and for transforming his office into "an instrument for the oppression of labor." Members of the state senate rushed to Hicks's defense and, bolstered by a ruling from the state supreme court, returned him to the bench. Once again, an attempt by Johnston to tip the balance of power in labor's favor had been blocked by the structure of government in South Carolina.[29]

What more could Tucapau trade unionists do? They had the allegiance of 80 percent of the workers who lived in the mill village, they had shut down the factory for four months, but still they could not force mill president McNab to make significant concessions. The union had already tested the TLRB and NLRB, securing favorable decisions from both, only to discover that management did what it pleased anyway. Union leaders were certain that the governor was on their side, but they lost their fight just the same. Many UTW members, resigned to defeat at least temporarily, decided to either lay low until they had another opportunity to organize or pack up and move to another town. The union in Tucapau was dead.

During the summer of 1935, while Johnston weighed whether or not to sign the workers' compensation bill and tensions mounted in Clinton and Tucapau, labor unrest ignited Pelzer. Located in Anderson County, ten miles south of Greenville, Pelzer was home to the Pelzer Manufacturing Company and little else. The company employed 1,650 workers at its four local factories.

Founded in 1881, the firm quickly gained a reputation for paternalism. Involving themselves in the personal and productive worlds of their laborers, the mill owners walked around the factories during the day chatting with workers. At night, they strolled through the villages, calling out "how-do-you-do" to people sitting on their porches. They built schools, churches, and libraries and chipped in for a YMCA, a park pavilion, and a swimming pool. In the mid-1920s the Bank of Boston bought out the original owners. Then the depression hit. Conditions in the villages deteriorated: sanitation was appalling, housing was substandard, and the stretchout ground workers down. Labor peace, a hallmark of the earlier era, was replaced by persistent strife. In 1929 and again in 1932, Pelzer employees struck against the new stretchout regime.[30] During the National Recovery Administration (NRA) era, workers swamped the code authority with reports of violations.[31] By the fall of 1934 more than three-quarters of the Pelzer workforce belonged to the UTW. The General Textile Strike shut down all four of the company's plants. Following the national walkout, general superintendent J. K. Blackmon launched a relentless campaign against the union coupled with a vigorous drive to recruit outside laborers. By the start of 1935 his efforts seemed to be paying off. The ranks of the once-formidable UTW local had shrunk to fifty-five stalwarts. Yet the passage of the Wagner Act breathed new life into the moribund union, and by the end of the spring three hundred Pelzer laborers belonged to the local.[32]

As the union expanded, holding weekly pep rallies and religious services, trouble started to brew.[33] To counter the UTW, management set up the Pelzer Good Will Association. Supposedly dedicated to fostering "goodfeeling [and] harmony," the Good-Willies, as they came to be called, further fractured the already divided community.[34] Another round of dismissals heightened tensions. Union adherents found themselves under constant surveillance both on the job and in the villages; any slip or mistake would be used against them. Insisting that they were acting impartially, Pelzer managers fired fifty employees in June for failing to meet "minimum standards of performance." All of the dismissed workers just happened to be UTW members or people who refused to join the Good Will Association. Yet when Blackmon initiated eviction proceedings against the ousted wage earners, the Anderson County sheriff and Governor Johnston refused to carry out his orders. Meanwhile, the UTW prepared to strike. Federal labor conciliators rushed to Pelzer and patched together an uneasy truce, avoiding a walkout, at least for the time being. Under the accord, mill officials agreed to allow the fired workers to remain in their homes until the NLRB ruled on their cases.[35]

The agreement, however, did not bring peace to Pelzer. Shop floor bosses continued to harass trade unionists, and the UTW continued to fight back.

On July 17 a recently demoted weaver, "Ump" Smith, waved a knife in the face of a particularly belligerent overseer. The company official fired Smith on the spot and ordered him to leave the factory at once. Smith would not budge. The mill police were summoned, and after a scuffle, Smith was disarmed and literally thrown out of the plant. Word of the standoff shot through the community. Aggravated by months of managerial intimidation, unionists burst into action. They cut off the power in the plant where Smith worked and within minutes threw up picket lines around the other Pelzer factories.[36]

The entire Pelzer community was on edge during the night of the Smith incident and the next morning. While armed pickets patrolled the mills, overseers reinforced all exits and entrances with steel beams. In the villages, roving bands of UTW members terrorized company loyalists, and Good Will supporters bullied trade unionists. Near midnight, gunshots went off. After surveying the area, the Anderson County sheriff urged the Pelzer superintendent to close the mills the next day. Blackmon refused to stop the machines, vowing to operate his factories the way he saw fit, even if that meant running them under the protection of a private militia. Pelzer trade unionists, meanwhile, wrote to their governor for help. Despite having less than half the workforce on their side, they asked him to do something unprecedented: to use the power of his office to shut down the mills and force management to negotiate with the union in good faith.[37]

Although he did not force the factories to close, Johnston did send the National Guard to Pelzer. The troops, he asserted as strongly as he could, were mobilized to maintain peace and protect human lives, which were "more precious than gold." Again unlike his predecessors, Johnston never mentioned the importance of keeping the mills running, the rights of nonstrikers, or the sanctity of private property. Repeatedly, he emphasized that he had mobilized the National Guard to prevent bloodshed, not to crush the strike. "I only wish," he told an idled Pelzer worker, "I had more power and authority in matters of this kind." Yet having concluded that he did not possess such "power and authority," the governor did what he could to bring both sides to the negotiating table. But here, too, he had little leverage, at least when it came to controlling the actions of the mill managers.[38]

In front of mill stores and in the lobbies of uptown law offices, Johnston's troop mobilization sparked debate. The vice president of the Ware Shoals Manufacturing Company applauded the governor's action. When Johnston was elected in 1934, industrialists like himself, he admitted, twitched with fear, but following the activation of the National Guard, he brimmed with confidence in the chief executive. Some workers, taking Johnston at his word, thanked him for saving their lives. "It is anomalous that he would break a 100% strike," wrote one worker in Johnston's defense, "but he is doing his best to help a strike of a minority." Others, however, were not so sure. "Labor is very much surprised," a weaver informed the governor. Like textile workers across the upcountry, mill folks in Pelzer had expected a new deal with Johnston's election, but the calling out of the troops looked to some like the same raw deal of the past. "The way we are being treated," protested a Pelzer man, "is worse than when *Blackwood* was Governor." Past experience had taught the Greenville Trades and Labor Council to consider the troops to be "strike breakers," and it demanded their immediate dispersal.[39]

The distinction between military men who were summoned to protect human lives and those who were mobilized to keep the mills running became a semantic one in Pelzer. Shielded by government bayonets, Blackmon reopened his factories. He staffed them with Good-Willies who lived both inside and outside the villages, as well as with replacement workers recruited from far and wide. Farmers' sons doffed and swept, tenants tended looms, spare hands from Anderson ran the card room, and sharecroppers broke up bales of cotton.[40] With the troops protecting the lives of everyone, no matter which side they were on, strikebreakers had little trouble getting past picket lines to enter or leave the mills. By the end of July federal labor investigators reported that the four Pelzer plants were operating at 90 percent of their capacity.[41]

With the armed forces in place and the mills running, the Pelzer management had no incentive to talk with the union, so it did not, despite persistent appeals from the governor and the U.S. Labor Department. At this point, with only a third of the workers on its side, the UTW possessed little raw power, but it did have a nucleus of steadfast followers who refused to abandon the strike. Militancy, however, was no substitute for strength in numbers, and without the governor's decisive intervention, the UTW had no chance of winning.

But Johnston was not done or about to give in to management. Claiming that the strike had turned into a lockout, he announced in late July that National Guardsmen would no longer escort strikebreakers who lived *outside* of the mill villages across the picket lines into the factories. Pelzer officials responded by evicting UTW supporters to create housing space for strikebreakers in the villages. They also persuaded company loyalists living in the villages to take in boarders who worked in the mills but resided in the country. This way, most people who worked in the factories would technically live in the villages and Johnston's order would therefore have little impact on production.[42]

A few days after the evictions, truckloads of UTW members from the

Saxon Mills, who were also on strike, arrived in Pelzer. Splitting up into small platoons, they set out to conduct a house-to-house canvass exhorting families not to accept out-of-towners "or else," they warned, "you'll have plenty to be sorry about." On the mean streets of Pelzer, it did not take long for a man to pull a gun on the group and threaten to start shooting. The Saxon workers beat a hasty retreat.[43]

Early the next morning, August 2, strikebreakers and pickets clashed in front of the Pelzer No. 4 plant. Small skirmishes continued throughout the day, and pistol shots rang out through the night. Desperate for a deal before the outbreak of a full-scale industrial war, Johnston imposed martial law in Pelzer and sealed off the village from the "disruptive influences" of outsiders. Under the governor's new decree, only persons employed in the mills *when the strike began* were now allowed in the area.[44]

Never before had a South Carolina governor used his authority during an industrial dispute for anything other than breaking up a strike. By "localizing" the Pelzer dispute, Johnston gambled that he could force management to the bargaining table and patch together a settlement before the outbreak of full-scale industrial war. Most UTW members applauded Johnston's actions, although the Good Will Association maintained that they aided the union and violated its members' constitutional right to work under any circumstances. A few, like Roy Sims, wanted Johnston to go further, urging him to shut down the factories altogether and not let them reopen until the owners recognized the union. Johnston was certain that his office did not give him this kind of power. He was equally convinced that such an action would cost him the votes of middle-class citizens, and if his electoral defeat in 1930 taught him anything, it taught him that he could not win an election without their backing.[45]

Standing behind barbed wire and makeshift wooden barricades, National Guardsmen blocked all roads leading into Pelzer the morning after the declaration of martial law. They stopped everyone—"the butcher, the baker, and the candlestick maker." Only local residents, food suppliers, and other vital personnel were allowed to pass through the blockade; at least this was the way it was supposed to work. As it turned out, enough strikebreakers lived in the villages or slipped through the military dragnet to keep the mills running. Behind the scenes, negotiations limped along without an end in sight. Although the union accepted arbitration, management stonewalled talks by declining to consider releasing any of the hundreds of replacement laborers hired during the walkout. Meanwhile, the Good Will Association threatened to strike if any UTW members were taken back.[46] "I have done everything humanly possible to get both sides together," complained a clearly frustrated Johnston at the end of August, "but the mill management has refused" to budge.

Superintendent Blackmon's intransigence, he said, called for "drastic action." On August 30 the governor pulled the troops out of Pelzer.[47]

On Labor Day, the first Monday of September, the long anticipated showdown finally took place. Before daybreak, unionists marched in front of the mill gate and loyalists assembled on a hill overlooking the plant. As the sun rose, Arthur Fleming, a lay minister, preached a sermon of fire and brimstone against the union. "It is the Devil's work," he shouted. UTW members yelled back biblical quotations of their own. The situation, according to an eyewitness, was tense, but there was no immediate threat of violence. Twenty minutes earlier, Rufus Newton had left his farmhouse and headed north along the Saluda River Highway toward Pelzer. He planned to drop off his son-in-law, who had begun working in the mill just after the strike started, and immediately return home. As he pulled up to the plant, strikers pelted his sedan with rocks. A UTW member hopped on the running board. Newton jerked the wheel, hurling the strike sympathizer across the dirt. Frantically trying to dodge his attackers, he lost control of his car; it skidded sideways toward the picket line, narrowly missing a group of laborers. "Come on let's go," cried a company loyalist. Jarred by the excitement, they charged down the picket line. Strikers scattered in all directions. Someone fired a shot. More followed. The gun battle ended quickly, but not before it left Laura Gertrude, a union booster and a twenty-three-year-old mother of two, dead, and twenty-eight others wounded. Kneeling in front of the mill gate as if it were an altar, Preacher Fleming raised his arms to the sky; he prayed not for the fallen, but for the mill managers. Even in death, the divisions at Pelzer were deep.[48]

When he learned of the killing, Johnston ordered the National Guardsmen to return to Pelzer. Under their watchful eyes, the mills continued to operate. The Labor Day shootings also jolted the stalled talks. Within days, Johnston, federal labor department officials, Pelzer managers, and UTW representatives hammered out an agreement. Not surprisingly, given the relative strengths of the sides and the fact that the local could not shut down the mill, the pact left trade unionists beholden to "the tender mercies of management."[49] Essentially, the UTW agreed to call off the strike in exchange for a vague commitment from the Pelzer Manufacturing Company to reinstate strikers—except for more than a hundred UTW members accused of violence—as jobs opened up. Discharged wage earners could appeal their cases before the TLRB. As union members would discover, however, the national labor board had a rather expansive definition of violence; it included everything from criminal acts to fighting to taunting strikebreakers on the picket line. Meanwhile, company officials rehired "nonviolent" trade unionists "with all deliberate speed." One year after the strike ended, only three dozen out of hundreds of eligible unionists had returned to their old jobs. Some hung on for months only to be offered positions as spare hands. If they refused the work, company officials evicted them. Managers continued to hire outsiders to fill vacancies, and the union faithful continued to press their claims before the national labor board. All the while membership in the local UTW dwindled. The union had lost again.[50]

Trade unionists around the state felt the sting of the Pelzer defeat. "We are very much concerned about the strike at Pelzer," Rosa L. Vollroth, a member of a nearby UTW local, wrote the governor in July 1935. "We have been trying to get organized here at Gluck Mill and the outcome of the Pelzer strike will effect [*sic*] us," she predicted. The Gluck union did not survive the year. W. E. Broderick, a union member from Jonesville, also felt the tremors from the Pelzer defeat. Recounting a conversation with his boss, he wrote: "They say that Governor Johnston can't do anything or will not do anything. They say look at what Johnston did at Pelzer sent troops there and made the union stand back and let loyal workers work."[51]

Millhands, who had expected Johnston's electoral triumph to be a turning point in their lives, were disappointed that he had not done more, and that when he did act, he had little impact on the outcome. "The public knows by this time," W. Everett Taylor observed in 1935, that Governor Johnston is "100% for the union but the fact that he does[,] does not solve any of our problems." Although workers' faith in New Deal Americanism and government action was dented, most apparently continued to believe in Johnston. "I voted for you, because I thought you was a fair man to laboring people," Bessie Bishop told him in the wake of the Pelzer strike, "and still believe you will do more for us in the future." Others were not so sure. "You was put in office because you was a square man and believed in equal right to all and special privealige to none," argued Bishop's neighbor Mary Guest, "this dirty Co. did not put you there or any other Co. and we are looking for some help."[52]

Poll watchers in and outside of Pelzer predicted dire electoral consequences for Johnston. "Do something with this thing or I am afraid you are done as Governor or Senate or any other office," warned one man. Another guessed that Johnston had squandered at least ten thousand votes in the mill towns when he decided to send the troops to Pelzer.[53] Johnston could not win for losing. Whereas some workers were angry that he had called out the troops, most town residents chided him for removing the National Guard units in August. Middle-class citizens blamed the governor for the Labor Day shootings and the death of Laura Gertrude even though a company loyalist pulled the trigger. Against Cole Blease, Johnston's respectability had won him some support in uptown wards, but his disdain for the mill managers in Tucapau and his refusal to maintain a military presence in Pelzer would cost him these precincts.[54]

For workers, the Pelzer, Tucapau, and Clinton strikes raised other troubling questions. Even after the bitter disappointments of the General Textile Strike, a significant minority of Palmetto State millhands remained committed to trade unionism. But their commitment was not enough. With Johnston as governor, mill laborers had a strategic advantage, one enjoyed by a very small number of workers, even those who successfully organized during the 1930s: a chief executive who supported their cause. Yet try as Johnston did to push aside the formidable barrier of state repression and ensure labor's right to strike, textile unions in South Carolina continued to crumble in defeat.

Even as he neutralized the repressive machinery of the state, South Carolina's political and economic structures hindered millworkers' attempts to unionize. The structure of the textile industry continued to provide manufacturers with few incentives to deal with labor. The depressed rural economy and the cultural differences dividing mill and country people continued to create a steady stream of strikebreakers. Johnston, despite breaking with past traditions by demonstrating a willingness to extend the law on labor's behalf, discovered that it would only stretch so far. He was handcuffed by the state constitution and the distribution of political power. When the governor, for example, exposed Inman magistrate Hicks's blatant pattern of antilabor actions and sought to remove him from the bench, members of the malapportioned, black belt–dominated, probusiness senate rushed to Hicks's defense, leaving him in a position of power over wage earners. Workers, often with the governor's endorsement, tried to circumvent the courts and the mill owners by pressing for legislation that would broaden their rights to organize and to strike, but the general assembly, deadlocked again and again by the senate, rejected these measures. On a number of occasions, as in Clinton and Tucapau, New Deal labor boards ruled against the textile manufacturers and tried to nudge them into compliance. But a much blunter instrument was needed against such vitriolic antiunion employers.

In the end, Johnston's election and the New Deal's liberal labor policies made little difference in the day-to-day lives of South Carolina laborers. Industrial relations in Clinton, Tucapau, and Pelzer in 1936 did not turn out to be much different from those in Ware Shoals in 1929, the Horse Creek Valley in 1933, and Rock Hill in 1934. The reason change did not come to the mill world of South Carolina was not because of the southernness of the workers or because they lacked class consciousness or because they pursued a racially exclusive organizing strategy, although this might have diluted their strength. Instead, it was the structure of power in the state that doomed workers' challenges. But millworkers and Johnston were not through; their struggles were not over. At the same time that millhands fought for the right to strike and kept the spirit of trade unionism alive, the governor led them into battle against the highway department and the state's image makers.

Fighting for the Right to Strike

CHAPTER TEN

They Don't Like Us because We're Lintheads

The Highway Fight, 1935–1937

"What the hell is going on?" a man shouted as well-armed, steel-helmeted soldiers marching in tight military formation passed him on the streets of downtown Columbia on a bright October morning in 1935. The troops turned at the capitol and headed toward Sumter Street. They stopped in front of a rather innocuous looking building. Grim-faced, they moved with quick precision to seal off all exits and entrances, set up two machine gun nests, and establish a checkpoint. They met no resistance at the building—the headquarters of the South Carolina Highway Department.[1]

The next morning Governor Olin D. Johnston called a press conference to explain the troop deployment. Journalists from around the state and nation crammed into a small briefing room at the governor's mansion. Reading slowly from a prepared text, Johnston said that Orangesburg Company D, 118th Infantry of the National Guard, had been called up to end the Ben Sawyer–led highway department's "unlawful assemblage in a state of insurrection, resistance and against the laws of South Carolina." His election, Johnston claimed, represented a mandate from the people to smash the highway department and restore democracy to the state. Since assuming office nine months earlier, he had tried everything from persuasion to intimidation to carry out this mission. Reviewing the record, he reminded the reporters that he had asked the highway commissioners to resign, and they had refused; he had tried to forcibly replace them, but the state supreme court had blocked his moves; and he had to tried to legislate them out of power, but the general assembly, filled with Sawyer backers, had stopped him. Having fought and lost against the highway department on all these fronts, the governor believed that he had only one option left to fulfill his campaign promise—brute force. That was the only language that Ben Sawyer and his partners in "trickery and subterfuge, favoritism and irregularities" understood.

The governor's action "amazed" and "surprised" many South Carolinians, even the hard-boiled politicians of the Charleston delegation to the general assembly. Longtime senator Cotesworth D. Means described the military takeover "as the most astounding development since my connection with public life."[2] Events around the capitol got even stranger over the next several weeks. Johnston commanded the troops to check everyone who entered the Sumter Street building to make sure that the ousted members of the highway commission did not try to slip back into their former headquarters. He also appointed Joe Calus, a Belgian-born accountant and longtime political ally, to replace Ben Sawyer. Calus immediately fired all highway department employees and then rehired most of them. He vowed to keep ongoing projects running but soon realized that he had been outmaneuvered by his enemies, who managed to freeze almost all of the department's funds. Pinched for cash, Calus ordered Frank Barnwell, the head of the National Guard unit, to go to a downtown bank armed with a rifle to get the highway bureau's money, but the attorney general prevented him from completing his mission. When another court officer came to serve Calus with papers to cease and desist from running the highway department, an overzealous guardsman hit him in the face. After that, little changed. National Guardsmen marched and passersby gawked. October ended, Thanksgiving came and went, and Christmas approached; all the while, the troops remained hunkered down around the Sumter Street building.[3]

What is next? the editors of the *New York Times* chuckled after the takeover of the highway department, the storming of the Board of Dental Health followed by an attack on the Chiropractic Examiners.[4] The buttoned-down Ivy League historian Henry Steele Commager must have read about the highway fight. Unlike the *Times* correspondent, the sober academic found the spectacle of National Guardsmen in a state capital punching law officers and setting up machine-gun posts more troubling than humorous. The situation, Commager judged, was "fraught with fear," and he decided to go to South Carolina to conduct "a first-hand study of conditions."[5]

Commager quickly discovered that the highway fight was not really about roads or spending. The South Carolina Highway Department was actually quite effective when it came to building roads and bridges. Even if Ben Sawyer

They Don't Like Us because We're Lintheads

and the commissioners did occasionally let one of their supporters skim a little off the top, they constructed roads for less money per mile than any other state highway authority in the nation. Despite getting a late start, South Carolina also had more paved roads per mile than any other state in the South. So if roads were not the issue, what was?

Patronage, Commager recognized, fueled the conflict. The South Carolina Constitution restricted the governor's powers. Beyond the veto, he could do little more than nominate a few commissioners to several rather meaningless boards and appoint fifty or so men to the constabulary and a few dozen to the state highway patrol. This was hardly the leverage needed to build a durable political machine. The highway department, meanwhile, oversaw an annual budget of $8 million, a figure that nearly equaled the entire state budget; it had projects in every corner of the state and employed 3,000 people. Although in theory it was supposed to be nonpartisan, in 1935 this formidable source of patronage was controlled by Johnston's electoral adversaries—cautious conservatives, business progressives, and low-country senators. Like most politicians, the highway men used their access to jobs and building projects to reward their friends and punish their enemies. Johnston, therefore, faced a dilemma: to establish himself as a permanent political force in the state, he needed patronage, and the key source of patronage was the highway department, but the road builders had locked him out of the game.

Commager grasped that there was another, closely related component to the conflict. Throughout his political career Johnston had watched a cadre of low-country senators, all of them allies of Sawyer and the highway department, check nearly every attempt to pass prolabor laws and other progressive legislation. Access to the spoils of patronage, Johnston reasoned, would strengthen his political network and weaken the power of probusiness conservatives. That is why, according to Commager, he was willing to risk everything to crush the "ring"—his code word for the alliance between antilabor lawmakers and the South Carolina Highway Department.[6]

Still, Johnston's bold grab for power alarmed Commager. Amid the clatter of troop movements, the Columbia University scholar heard the dissonant, eerie echoes of extremism, Longism, and perhaps even European fascism. The governor's actions prompted Commager to dub him the "South Carolina dictator." Even more troubling was the attitude of Johnston's supporters. Like sheep heading for slaughter, they backed him no matter what: regardless of whether he broke the law or played by the rules. Commager cringed when a Johnston defender told him: "The courts are packed . . . there was no justice there. It was necessary to call out the military in order to get justice." Asked if he was disturbed about setting a dangerous precedent, the working man evaded the question and when pressed, answered, "there was . . . no other way."[7]

To Commager, law and order were the cornerstones of American democracy and they were imperiled in South Carolina. Johnston's backers agreed: democracy was indeed under siege in the state. But they did not cast the governor in the role of the Palmetto State fascist; rather, he was the hero. Although he had been elected by a majority of the people to bring "a little New Deal" to South Carolina, senators, business leaders, and others foiled his every move. To the governor's supporters, the highway fight symbolized the larger struggle for control over the machinery of state government. In this sense then, Commager read the situation correctly. The highway fight was not about roads and only remotely about patronage, it was about who would rule South Carolina.

There was little doubt about which side most millhands took in the highway fight. Toward the end of 1935, Charlotte's Arthur Eargle spent three days in Newberry County and did not find a single millworker who opposed the governor's actions.[8] More than 12,000 people from mill districts signed postcards, poems, pictures, and petitions in support of Johnston's attack on the highway department.[9] J. W. Koon mailed the governor a jawbone of an ass and told him to use it just like Samson did to slay a thousand men.[10] Greenville "citizens" applauded his efforts "on behalf of the citizenship of our state as against entrenched power." "Attaboy still for you hook, line, and sinker," wired a York County resident.[11] "You are right," a Spartanburg worker declared, "I'm with you all the way in your fight for the people of South Carolina." "All the textile people are for you," added Gaffney's Mary Biddex. Five hundred and twenty Richland County millworkers declared their "one hundred percent support" for the governor, as did 124 employees of Lexington's Red Bank Mill and 832 people from West Greenville. Twenty-eight UTW chapters also sent Johnston enthusiastic letters of encouragement.[12]

Along with writing letters and marking referendums, millhands volunteered to join the fight against Ben Sawyer. "If you need any further help call on Local 2014," resolved several hundred employees of Newberry's Oakland Mills just after National Guardsmen took over the highway department. Other workers offered military assistance. "I carried a rifle in 1898 and can carry one in 1935, if necessary," a wage earner told Johnston. "If the situation should arise . . . calling for volunteers," a Greenwood man wrote, "Don't fail to call on me." "Citizens of York County" agreed: "If the bunch of law makers we have sent to Columbia to represent us get it in their heads they

They Don't Like Us because We're Lintheads

can abolish the National Guard to make their own personal points—call on us quick, for many of our older citizens still have our uniforms of 1917-18 and if it becomes necessary we can go without our uniforms. By all means keep Ben Sawyer and his gang out of our Highway Department."[13]

Class loyalty pulled mill people into the fight against Ben Sawyer. They accepted Johnston's characterization of the highway department as a threat to democracy, because, in part, he was one of them, and they trusted his analysis of the world. Textile workers also stood by the governor because they saw him as a man of principle. Unlike other politicians who came around the mill hills making endless campaign promises, only to forget them as soon as they assumed office, Johnston kept his word. He said he would crush the highway department, and that was exactly what he was doing. "We want you to know," wrote a labor leader, "that your friends and people are behind you 100%. . . . You have kept your word and no one can say otherwise. You are our governor and we are proud of you." Praised for not being a "pussy footer," Johnston stood up to the "big guys," just like workers imagined themselves doing.[14]

The governor's message also made sense to millhands because it fit with what they saw happening around them. Though the Sawyer-led highway department built miles of roads, not many textile workers noticed, because few of the new routes passed by the mill villages. Moreover, not many mill people were hired for high-paying jobs on the road crews; in fact, rumor had it that the highway commissioners only employed their friends or friends of friends. According to other reports, the highway men paid African Americans more than white men for the same work. Mill people also recognized that the highway commission was a powerful force in South Carolina's fiscal and political affairs, and that it was championed by a clique of low-country senators who regularly rejected labor legislation. There seemed to be an element of duplicity here as well. Although politicians clamored for economy, slashing teachers' salaries and killing workers' compensation legislation because of the cost, the highway department thrived. When Johnston took office in 1935, workers knew that the commission controlled a war chest of funds.[15] But from the start, millhands suspected that there was more to the highway fight than the issues of political and fiscal power and the high-minded arguments about the constitution featured on editorial pages. They detected a subtext of "us" versus "them" in the road battle.

Locked out of power for so long, textile workers believed that with the advent of the New Deal and Johnston's election their time had come. But low-country planters, upcountry manufacturers, and conservative senators refused to step aside or share even a little of their authority. "Just to commend you," wrote a supporter from Union, "for being the only Governor this state has ever had who cared a little picayune for laboring people. . . . I think that is at the bottom of the severe fight against you." A Greenville man compared Johnston's enemies with FDR's rivals: "The first step taken by President Roosevelt after becoming chief executive of the United States was to relieve conditions which existed because of the power of money, this same class jumped on him, and they continue to fight him." [16]

This was class war. In the minds of many South Carolina workers, an unholy alliance of "blue bloods," "highway gentlemen," "autocrats," "people willing to fatten on the crumbs that fall from Ben Sawyer's table," and "Hooverites" fought as a united front against Johnston.[17] Why? Because he was the son of a tenant farmer, a mill boy, and a linthead. S. J. Grady explored these themes in a poem about the highway fight, and the "linthead" governor:

Hats off to the governor
   Of the Palmetto State!
They may call him linthead
   But I think he's great
He may be a linthead, but he's
   Full of spizzerinktum
I just think he is the
   Very dinktum.
Why, what if he did work in a mill?
   Remember, he is governor still.
What difference if he had
   Been a coal miner?
He is now governor of
   South Carolina.
What's the difference if he was
   Brought up poor?
He now carries the keys to the
   State mansion door.
Now you fellows that are making
   So much noise,
Remember that Olin is one of
   The Johnston Boys
He started at the bottom, and
   Climbed to the top
And you fellows in the middle
   Are going to "flippety-flop."

Well I guess I had better stop this thing
   Before someone accuses me of
Belonging to some ring.[18]

At a capital city rally held in December 1935, six weeks after the initial troop deployment, Olin Johnston himself framed the highway fight in class terms. Organized by "Johnston supporters" to "let the popular will of the people be known" and "show the Governor that we deeply appreciate his efforts," the demonstration attracted thousands.[19] More than fifty cars caravanned to Columbia from Greenville trailed by millhands from Pelzer and Ware Shoals and dozens of other points in the Piedmont. Standing on top of the "Voice of Labor"—the UTW's sound truck, described at its dedication as a "symbol and a weapon . . . of our determination to fight for complete unionization"— Johnston began with a blistering attack on Sawyer.[20] So wicked was the highway chief that the governor had no choice but to call out the troops. With the crowd stirring, Johnston reminded everyone who he was and who they were. "They referred to me as the linthead boy, they now refer to me as the linthead Governor," he shouted so loud that the microphone hissed, "I accept these remarks on the part of my enemies as compliments." "Of course," he continued, "my election as Governor did not meet with the approval of the blue bloods and aristocrats because I had come from poor, but honorable parentage and had by earnest and conscientious effort been elevated from a cotton mill hand to Governor." Because of "my having come up from the ranks," wealthy South Carolinians had joined together "to undermine my administration." He asked the onlookers for their support against his silk tie-, top hat-wearing adversaries. They roared back with applause. Following the address, millhands in well-worn overalls and simple cotton dresses hovered around Johnston, praising his speech and pledging their assistance in the war against Sawyer and all others who scorned the "linthead governor."[21]

Proudly identifying himself as a linthead, Johnston transformed the highway fight from a debate over roads and public policy into a battle over class dignity and social equality. In framing the discussion this way, he slyly turned Ben Sawyer into anyone who had ever looked down on millhands. The highway chief became every well-dressed man who passed a group of millhands window-shopping on a Saturday afternoon and whispered just loud enough for them to hear, "damned lintheads." He became every shopkeeper who watched mill people like a hawk in his/her store, waiting for one of them to try to steal something. He became every rural resident, every Buck and Shaw Walden, who was sure he was better than "those lazy good-for-nothing lintheads." Millhands saw the highway commissioner as every merchant's son or daughter who rejected a textile worker, who said when asked out on a date, "no, I can't, you're a linthead." The road chief stood finally for every doctor, lawyer, or banker who would just as soon have an African American over for dinner as a linthead.[22]

For millhands, the highway fight was part of a broader New Deal era struggle to construct a new public identity for themselves. Every time Buck, Shaw, or anyone else spat out the word "linthead," they covertly defined workers as second-class citizens. To be seen as something less than a full citizen in a place like Jim Crow South Carolina meant being categorized as less than totally white. By calling mill people lintheads, planters, professionals, and country people attempted to naturalize their political dominance. Lintheads, by definition, were too stupid and too ignorant—not quite white enough—to run the state. These assumptions, in turn, served as a justification for preventing mill people and the mill boy governor, Olin Johnston, from entering the corridors of state power.

By enlisting mill people as lintheads in the struggle against the highway department, Johnston urged them to join him in sending a message to South Carolina's rich and powerful that white laborers were as good as anybody and as "white" as anybody. He also told wage earners that they were first-class citizens, worthy and capable of running South Carolina. In this way, he created a link between the highway fight and the New Deal. From where workers stood, both revolved around demands for full citizenship rights and both required using their electoral muscle to gain these rights. Something else was going on at the same time. Every time Johnston and his millworker allies called themselves lintheads, they took some of the sting out of the epithet, snatching it away from their enemies and turning it into a playful expression of class unity and pride.[23]

Millhands did not confine their battle for social respect and first-class citizenship during Johnston's first term as governor to the highway fight. Another less famous showdown took place on the campus of Wofford College, a Methodist school on the northern border of Spartanburg. The focus of this controversy was as unlikely as the setting. It was over a poem.

A few months before the highway fight started, Peter R. Moody enrolled in a poetry class at Wofford. His teacher probably told him to write from experience. Moody had grown up in a Cooleemee, North Carolina, mill village and during the previous summer had worked at the plant down the street from his parent's house. Inspired by Carl Sandberg, he decided to describe the familiar topography of the cotton mill world in what he dubbed "free verse." Rather than a tender portrait of kin and family, his poem was a searing saga of physical and intellectual degradation. In "To a Cotton Mill Worker," Moody wrote:

Your shoulders are humped and your head is bent; your gray eyes are spiritless and your mouth is just a hard straight line in a yellow face under the blue lights of the mill.

You are diseased and unhealthy looking, standing there in your faded overalls with one suspender loose. Your voice is cracked and your throat and lungs are lined with cotton.

Every night the whistle blows and you plod home to swallow your bread and beans, comb the cotton from your straggly gray hair, wash your wrinkled face, and then lie down on your hard, unclean mattress until the whistle's blast calls you back to your machine in the mill.

In these close, four-room green and yellow houses filled with soot from the mill's smokestack and dust from the road, you breed countless children, dirty and ill-fed, who grow up to take your place in the cotton mill.

You are narrow-minded and ignorant, you with your six years of schooling. And you are afraid, afraid of your bosses, afraid of being laid off. You are desperately frightened by knowledge. Therefore you shun it, and are content to stay a coward.

Recreation for you is talking baseball and in seeing, on Saturday nights, some cheap Western movie full of guns and ropes and horses and fights. And your pleasure is wasting your nickels in the drug store slot machine.

On your day off, dressed in your shiny cheap suit and dingy white shirt, you come down to the village square and sit in the sun in front of the company store and spit tobacco juice on the sidewalk from between your decaying yellow teeth. You gossip with other factory bucks, and miss the clamor of the mill.

You join a union and pay your dues. And you attend meetings where loud-mouthed bunk-shooters shout lies at you and yell against the stretch-out, and tell you that if you strike and lose your jobs you will no longer be poverty stricken. And you believe them. These mealy-mouthed hypocrites tell you that you are the salt of the earth and the bulwark of the nation, and then grab your dollar contribution and put it in their pockets, while your children go without shoes.

On Sundays you put on your red tie and go to church with your consumptive wife, and while she goes in and sits on the left side of the narrow wooden church you stand outside, you and your cronies spit tobacco juice. And then you go in and sit down on the right side away from your wife. You hear the preacher speak of Christian living and high ideals. What do you know about high ideals, you broken, $16 a-week mill hand?

Listen, you linthead, you are just another poor, illiterate, cotton mill worker. You stand with a thousand others just like you for five days a week, eight hours a day, running and watching and nursing and tending a power loom all for 40 cents an hour.

What do know about life?

What do you know about music?

What do know about art or literature?

What do know about "love"?

What *could* you know about anything?

You are dead!

You died on your 16th birthday when you went to work in the cotton mill.[24]

Moody's brutal depiction of millhands first appeared in April 1936 in the *Wofford College Journal*, a student literary magazine. Eventually, it reached a wider audience when several upcountry newspapers and weeklies reprinted the poem. Moody's savage picture wounded mill people. One wage earner thought that it was "probably the most vicious attack ever aimed at cotton mill workers." "Just think of what was said about us," a millhand-turned-preacher-turned-lawmaker gasped, choking back tears. When a student read the poem at a local high school, mill folks booed and hissed, denouncing Moody as a mean-spirited fraud. A few nights later, an angry band of textile workers headed over to Wofford College to "get" Moody. Alarmed by their presence on campus, the president of the college telephoned a local labor leader, who rushed over to the school and helped disperse the protesters. For the next several days campus security remained on alert, braced for another late-night visit from workers, but the millhands stayed away.[25]

The campaign against the poet quickly became politicized. Revealing the depths of their New Deal faith in government action, millhands called on their elected representatives to punish Moody and uphold their collective dignity, just as they urged them to pass labor legislation and guarantee the right to strike. "We Citizens of South Carolina ask the Honorable Olin D. Johnston," fifty-five Laurens County millhands petitioned, "that the said Peter Moody be asked to leave the state of South Carolina and never return, because of his being indecent, immoral, and of an undesirable character." Displaying a continued commitment to racially bracketed citizenship, these workers argued that Moody's poem showed that he was not an honorable white man. For this, they said, he should be ostracized, de-raced even. "We would prefer in his stead as a citizen of South Carolina the most unlearned negro man in our Grand Old State." In a gendered attack, another upcountry writer insisted that Moody's "slanderous statements" revealed an "[un]manly man."[26]

Not long after the publication of "To a Cotton Mill Worker," the South Carolina General Assembly took up the matter of Peter Moody. Spartanburg representative William Fred Ponder, a Chesnee mill boy described by an upcountry newspaper as an "active adherent of . . . textile labor measures," spearheaded the legislative offensive against the poet.[27] Moody's verse, the lawmaker charged, "grossly exaggerated" conditions in the mill villages. Even worse, Moody did not bother, as New Dealers and Johnstonites had, to "deplore the alleged conditions, nor does he look with compassion on those he purports to describe." Playing on the theme of "us" versus "them," while glossing over Moody's own mill village background, Ponder continued: "The writer has no common sense; he knows the tennis racquet [and] the golf club, and would not know a frame or a loom if he saw one." Ponder concluded that Moody suffered not only from elitism, but insanity as well. Public safety demanded that such a "deranged mentality" be locked up. He urged the general assembly to send a psychiatrist "to examine . . . Peter Moody and report such findings to this body at the earliest date possible."[28]

During the debate over Ponder's resolution, upcountry legislators interspersed their views on Moody's mental health with tributes to mill people. "It [the poem] is a slander on the people in the cotton mills," an Anderson representative protested. One of his house colleagues declared that "it is an absolute insult." Textile workers, another chimed in, were "refined, good-looking and a credit to the state." Still another professed, "Textile operatives are an honorable[,] law-abiding and God-fearing people." Eventually the motion passed, and Dr. E. L. Hoerger, the superintendent of the state hospital, traveled to Spartanburg to examine Moody. The doctor and the student spent an hour together. After the meeting Hoerger declared Moody sane, adding that the undergraduate had "more sense than the members of the legislature." Within days, the general assembly voted to "expunge from the record the original resolution concerning the Wofford College student." The Moody episode was over.[29]

This obscure literary controversy involving an unknown undergraduate poet and a long-forgotten lawmaker might seem like an odd detour in the larger discussion of the highly publicized highway row. For all of their apparent differences, however, both were about the same thing. Both represented public rejections of the "linthead" label and all that went with it, including second-class citizenship and de-whitening. Both demonstrated millhands' continued faith in government action, the idea that political organizing could address gnawing grievances and long-standing problems. By rising up to challenge the highway department and the college poet Peter Moody, South Carolina lintheads indicated that they would no longer be passive victims of class prejudice. At the same time, they demonstrated that they were potent agents capable of shaking up the existing power structure. Millhands, in other words, announced in the first years of the Johnston administration that they intended to have a say in the running of the state no matter what Ben Sawyer, Peter Moody, and their blue-blooded buddies thought.[30]

If textile workers went to battle against Sawyer and Moody to win the respect of others, they seemed to have lost. Distorted images of mill people persisted long after the cultural clashes and road wars of the winter of 1935–36 ended. Factory owners continued to allow supervisors to sexually harass female laborers. Shopkeepers and town residents continued to greet workers and their families strolling through town on Saturday afternoons with unwelcome stares. Rural people continued to insist that they were better than mill folks. And college students and professionals continued to poke fun at how textile workers dressed, talked, played, and prayed. Take the case of David D. Wallace. The noted South Carolina historian recounted the Moody episode in his 1951 study of Wofford College. Although, he acknowledged, South Carolina millhands had "advanced mightily" since the beginning of the century, "the Moody affair revealed like a lightening flash how deep is still the chasm between them and other elements of our society."[31]

On the political and patronage fronts of the highway battle, Johnston and his allies fared no better. Five tense weeks after the initial mobilization of the National Guard in October 1935, the troops remained in place. On December 5 the state's supreme court justices—almost to a man close allies of Ben Sawyer—delivered a sharp blow to Johnston. Although affirming the governor's right to declare an emergency, the judges argued that in the case of the highway department he had overstepped the law. The Sawyer-run road board, they maintained, had never risen up in a "state of insurrection" as Johnston had charged; moreover, the chief executive could not "use the militia to discharge . . . a civil officer." The knockout punch came when the court ruled that Joe Calus and the interim highway authority were "trespassers" and that

Sawyer and the original fourteen commissioners could return to their posts immediately.[32] Complying with the decision, Johnston's appointees gave up their positions at the highway department. The governor, however, refused to back down.

Brazenly defying the court order, Johnston left the troops in place and put the highway department under direct military rule. A National Guard major, Frank Barnwell, who knew nothing about roads or finances, now headed the highway department, the state's largest and most important agency. The situation was chaotic and no one knew who was in charge.[33] Was it the governor? Sawyer? the courts? A few days after the December legal decree, in Charleston, a Johnston appointee bit a Sawyer man as they fought over a telephone, keys, and a cash box for control of the road department's local headquarters. This was the first and only casualty of the highway war.[34]

With his critics' voices getting louder each day, Johnston convened a special session of the state legislature to resolve the highway matter. On December 10, 1935, lawmakers arrived in Columbia in an angry mood. Many talked of impeachment. Still, Johnston did not use his opening remarks to strike a conciliatory note. Fanning the fires of class discord, he thundered: "The blue-bloods and the aristocrats" opposed him for no other reason than he was "a linthead boy." He vowed to make them pay for their arrogance. Not until the "will of the people" as expressed in his electoral mandate was carried out would he remove the National Guard. Predictably, the speech polarized the legislature.[35] "It was all right in the past for a governor to call out the troops on those poor boys in the cotton mills," observed one of Johnston's senate supporters, "but when this governor called them against the big boys in the highway offices, the rulers for so long . . . think its [sic] awful." Yet few lawmakers agreed with this or the governor's analysis. A majority refused to move on any legislation until he sent the troops home. After a week of heated accusations and fervent rebuttals, Johnston finally relented. The National Guard took down its machine gun nests and marched out of Columbia on December 18, 1935.[36]

With Christmas only four days away, the two sides in the highway fight reached an uneasy truce. The legislature passed a compromise temporary highway control act that set up a "nonpartisan" supervisory board of state officials to direct the highway department until a final solution could be approved. Both sides claimed victory. Highway supporters bragged that they had held firm, forcing the governor to remove the military dragnet, while Johnston told his backers that they had won. Keeping "the Hooverite" Ben Sawyer and the old commissioners out of power, which the statute did do for

a time, meant, Johnston boasted, that he had stuck to his campaign promise to break up the ring. Bluster aside, most South Carolinians knew that the
"Olin-Ben War," as one newspaper called it, was not over.[37]

As soon as the 1936 session of the general assembly got under way, it became clear that the governor's support in the house had slipped. Greenville
representative B. M. Gibson had backed Johnston in the 1934 election and
throughout most of the 1935 legislative session, but in the wake of the chief
executive's military maneuvers and his disregard for supreme court decisions,
Gibson went over to the other side. "[T]he die is cast," he told a reporter,
"and I am on the side of constitutional government." With lawmakers like
Gibson defecting from his camp, Johnston failed to win a string of crucial
votes in 1936. Most important, he lost the backing he needed in the house to
sustain his veto. Now nothing prevented the prohighway forces from devising
a road program for the state on their own.[38]

At the close of the 1936 legislative session, the longest in the state's history,
the general assembly passed the Highway Reorganization Act. Better known
as the "Triple Road Bill," the legislation hit the governor, as one paper headlined, like "a slap in the face."[39] Details about finances, license plates, and
bridges aside, the measure essentially diluted the governor's power. It took
the authority to sign road bonds and appoint and dismiss highway commissioners away from the chief executive and gave it to the legislature and the
courts. The law also empowered representatives, not the governor, to appoint
a new highway board. By June 1, 1936, South Carolina did indeed have a new
highway commission, made up of nine members from the "old" road administration and five "new" ones. These men promptly tabbed Ben Sawyer to once
again serve as the state's chief road builder.[40]

Defeat did not deter Johnston. Convinced that he had the people behind
him, the governor crisscrossed the state in the summer of 1936 campaigning
for a friendly legislature.[41] Out on the stump Johnston cast the highway fight
in broad terms, equating Sawyer with elite dominance and announcing that
he himself, like FDR, was fighting for "liberal democracy." "The immediate
object [is] to break the grip of the state Highway Department," he told a campaign crowd, but "the fundamental issues transcend this question." His overall
plan for the state included unemployment insurance, old-age pensions, and
"other measures of vital interest to the farmers and workers of trades, occupations, and industries." Before this could happen, the "people" had to get rid
of Ben Sawyer. Hammering home the point, Johnston compared Sawyerism
to the dark days before Ben Tillman had chased the aristocrats out of power
with his pitchfork, when "government . . . passed from the representatives
of the people into the hands of a legislature controlled by greedy and selfish

They Don't Like Us because We're Lintheads

men . . . indifferent to the sufferings of the masses and hostile to their aspirations and longings for economic freedom." Like Pitchfork Ben, he scoffed at those "mugpies of the entrenched powers and predatory interests" who derided his attempts to recast the legislature with cries of "Dictator! Dictator!" "Then, as now," Johnston professed, "the dictator these enemies of the people feared was the dictation of the people as expressed at the ballot box."[42]

Wherever Johnston went in 1936, he warned that Sawyer, "the high priest of ring rule," would climb down from his yacht and try to buy the legislature in order to "stem the tide of liberal democracy in South Carolina." But Johnston was not worried, he had faith in the "downtrodden toilers," the people, who had as much "blue-blood" coursing through their "veins as any of the Sons and Daughters of the American Revolution." He believed that "[m]oney, intimidation, propaganda, and other malicious influences" would not affect "the incorruptible nature of the masses."[43]

Millhands, not surprisingly, joined Johnston's 1936 crusade for "liberal democracy." "What the people of South Carolina need to do," W. Kay Proctor suggested, "is to kick the pants off the present general assembly and put men (I said men) in their places who will cooperate with Governor Johnston and make our state government, a government of the people, by the people, and for the people."[44] As house and senate members headed home in the spring of 1936 after passing the Triple Road Bill, letters from mill laborers poured into the governor's office. Greer millhand Y. A. Edwards wondered "who from Greenville County if any of the Legislature stood by you and suported [sic] you in the Highway mater [sic]?" "I am a Johnston man," Babb Smith wrote, "and therefore I want Johnston men in the House. Who are they?"[45] Millhands from Easley, Inman, Bennettsville, and Spartanburg asked the same question. Johnston answered every letter.[46] Although he almost never endorsed a candidate outright, he did send all of his correspondents a pink copy of the roll call from the Triple Road Bill; that way they could find out for themselves how their representatives had voted.[47]

Dozens of workers volunteered to take on Sawyer and his ring themselves by running for office on a pro-Johnston platform. A weaver and loom fixer for nearly three decades, Ralph L. Sullivan weighed whether or not to enter the race for the house in Laurens County. Sounding a familiar theme, he told the governor: "I am in sympathy with all the mill people as it is almost *slavery* [his emphasis]. Something must be done. All of your efforts have been blocked by a so-called ring. . . . If I make this race I will stand by you 100%." L. A. Kinard of Prosperity put himself up for office as well. Pledging all-out support for the governor, he explained, "I am in favor of change in the highway department and I am with the textile uion [sic] and am in favor of the

40hr week law." Twenty-four-year-old Honea Path millhand James McDonald also planned to run for the house on a "100% Johnston platform," saying that he favored "the election of [highway] commissioners by the voters of this state and also the Supreme Court judges by the people of their district" and "no additional hours on the textile man, no decrease in pay."[48] For McDonald, Kinard, and Sullivan, support for labor legislation and opposition to the highway department were two sides of the same coin. According to them, conservative domination of the general assembly meant the continuation of ring rule, low pay, and long, hot days in the factory.

Spartanburg workers also bundled these issues together. In 1936 a revived local textile labor movement presented a slate of candidates for just about every office in the county, from state senator to sheriff.[49] "The thing labor should be concerned about," advised the leaders of UTW Local 1705 of Beaumont, "is the election of some public officials whom we know to be fair to labor and our greatest Governor of all times, Olin D. Johnston." Without men like Johnston in power, the union warned, "we would be a more down trodden people than the slaves." But the governor could not do it alone; freedom would come only through the election of men like Furman Garrett, secretary of Lyman's UTW Local 2191. Garrett ran for the state house of representatives on a platform advocating higher wages, shorter hours, the right to strike, amendments to the workers' compensation statute, and full support for Johnston's battle against Sawyer.[50] So crucial was it to elect men like Garrett that Spartanburg trade unionists went out of their way to urge women to vote. "It is time," Martha Crow contended, "we women began to take part in politics if we ever expect to get the right men in the public offices." Otherwise, working people would "be slaves forever."[51] Whether women from Spartanburg mill hills flooded to the polls in the summer of 1936 is hard to determine. Furman's story is easier to fill out. While running well in the mill precincts, he lagged far behind his competitors in city wards and rural districts and lost the election.[52]

Elsewhere pro-Johnston candidates picked up a dozen or more seats in the house and two or three in the senate. Most observers agreed that the governor had done pretty well for himself in 1936, but not good enough to push his prolabor, anti-Sawyer legislative agenda forward. Once again, he knocked up against the hard walls of government structures in South Carolina. Skewed apportionment and the fact that only half of the seats in the crucial senate were up for grabs at a time meant that the upper house would remain in the hands of low-country conservatives who were hostile to the governor and organized labor. A breakdown of the house election returns revealed Johnston's other problems. "Outside of the mill," Arthur Eargle noted after his visit to Newberry County in 1935, "easily three-quarters of the towns people are opposed" to the governor and "lots of them like to tell you so."[53] Two years earlier, some of these people probably backed Johnston. Perhaps they voted for him because he was a millworker who had made good, or because he did not drink and went to church, or maybe because he appeared at the time to be less reckless than Cole Blease. When he mobilized the National Guard and snubbed the state supreme court, Johnston no longer appeared to be so respectable or upstanding. A few town residents laughed at the governor's actions, but most others, exhibiting a somewhat typical regional defensiveness toward "Yankee" criticism, could not stand to hear the likes of the *New York Times* poke fun at South Carolina. Still others feared that an emboldened Johnston would continue his attack on constitutional principles, not stopping until anarchy reigned.[54]

Johnstonites triumphed in house races in the medium-sized, white majority, upcountry industrial counties of Anderson, Laurens, Pickens, and York. His allies also ran strong in Richland County. Yet in the two counties with the largest number of spindles, Greenville and Spartanburg, pro-Johnston candidates lost badly in both the city wards and the countryside and ended up splitting the seats up for grabs with their opponents. In the sections of the state with smaller manufacturing bases, such as Lancaster, Chester, and Fairfield Counties, areas that Johnston carried in 1934, he failed to extend his electoral reach much beyond his base in the mill precincts. The returns from 1936 showed that Johnston still had considerable backing across the state, but he increasingly relied on the votes of textile laborers. Although it was difficult to win a statewide election in South Carolina without gaining some votes in the mill villages, it was impossible to prevail if a candidate only won these areas. Johnston would learn this lesson the hard way in 1938.[55]

But even before the next election cycle, he once again felt the sting of defeat. The more fairly apportioned house of representatives, a stronghold for the governor and for labor throughout much of 1935, delivered the most telling blow. As house members gathered in Columbia in January 1937, some journalists predicted a close race for the speaker of the house between Johnston's candidate, L. C. Wannamaker of Chesterfield County, and his opponent, Sol Blatt of Barnwell County, a close ally of senate conservatives and the highway department. As it turned out, the governor's support, weakened by last-minute defections, collapsed in the final days of the campaign.[56] Blatt cruised to a 74 to 8 victory. In his acceptance speech, he proudly announced that "factionalism is dead." Blatt was right. Factionalism had been killed, yet not because of a grand accord between the state's two warring parties, but because Johnston had been routed.[57]

Everyone drew his or her own conclusions from the highway fight. Senator Harry Hughes of Oconee County determined that the governor, whom he called "the little Spartan lawyer," was a "despot," cynically willing to "magnif[y] . . . the [highway] issue to sweep himself in to the United States Senate." Another Johnston critic grumbled that the governor "abused his executive powers, disregarded the constitution, and defied (that honorable body) the state Supreme Court." The *Greenville News* dubbed him "Herr Johnston," and the *Greenville Piedmont* worried that an odious strain of "Talmadgism" had seeped across the Georgia border, infecting the governor with the virus of lawlessness. Others, including Barnwell state senator Edgar A. Brown, simply called Johnston a dictator.[58]

Something of a tyrant himself, Brown, the so-called Bishop of Barnwell, had joined a coterie of like-minded low-country lawmakers and a handful of legislators from other parts of the state with close ties to the business community to dominate the powerful state senate through a combination of longevity of service and backroom deals. Dominance of the senate gave them control of the supreme court. Brown's clique was also close to Sawyer and the highway department. This was a formidable assemblage of political clout. The alliance was strengthened by the fact that Brown and his allies in the senate, on the bench, and at the road bureau shared a common conservative ideology. Opposed to change unless they could manage it, they battled tooth and nail to uphold the status quo of white supremacy, cheap labor, low taxes (although bonds were okay), limited social services, antiunionism, states' rights, and the malapportionment of the general assembly.[59]

Then Olin Johnston came to the state capital preaching about the need for change. He talked of diverting authority away from the legislature to the chief executive's office. He also wanted to amplify the voices of workers in state affairs. Yet what made Johnston so scary to Brown and his conservative allies, much scarier than Blease, was his willingness, as demonstrated in the highway fight, to use every means necessary to push forward his agenda of "liberal democracy."

In the weeks, then months, then years after the highway war, Brown and his supporters made Johnston pay for his attack on their constitutionally safeguarded positions of privilege. Beginning with the Triple Road Bill, the conservative lawmakers reasserted the principle of legislative rule, hammering this point home whenever they could. Following the highway fight, the legislature curbed the governor's fiscal responsibilities, limited his authority to select judges, and reduced the number of his constabulary appointments. "That episode," Senator Brown said of the highway fight more than a decade later, "is one of the reasons the governor of South Carolina has less power today than he had before, and even before that he didn't have much."[60]

Like Brown, workers also worried about the spread of dictatorship. For them, democracy meant that power should be derived directly from the people: majority rules. Yet during the road war, democracy, in their eyes, stumbled as the few imposed their will on the many. "May you keep the fight up and place the responsibility where it belongs, [with] the general assembly," an Aiken man urged Johnston, adding that "ninety percent of the people in this county are with you." A Florence barber offered a more modest, but still pro-Johnston, assessment of the situation. He estimated that the governor had "100% support of 75% of the people." J. C. Vaughn reminded "the linthead critics" that Johnston had been elected by more than 35,000 votes. But from his vantage point, a minority of politicians, jurists, and road commissioners imposed their will on the majority.[61] Defeated in the legislature and the courts, Johnston's backers showed once again that they understood their world and searched for ways to alter the structure of government so the people could never again be "dictated" to by a selfish minority.

"Who most nearly represents the will of the people[,] the governor or legislators?" asked Wilton Hall, editor of the pro-Johnston *Anderson Independent*.[62] The answer was one of simple arithmetic; the majority of all white people voted for the governor. Yet it seemed to G. W. Anderson of the Horse Creek Valley that the "house and senate has tried to make Ben Sawyer Governor."[63] Orangeburg's J. Z. McConnell echoed this view. The general assembly, he charged, "by every means known . . . chicanery, parliamentary procedure and even intimidation" sought to "wrest all authority from the governor of our great old state." "For years," commented a prolabor newspaper, "the Senate has been a rain check on the Governor. What an absurdity for a Senator elected by possibly 2500 votes and often . . . less [to] stand in the way of a Governor elected by 150,000 votes." "The slogan is now," wrote one of the chief executive's more zealous boosters, "More Power to Johnston."[64]

"I think the Senate," a Spartanburg millhand complained, "has gone back on the people by not passing on legisla[tion] for which it was called to pass on regardless of personal views." More than the lower house, the senate remained the most imposing obstacle to Johnston's highway reorganization plan and, more significant, to labor legislation. In 1935 another South Carolinian bemoaned that senators whom he had no part in electing held a firm grip on his life. A low-country, prolabor legislator who labeled the senate a "stumbling block to progress" and "a refuge of privilege" advocated the abolishment of the upper house. Although only a handful of citizens favored such drastic measures, many certainly felt that the senate had too much power, and they wanted something done about it.[65]

Workers also identified the South Carolina Supreme Court as a bastion of antidemocratic sentiment. Events in Washington, perhaps more than what happened in Columbia, shaped their thinking on the judiciary. In the spring of 1933 the specter of shop floor slavery haunted mill people. Then, came the National Recovery Administration (NRA), a New Deal measure embraced by South Carolina workers as their "industrial declaration of independence."[66] On May 27, 1935, a day Roosevelt grimly called "Black Monday," the U.S. Supreme Court ruled the NRA unconstitutional.[67] Laborers feared that they were back to square one in the fight against industrial slavery. No longer did the Court seem like the unassailable bulwark of democracy described in grade school readers. "If a man has money he can do anything he pleases[,] kill, steal [and] get pardoned," an upcountry resident raged. "Yet when the President and Congress figured a way to help the poor . . . who were down and out they say it is unconstitutional." To those who spoke of the sanctity of the Supreme Court, he added, "We know that the writers of our constitution never intended it to be a hindrance to the welfare of the poor."[68] Working-class South Carolinians did not quickly forget the betrayal of the horse-and-buggy decision—again, Roosevelt's words—that killed the NRA.[69]

Millhands came to see the South Carolina Supreme Court in the same harsh light as the federal bench. Citing articles of the state constitution, the high court repeatedly blocked Johnston's moves during the highway fight. "There is a higher tribunal in South Carolina than the state supreme court and that is the court of public opinion," contended W. Fred Ponder, the poet Peter Moody's legislative adversary.[70] "The welfare of the public," Wilton Hall observed, "is paramount to any law and the voice of the people is the highest tribunal." The worker interviewed by Henry Steele Commager during his trip to the state told the historian that the court was packed and that there was no justice.[71] Another South Carolinian accused the high court of doing the dirty work of the state senate. In place of repeated military mobilizations to uphold the will of the people, some proposed using popular elections to fill the bench of the state supreme court. "Public opinion," argued the Citizens of McColl, "should direct the affairs of the state."[72] Only in this way would the courts truly represent the majority of citizens, not the interests of a few. This was what the highway fight had been about from the beginning. Who would run South Carolina?

In the end, discussions about the supreme court and the senate, the highway fight, and labor legislation were really debates about democracy and American political traditions. Forged from the writings of John Locke, select passages of the constitution, and the "tragic era" view of Reconstruction, one tradition, the one embraced by Edgar Brown and his cohorts, stressed the separation of powers. The senate and supreme court acted as a check against the despotism of a power-hungry leader and the tyranny of the unlearned masses. To millhands, this tradition was little more than a sanction for business as usual. The events of the first years of the New Deal and the Johnston administration demonstrated to them that the courts and the legislature acted less as counterweights to dictatorship than as obstacles to democracy. Too often, these institutions bolstered the privileged few—the blue bloods, the Magistrate Hickses, the Ben Sawyers, and the Peter Moodys—and blocked the mandate of the people.

Without issuing long manifestos or wearing bright badges, workers embraced another American political tradition, one that borrowed its ideas from Tom Paine, the Declaration of Independence, and New Deal liberals and highlighted an expansive notion of equality, at least for whites. Equality meant the right to a job, a decent home, and adequate clothing. Politically, workers expected to be treated like first-class white citizens who not only had the right to vote, but, just as important, the right to have each vote counted equally with power going to whoever had the support of the majority. Based on this version of equality, mill people concluded in the wake of the highway fight and other setbacks that only chief executives, both on the state and national levels, truly represented the will of the majority of the people. All power should, therefore, go to them.

CHAPTER ELEVEN

The Carpetbaggers
Are Coming

The 1938 Senate Race

 The carpetbaggers are coming. That is what some South Carolina conservatives said in 1938. According to these neo-Bourbons, wave after wave of carpetbaggers were pouring into the South aiming to turn the region into a socialist, communist, fascist—one could pick the peril—colony of the North. With the cold efficiency of a bulldozer plowing over an antebellum mansion, they had set out to eradicate the South's proud traditions of state's rights, patriarchy, local control, and white supremacy. What would happen next was almost too horrible to say. First, these sinister individuals would do away with Jim Crow laws. Next, African American men would tend looms in steamy factories, rubbing elbows with sweaty white women. Everyone would do the same work and everyone would be paid same. The color line would be erased. Social equality and miscegenation were sure to follow. Ultimately, the white race would be destroyed.[1]

"There is," a South Carolina newspaperman warned in 1938, "a long fight ahead of us. We are in graver danger than we were in 1876." That was because the new carpetbaggers had more money than the old Radical Republicans, and, worse, they were "shrewder." According to conservatives, the newcomers never came out and said exactly what they intended to do. They waved the flag while they undermined the U.S. Constitution. They talked abstractly of equality without mentioning African Americans, but they crept around trying to weaken white supremacy. Most alarming, they were more vindictive than their predecessors. If the carpetbaggers of the 1930s had their way, they would turn every white southerner into "little better than a slave." The same fierce unity that had "redeemed" the South in the nineteenth century would be needed to put down these new foes. It was time, conservatives announced, to revive the "spirit of '76"; for men to once again don "red shirts" and drive the Yankee invaders back across the Mason-Dixon line.[2]

Just who were these new carpetbaggers that so troubled South Carolina conservatives? They were New Dealers. Only a few lumped the president with this group. Most, instead, pointed an accusing finger at the champions of liberalism in the federal government, the NAACP, and the labor movement.

Charging New Dealers with treason was an unexpected turnabout, at least when viewed from the perspective of 1936. That year, President Franklin Roosevelt stood for reelection. During the summer and fall he crisscrossed the country pledging to establish a "democracy of opportunity for all the people." A vote for him, he said, was a vote for the New Deal.[3] By this measure, the New Deal won big. Roosevelt stormed to victory in every state but Maine and Vermont. In this landslide, no state in the nation was more firmly behind the president than South Carolina, which gave him a whopping 99 percent of its vote.[4] South Carolinians, it seemed, spoke with one voice for the New Deal and for the president. But this was before the antilynching bill, before the Congress of Industrial Organizations (CIO) went south, before the introduction of the Fair Labor Standards Act (FLSA), and before the purge of 1938. Together these developments gave rise to the siege mentality in South Carolina, to the fear that the carpetbaggers were coming and that social equality and intermarriage were sure to follow.

Not everyone in South Carolina anticipated a return of the carpetbaggers or wanted to revive the spirit of '76. Textile workers, in particular, continued to demand the same things they had demanded during the tense days of the general strike and the highway fight: first-class citizenship, new laws to spread out work and balance the distribution of power on the shop floor, and the centralization of authority in the hands of chief executives. Olin Johnston remained their main spokesperson. Still standing after his battle with Ben Sawyer and black belt conservatives, Johnston entered the 1938 U.S. Senate race broadcasting that he would run on a liberal, New Deal platform, at least where whites were concerned. His opponent was the incumbent, Senator "Cotton Ed" Smith, a man *Time* later called a "conscientious objector to the 20th century."[5]

Paralleling the lines of conflict in the highway fight, Johnston and Smith had come to represent two distinctly different visions of democracy. The senator railed against the excesses of New Deal liberalism. He saw the state

Olin D. Johnston chatting with another politician in 1943.
(Modern Political Collections, South Caroliniana Library,
University of South Carolina)

Democratic Party as white South Carolinians' last line of defense against an intrusive federal government. The governor, on the other hand, viewed it as the state's New Deal agent. Opposing the expansion of government power, Smith stood for the status quo and the maintenance of the South's political, economic, and cultural practices. By contrast, Johnston spoke for the cutting edge of national liberalism; he wanted to transform the political economy of the region through state action and trade unionism. Mirroring battles being played out nationwide pitting New Dealers against members of the emerging conservative coalition, the South Carolina Senate contest of 1938 became a referendum on the role of government in a racially and economically polarized society.[6] The keys to the election were how people defined themselves in terms of race, class, and gender.

When Ellison Durant Smith looked out at the world, he saw a different landscape than did Olin Johnston. He noticed cotton fields, not textile mills; he spotted small homesteads, not rows of company homes; and he saw callous-handed, bent-backed farmers toiling in the fields, not tired millhands leaving

The Carpetbaggers Are Coming

"Cotton Ed" Smith and his wife shaking hands with voters in 1944.
(South Caroliniana Library, University of South Carolina)

red brick factories. Smith's background, like Johnston's, molded his outlook
and provided material for a carefully crafted autobiography. Born in 1864 in
Lynchburg, a tiny town in Florence County where the sandhills meet the low
country, Smith, the son of a Methodist minister, grew up in modest comfort.
His family lived at Tanglewood, a small plantation or big farm, depending on
how you saw it, that had been handed down through several generations to
his father. Following stints at the University of South Carolina and Wofford
College and an apprenticeship as a full-time farmer, Smith became a politician. After only two undistinguished terms in the South Carolina House of
Representatives, he shocked the state's political establishment in 1908 by winning a seat in the U.S. Senate. There he remained for the next three and a
half decades.[7]

Civilization, Smith often remarked, rested on white supremacy, but day-
to-day life depended on agriculture, cotton agriculture to be precise. On the
stump, he paid homage to whiteness in both a racial and a commercial sense.
Wearing a wrinkled white linen suit with a big cotton boll pinned to the lapel,
the walrus-mustached senator rode to campaign rallies on a wagon stuffed

with cotton bales. After a local magistrate or some other well-known figure introduced him as "the farmer's friend," he sauntered to the middle of the stage and stood there for a moment soaking up the applause. As the clapping died out, he serenaded the crowd with "Cotton, Cotton, My Sweet." Obviously, his nickname—Cotton Ed—was another part of the performance.

"I am one of you," he always said. In a way, he was. Throughout his Senate career, he remained in charge of the family farm in Lynchburg and listed "dirt farmer" as his official occupation. Over the years, if cotton prices were high, Smith took credit; if they were low, the lawmaker, lifting a few lines from well-worn populist scripts, denounced Wall Street speculators, greedy railroad men, and crooked Yankee politicians. Federal programs, he argued, rarely provided rural people with the aid they needed because the lawyers in Congress knew nothing about farming. In 1926 he joked that his fellow senators were so ignorant of husbandry that when he called on one of them to support a nitrate soda bill, his colleague asked if that was "the stuff for cooking." No sense letting these people run the family farm, Smith would say with a smile. Rural audiences howled.

Next, Cotton Ed turned to race. He dredged up the imagined horrors of Reconstruction—black voting, corruption, and sexual assaults on white women. This is what would happen if Washington once again told southern men what to do. As he defined it, the job of a southern senator was to defend states' rights and make sure that the federal government stayed out of southern affairs. Summing up, Smith vowed to stand tall in the nation's capital as a farmer, a southerner, and a lonely "tobacco spitter" against all Yankee attacks on segregation and cotton culture.[8]

Smith did not say much about the status quo on the stump, but he believed in it as steadfastly as he did in Jim Crow and cotton. That the many should sweat for the few, that wages should remain low even for whites, and that the government could not do much to aid the poor—Smith never questioned these things. To him inequality was as natural as the seasons. He was, to borrow a phrase, a "born-aginner": against organized labor, against social welfare legislation, against progressive taxation, and against federal intervention. The Great Depression tested, but did not break, Cotton Ed's faith in lassiez-faire government. True to the end to the holy trinity of white supremacy, cotton, and states' rights, he fought to preserve the southern system of economic and racial privilege ahead of relief and recovery.[9]

When Roosevelt became president in March 1933, a crisis of overproduction battered the South. Unsold cotton exceeded the previous year's total world consumption, and another bumper crop lay in the fields, threatening to flood the already glutted market and push prices down to an all-time low.[10]

The Carpetbaggers Are Coming

Despite these problems, Cotton Ed Smith, then the head of the powerful Senate Agricultural Committee, saw no structural faults in the economic foundation. He blamed the farm depression instead on the weather, bankers, high tariffs, and discriminatory freight rates and advocated a program of currency inflation and temporary government guarantees to cover the cost of production along with the usual mixture of balanced budgets, lower taxes, and fiscal austerity.[11] FDR rejected Smith's timid conservatism in favor of the more ambitious schemes of his northern and midwestern agricultural advisers, like Henry Wallace. Hard times and World War I planning led these men to press for a permanent federal role in maintaining agricultural stability. The Agricultural Adjustment Act (AAA), passed by Congress in the spring of 1933, embodied many of their ideas.[12]

Based on the notion of planned scarcity—that is, of solving the riddle of want in the midst of plenty by removing the plenty—the AAA urged farmers to plow under crops and cut the number of acres under cultivation. Wallace and other New Dealers predicted that this would reduce supply, drive up prices, and boost income levels. Complaining that the original bill was "too complicated and required too much regimentation," Smith and his colleagues rewrote the legislation, especially the portions that affected the South. They made sure it would pour millions of federal dollars into their region without addressing the inequities of the plantation system.[13] Convinced that in the end the plan would not disrupt the status quo, Smith, still grumbling about this and that, finally put aside his reservations and voted for the AAA.[14]

With his vote for the AAA, Cotton Ed did not, however, join the ranks of zealous New Dealers. Although he tolerated federal projects that brought new highways, power plants, and opportunities for local patronage to the state, he opposed other, more ambitious initiatives launched during the Roosevelt administration's first one hundred days. Programs that expanded the size and scope of the federal government, giving it the power to regulate wages, commerce, banking, and relief, made Smith particularly nervous. Unlike his junior Senate colleague, James F. Byrnes, Cotton Ed did not hail the establishment of the CWA (Civilian Works Administration), TVA (Tennessee Valley Authority), NRA (National Recovery Administration), PWA (Public Works Administration), or any other alphabet agency.

In Smith's mind, Roosevelt was all too willing to take power away from scrupulous southern men and give it to shady New York liberals. As early as 1934 he started to voice his uneasiness with the New Deal, but the senator picked his fights carefully. Like Martha Gellhorn, he noticed the pictures of the president on his constituents' walls, and he knew that a direct attack on FDR would cost him mightily at the polls. Playing the game of guilt by association, he went after the president by ambushing his advisers, especially his eager, young, liberal Ivy League–educated aides.

Smith singled out Rexford Tugwell, a member of the president's brain trust, as his first New Deal punching bag.[15] According to the *New York Times*, the Columbia University professor "symbolized the New Deal." The South Carolina senator seemed to agree. Heir to populism's antipathy toward Wall Street and New York bankers as well as its razor-edged provincialism and thinly veiled anti-intellectualism, Smith imagined the "Big City" as both effete and menacing. Tugwell, with his golden tongue and gray flannel suits, epitomized cosmopolitan culture. To the senior senator, Tugwell's prominence in the Roosevelt administration represented a disturbing shift in the Democratic Party away from virile rural conservatism and toward amoral liberalism. He worried, for instance, that the professor's highfalutin ideas about resettling African American sharecroppers on wasted farmlands would reduce the supply of cheap labor in the South. During Tugwell's confirmation hearings for the post of undersecretary of agriculture in 1934, Smith fired question after question at the nominee: "Did you ever follow a plow?" "Did you ever have mud on your boots?" "Do you know how hard it is to get a dollar out of the soil?" The answers hardly mattered. The senator did not care that Tugwell had raised livestock or worked in the family orchard. Because he was not a "dirt farmer," the most important credential for the job, but a "window-sill agriculturist" who could not distinguish a "cotton stalk from a jimson weed," Smith opposed him. "He is a handsome, splendidly equipped gentleman," the senator said, taking a swipe at Tugwell's masculinity, "but throw him into the cotton fields and he would starve to death." Effete men like Tugwell could not, in Smith's mind, be trusted to take care of agricultural policy let alone white supremacy. From his position at the head of the agricultural committee, Smith held up Tugwell's appointment for weeks, forcing the president's men to ram the nomination through the full Senate.[16]

For Smith, Tugwell represented the takeover of the Democratic Party by arrogant northern liberals. Big-city folks were trying to tell rural people what to do with their farms. What about the next time? Maybe some bureaucrat or some intellectual would try to tell southerners how to deal with African Americans. After all, Smith noted, African Americans were gaining power in the national Democratic Party. He was alarmed that the president occasionally met with members of the so-called Black Kitchen Cabinet at the White House and that his relief schemes did not discriminate, at least not enough for Smith.[17]

By 1934 Smith was developing a sense of regional victimization. In his mind, southern control of the Democratic Party was ebbing as northern liberals, foreign-born big-city bosses, and African Americans increasingly held positions of authority. At the same time, an overbearing federal government, acting under the New Deal's reformist guise, oppressed the South, disrespecting its traditions and customs. Southerners, in other words, not African Americans or the poor, were the real victims in the 1930s. The introduction by Senators Edward Costigan of Colorado and Robert Wagner of New York of an antilynching bill confirmed Smith's suspicions that New Deal Democrats held the South in contempt.

Originally drafted by Walter White and his staff at the NAACP, the Costigan-Wagner bill would have empowered the federal government to prosecute lynchers when state courts did not do so and to levy fines against the county in which the crime took place with the proceeds going to the victim's family. No respectable southerner, Senator Smith claimed, condoned lynching.[18] But the proponents of the Costigan-Wagner bill did not really care about the offense either; instead, they willingly dived into the "dregs and scum of politics in a miserable effort to get negro votes." Big-city politicians were so hungry for the black community's approval that, according to Cotton Ed, they were eager to humiliate the South—"the section . . . that kept the Democratic fires burning on the nation's political altar during the long years of Republican rule."[19]

"Long-haired men and short-haired women" drafted the noxious legislation, Smith theorized on one occasion, which, in turn, reminded him "of the iniquitous Force Bill." The Force bill, furthermore, recalled Reconstruction, when "every element of society was threatened with debasement and extinction." Smith infused his account of that era with sexual, almost pornographic, imagery. The immediate postbellum years, he said, were marked by an "unspeakable orgy of lawlessness, corruption, and vice." "[L]ust" filled the legislature, and carpetbaggers "prostituted" elected offices. He promised to protect "southern womanhood" as well as to carry out his solemn duty as a southern gentleman and senator to defend the region against the "obnoxious and unconstitutional" offensive of congressional liberals. Back in Washington, Smith and other southern conservatives, invoking the glories of the Redeemers, filibustered the antilynching bill to death.[20]

Then came the 1936 Democratic National Convention in Philadelphia. Late in arriving, Smith, the nation's most senior senator, rushed over to the convention. On reaching his seat, he looked up to see Marshall L. Shepard, a local African American minister, delivering the evening's benediction. Smith leaped from his chair and stormed out of the hall, telling trailing reporters that "this mongrel meeting ain't no place for a white man."[21]

The next day Smith rejoined his fellow South Carolina Democrats, but only, he said, to ward off an attempt by northern liberals and labor officials to jettison the party's two-thirds rule. For nearly a century, a Democratic presidential aspirant had needed two-thirds of the votes of convention delegates to win the nomination. In this way, the solid South held a virtual veto over all candidates. Smith failed to save this rule of procedure. Soon after its defeat, Illinois congressman Arthur Mitchell, an African American, addressed the delegates. Again, Smith bolted from the convention, this time for good. When Franklin Roosevelt delivered his acceptance address in Philadelphia, chiding "economic royalists" and decrying "industrial dictatorship," Cotton Ed was off fishing in the South Carolina backwoods. Before he left, though, he had fired off a few parting shots. True South Carolinians, he hollered, could not remain in a "political organization that looks upon the Negro and caters to him as a political and social equal" because it would lead to "intermarriage and . . . the mongrelization of the American race."[22]

After Philadelphia, there was no going back for Smith. He interpreted every move by New Deal liberals as an attempt to humiliate the South. Just about everything reminded him of Reconstruction. The Roosevelt administration's efforts to bolster the authority of the executive branch looked to Cotton Ed like a naked attack on states' rights. The president's plan to restructure the Supreme Court was another assault. "It is the keystone of the arch to our form of government," Smith said of the high court. "Every American should resist with all the power in him any attempt to subject the Supreme Court . . . to the plane of politics." Behind Smith's objections was the conviction that the Court served as a check against the New Deal's electoral popularity. If Roosevelt got his way on this matter, like he had on the two-thirds rule, another of the region's defenses would be down. The carpetbagger's march through the South would be that much easier.[23]

Smith's running feud with the New Dealers heated up again in 1937, when Alabama senator Hugo Black, a liberal not just in southern terms, introduced the Fair Labor Standards Act. Promoters of the bill said it would spread employment and spark purchasing power by fixing a maximum workweek and mandating a national minimum wage, but Cotton Ed sensed a different agenda. "Any man on the floor," he lectured his fellow senators, "who has sense enough to read the English language knows the main objective of this bill is by human legislation, to overcome the splendid gifts of God to the South." "If South Carolina's living conditions are so kindly that it takes only fifty cents a day, for illustration," while it "costs three times as much to live" in New England, that was no reason to triple southern wages. Hiding behind the mask of kindhearted liberalism, mercenary northern politicians wanted to use the FLSA to weaken states' rights and cripple the southern textile industry. "All our cotton mills have gone South," Smith said one of his colleagues told him, "and we want them back." The South Carolinian also grumbled that the hours and wages bill would force employers to pay whites and blacks exactly the same wages. Farmers would lose out as well. The legislation, he predicted, would increase retail prices, making it impossible for rural families to afford the basic "necessities of life." Citing his senatorial duty to protect his region from federal encroachment, Smith battled against the FLSA through two congressional sessions, leading several filibusters, before the bill finally won approval in 1938.[24]

If the Fair Labor Standards Act worried Smith, the rise of the CIO scared the daylights out of him. Founded in 1935, when John L. Lewis of the United Mine Workers plastered William "Big Bill" Hutcheson of the Carpenter's Union with a stiff right hook at the convention hall along the Atlantic City boardwalk, the CIO beat a different organizational path than the American Federation of Labor (AFL).[25] Built around a constellation of craft unions, the AFL mostly represented the "aristocracy of labor," relatively well-paid, largely white, older, skilled workers: plumbers, musicians, machinists, and tool and die makers. Semiskilled machine tenders, the women and men who ran the nation's largest and most modern factories, remained without a voice in the venerable labor federation. The CIO stepped into this void, committing itself to bringing industrial wage earners—miners, meatpackers, mill-hands, and steel workers—into the house of labor. The differences between the AFL and the CIO did not stop there. Whereas the AFL kept radicals at arm's length, the CIO offered membership to just about anyone willing to join. In fact, Communist Party loyalists and fellow travelers held key posts in a number of affiliated unions. At the same time, the CIO, recognizing that organizing the factories required bringing African American workers into the labor movement, explicitly barred discrimination and trumpeted racial equality. Deeds did not always match words, but through unionization drives that reached out to African American community groups, churches, and civil rights organizations, the CIO revived an older tradition of biracial unionism that the AFL had allowed to lapse.[26]

Projecting an image of "manly strength," the CIO steadily grew during its first eighteen months of existence.[27] Then came the Flint sit-down strike. For forty-five days between December 1936 and February 1937, determined members of the United Auto Workers (UAW) occupied several General Motors (GM) factories seeking union recognition. Twice the automobile giant tried, and failed, to secure injunctions to oust the men. Professing neutrality, President Roosevelt made it clear that he would not intercede, and Michigan governor Frank Murphy refused to mobilize the militia to recapture the plants.

Pressed by financial constraints magnified by its interlocking industrial structure, GM finally capitulated and signed a contract with the UAW. During the next six months, workers across the country staged 170 sit-down strikes. The editors of *Time* magazine worried that sitting down had replaced marathon dancing and miniature golf as the nation's latest craze. Whatever journalists thought, this new form of protest proved to be an effective organizing tool. Workers in the coal mines and garment factories, steel mills and rubber plants joined the CIO after the Flint strike. By the time of its second anniversary in March 1937, the new union federation had nearly 3 million members, almost as many as the AFL. At the same time, it dominated the news. Scarcely a day went by when the CIO and its daring, grandiloquent leader, John L. Lewis, did not appear in the headlines. Reporters marveled, and sometimes cringed, at the group's militancy, bravery, and virility.[28]

From the outset, the CIO was as much a political movement as a trade union. Recognizing, as South Carolina workers did, the need for a prolabor, or at least neutral, state, Lewis eschewed the AFL's outdated creed of voluntarism, or trade union political nonengagement. In 1936 Lewis's United Mine Workers raised more money for the president's reelection campaign than any other organization. The union leader regarded his contributions as a payback for past favors, such as the Wagner Act, and as a down payment for future actions, and he made no secret of his intention to cash in on his investment. Throughout Roosevelt's second term, the CIO remained politically active, supporting the administration's liberal programs and trying to nudge it further toward the left.[29]

Recasting the nation's political economy stood at the top of the CIO's reform agenda, and the South figured prominently in this strategy. To union leaders like Sidney Hillman of the Amalgamated Clothing Workers, the region's abysmally low wages weakened the purchasing power of workers everywhere. Redressing this problem, Hillman argued, required establishing a national minimum wage along with unionizing the textile industry. Not only would the organization of the mills and federal labor legislation raise wages in the South, but together they would help to build an electoral base for liberal-labor candidates in the region. Better-paid, unionized workers, Hillman anticipated, would reject conservative lawmakers like Cotton Ed Smith, voting instead for New Deal candidates such as Olin Johnston. Once in office, men like Johnston were sure to support additional labor laws, making it easier to organize other workers, which in turn would strengthen liberalism and the CIO.[30]

In July 1937, five months after bearded UAW militants marched out of the Flint factory with a contract in their hands, the CIO moved into South Carolina. The union movement arrived under the banner of the Textile Workers Organizing Committee (TWOC), an alliance between the United Textile Workers of America (UTW), which had left the AFL, and several other unions. Like its forerunners, the new textile labor force immediately looked southward. Organizing the textile industry, TWOC leaders recognized, meant cracking Dixie.[31] As summer began, dozens of southern organizers and a handful of northerners fanned out across the mill hills of the Piedmont, preaching the message of trade unionism and the social gospel.[32] Management answered the challenge with a familiar carrot-and-stick approach. Within weeks of the TWOC's arrival, nearly all of South Carolina's two hundred mills boosted wages between 5 and 10 percent and cut the workweek from fifty to forty hours.[33] At the same time, mill owners and the press tagged the TWOC and its supporters enemies of all that was decent, white, and southern. The CIO's identification with the left, militant sit-down strikers, and African American trade unionists made it an easy target in the South. CIO members were branded communists, no matter what their political affiliation. When white southerners spoke of communism, they were thinking less of Karl Marx and more of social equality; when they thought of social equality, they thought of Reconstruction; when they thought of Reconstruction, they thought of racial disorder; and when they thought of racial disorder, they thought of black men and white women.[34] By this logic the CIO advocated free love and miscegenation, not higher wages and better conditions. Obviously such people had to be stopped.

South Carolina newspapers led the charge against the TWOC and the CIO. Loyal to the crimson banner of communism ahead of the American flag, an upcountry editor insisted that the CIO would "run this country quite differently," most notably, by ending all "race distinctions."[35] Egged on by press reports about free love, crazed sit-down strikers, and bomb-throwing communists, the South Carolina General Assembly thought about barring John L. Lewis from the state and levying a crippling tax on all dues paid to "foreign labor organizations."[36]

With the TWOC holding rallies in Spartanburg and Seneca, Clover and Chesnese, and with his reelection campaign less than a year away, Smith joined the attack against the CIO. According to Cotton Ed, the CIO was the bastard amalgamation of all that was wrong with the Yankee New Deal. It ridiculed the South and expressed an alarming contempt for white supremacy. But because of its combativeness and aggressive manliness the CIO, the senator exhorted, had to be taken seriously. Playing a game of word association, Smith, when asked about the CIO, retorted, "John L. Lewis, sit-downers, foreigners, Communists, and equality with Negroes." He warned that after the TWOC organized the mills, white textile workers would "be replaced by Negroes at the looms." Next, "John L. Lewis," "Yankee Negroes," and their "un-American" followers would snatch control of the state away from "true Democrats." Applying the familiar doctrine of guilt by association, Smith accused New Dealers and those who won the CIO's backing of the same crimes. In his view, supporting industrial trade unionism was the same as supporting communism, and communists were nothing more than carpetbaggers dressed in the latest big-city fashions, committed to bringing white women and African American men together. Appealing to white citizens' identities as white South Carolinians first and foremost, Smith tried to cut the string that tied state Democrats, especially millhands, to Roosevelt, Johnston, the New Deal, and the CIO.[37]

While Cotton Ed Smith distanced himself from the New Deal, Olin Johnston veered closer to the CIO's version of economic, although not racial, liberalism. In 1936 Johnston wrote a third-person magazine article, entitled "Olin D. Johnston: Labor's Governor," in which he talked about his youth in the mills. After chasing up and down rows of looms for years on end, Johnston was sure that he grasped the "problems that daily confront those who work with their hands for a living." Neither financial nor political success, the essay maintained, erased his proletarian identity. "One of his pet prides today is his ability to repair a loom, put a spooler in operation, take off bobbins, and guide other intricate machinery." Speaking to trade unionists in 1937, he bragged about his working-class background and extolled wage earners' contributions to society. "The foundation stone of America's greatness is the working man," he declared, "he is the man upon whom we all depend." "As a working man myself," Johnston summed up, "Your problems are my problems, and your joys are my joys."[38]

Johnston offered workers more than rhetorical identification. He emerged as South Carolina's leading advocate of a laborite political economy, and he did so virtually without mentioning race. Maintaining that Roosevelt had the best interests of white wage earners in mind, he disregarded the widely presumed lessons of Reconstruction and supported concentrating power in the White House. He praised the Executive Reorganization Act and the president's plan to alter the Supreme Court.[39] He backed each of the administration's tentative steps toward building a welfare state, especially the Social Security Act. The governor also talked the anti–big business talk of New Deal liberals. "The rich men have cried out," he wrote, "because some of them had to dig into their fortunes to pay higher taxes . . . [and] . . . sacrifice a few of their luxuries so that more humble people could have jobs and something to eat." They called "Roosevelt . . . extravagant" and said that "he is an imitator of Moscow." Rubbish, Johnston asserted. "Every champion of the rights of the common man has received such ridicule and malicious abuse."[40]

Never much of a theoretician himself, Johnston nonetheless accepted the economic analysis of liberals like Rexford Tugwell who blamed the Great Depression on the maldistribution of wealth. Johnston's own view of the economic catastrophe went something like this: Following World War I, "modern factories [became] marvels of efficiency and organization." Output and profits soared. But business leaders did not pass a "fair share" of the rewards of the new economic order on to labor. Instead, they stretched out workers and left too many consumers with too little money. As purchasing power dwindled, the economy ground to a halt, and in a shameful moral irony, people went hungry as crops rotted in the fields and goods piled up in stores. Fair wages and full employment, Johnston repeatedly stated, would ensure economic health and stability, whereas low wages and joblessness would trigger endless depression and enable a few "malcontents" and members of the Liberty League to profit at the expense of others.[41] Unafraid of putting economic power in the hands of the federal government, Johnston called for massive state intervention to boost purchasing power.[42]

"I am not speaking tonight for the working man alone," the governor began a 1937 radio speech in support of the Fair Labor Standards Act, "but . . . for the general welfare of all our people." Higher wages for labor would usher in an era of prosperity, but capital, blinded by short-term greed, could not be trusted to protect society's, or even its own, long-range interests. Insisting that southerners should make as much as northerners as a matter of principle, he argued that the more they made, the more they could spend, and the more they spent, the faster the nation would climb out of the depression. Addressing farmers' skepticism about the bill, Johnston said that the purchasing power of labor governed crop prices. "When the working man gets a decent wage," he reasoned, "the farmer, the merchant, and everybody else prospers." "The only way to circulate money is to release it into the hands of the people who spend it, and the only way to release it is to give people [who] work . . . a decent compensation for what they do." Higher wages alone were not enough. Reduced hours were necessary to create more jobs.[43] Beginning in 1936, Johnston spearheaded a campaign for a forty-hour workweek in South Carolina's textile mills. Together, he forecast, state and federal labor reforms would end the "slave-driving" of workers by "greedy employers."[44]

Johnston's campaign for a more equitable economic order reached in several different directions. Blaming the Great Depression on selfish Republicans and business leaders, he pressed for state action against monopolies. This was not to say, as some critics charged, that he envisioned ending private ownership of the means of production. Rather, he wanted the government to rebuild the economy so it would function in the interests of labor, not capital; the many, not the few. Johnston also urged workers to organize. Labor unions, operating as a check on rapacious factory owners, could, the governor believed, play a key role in bolstering purchasing power and fashioning a more equitable capitalist system both in South Carolina and nationwide.[45]

Johnston's faith in trade unionism eventually led him to support the CIO. When TWOC organizers first entered South Carolina in March 1937, editors and politicians pressed the governor to say what he thought of the new labor organization. Trying to avoid alienating potential supporters, he initially kept quiet. Many interpreted his silence as a tacit endorsement. "Is Governor Johnston a member of the CIO, an honorary member?" asked the editor of the *Union Daily Times*. "It would not be surprising!" Over the next six months, thousands of South Carolina millhands signed TWOC membership cards. But just as the CIO offensive was picking up momentum—winning a contract covering the Marlboro Mills' three plants in McColl and Bennettsville—the "Roosevelt recession" hit.[46] With this sharp economic downturn came widespread unemployment and deep wage cuts in the textile industry. The collapse in production stalled the South Carolina unionization campaign.[47]

With the union drive disabled, Johnston, hoping to jump-start the campaign, made public his support for the Textile Workers Organizing Committee. Speaking at the TWOC's "On to Victory" rally in Columbia, he announced that he was behind the CIO's push to organize the textile industry and its fight for shorter hours, higher wages, and better living conditions.[48] One month later, the governor once again tried to use his limited authority to aid trade unionists. He offered TWOC organizers in Gaffney—an area once described as "the roughest place this side of Harlan County"—the use of a state armory building after local ruffians attacked them with pipes and rocks and the sheriff would not guarantee their safety if they returned.[49]

Johnston's public support for the CIO enraged many, but none, it seems, more than the Greenville Ku Klux Klan (KKK). Blending race and class fears into an explosive mix, these upcountry night riders combined racist vigilantism with antiunion harassment. Made up largely of "second hands, overseers, superintendents, and scabs," the KKK had a long history of harassing prolabor workers in Greenville. When the TWOC entered the area in 1937, the Klan tried to hamper the union drive and even took a shot at Johnston.[50] In a letter leaked to the press, Grand Klakard Fred V. Johnson ordered the governor to clarify his views on the CIO. Did his actions in Gaffney and Columbia mean that he advocated "the unlawful seizure of property, lawlessness, bloodshed . . . [and] . . . Communism?" No, Johnston shot back, he did not believe in such alien notions, but he did proudly support "any organization . . . devoted to the improvement of the living conditions of the working people of the State, the shortening of the hours of labor and the increase of wages so long as they do not violate the laws and statutes of South Carolina."[51]

As expected, Cotton Ed Smith and Olin Johnston entered the 1938 Senate race. A third candidate, state senate kingpin Edgar A. Brown, also joined the campaign. A powerhouse inside the general assembly, the Barnwell lawmaker also had experience in statewide contests. In 1926 he had run for the U.S. Senate and narrowly lost to Smith. Now, twelve years later, he jumped into the battle again, praising President Roosevelt and boasting that he could bring home more federal "bacon" than anyone else. His formidable credentials not withstanding, Brown's candidacy never took off.[52]

Fittingly, Johnston kicked off his campaign on the steps of the White House. Following lunch with two prominent Senate southern liberals, Florida's Claude Pepper and Alabama's Lister Hill, and a conference with Roosevelt, the governor formally declared what was already widely known in South Carolina, that he would challenge Smith for his Senate seat. Allegiance to FDR and the New Deal, Johnston predicted, would be the main issues in the contest. For his part, the governor proclaimed himself to be "one-hundred percent" behind the "reforms and policies of President Roosevelt."[53]

Johnston's promise of unflinching fidelity to the New Deal earned him the backing of liberals across the state and the nation. But none of these endorsements proved to be as vexing as the one he received from the Labor's Nonpartisan League (LNPL), a forerunner of the modern political action committee and an organization, despite its name, with much closer ties to the liberal CIO than the more moderate AFL. Late in the spring of 1938, the LNPL placed Senator Smith at the top of its congressional hit list and pledged funds and volunteers to the Johnston campaign. The CIO's craft union rivals, the AFL and the railroad brotherhoods, responded by supporting the incumbent.[54]

Like a veteran boxer sensing a weak spot, Smith pounded away at Johnston's LNPL-CIO backing, economic liberalism, and "one-hundred-percentism." Jabbing him with scorn, the senator swung as hard as he could at his opponent's manhood. Because Johnston was not his "own man," but "a yes, yes, me too man," the senator charged, he had to go "creeping up to Washington to see if he could run." Throughout the race Smith referred to him as one of "those . . . things running against me" and on one occasion depicted him as a "beautiful one-hundred percenter." Bobbing and weaving across campaign stages, Smith hit at the governor's independence, which, according to him, formed the core of manly virtue. Johnston clung so tightly to "Frank" Roosevelt's coattails, Smith sneered, "that he didn't know the way the man whose coat-tails he is swinging on is going." By challenging Johnston's masculinity, the senator also questioned the Honea Path native's commitment to white supremacy. "This yes-yes man endorsed the nigger, and went one hundred percent for anything belonging to the New Deal, right or wrong, because he does not have guts enough to disagree." Asserting his own independence, Smith bragged, "God gave me a head and I am going to use it. . . . I'm one-hundred percent for everything I think is right for my state and the nation under the Constitution, and one-hundred-and-ten percent against what I think is wrong."[55]

If Johnston was a one-hundred percenter, Smith asked, did that mean that he favored such wild government extravagances as "the federal housing bill, seven or eight TVAs, [and] permanent relief for the unemployed"? Did it mean that he supported the takeover of the Democratic Party by big-city bosses and immigrants from the North? Did he approve of John L. Lewis and his sit-down-crazed associates "dictating" policy to the president? Did he agree with the CIO that "blacks shall be in your schools and in your factories"? Did he condone communism, free love, and interracial marriage? After all, Smith reminded his audiences, LNPL—that "Yankee Nigger Gang"—espoused these values and they backed Johnston, and as he understood it, they did not give away their money for nothing. If Johnston was a one-hundred percenter did he approve of "obnoxious and unconstitutional anti-lynching laws?" Hadn't the governor's father told him, Cotton Ed wondered, about the horrors of Reconstruction, when "black feet pressed on white heads . . . [and] . . . the flowers of the solid South?"[56]

As soon as Smith raised the flag of white supremacy, someone in the stump crowd would holler: "Ed tell us about Philydephy!" The senator would feign resistance. "I have been trying to keep this campaign on a high plane," he would say, looking away. Then another spectator would demand to hear what had happened at the convention, and then another and another until Smith mumbled something like, "Well, okay if you really want to hear about it." There would be loud cheers from the audience. Starting off slowly, his voice low and serious, he quickly got rolling:

[W]hen I came out on the floor of that great hall, bless God, it looked like a checkerboard—a spot of white here, and a spot of black there. But I kept going, down that long aisle, and finally I found the great standard of South Carolina—and, praise God, it was in a spot of white!

I had no sooner than taken my seat when a newspaper man came down the aisle and squatted down by me and said, "Senator, did you know a nigger is going to come out up yonder in a minute and offer the invocation?" I told him, I said, "Now don't be joking me, I'm upset enough the way it is." But, then, Bless God, out on that platform walked a slew-footed, blue-gummed, kinky-headed Senegambian!

And he started praying and I started walking. And as I pushed through those great doors, and walked across that vast rotunda, it seemed to me that Old John Calhoun leaned down from his mansion in the sky and whispered, "You did right, Ed."

Smith mopped the sweat off his brow. The crowd clapped and yelled "pour it on." They recognized a good show when they saw one.[57]

Johnston had a tough fight on his hands. Some said Cotton Ed was the best stump speaker ever to barnstorm across South Carolina, better even than Ben Tillman and Cole Blease. Although Johnston was not in the same league as these storytellers, he was no pushover. Six-feet-four-inches tall and well over two hundred pounds, the governor had a booming voice. When it was his turn to speak, he would take a few long steps up to the podium and start to retell his life story. Always looking for a way to make contact with the crowd, he would stop right in the middle and call out to someone in the audience: "Isn't that you Roy Lee Brooks? How are you? And how is that daughter of yours, Bertha?" Next came the attack.[58]

Turning and pointing his finger at Smith, Johnston would shout: "There is the sleeping Senator." When vital farm legislation came before Congress, where was Cotton Ed, the farmer's best friend? he asked. "Out of town," he shot back, just as he was in 1936 when it was time for him to vote for President Roosevelt's reelection. "Your senior senator hasn't done anything for you"; instead, the governor charged, "he just about put all of the cotton farmers out of business." Workers would be even worse off if Smith had his way. "Is it undemocratic," Johnston asked, "for our government to say that a mill worker should receive enough to feed and cloth his family and save them from destitution and want?" Touching on Cotton Ed's opposition to the hours and wages law, he scoffed, "If Olin Johnston ever says that laborers can live on fifty cents, I'll either be crazy or I'll never have the nerve or gall to face you people again."[59]

Having done nothing for the people of South Carolina, Smith, Johnston warned, was trying to slip into office on the race question. Unlike some New Deal liberals, Johnston did not defend the rights of African Americans. Yet he rarely played the race card. Insisting that the race issue was a false one and that it had been settled years earlier by Wade Hampton and Ben Tillman, he laughed, "It's a joke to me, [y]ou don't find Senator Smith trying to ride into the Senate on a cotton bale these days, he's trying to ride in on a poor nigger."[60] With the same contempt, he brushed aside Smith's harangues about the antilynching law: "A northern senator introduced the anti-lynching law . . . to get negro votes," but "every real Southerner is opposed to . . . the bill and it's not an issue in this campaign." For anyone still worried about his loyalty to Jim Crow, the governor pointed out that he had signed a law earlier that year making sure that "no negro will vote." Toward the end of the campaign, Johnston even race-baited Smith, the master himself, by accusing the senator of supporting Alexander Haskell's 1892 biracial challenge to Tillman. But these were sideshows; the governor tried to keep the contest tightly focused on the New Deal and class issues.[61]

"Shall we the people of South Carolina," Johnston asked, "elect to represent the most Democratic state in the union a senator opposed to . . . Franklin Delano Roosevelt?" No matter what Smith said, Johnston remained "100 percent for the humanitarian policies of Franklin Roosevelt." "I would be a traitor to my people," he proclaimed, "if I wasn't with Roosevelt in his great program." Before the New Deal, he continued, the sound of failing banks echoed across the land, hungry mothers and children waited in breadlines, and desperate fathers walked desolate roads searching for work. "Hooveriteindividualism," Johnston contended, caused this suffering. "This great individualist," he said of Smith, "means that if you are blind, you should stay that way, if you are too old and without means of support you should be left to shift for yourself." "Thank God," Johnston declared, that he and the president embraced a different outlook; they saw themselves as "my brothers' keepers" and recognized a "moral responsibility to [their] fellow man." Through the NRA, the Works Progress Administration (WPA), rural electrification, the Civilian Conservation Corps (CCC), the introduction of social security, the hours and wages law, and the establishment of a stable banking system, people's spirits had been lifted, purchasing power had expanded, and families had food on their tables. Johnston bragged that his administration had done all that it could, and then some, to aid the president's "humanitarian" mission.[62]

Fighting to bring a New Deal to South Carolina, Johnston, of course, made some enemies, and not just in the highway department. But he did not care; in fact, he welcomed them. "I expect the big interests to fight me," he said on one occasion. "When the forty hour week law came up," he boasted, "the manufacturer did not like it, I went before the committee and we passed it and I signed it." Then he asked: "Whom do you think the big interests want to see elected this year? Whom do you think the capitalist press wants to see elected?" "They don't want Olin Johnston," the governor proudly declared. In another town, he joked that if someone walked up to "the big man and asked him what he thinks of me . . . he will probably want to kick me in the pants. . . . But ask the little man, the farmer, the mill worker, he is for me."[63]

As Smith and Johnston slugged it out in town after town in the heat of the South Carolina summer of 1938, Roosevelt contemplated a break with tradition. Two years earlier he had scored one of the greatest landslides in American electoral history. A slew of Democrats rode into power on his coattails. In the House, 330 Democrats, 8 Progressives, and 5 Farmer-Labor Party members faced off against 89 Republicans, and in the Senate all but 16 were Democrats. But despite FDR's popularity, lawmakers refused to follow his legislative lead. Of the president's half-dozen "must" proposals for 1937, only the housing bill cleared every congressional hurdle. Among the five others, the restructuring of the Supreme Court was scrapped in the face of certain defeat, crop controls were held over until the next session, the hours and wages act was tabled, the executive reorganization scheme was rejected, and the regional conservation program was ignored. (The farm bill and the FLSA passed the next year.) Much of the legislation was killed by an emerging conservative coalition of Republicans and southern Democrats. Some of Roosevelt's aides urged him to take his case for a more cooperative Congress directly to the American people where his support was strongest. Eventually, he decided to follow this advice. During a fireside chat in June 1938, the president told the nation that he planned to speak out against conservatives, even if they were members of his own party, pointing out who was a New Dealer and who was not.[64]

Roosevelt's contempt for Smith's reactionary politics was well known. As the South Carolina primary approached, however, no one knew whether he would intervene. Meanwhile, a great deal of politicking went on behind the scenes.[65] Senator James F. Byrnes and several of the president's closest advisers opposed his entry into the Palmetto State Senate race, but Roosevelt had a mind of his own.[66] On August 10, addressing a rural electrification celebration in Georgia, the president showed his hand. Like its northern neighbor, the Peach State was embroiled in a tight Senate race that pitted an incumbent conservative anti–New Dealer—Walter F. George—against a young liberal—Lawrence Camp.[67] "My friends," FDR began with his familiar greeting, "the senior senator from this state cannot in my judgment be classified as belonging to the liberal school of thought." Then he dropped the bomb: "I am impelled to make it clear that on most public questions he and I do not speak the same language. I most assuredly would vote for Lawrence Camp." Following the speech, the president told reporters that he was heading to South Carolina, where he planned to "go out on the platform" and say "how do you do" the next day in Greenville.[68]

Fifteen thousand people waited for Roosevelt in Greenville. Millworkers made up the bulk of the crowd. They held up placards that read "Our Friends: Olin D. and Franklin D." and "A Vote For Olin D. Is a Vote for Franklin D.— We Need Them Both." The Presidential Express finally pulled into town around midnight, nearly two hours later than expected.[69] When FDR stepped to the rear of the train, he was accompanied by Brown, Johnston, Smith, and a few other state officials, but the press soon learned that only the governor had accompanied him all the way from Georgia; the others had climbed aboard just outside of Greenville. Governor Johnston introduced the president to the drowsy crowd "as a man who has meant so much to the people of the United States." "Some of you," Roosevelt began, "may have heard what I said down in Georgia." For those who did not, he reiterated his plea "for more team work in Washington." "If you believe in the principles for which we are striving," he continued, the wider "distribution of natural resources," increased "purchasing power," and the establishment "of a definite floor under wages . . . then I hope that you will send representatives to the national legislature who will work toward that end." Turning toward the grinning governor, he pledged to "come down this year to visit the capital." Roosevelt then backed away from the microphone. The train whistle squealed and the engine started to grind. Just then, FDR edged back to the rostrum, adding, "You don't impress me as being a people willing to work for fifty cents a day as one of your Senators has said." Suddenly the train jerked forward, ripping the microphone cord out of its socket. The sound went dead, and the president never finished his address.[70]

Over the next few days, South Carolinians debated the meaning of FDR's remarks in Greenville. Johnston treated them as an outright endorsement. "I am for the President and you know now whom he is for." Reminding people that he got on the train first, the governor said, "I guess you know whom he is friendly with—you saw who rode with him, you saw who introduced him." Recalling the fiery rhetoric of the highway fight, Johnston once again detected a subtext of class hostility in the reactions to the event. "Some of the bluebloods of South Carolina," he suggested, "are jealous because he [FDR] . . . sent an invitation to Olin Johnston to come over and ride on the train with him."[71]

The Smith team put their own spin on the president's speech. FDR, they pointed out, never referred to Johnston by name, as he had Georgia's Lawrence Camp. "It is to be assumed," editorialized a pro-Smith newspaper, "that Governor Johnston is still in the race for the US Senate. Even so, President Roosevelt, his alleged sponsor . . . made no mention of the matter as he skirted through South Carolina . . . fishing for 'yes men' in the US Senate."[72] Smith also defended himself against the fifty-cents-a-day shot. Insisting that FDR had misquoted him, he maintained that his statement about wages had been a defense of the South's natural advantages, not an endorsement of low pay. Yet he did not blame the president for the confusion. Roosevelt, he charged, had been duped into repeating "falsehoods" passed along by "my opponents" — "those terrible coat-tail riders." Trying to take the sting out of FDR's remarks, Smith mailed out 20,000 copies of his Senate floor speech about the FLSA, which he thought cleared up the matter. He also read from it on the stump.[73]

Cotton Ed, in addition, tried to identify with labor. Sometimes the strategy worked; other times it did not. "I am a working man," Smith told 5,000 Spartanburg residents. The crowd "broke into wild laughs." Smith turned bright red. Despite the rebuff in the textile belt, the senator never failed to mention his endorsements from the racially exclusive AFL and railroad brotherhoods, and he took every opportunity to remind crowds that the CIO supported his opponent. "The AFL is supporting Smith and the CIO is opposing him—Enough Said," headlined a Smith advertisement. Just in case this was not, in fact, enough said, the handbill explained that the senator was "opposed to the Communistic influence which dominates the CIO—an organization that lobbied for the anti-lynching bill and favors putting negro workers in factories side by side with white employees."[74]

Broadening his attack, Cotton Ed portrayed Roosevelt's, and the CIO's, intervention in the contest as an assault on white supremacy. In so doing, he once again dredged up the inflated glories of the Civil War and the imagined horrors of Reconstruction. Comparing the actions of the president and the CIO to the original invasion of the carpetbaggers, Smith vowed to resist any attempt by liberal politicians and labor activists to take over South Carolina.[75]

Meanwhile, the president's brief speech in Greenville created turmoil in the Brown camp. On August 27, three days before the primary, the Barnwell senator, trapped in what he tabbed "the unfortunate position of the third man," withdrew from the race. When he learned of this development, Roosevelt briefly commented that Brown's exit "clarifies the issue." On the eve of the primary, the president again addressed South Carolinians, this time more decisively than before. "The voters of the State," he said, "now have their choice between two candidates representing entirely different political schools of thought. . . . One of the candidates thinks in terms of the past," while the "other thinks in terms of 1938, and 1948, and 1958 as well."[76]

In the closing hours of the campaign, Johnston and Smith drew their differences in bold, stark lines. A vote for Olin Johnston, the governor stressed, was a vote for Roosevelt and the New Deal, for shorter hours, higher wages, social security, workers' compensation, and first-class citizenship. It was a vote against sleeping senators, persistent poverty, selfish individualism, and economic slavery. Smith, on the other hand, defined his candidacy in terms of the threats that lurked in the shadows of the New Deal. "You red-blooded men," he hollered to a Greenwood crowd, "If you vote against me you will vote for that negro white man [NAACP chief Walter White] who is trying to blacklist me because I was against the anti-lynching bill." [77] He told crowds that a vote for his opponent was a vote for equal rights for African Americans, antilynching laws, the "Commie-Nigger-loving CIO," and the destruction of white civilization. He vowed to safeguard the Old Democracy—states' rights, white supremacy, and cotton culture. On the next to the last day of August 1938, South Carolinians turned out in near-record numbers to choose between these two visions, between Olin Johnston and Cotton Ed Smith. [78]

When the returns came in just after dark on August 30, they showed Smith the clear victor. The senator won 56 percent of the vote. Even before all the ballots were counted, pundits began to analyze the campaign. "The negro issue— if it is an issue—helped Senator Smith," one newspaper reported. Turner Catledge, who covered the contest for the *New York Times*, identified the highway fight as the key factor. "While useful to him in gaining the office he holds," Catledge wrote of the Johnston-led road battle, "it did not help him after he won that office." Given South Carolina's tradition of "local determinism," the *State* and Lewis Hamby, a poll watcher from North Carolina, doubted the wisdom of Roosevelt's intervention. The Columbia paper also criticized Johnston's "one-hundred percentism." "No man," the editors wrote, "is right all the time." Anderson journalist Wilton Hall blamed Johnston's defeat on the racially liberal, radical CIO's endorsement. [79] One way or another, all of these assessments were right: Johnston lost because of the highway fight and because of his ties to liberals in the White House and in the CIO. What linked Senator Smith's backers together were not just their obvious fears about the stability of white supremacy, but also class fears about what Olin Johnston and the New Deal, industrial trade unionism and liberalism would do to their economic and social positions. Using the incendiary language of Reconstruction, Smith knitted together a coalition of citizens afraid of losing something.

Cotton Ed clobbered Johnston in the black majority counties of the low country. Whites across the state, but more aggressively below the fall line, fabricated an economic and social system based on the subjugation of African Americans. Any change in the racial balance of power, many believed, would be cataclysmic. Black belt citizens feared that northern liberals' courting of the African American vote would eventually bring an end to disfranchise-

The Carpetbaggers Are Coming

ment. Once African Americans obtained the right to vote, whites feared, they would no longer work in the worst jobs for next to nothing. If they could vote and earn a decent living, they might think that they were white. After that, the unthinkable, the unmentionable act, would surely take place.

Searching for the most ominous metaphor available, Smith voters, like the candidate, described the CIO's emergence, the expansion of federal authority, and the rise of black political participation in the harsh light of Reconstruction. "To keep the South Carolina Democratic party a white party is the duty of every Democrat," proclaimed a Colleton County man, "and those who scoff at what Senator Smith did [in Philadelphia] are not true South Carolina Democrats." Some black belt residents equated support for Johnston and Roosevelt with interracial marriage or worse—the rape of a white woman. "A VOTE FOR ROOSEVELT," an unsigned handbill proclaimed, "means that the day is coming closer when dirty, evil smelling negroes will be going to church with you, your sister, your wife, or your mother." To some, being a man meant standing up for white women. By voting for Smith, black belt white men asserted their own racialized version of masculinity.[80]

Economic development also mattered to black belt voters. As residents of the state's most economically backward areas, they wanted the government to help lift them out of poverty without disrupting the racial order. While planters attacked the New Deal as a threat to white supremacy, states' rights, and cheap African American labor, they backed any program, state or federal, that would bring funds into their sections of the state. The South Carolina Highway Department's road-building scheme fit this model of government-sponsored growth, and, not surprisingly, many of Ben Sawyer's most ardent backers were from the black belt. In the 1938 Senate contest, some of these people punished Olin Johnston for waging war against their plans for economic revival in the highway battle three years earlier.[81]

In addition, it did not help Johnston in the low country, or anywhere else for that matter, that James F. Byrnes, South Carolina's popular junior senator, was hard at work behind the scene writing letters and raising money to seal his defeat. Although born in Charleston, where he retained important political ties, Byrnes lived in Spartanburg in 1938, not too far from Olin Johnston. At a glance, Byrnes and Johnston should have been on the same side. Both were New Dealers. Byrnes, in fact, had served as Roosevelt's Senate point man on several key legislative initiatives in 1933 and 1934. But after FDR's reelection in 1936, Byrnes, like Smith, although to a lesser extent, fumed over the New Deal's drift to the left. Though he backed the reorganization of the Supreme Court, he opposed the hours and wages bill, introduced legislation to outlaw sit-down strikes, and once publicly charged that "[n]egroes are in control of the Democratic Party."[82] For Byrnes, the purpose of the New Deal was to foster recovery through reforms that tampered as little as possible with existing social structures. Johnston, on the other hand, looked at the New Deal as an engine of change. Certainly the governor wanted to see the health of capitalism restored, but when the economy regained its vigor, he hoped that workers' contributions to society would be recognized and rewarded. Byrnes never shared this laborite view of the New Deal.[83]

The senator was also concerned about his own political future. "Byrnes does not wish a governor who might run against him in 1942," Charleston editor W. W. Ball told a friend, "Maybank would not run against him, they are too close." The Maybank to whom Ball referred was Burnett Rhett Maybank, scion of a prosperous Charleston family, the popular mayor of his hometown, and the front-runner and eventual victor in the 1938 governor's race. A New Deal moderate, a critic of sit-down strikes, and no friend of the workingman, Maybank figured prominently in Byrnes's political plans.[84] The senator wanted to make sure that Maybank rolled to victory in 1938, while Johnston went down, hard if possible, to defeat. Then in 1944, according to Byrnes's scheme, Smith would retire. Maybank, fresh from his gubernatorial triumph, would run for his seat, unopposed by the badly wounded Johnston. Heavily indebted to Byrnes, Maybank would repay his benefactor with unflinching loyalty. Tightly controlling federal patronage, the Charlestonian and the Spartanburg resident would go on to build a powerful middle-of-the-road political machine linking the upcountry and the low country. Personal issues were also involved here. During the highway war, Johnston had bloodied some of Byrnes's closest associates. Style mattered as well. To Byrnes, who himself was raised in a working-class family, Johnston, despite his respectability, was still a linthead in a lawyer's suit who remained rough around the edges, and he did not want him as a colleague in Washington.[85]

With Byrnes and Maybank against him and the highway fight behind him, it was no surprise that Johnston did poorly in the black belt. His sub-par performance in the upcountry, however, was startling. In previous statewide campaigns, the counties above the fall line had been Johnston country. Yet half of Smith's votes in 1938 came from these areas. Here, the New Deal and the CIO's racial moderation combined with economic and cultural concerns to form the central issues of the senatorial contest.

Predictably, manufacturers preferred Smith over Johnston. They backed the incumbent because he had battled to safeguard their chief competitive advantages—the regional wage differential and the South's low rate of unionization. Indeed, reports indicated that the mill owners bankrolled Smith's campaign, underwriting, for instance, his rebuttal to Roosevelt's "fifty cents a day" remark.[86] The senator's opposition to the CIO and the reorganization of the Supreme Court coincided with the manufacturers' interests. Beginning with Roosevelt's second inaugural address, when he attacked "economic royalists," industrialists nervously watched as New Dealers blamed them for many of the nation's ills. At the same time, corporate leaders felt that liberal politicians in Washington and Columbia sanctioned militant trade unionism. Troubled by the tenor of the public debate, South Carolina industrialists looked to Smith not only to defend their economic interests, but also to help restore their declining social position. Even if Cotton Ed did nothing, businessmen knew that he would serve them better than the CIO's candidate, Olin Johnston.[87]

Townspeople, small businessmen, and professionals, who had probably been evenly divided for and against Johnston in 1934, joined their wealthier neighbors in voting for Cotton Ed in 1938. Most of these people honored the Supreme Court. Some suggested, in language reminiscent of the highway fight, that Roosevelt's attack on the justices was leading the country "pretty well along the road to dictatorship." A few blamed the brain trusters for the New Deal's drift away from "democracy." "Why doesn't President Roosevelt get rid of the . . . Communists of the Tugwell type?" an upcountry man asked. Like the industrialists who lived in their neighborhoods, middle-class citizens also objected to the administration's antibusiness and prolabor pronouncements.[88] Some bemoaned the expansion of state power, warning that the nation was barreling down the road of wasteful spending and debt, careening toward the wall of inflation. Still others railed against New Deal programs, claiming that they were sapping the country's drive. Laborers now expected the government to do everything. Once the hours and wages act was in place, one man predicted, it would be impossible to find a single person willing to work overtime. If CIO communists had their way, wage earners would not even work forty hours a week.[89]

Equally troubling to middle-class citizens was the New Deal and Johnston's supposed disrespect for law, order, and private property. From the moment that the former weaver stepped onto the political stage, a cross section of South Carolinians worried about how he would interpret the law. Johnston's all-out war against the road commission, his disregard for the rulings of the state supreme court, his steadfast support for Roosevelt's court-packing plan, his defense of the right to strike, and his encouragement of the CIO amplified these concerns. "Smith believes," explained a devotee, "in law and order and not in the reckless use of armed forces such as taking over the highway department by the national guard and contempt for the Supreme Court."[90]

"Smith," added a Greenville supporter, "has been a friend to labor but not the sit-down variety." The sit-down strikes tweaked a raw nerve uptown. Not only did they dramatize the growing militancy of labor, which was ominous enough, but also some saw this new form of protest as the opening red wedge of communism. Johnston's liberalism and advocacy of the TWOC made him guilty by association of "toleration . . . of lawlessness in connection with CIO labor disputes."[91] South Carolinians, an upcountry editor argued, opposed organizations that favored violence and lawlessness. One state resident worried that the forces behind the sit-down strikes "once unleashed, become difficult or impossible to control, and naturally result in a serious disorganization of society." Throughout the 1938 Senate campaign, rumors circulated that if Johnston were elected, CIO radicals would celebrate his victory with another, more vicious general strike. With the chaos of the 1934 walkout still fresh in their minds, people who had barricaded themselves in their homes through the last uprising were understandably nervous about another one. For those town residents not frightened by the CIO's militancy, there was always the union's racial policy and tolerance of left-of-center politics to scare them off. *Anderson Independent* editor Wilton Hall's assessment of the election was probably right: for every vote that the governor gained as a result of the CIO's endorsement, he probably lost three or four other votes in the middle-class precincts.[92]

Perhaps no group of South Carolinians, or U.S. citizens in general for that matter, was more property conscious than farmers. Whereas less than two-thirds of the people interviewed in a Gallup Poll thought that states "should pass legislation making sit-down strikes illegal," 73 percent of the nation's farmers endorsed such measures.[93] "[P]eople in open spaces are against organizations," the *Anderson Independent* observed, "which favor the violent seizure of private property and violent suppression of the liberties of individual Americans."[94]

The sit-down strikes were only part of the reason that rural whites voted for Smith. Farmers, like business leaders, also suffered from anxiety over their declining social status. Long before the stock market crash, hard times hit the South Carolina countryside. The market seemed to punish farmers for their efficiency: the more they produced, the less they earned. New Deal agricultural reforms helped some growers, but not everyone. As a result, many rural white folks were forced to recognize that neither land ownership nor hard work guaranteed subsistence, let alone social respect.

Between 1934 and 1938, as farm families struggled to make ends meet, politicians seemed to speak only of workers' virtues and industrialists' vices. Agricultural issues no longer dominated politics. Candidates for statewide and local offices regularly made direct appeals to wage earners, celebrating their contributions to society. "I'm labor's true friend," became one of the era's most familiar political refrains. Olin Johnston talked this prolabor talk louder and better than anyone else in South Carolina. "Let me show you how my heart beats," the former weaver said to a campaign crowd in 1938: "at the governor's conference of 1935, I urged that something be done for labor[,] that they put a limit to the hours of work and a floor to wages that would have to be paid."[95] Opposed to the hours and wages bill and disdainful of mill village culture, many rural folks obviously did not like the way Olin's heart beat. When the Roosevelt recession hit the mill towns in 1937, putting thousands out of work, Johnston, some farmers noted, rushed to Washington to secure relief for textile workers, but he never moved that fast to help them. "Lately," a Smith partisan wrote in 1938, Johnston "has possessed a great interest in the farmer, yet everybody knows that all he can see is a labor union, and that all other people have no place in his mind." Besides, another of Cotton Ed's backers contended, Johnston's knowledge of farm issues was "negligible."[96]

Smith, by contrast, portrayed himself as "a small dirt farmer." Rural voters trusted that he understood and cared about their problems. Just as important, Smith told farmers that they, not millworkers, were the "backbone of society," the "foundation of American greatness," and the "purest strain of Anglo-Saxon blood in the world." All too often cotton growers, he explained, did not "obtain . . . their share of the national wealth." Farmers did not fail, Smith said again and again, because of their own mistakes, but due to forces far beyond their control: "unfair tariff walls, unfair freight rates, and many other handicaps." Assuring farm families that he would remove these obstacles, the senator, in his 1938 speeches, one observer noted, filled rural families with "hope in the future." Farmers repaid Smith with their votes.[97]

The divisions between Smith supporters and Johnston backers extended beyond the countryside, the town, and the low country. Working people were also divided in 1938. Even during the gloomiest days of the Great Depression, Aloysius Flynn had earned a decent living as a boilermaker. A highly skilled craftsman, Flynn doubled as president of the South Carolina Federation of Labor. Like many AFL members, he voted for Smith in 1938. His organization, along with two dozen of the state's railroad brotherhoods, officially endorsed Senator Smith that year. Even William Green, the national leader of the AFL, wrote a personal letter of support for Smith. How had Olin Johnston—"Labor's Governor" and a "laboring man himself"—come to arouse the antipathy of the head of the country's largest labor body?

The arrival of the Textile Workers Organizing Committee in South Carolina in 1937 touched off a trade union turf war in the state.[98] Resembling the national fray, members of the South Carolina AFL lashed out at their organizational rival, charging it with the crime of dual unionism and comparing its leader, John L. Lewis, to Adolf Hitler. Matching Smith's own virulent anti-radical, white supremacist rhetoric, the AFL red-baited and race-baited the TWOC. "No Red Flag, No Communism, but a display in deed and thought of 100% Americanism, with no gauntlet thrown down to capital," read an AFL pamphlet. Other AFL fliers warned that the CIO would integrate the textile mills.[99] After 1936, in fact, the AFL's political agenda sounded more like Smith's than Johnston's. Like the senator, President Green spoke out against the hours and wages act, voiced concern over the government reorganization bill, and objected to FDR's plan to purge the Supreme Court.[100]

Although the evidence is sketchy, Smith appears to have gained the backing of some South Carolina labor aristocrats. In the railroad shop districts of the state—the easiest to identify of skilled working-class precincts—the senator outran, and in some cases walloped, the governor. Returns from the Abbeville Railway shops, for instance, showed Smith with 82 votes to Johnston's 2. In Greenville City's Ward 4, another craftsmen's neighborhood, Smith edged Johnston 228 to 212.[101]

Working as most did in small shops, "skilled" workers set their own pace of labor. Away from their jobs, many had carved out for themselves and their families a middle-class lifestyle. They owned their own homes, belonged to clubs with a few local businessmen, worshipped at a mainstream church, and maybe even sent one of their children to the University of South Carolina along with the sons of manufacturers. Craftsmen suffered less from the social and economic alienation that afflicted mill people. For them, class lines did not seem so impermeable. New Deal liberalism and the CIO's plan for industrial unionism were irrelevant, even unappealing. Scores of skilled laborers cherished private property, hard work, and independence, and, like middle-class citizens, some feared that the New Deal was giving something away for nothing. For others, the prospect of uniting with millhands represented not a grand alliance of labor, but a repudiation of the social gains and respectability they had fought so hard to secure. A vote for Smith, therefore, was something of a declaration of their membership in the white middle class.[102]

Throughout the 1938 campaign, Smith and his supporters tried to lure textile workers away from Johnston and the New Deal into their coalition of fear. White supremacy was the bait they used. AFL leaders pointed out with alarm that African Americans sat on the CIO's executive council. Smith, they assured voters, opposed organizations "controlled by Communists, people who do not believe in God, church, or Marriage, and who advocate racial and social equality." Even the president, Johnston's benefactor, was fair game when it came to issues of race, class, and the CIO. "Does the President," asked the *Greenwood Index-Journal*, "believe that Negroes should be excluded from employment in South Carolina cotton mills and from dwelling in our cotton mill villages among white people?" "Could he tell us," inquired the same paper the next day, "how he feels about the CIO and its urge to colored workers to join with it and enable such workers to force employment in any industry, cotton mills or what not, in the South?"[103]

W. W. Ball, the editor of the *Charleston News and Courier*, also took it on himself to alert textile workers to the presumed racial liberalism of the CIO and its loyal servant Olin Johnston. "The contest for a Senator is now a race question," Ball wrote in a widely syndicated editorial after the CIO and LNPL stepped into the campaign on the governor's behalf. In another editorial addressed to "Mill Workers," Ball warned: "We cannot surrender states rights in respect of business and industry, we cannot amend the constitution and deliver control over them to Washington without giving up traditions." One of the traditions supposedly in jeopardy was the exclusion of African Americans from the textile mills. If the New Dealers had their way, the editor asserted, they would force blacks and whites to compete as equals in the labor market. "Think about it," he seemed to be saying to the state's millhands.[104]

Millhands thought about it, and they voted for Olin D. Johnston. "White supremacy," declared the editors of the prolabor *[Una] News-Review*, "is not the issue." Workers had more pressing concerns, wrote a trade unionist summing up the views of many mill laborers, than "the negro, the tariff, and states rights." "We have the unemployment problem, the matter of shrunken earnings, monopolistic control of basic industries, . . . hours and wages legislation, labor relations, child labor, etc." He concluded: "No respectable union man would let his hatred for a poor negro make him commit political scabbery by voting for" Smith.[105]

The electoral behavior of millhands in 1938 flies in the face of most portraits of the political consciousness of white southern industrial workers. Usually these people are depicted as the most viciously racist of all southerners. Jarred by the mere mention of white supremacy, they cease to be influenced by economic issues. But in 1938 this was not the case. Johnston, campaigning on a platform of New Deal liberalism, rolled to victory in the state's mill precincts. He won 75 percent of the vote at Matthews Mill and 80 percent at Appleton Mill. Indeed, in most textile towns he widened his margin of victory from four years earlier; he did so despite workers' mounting frustrations with how the political system operated and despite the fact that he faced a more formidable candidate than in 1934. More fearful, for now, of the manufacturer than the carpetbagger, of the stretchout than interracial marriage, of a return to laissez-faire government than sit-down strikes, mill people continued to try to use their access to the ballot to redistribute power on the shop floor, not to cut down African Americans or northern liberals. Asked to choose between their identities as white South Carolinians and as laborers, most chose the latter. South Carolina workers were certainly not converts to racial liberalism nor were they even ardent supporters of the CIO. They remained committed to racial segregation at home, at the polling station, in unions, and in the factories, but for a brief time they did put their class interests ahead of their racial ones.[106] Once again, however, the votes of millworkers were not enough.

On election night, 1938, Cotton Ed Smith and two hundred of his supporters in Orangeburg got together to revive the spirit of '76. Donning bright red shirts, they celebrated Johnston's defeat. The senator compared his victory to the Redeemers' overthrow of the radical Republicans sixty years earlier. "Boys," Smith told his followers, "the symbol you wear tonight is the symbol we hurled to the world after the Confederate War when Negroes and carpetbaggers got control of the State government." The crowd let out a rebel yell. "No man dares to come to South Carolina," he continued, "and try to dictate to the sons of those men who held high the hands of Lee and Hampton." On leaving the rally, one red-shirted man pointed to Smith and, breathing a sigh of relief, announced, "He was re-elected so we are safe." The threats posed by labor and liberalism, the New Deal and Olin Johnston, he trusted, had been put to rest. His faith was not misplaced.[107]

Observers at the time, and later, have suggested that in 1938 the politics of race defeated the politics of class in South Carolina, that Cotton Ed Smith raised the bloody red shirt of Reconstruction to extinguish the hope of the New Deal.[108] Undoubtedly race mattered in this campaign, but so did class. Most political languages are polyvocal, that is, they say more than one thing at a time. When Smith talked about race, carpetbaggers, and red shirts, he also assured the already powerful that he was on their side and that if they voted for him, they would remain where they were on the social ladder. As a result, upper- and middle-class South Carolinians, farmers and skilled laborers overwhelmed millhands at the polls in the 1938 Senate campaign just as they had on the pickets lines and in the factories, and just as they had in the debate over workers' compensation and during the highway fight. This was the main theme of politics in South Carolina in the thirties. Class tensions dominated the discussions, and millhands played this game quite well, but not well enough. Yet it hardly mattered. The game, as it turned out, was stacked from the beginning.

CHAPTER TWELVE

The New Politics of Race, 1938–1948

 Throughout World War II, white South Carolinians told each other wild rumors about bloody race wars and impending rebellions. Charleston whites were convinced that African Americans were stockpiling ice picks. A salesman warned, and people believed him, that blacks planned to use these sharp objects to kill all whites during a Labor Day uprising. Meanwhile, it was said, black domestics were joining quasi-unions called "Eleanor Clubs," named after the crusading liberal first lady. When their white employers were not looking, club members plotted mayhem. Reportedly, by Christmas they intended to be living in the big house, eating roast beef and fresh asparagus cooked and served by their ex-bosses. As white soldiers pulled out of an up-country town and headed for basic training, it was alleged, a few grinning African American men waved and told them not to worry, they would take care of their mothers, wives, sisters, and daughters.[1]

After investigating these stories, both the Federal Bureau of Investigation (FBI) and South Carolina authorities concluded that there were no race wars on the horizon or Eleanor Clubs in the kitchens. Based on half-truths and sheer invention, rumors like the ones that spread through the white communities of South Carolina during World War II nonetheless still provide a map of social anxieties and psychological pressure points. By repeating rumors, frightened whites created space to express their anxieties about the uncertainty of the system of white supremacy that they felt uncomfortable talking about out in the open.

More than a decade before the *Brown* decision and the Montgomery bus boycott—the textbook starting points of the modern civil rights movement—African Americans started to mobilize for an all-out raid on Jim Crow.[2] Black activism alarmed whites, especially working-class whites, but few discussed their uneasiness in public. Such talk would make African American agency clear and expose white supremacy's flimsy foundations. Instead, whites invented stories and rumors that, in the tense climate of the 1940s, allowed them to voice their fears and at the same time assure themselves that they remained on top of the racial order.[3]

The same racial anxieties that fueled these rumors propelled a political change in the state. During the war, the focus of South Carolina politics—and, for that matter, national politics—shifted away from class concerns toward issues of race and the defense of white supremacy against African American insurgency and federal intervention. As blacks pressed for civil rights, economic issues drifted further and further into the background of white politics, but certainly not out of sight.

Looking back, "Cotton Ed" Smith's defeat of Olin Johnston marked a transition in the politics of white textile workers. It was the end of millhands' faith in New Deal Americanism and the federal government; it was the last time that these laborers stressed their economic interests ahead of their concerns for white supremacy. Slowly, unevenly, in the wake of the 1938 election, race moved to the center of the political world of South Carolina. Since the days of Cole Blease, working-class whites took white supremacy for granted. The best jobs were reserved for whites only, and only whites voted. That was the natural order of things. As long as blacks were barred from politics and kept out of the factories, white workers felt free to disagree with other whites on a wide range of issues. In fact, during the twenties and thirties voters repeatedly split along class lines without race being a factor. Before 1938 it was possible, as Olin Johnston and a host of local candidates demonstrated, for a South Carolina politician to avoid talking about race, to consider it a given. Afterward this was impossible. Admission into the political game required that players announce at the outset their unyielding support for white supremacy. That was the first order of business, much like during the depression, when candidates started their campaign speeches by spelling out their positions on labor and capital. After 1938, politics revolved around who was the most determined to keep African Americans down and the federal government and courts at bay.

Before 1938 white workers stood on the liberal edge of South Carolina politics. They were FDR's most fervent supporters. In their eyes he could do no wrong. They were the most vocal proponents of government action and the

The New Politics of Race

expansion of federal power and the leading critics of corporate wealth and private property. Jarred by African American attempts to push themselves into the political process, however, white workers emerged after 1938 as a reactionary political force.

Black men and women never accepted the South's repressive racial order or willingly wore its ugly brand of inferiority, but they often hid their pain behind many masks of getting along. Whites read African American gestures as clear windows into their collective psyche. They believed all of the mumbled "yes sirs," tipped hats, and moving off of wooden sidewalks. They convinced themselves that African Americans accepted, even liked, segregation, Jim Crow, and disfranchisement. Beginning in the late 1930s, this fantasy became harder than ever to believe.

Sometime between the last days of the New Deal and the first moments of World War II, a gear in the machine shifted, the world moved a little, and nothing would ever be the same.[4] African Americans broadcast in hundreds of both quiet and dramatic ways that they would no longer endure the humiliations of discrimination and second-class citizenship. They intended to grab hold and not let go of their long-denied freedoms. Tens of thousands protested with their feet. Cramming what they could into cardboard suitcases and flimsy trunks, many crowded onto trains headed to the promised lands of Chicago, Detroit, Atlantic City, New York, and Hartford. Most African Americans, however, stayed behind in the land of their parents. In 1945 more than half of the nation's black community remained in Dixie. Even here in the heart of the old Confederacy, African Americans had freedom on their minds, and whites could not help but notice.

In a place like prewar South Carolina, joining the NAACP represented a brave act of defiance, a clear vote by the disfranchised against Jim Crow. In 1938 fewer than 1,200 African Americans in eight Palmetto communities belonged to the NAACP. The next year, Levi Byrd, a plumber's helper from Cheraw, brought these separate groups together to form the State Conference of Branches of the NAACP. From then on, the organization's membership grew. By 1945 perhaps as many as 30,000, although the number was probably closer to 13,000, blacks belonged to one of South Carolina's forty branches of the NAACP.[5]

Throughout the 1940s the South Carolina NAACP represented, according to one historian, "the vanguard" of the African American struggle for civil rights in the South.[6] "To meet the challenge of the times" and "let the world know that democracy . . . is an actuality, rather than a far fetched ideal," the statewide organization pressed for—along the lines of the national call for Double V—"Democracy in America, Democracy Abroad." "JOIN the

NAACP," read a 1942 flier, "Stay on Guard Against" educational inequalities, police brutality, unfair treatment in the courts, and discrimination in parks and playgrounds. Above all, NAACP activists demanded the badge of citizenship, the right to vote; that, they trusted, was the key to democracy in America and in South Carolina.[7]

The South Carolina story was a familiar Deep South story. In 1940 African Americans made up 43 percent of the state's population; only Mississippi had a larger proportion of black residents. In almost half of the state's forty-six counties, African Americans outnumbered whites. Yet the poll tax, fraud, easy-to-manipulate registration rules, and raw racism kept all but a few black Republicans away from the polls. In Beaufort, African Americans comprised more than two-thirds of the population, but not a single black resident could vote. More than 30,000 black men and women lived in Greenville County, but only 35 were listed on the voting rolls, and they could vote only in the rather meaningless general election, not the decisive Democratic primary.[8] Beginning in the late 1930s, a few African Americans tried to force their way into power and into the Democratic Party.

Cherokee County schoolteacher and NAACP member Lottie P. Gaffney was one of these people. On the first Tuesday of August 1940, Gaffney, four other women, and a couple of ministers went at the designated time to the designated place to register. They rapped hard on the door. Looking out, the registrar could not believe what he saw. "Darkies," he told them, "have never registered in the South and especially in Cherokee County." Then he slammed the door in their faces. They kept knocking all afternoon, but the registrar would not answer.[9] Following in Gaffney's footsteps, African Americans in Columbia, Greenville, Charleston, Cheraw, and Spartanburg tried to register. Very few people got past the registrar. Most were treated like a Spartanburg man who was told that if he continued to ask to have his name placed on the voting roll, his house would be torched and he would be "scalped."[10]

Shifting currents in political thought during and after the war promoted the grassroots efforts of African Americans in South Carolina. Outside of the South, tolerance for white supremacy withered as the nation geared up for battle against racist, fascist foes. At the same time, race became more central to liberalism. Throughout his first six years in office, Franklin Roosevelt, afraid of alienating southern congressional conservatives, refrained from talking about the nation's tortured race relations, concentrating his recovery efforts instead on economic issues. Yet as the New Deal lost steam after the setbacks of 1937–38, a new version of liberalism started to take shape. "This new liberalism," writes Alan Brinkley, "has focused less on the broad needs of the nation and the modern economy than on increasing the rights and freedoms of individuals and social groups." [11]

Typically, politics are cast as morality plays and filled with stock characters. In the dramas staged by the newer liberals, the fat, bloated southern Bourbon replaced the fat, bloated "economic royalist" as the nation's leading bad guy. Long-victimized African Americans, meanwhile, replaced brawny industrial laborers as the driving force to a fairer, more just society. Liberals now envisioned reshaping America starting with the South. They pointed to Dixie conservatives as the major impediment to reform and considered extending the vote to African Americans as an essential first step to remaking the nation. With blacks participating in elections and backing liberals, the Bourbons would be doomed. With these conservatives out of the way, liberals could begin to reform American democracy. In the end, then, it was not that the new liberals did not care about economic issues or the distribution of wealth, it was that these issues, central to the political debate during the first days of the New Deal, now took a backseat to the quest for racial equality.[12]

Developments in Washington and elsewhere during the war years encouraged the new brand of liberalism. Activists applauded when President Roosevelt, prodded by A. Phillip Randolph and his March on Washington movement, signed Executive Order 8802 outlawing racial discrimination in hiring on war-related projects and establishing the Fair Employment Practices Committee (FEPC) to investigate violations. Up the hill, liberal lawmakers did battle with southern Democrats over voting rights, winning some fights and losing others. In 1942 Congress passed the Soldiers Vote Bill, making it easier for servicemen, including African Americans from southern states, to cast absentee ballots in federal elections. Liberals also came close to getting rid of the dreaded poll tax. An anti–poll tax measure passed in the House in 1942, only to be filibustered to death by southern conservatives in the Senate.[13] Then in the spring of 1944 came the Supreme Court's *Smith v. Allwright* decision.

Throughout the South, cunning Democrats had kept African Americans out of their party by claiming that it was a private club, which could set its own rules and requirements for membership. Undercutting this pillar of white supremacy, the justices ruled in *Smith* that political parties were not private clubs, but agents of the government. As an arm of the state, the Democratic Party could not bar blacks from participating in primaries—the real elections in the South—without violating the Fifteenth Amendment.

Led by the increasingly combative NAACP, African Americans in South Carolina jumped at the opportunity created by the *Smith* ruling. Neatly dressed ministers, teachers, undertakers, and plumbers, in both cities and small towns, lined up outside registrar's offices in the spring of 1944, demanding a voice in the Democratic Party. Predictably, party regulars tried to keep them out, but these black citizens would not go away easily or quietly. That summer, a group of African American pro-Roosevelt Democrats along with a few whites, organized under the banner of the Progressive Democratic Party, traveled to Chicago to the national party convention. They petitioned delegates to seat them in place of the state's all-white, largely anti–New Deal contingent. Treating the insurgents as something of a nuisance, party leaders sent them back to South Carolina with vague promises of an investigation and future consideration. The Progressive Democrats had lost, but at the same time they had delivered a clear message to white South Carolinians that they intended to be heard in the political arena.[14]

Black teachers banging on the door of the registrar's office, black activists publicly challenging the leaders of the state Democratic Party, black men in crisply pressed uniforms with rifles slung over their right shoulders, the Supreme Court toying with primary laws, Soldiers Vote Bills, and federal sanctions against job discrimination—these developments were too much for many white South Carolinians. These sons of yeomen, planters, and laborers had been taught to see suffrage as a racial privilege, not a generic democratic right. Now African Americans laid claim to the franchise in the most aggressive public manner. Worse yet, with the ballot in hand, or at least in sight, and with northern lawmakers and their Yankee army buddies telling them that they were as good as anybody, African Americans, according to whites, began to descend into a spiral of lawlessness and disorder.[15] Some even began to do the unthinkable, that is, to act "like white folks." Anxiety over social equality generated those wartime rumors about ice picks, guns, and Eleanor Clubs. Whites told each other that blacks would no longer adhere to the rules of the Jim Crow order and step off the sidewalks to let whites pass, move to the back of the bus, or happily accept the worst and most dangerous jobs for next to nothing in pay. And then, of course, came wild talk of interracial sex. In this electric climate, a brush became a touch, a glance became a leer. Whites nervously discussed the alleged propensity of African American men to suggestively squeeze white hands when getting change at stores, whistle at white women, call them for dates, and send chocolates to young white girls, just like white boys did. While blacks registered to vote and left their jobs as domestics for higher-paying positions in war-related industries, whites thought they overheard them say that after the conflict, "Negroes will marry white girls and run the country."[16]

"I read your article in the newspaper," Bertie Mae Loner of Iva told Eleanor Roosevelt, "where you thought white girls should dance with negroes." Even

The New Politics of Race

though she already knew that the first lady was "a negro lover," she still could not believe it. "I think it is mighty sorry in you to even ask us to dance with those negroes." Retelling a rumor, Loner said that she saw African American women, who "think white people should work for them," carrying a picture of Eleanor Roosevelt. "When our soldier boys return home," she wrote, "the negroes will get the daylights knocked out them if they even talk back to one boy. . . . We can always bet on our boys."[17] Whites did, in fact, respond to the African American challenge with violence.

During the 1940s white South Carolinians launched a bloody campaign of terror, reminiscent of Reconstruction, to shove blacks back into their "place." An older man, Louis Nesbitt of Greer, talked "very bold . . . in regard to the equality of the two races" and wondered aloud whether black men should volunteer "to fight and die in a white man's war." Several times, Nesbitt tried to register to vote. Whites speculated, further, that he was behind the organization of a mythical Eleanor Club in Spartanburg. On November 5, 1942, white vigilantes grabbed Nesbitt, drove him across the county line, and whipped him with leather straps.[18]

Uneasy seeing African Americans in uniform, angry whites, especially near military encampments, targeted soldiers for attack.[19] Black political activity and military service also sparked a Ku Klux Klan revival in the state. Even before the war began, Greenville Klansmen, aided by the police, ransacked eight homes in search of a school principal who was an NAACP member and the head of a local voter registration drive. When the police found the frightened educator armed with a gun, they arrested him for carrying a concealed weapon. Before long, the white-controlled school board fired him.[20] In 1941 two thousand knights and their supporters met near Wade Hampton's statue in downtown Columbia and listened to speeches by hooded Klansmen about the evils of communism and racial mingling.[21] A few years later, the Klansmen returned to the capital. After a short parade, they went on a rampage, burning wooden crosses in front of several black churches.[22] According to the FBI, in 1942 male millhands from Anderson, Spartanburg, Ninety-Six, and Greenwood formed chapters of the Blue Shirts, an organization reportedly similar to the Klan. Following a twilight July meeting in an upcountry brickyard, Blue Shirts fanned out across the region and beat and molested dozens of African American men and women.[23]

White rage took an even uglier turn in the immediate postwar years. A few short months after South Carolinians went "slightly mad" celebrating V-J Day, Isaac Woodward, a black serviceman anxious to get home to New York after fifteen months in the South Pacific, downed a few drinks and boarded a bus in Augusta, Georgia.[24] Just after crossing the Savannah River into South

Carolina, Woodward and the white bus driver got into a shouting match. When they reached Batesburg, a midlands town twenty miles southwest of Columbia, the driver called the local sheriff's office, saying he needed help with an unruly black passenger. Two law officers rushed over to the bus station. They ordered Woodward off the bus, then dragged him around a corner and beat him. The next day, the veteran could not see. A medical report revealed that a billy club had been shoved into his eye sockets with such force that "both of his eyes were mutilated beyond repair." An all-white jury later acquitted Woodward's attackers. A few months after the decision, a black man was killed in Elko, South Carolina, after trying to register to vote.[25] Then in 1947 there was a lynching, perhaps the last ever in the state.

Sometime in the evening of February 16, 1947, in one of the black sections of Greenville, Willie Earle got drunk. That was not so unusual. Earle had been drinking a lot since his boss had discovered that he suffered from epilepsy and fired him from his job as a truck driver. Later that night, Earle called a cab to take him to his mother's house near Liberty. Cabs had long been sites of racial confrontation in the region. They were one of the few places in the South where African Americans could tell whites what to do and they would listen. A white driver from the Bluebird Taxicab Company, Thomas W. Brown, picked Earle up around 9:00 P.M. Something happened—a fight, maybe Earle said something about a white woman or about African Americans taking over after the war, or maybe Brown spit out a racial epithet or made a lewd remark, or maybe nothing happened between them. We do not know. But one thing was certain: the cabdriver ended up on the side of a country road bleeding from a deep knife wound. As he lay dying in a nearby hospital, the police picked up Earle and took him to the Pickens County jail. Meanwhile, word of the knife attack and Earle's arrest spread quickly as one cabbie told another, who told another. Within hours, fifty men in two dozen cabs were on their way to the jail. The jailkeeper, an older white man worried about his wife's safety, handed over the keys without a fight. He even pointed the angry white men to Earle's cell. They grabbed the twenty-four-year-old African American and drove off into the night. After a fast ride out of the city, they yanked Earle out of the car. They punched him and kicked him. They cracked his skull with a pistol butt, and then they shot him. After he was dead they shot him again. "The bushes around him," wrote a reporter, "were splashed with his brain tissue."[26]

Many people knew that cabdrivers had killed Earle, but thirty-six hours after the crime the local police had still made no arrests. Under orders from the U.S. attorney general, the FBI went to Greenville to take over the case. Agents interrogated drivers. Many of the cabbies admitted that they were at

The New Politics of Race

the scene, but all of them denied actually participating in the killing. Several, however, blamed one coworker or another for Earle's death. Based on this evidence, the state prosecuted twenty-eight cabdrivers and three others including a mill owner's son, who had heard about the crime at a downtown café and joined the mob. Despite graphic testimony detailing the brutality of the murder, the jury of twelve white men — nine millworkers, two salesmen, and a farmer — voted to acquit the accused.

Obviously, defense attorneys spoke the same language as the men on the jury. Well known around Greenville as a friend of the workingman, John Bolt Culbertson represented several of the cabdrivers. He told the jury that Greenville was white man's country and that Earle was a "bad nigger" who got what was coming. "Willie Earle," he announced, tapping into white fears of a postwar black crime wave, "is dead, and I wish more like him was dead." The defense team also stirred resentments against the FBI, transforming the agents from dutiful investigators into evil carpetbaggers. Heaping abuse on "northern agitators, radio commentators, and certain publications," another defense lawyer asserted, "We people get along pretty well until they start interfering with us in Washington." If the FBI stood for a malevolent federal government, then the thirty-one defendants became every beleaguered white man under attack by the unholy alliance of aggressive African Americans like Willie Earle and pro-civil rights liberals like Eleanor Roosevelt. This argument made sense to the largely working-class white jury.[27]

Within a short a time, the violence and mayhem of dark country roads and steamy courtrooms spilled over into the political arena. Elected leaders and candidates for office, however, rarely mentioned African American political mobilization; that would mean recognizing the power of blacks to shape the thoughts and actions of white people. Few spoke of the Ku Klux Klan, the Blue Shirts, or cabdrivers, either. Instead, highlighting themes first previewed by Cotton Ed Smith in 1936 at the Democratic National Convention and again during the 1938 Senate race, South Carolina politicians described their state as under siege by ruthless Yankees. These sons of William T. Sherman loathed the South and egged on African Americans, urging them to vote even when they did not want to, just to humiliate white men and scare white women. Behind Eleanor Roosevelt's pleas for civil rights, the Soldiers Vote Bill, antilynching legislation, assaults on the poll tax, and the *Smith* decision, Dixie lawmakers saw another well-coordinated assault on state sovereignty by arrogant northerners. They saw a replay of Reconstruction.

After a decade in which racial themes could be heard only in the background, the tone of South Carolina politics became meaner and more hateful during the 1940s. The Charlestonian Burnett R. Maybank, for instance, had walked out of the 1936 Democratic convention behind Cotton Ed Smith but was never known as a hard-line segregationist. In the new racial climate of the 1940s, however, he had to play the race card to survive at the polling station. In the 1941 Senate contest, then Governor Maybank said little about the New Deal or labor, but he boasted that of all the candidates he was the best prepared to "fight any anti-lynching bill."[28] Following the *Smith* decision in 1944, he threatened that South Carolina would do whatever it took to "protect our primaries." Later that year, as he prepared to leave for the Democratic National Convention, Maybank told a *New York Times* reporter that white supremacy was *the* issue to be resolved in Chicago.[29]

White supremacy was also *the* issue back home. In August 1941 five thousand people gathered in Saluda to celebrate the forty-sixth anniversary of the 1895 constitutional convention. The air was thick with heat and humidity. As in the old days, a band played patriotic songs and soldiers marched in formation. The local American Legion post served everyone heaping plates of barbecue free of charge. Former chief justice of the South Carolina Supreme Court, Eugene Blease, Cole's brother, was the keynote speaker. When it came time for the talking, the music stopped and the people put down their plates. Feeling the pressure of the new liberalism and the NAACP's push for civil rights, Blease delivered a fervent defense of white supremacy. He charged that the national Democratic Party had given too much encouragement to African Americans in "several places of the country to get his vote." There was danger in this trend, he warned, a danger that the federal government would once again force black voting on South Carolina. Blease ended his speech praising the 160 men of the constitutional convention who had "wiped out the last vestiges of government forced on South Carolina by the carpetbaggers of the North and the scalawags of the South."[30]

Two years later Representative John D. Long, who had been a Johnston ally during the highway fight as well as a frequent supporter of labor legislation, condemned as "un-American," "agitators of the North" who were "seeking the amalgamation of the White and Negro races by a co-mingling of the races upon any basis of equality." In the spring of 1944, Long urged his house colleagues to vote for a resolution declaring "our belief in and our allegiance to established White Supremacy as now prevailing in the South and pledging our lives and our sacred honor to maintain it, whatever the cost, in war and in peace."[31] After the measure passed with only a few dissenting votes, Cotton Ed Smith sent a congratulatory telegram, saying "we are damned tired of these butterfly preachers who do not know conditions in the South."[32]

The reactionary climate in South Carolina got even hotter after the Supreme Court outlawed the white primary. Sounding the tenor of the times,

Richard M. Jeffries, a onetime governor and longtime state senator from low-country Colleton County, wrote a friend, "It seems impossible for us to entertain, even for a minute, the possibility of acquiescing in the voting of Negroes in our primary elections." The reason why, he said, was that "The Negro race has not yet developed to the point that it can assume properly this vital function of citizenship." Still, if African Americans obtained the right to vote, "it would not be long before candidates for political offices and factions in the party would be calling upon the Negroes to settle differences between the white people." "In my opinion," Jeffries concluded, casting an eye back to Reconstruction, "we must meet this challenge in the spirit of our fathers and solve the problem for the protection of southern civilization."[33]

Not every white South Carolinian was swept along by the waves of reaction. There were a few homegrown white liberals and integrationists, people like James McBride Dabbs, in the state. Never a large number, these liberals belonged to either the Southern Conference for Human Welfare, the Southern Regional Council, the South Carolina Council on Human Relations, or the Progressive Democratic Party. Committed to ending, or at least adjusting, the Jim Crow order, these people, concentrated mostly in Charleston and Columbia, repeated the arguments of national liberals, saying that the only way to reform the nation was to reform the South, the only way to reform the South was to get rid of the Bourbons, and the only way to get rid of the Bourbons was to extend suffrage rights to African Americans.[34]

The state's unsteady racial climate also produced some strange hybrids of liberalism. Praised by the *New Republic* as one of the "true liberal leaders of the South," the lawyer John Bolt Culbertson backed African American demands for better schools and expanded civil rights. He was, wrote the journalist Rebecca West, "one of the very few white people in these parts who shake hands with Negroes and give them the prefix Mr. or Mrs. or Miss." Culbertson's ties to the Congress of Industrial Organizations (CIO) further bolstered his liberal credentials. But he also represented several of the Greenville cabdrivers accused of lynching Willie Earle and built their defense around vicious racism and twisted analogies to Reconstruction.[35] The South Carolina CIO was another odd liberal hybrid. "Personally," an organizer for the group's textile branch said, "I think the niggers ought to have the right to vote. They're citizens, like everybody else." Yet in the same breath he admitted that he would not jeopardize his union's standing with millhands by pressing for civil rights.[36]

In the end, the racist diatribes of Maybank, Long, and Smith drowned out the voices of liberalism in the state, even the odd ones. Without question, the reactionary forces in the South put together something resembling a mass movement, one that was clearly bigger, stronger, and more powerful than anything the Southern Regional Council or the Southern Conference for Human Welfare had ever imagined for themselves. Following a visit to low-country Jasper County just after the war, a *Newsweek* reporter made a similar observation. Hearing the speeches and the lusty applause, he concluded that the South's conservative white politicians "were not stirring up a popular revolt. They were reflecting it."[37]

Olin Johnston was not the kind of man who swam against history. Ambitious to the core, he was the sort of person who reflected, amplified, and confirmed what people already believed or what they wanted to believe. That is what he did in the 1930s. Sensing workers' identification with New Deal Americanism, he became their messenger. In the 1940s, after a few miscues, Johnston once again tuned into what the majority of South Carolinians were thinking. Judging from poll returns, they were thinking about race. That is not to say that labor issues or gender anxieties disappeared, but after 1938 they took a backseat to white supremacy.

Having refrained from playing the race card earlier in his career, saying that the issue had been settled by Wade Hampton and the Red Shirts, Johnston eventually got in line with the shifting tenor of southern politics. His turn-about stemmed not only from the mounting pressures of African American protest, but also from his own dwindling political fortunes. In 1941 Johnston lost a second bid for the U.S. Senate. Just as during his 1938 run to unseat Cotton Ed Smith, the mill-boy–turned-lawyer–turned-politician built his campaign around working-class issues. He told voters that they had a choice between himself and his Charleston opponent, or between "a cotton mill boy and a wealthy aristocrat." "Cotton mill workers," he argued on another occasion, "should vote for Johnston if only to prove that the son of a textile worker is as good as an aristocrat." After winning big in the mill precincts but losing another election, Johnston sought to broaden his constituency.[38]

In 1942 he returned to the political victory circle, winning a second term as governor. Making race the central theme of his campaign, he used his earlier reluctance to play the race card to his advantage. "Have [I] been one to exaggerate the issue of white supremacy?" Johnston asked. But now, he warned, threats to the "southern way of life" were everywhere. Promising to erect "new barriers against the invasion of the white party in the South," he proclaimed, "This is a white man's state, and Olin Johnston will always be in there fighting hard as he can to keep it that way." Eliminated from his speeches were avowals of one-hundred-percentism and unyielding support

The New Politics of Race

for the New Deal; in their place came a pledge of allegiance to "South Carolina first, last, and always."[39]

True to his word, once in office Johnston pursued the politics of white supremacy ahead of his older agenda of the "greatest democracy for the greatest number." Even as he made peace with Edgar Brown and the Barnwell Ring and urged South Carolinians to "act alike with a oneness of purpose to win the war," race lurked in the background. In the summer of 1943, Johnston addressed the state's Home Guard. "God didn't see fit to mix them," he asserted, "and I am tired of people agitating social equality of the races." "If outsiders come into our state and agitate social equality," he warned, "I shall deem it my duty to call upon you men to expel them."[40]

Then the bombshell hit. On April 4, 1944, the Supreme Court outlawed the white primary. Initially, Johnston said that he was "not alarmed" by the decision. Other people, however, panicked. They urged, implored, demanded, and begged the governor to do something to save the white primary.[41] Six days later Johnston called the members of the general assembly back to Columbia for a special session. Addressing the lawmakers, he spoke like a tent preacher, his voice rising and falling with emotion. The text that night was drawn from D. W. Griffith's *Birth of A Nation*; the lesson was the horrors of Reconstruction. "Where you now sit," the governor reminded the packed audience, "there sat a majority of negroes." His voice rising to fever pitch, he lifted a line or two from the stump speeches of Pitchfork Ben Tillman and Cotton Ed Smith and embellished on them:

> The records will bear me out that fraud, corruption, immorality, and graft existed during that regime that has never been paralleled in the history of our State. They left a stench in the nostrils of the people of South Carolina that will exist for generations to come. The representatives of these agitators, scalawags that called themselves white men and used the colored race to further their own course, are in our midst today, and history will repeat itself unless we protect ourselves against this new crop of carpetbaggers and scalawags who would use the colored race to further their own economic and political gains.[42]

Inspired by Johnston's savage rhetoric, the "Killbillies," as *Newsweek* nicknamed the South Carolina legislators, followed his advice "to repeal all laws pertaining to our primaries, thus making the contest a private matter outside the scope of Supreme Court decisions." Over the next few days, representatives combed through state law books looking for any mention of elections, primaries, and the Democratic Party. In all, they got rid of more than 130 laws in less than a week. "Should this prove inadequate," Johnston vowed at the end of the session, "we South Carolinians will use the necessary methods to retain white supremacy in our primaries and to safeguard the home and happiness of our people." For now, the white primary had been saved, but not for long; in 1947 Charleston's Judge J. Waties Waring, bravely turning against his region, ruled this legal subterfuge unconstitutional.[43]

Recognized now as an "ardent segregationist," Johnston, meanwhile, once again set out on the campaign trail to topple Cotton Ed Smith. In the summer of 1944 the contest revolved around who could best defend the state's entrenched system of segregation, not the New Deal and the CIO. Slowed by age and a flagging voice, Cotton Ed succumbed to his younger, more vigorous opponent. Soon afterward, as Johnston headed to Washington pledging to defend white supremacy, Smith died.[44]

Six years later, in 1950, J. Strom Thurmond, fresh from his presidential run on the Dixiecrat ticket, entered the Senate race against Johnston. Both men swore their allegiance to Jim Crow, and each tried to pierce the other's white supremacist armor. "I am for segregation of the races. God started it and I believe in keeping it that way," the senator bellowed in Florence, "I defy anyone to say that Olin Johnston didn't fight civil rights." At the Newberry stump meeting, Thurmond accused him of sitting by "silent as a tomb" as President Harry S. Truman integrated the armed services in 1948. "If that's not so, Senator, stand up and deny it!" Thurmond yelled. "That's a lie! That's a lie! That's a lie," the incumbent hollered back. The two candidates almost came to blows. In the end, Johnston narrowly defeated Thurmond.[45] Besting the Dixiecrats' first man further bolstered his segregationist standing and made him a leading member of a new breed of postwar southern reactionaries that included archconservatives James Eastland and John C. Stennis. So solid were Johnston's credentials on the race question that no one dared to run against him in 1956.[46]

Even as Johnston drifted away from the politics of New Deal liberalism to the politics of reactionary racism, he remained just about the only politician in South Carolina who stood up for the workingman. "I am for the laboring man," Olin D. Johnston told an Aiken stump crowd during his last run for the Senate in 1962, although it could have been 1944 or 1950 or 1956. "I worked in the mills," he said everywhere he went, "my whole life has been dedicated to the working people." After his opponent ripped him for being endorsed by "all those foreign labor bosses," Johnston shot up to defend himself. "Do you blame labor?" Thirty years earlier, during his first term as governor, he noted, he had signed the state's first workers' compensation bill and authorized the establishment of a separate department of labor. "I am proud of my labor record," he declared.[47]

Occasionally during his Senate career, Johnston reinforced his ties to the working class with action. He was one of a handful of southern senators to oppose the Taft-Hartley Act, a conservative piece of legislation aimed at curbing trade union power, most notably by permitting states to enact right-to-work laws. Readily acknowledging the sins of some labor leaders, Johnston nonetheless insisted that the Republican proposal went "too far penalizing . . . those who live by the sweat of their brow."[48] A decade after Taft-Hartley passed over President Truman's veto and Johnston's opposition, the South Carolinian objected to fellow senator John McClellan's plan to expand the secretary of labor's authority to investigate and root out union corruption. Although Johnston assailed "gangsterism in labor unions," he refused to let any federal official grab hold of enough power to threaten states' rights or possibly integrate the factories. "I cannot fight in the Judiciary Committee," Johnston explained, "[t]o kill such legislation on civil-rights matters and vote for such matters in the field of labor. . . . This is inconsistency."[49]

When Johnston complained about the proposed McClellan act, he was doing more than reaching out to his reliable labor constituency. Crafting a message similar to his New Deal appeal, he spoke in a populist vernacular of the people against the interests, us against them.[50] The big difference was that in the postwar era, Johnston's "them" changed. Leaving Ben Sawyer, the money changers, and greedy capitalists alone, he pointed out new threats to working-class whites posed by liberal authorities from above and aggressive African Americans from below. Meeting in some far off place, probably Washington, these twin forces of evil were plotting to snatch the privileges of whiteness away from millhands and others. Sounding more like Blease and Smith than a New Dealer, Johnston now favored using government power to uphold white supremacy, and perhaps to bring a little pork back home, but little else. Again like Coley and Cotton Ed, he couched his opposition to government action in the intertwining idioms of race, class, gender, and sex.

Unnerved by African American insurgency, white millhands embraced Johnston's new-found antistatism. For years they had placed their faith in Roosevelt and centralized authority, but no more. After 1938 millhands mobilized to limit the scope of the federal government's power. That meant voting for politicians, like Olin D. Johnston, who vowed to uphold states' rights and white supremacy. Racial identity, however, was not the only factor that eroded workers' faith in the power of the federal government. No doubt the many defeats they had endured through the Great Depression, the New Deal era, and Johnston's first term as governor soured some on class-based political activism. Throughout the 1920s and 1930s, looking back at one example, textile laborers had demanded government-sponsored workers' compensation.

Finally, in 1935 they got their wish, only to discover that the law did not operate in their interests. For all of their hope, imagination, and grit, millhands, as the workers' compensation case illustrated, could not transform their world. Many, in fact, seemed almost politically exhausted from the long fight.[51]

As early as 1939, some millhands voiced their political resignation. "Somehow," explained Columbia's Collie Croft, "I didn't feel like I wanted to vote this time, and I just decided I'd stay at home and pray." Another capital city millworker said: "I don't like Roosevelt. Got no patience with him. I'm working hard as ever I did and ain't getting a cent more for it. If I'm going to starve, I just as soon kick my feet up on a dry goods box, get a good book to read, and sit right there and starve." Few were as bitter as this man, but many began to rethink the value of political mobilization along class lines and some decided that it was a dead end. But this is not to say class did not matter.[52]

The echoes of the language of labor that reverberated through Johnston's wartime and postwar campaign speeches resonated with workers' continuing concern with class issues. Even after 1938, millhands still complained about wages, workloads, promotions and dismissals, the heat in the factories, injuries, the deadly lint in the air, and being called lintheads. Occasionally, they pressed for labor legislation and backed labor candidates for state and local offices. Thousands joined unions and went on strike. Whether they enlisted with the more conservative American Federation of Labor or the liberal-leaning CIO or eschewed trade unionism all together, workers in the postwar period were trying to hang on to what they had gained.[53]

World War II pulled the textile industry out of its depression-era doldrums. Even before Pearl Harbor, orders for material for tents, khaki shorts, mosquito netting, and army-issued baseballs and softballs poured into South Carolina. Mills ran around the clock trying to keep up with demand. As the war also jump-started other industries, mill owners raised wages in frantic bids to keep their labor force intact. Conditions continued to improve throughout the war years. The conflict put a new shine on the public image of textile workers. Although they had been portrayed in the past as white trash, tin-bucket totters, and cotton mill drones, journalists now penned stories about patriotic laborers doing their part to defeat fascism. Prodded by federal statutes and war production boards and trying to prevent their employees from drifting into other jobs, mill owners raised wages again and again during the war. Labor shortages also presented women with new opportunities to work outside the home. More people at work and more money for each hour of work translated into a dramatic jump in mill people's standard of living.[54]

Even more than the First World War, World War II allowed southern millhands and their families to enter into the nation's consumer economy. After

The New Politics of Race

saving much of what they had made during the conflict, simply because there was nothing to buy, southern workers joined the national postwar spending frenzy. Taking advantage, at the same time, of the GI Bill, many bought their own homes either in the mill village or just outside of it in newly constructed working-class suburbs. They purchased new cars, shiny white refrigerators, automatic washing machines, and imitation mahogany high-fidelity radio consoles. Others put away enough money to send their children to college and out of the working class.[55]

By the late 1940s white millhands were beginning to be people with something to lose, and they desperately clung to their corners of the American Dream. Casting aside their older faith in New Deal liberalism, they lined up behind Olin Johnston and other reactionary politicians in an all-out campaign to save segregation. They believed that the wages of whiteness were worth more than the latest promises offered by liberals, and they were not entirely wrong, at least not in the short run. Postwar liberalism, which one observer described as "progressivism shorn of any economic critique," all but abandoned white laborers. Downplaying economic issues while moving civil rights and expanded opportunities to the top of their domestic agenda, postwar liberals offered white workers, according to Numan Bartley, "little aside from contempt and the right to compete for scarce jobs with black workers."[56]

By this time millhands had moved away from the politics of the New Deal toward an early version of massive resistance. For poor whites, the key to holding onto their precarious social position was keeping African Americans down. That meant making sure that jobs and suffrage remained racially defined. If liberals prevailed, millhands and people like them—semiskilled, undereducated, mostly nonunion white workers—would be forced to compete with African Americans for opportunities that had long been reserved for whites only. Fearing the worst, these workers worried that expanding options for African Americans would increase the labor supply and drive down their wages, forcing them into lower-paying jobs, and edging them out of the consumer economy, back into used cars, second-hand appliances, and worn-down neighborhoods.[57]

Millhands embraced a view of democracy similar to their view of the economy. Unlike liberals, who saw democracy as elastic, many white South Carolinians saw it as finite. There was only a fixed amount of citizenship to go around, barely enough, it seemed, after 1938.[58] If African Americans were given full democratic rights and allowed to vote in the primaries, there would be less "democracy" for others. Working-class whites feared that if democracy stopped being racially exclusive, wealthy whites, whom, going back to the days of Blease, they never really trusted, would leave them out.[59] If poor whites were written out of the dominant group, what would happen? Would they end up like African Americans, pushed into the worst jobs and the worst neighborhoods, despised and humiliated, tortured and exploited? Would someone treat them the way they treated African Americans? Would they end up not being white anymore?

For millhands, African American protest and the new liberalism that started to emerge during the late 1930s jeopardized their lives as white people and participants in the consumer economy. If blacks could vote and work alongside whites in the factory, then whiteness would be meaningless. White workers did not intend to let the whole idea of race and racial privilege evaporate without a fight. They attacked African Americans who attacked their whiteness, and they lashed out against politicians who favored easing racial distinctions.

They also incessantly talked of sex across the color line. Interwoven into these discussions were complicated metaphors about race and power. Defining race as natural, as a question of blood, as most white southerners did, meant that interracial sex symbolized an end to racial distinctions. In this coded language, race, then, would no longer matter. Whiteness would no longer matter. Poor whites would no longer receive the benefits and social privileges of whiteness. They would be nobodies. South Carolina millhands were not about to give up their whiteness, their jobs, and their status as citizens so easily, especially when the latest version of liberalism seemed to offer so little in return. Beginning during the war years, therefore, they dedicated their political efforts to making a hard fact out of the slippery fiction of race.[60]

CONCLUSION

Olin D. Johnston died on April 18, 1965. Millhands, mostly older, many retired, bowed their heads. Dressed in faded blue overalls and simple print
dresses, thousands of workers, some still "with lint in their hair," traveled to
Spartanburg to attend the former mill boy's funeral. Hundreds more filed
passed Johnston's casket in the rotunda of the state capitol in Columbia a few
days later. These "lintheads" came to pay their respects to Olin D., but they
also came to relive, for one last moment, a time in South Carolina history
when they stood at the center of state politics and better days seemed just
around the corner. That opportunity, however, had long since vanished.[1]

There can be little doubt that South Carolina millhands lost in their New
Deal–era bid to transform the state. Edgar A. Brown, ever hostile to labor,
remained in control of the malapportioned state legislature in 1948, and he
was still there when Johnston died. Business leaders continued to be the pre-
eminent force in the capital after World War II. Over the next decade, they
consolidated their grip on power, turning the state government into a virtual
professional booster association that marketed South Carolina to investors as
a paradise of cheap labor, sunny skies, and warm smiles. Despite some organizational gains during the war, few textile workers were represented by a
union in 1948. Although they made more money than ever before, they had
no say on the shop floor and no voice when it came to hiring and firing. Factories remained dangerous places; the air was thick with layers of deadly lint,
and the fast-moving machines were a constant threat to limbs and fingers.
Plant inspections were few and far between. Lawmakers, crying poor, said
that there was no room in the state budget to check on safety and working
conditions, not with all the tax breaks they were giving to companies to lure
them to the state. And "lintheads" were still disparaged and ostracized. Scorn
became an excuse for neglect. The schools in working-class neighborhoods
were overcrowded and underfunded, and there were few parks or playgrounds
in these areas.

In the postwar era textile workers could not even protect the flimsy privileges of whiteness. By the mid-1960s mill owners, pressured by the federal

government and anxious to drive down labor costs, for the first time hired African Americans in large numbers to work inside the mills next to whites. Following the stirring campaigns of the civil rights movement and a brief moment of liberal triumph in Washington, African Americans finally regained the ballot, stolen during Reconstruction. Now, blacks could vote, even in the once all-white Democratic Party primary.

White workers were dismayed. While most of the nation seemed to be rushing ahead into Henry Luce's ballyhooed "American Century" of newfound prosperity and security, they felt like they were going backward. Lifelong millhand Earl Jeffcoat voiced white frustrations. He complained a few weeks after Olin Johnston died that the "nigger is just about where the white was twenty or thirty years ago." [2]

Undoubtedly the thoughts and actions of white workers contributed to their ultimate defeat. They were perhaps too quick to strike, too quick to invest their faith in the New Deal and the idea of state action, and too quick to embrace political leaders as their saviors. Although they conscientiously went to the polls on election day and repeatedly pressured lawmakers to enact parts of their legislative agenda, they failed to build a durable and lasting political organization. Finally, their ideas about whiteness narrowed their vision. Unable to picture, even for a moment, a world where race did not matter, they could see African Americans only as enemies, as emasculating sexual predators and constant threats to their social position and economic status. Despite their economic liberalism, they could not imagine a biracial labor movement or a political challenge of the have-nots, black and white across the color line.

But the stories written on the streets, in the red brick factories, and in the four-room yellow houses in South Carolina's mill towns were not simple dramas about vicious racism. Certainly racism, in all of its ugly brutality, was always there, as evidenced by the grisly murders of Joe Brinson, Frank Whisonant, Dan Jenkins, and Willie Earle. Yet the white racists who made the looms and spindles whirl and spin in the 1930s also exhibited tremendous imagination and grace, resilience and persistence when it came to the politics of class. They came close to controlling the state government in the middle of the decade. They reached out in many directions to change the balance of power and nudged the world at the polling station, but in the end the weight of South Carolina's bulky economic and political structures proved too heavy for millhands to topple. They could not overcome the fact that, although a significant political force, they still represented only one-fifth of the state's white population. The malapportionment of the legislature diluted their political strength, making it hard for them to be heard in the corridors of power, especially in the all-important senate. At the same time, the savagely competitive structure of the textile industry and the region's relentless rural poverty, which created an endless surplus of cheap labor, combined to weaken mill village trade unionism and blunt the strike weapon.

Then there was the final blow. The nature of national liberalism changed. Pushing issues of racial justice ahead of economic democracy, liberals left racist white workers without powerful allies in the government and with no place to go but to the right. And that is where they headed, to the side of the reinvented and more racist Olin Johnston, Strom Thurmond, and, eventually, George Wallace. After casting their lot with these reactionaries, poor whites became stock Hollywood characters, tobacco-spitting, Confederate flag-waving rednecks. Films and television shows made fun of these not-so-good, good ol' boys, and audiences in all-white, middle-class suburbs congratulated themselves for not being anything like them. The defeat of the millhands became a rout.

"The tragedy of Man," Eugene O'Neill wrote, "is perhaps the only significant thing about him." After watching one of his stories unfold, he wanted his audiences to walk away from the theater with "an exultant feeling from seeing somebody on stage facing life, fighting against odds, not conquering, but perhaps inevitably being conquered."[3] Like O'Neill's tragically flawed, but somewhat noble, characters, the working people in this story were also conquered, maybe not inevitably, but they lost all the same. During their struggle between 1910 and 1948 for respect, higher wages, a slower pace of work, and a share of state power, South Carolina millhands revealed something of themselves. They showed how identities shift and how meaning is constantly being created and re-created. They also demonstrated how complicated are the tensions among race, class, and gender. Again, millhands lost nearly all of their battles, but the stories they wrote add up to more than just another sad tale from the gothic, pre–Sun Belt southern past. They are the stories of real, everyday working people, capable of love and hate, racism and heroism, who understood the world they lived in but were unable to change it.

Data for Tables A.1 through A.5 are from a variety of sources. For countywide returns, I consulted Alexander Heard, *Southern Primaries and Elections, 1920–1949* (1950), 106–11. For precinct-level returns, see *Anderson Independent*, September 12, 1934, August 31, 1938; *Beaufort Gazette*, September 13, 1934; *Easley Progress*, September 10, 1924, September 10, 1930, September 13, 1934, September 1, 1938; *Gaffney Ledger*, September 11, 1924, September 11, 1930, September 13, 1934, September 1, 1938; *Georgetown Times*, September 14, 1934, September 2, 1938; *Greenville News*, September 10, 1924, September 10, 1930, September 13, 1934, September 1, 1938; *Lee County Messenger*, September 1, 1938; *Manning Times*, September 12, 1934, August 31, 1938; *Orangeburg Times and Democrat*, September 12, 1934, August 31, 1938; *Rock Hill Evening Herald*, September 10, 1924, September 10, 1930, September 12, 1934, August 31, 1938; *Spartanburg Herald*, September 10, 1924, September 10, 1930, September 12, 1934, August 31, 1938; and *Union Daily Times*, September 10, 1924, September 10, 1930.

For the purposes of these tables, I defined the low country simply as a geographic area. My sample for the low country includes returns from the counties of Allendale, Bamberg, Barnwell, Beaufort, Berkeley, Charleston, Clarendon, Colleton, Dillon, Florence, Georgetown, Hampton, Horry, Jasper, Marion, Orangeburg, and Williamsburg. Upcountry counties include Abbeville, Anderson, Cherokee, Chester, Fairfield, Greenville, Greenwood, Lancaster, Laurens, Newberry, Oconee, Pickens, Saluda, Spartanburg, Union, and York.

Town precincts are defined as those precincts within city limits; only town precincts in the upcountry are included. Therefore Charleston and other low-country cities are excluded. Almost without exception, these precincts are listed in the newspapers as wards. For instance, the *Greenville News* listed returns for four city wards. For mill precincts, I counted the returns from all precincts that bore the same names as the mills in the areas. For rural areas, I considered any precincts not clearly urban or mill, with less than 150 voters, to be rural.

Unfortunately, it is hard to know exactly who lived in each precinct. However, the South Carolina Division of Archives and History does have some, although certainly not all or even a majority, of the state's Democratic Party Club Records. These are lists of all registered voters in a given precinct. Most important for my purposes here, they include the occupations of most voters in a given precinct. A quick look at the occupational profile of several precincts underscores the occupational and residential divisions in the state in 1930s and 1940s.

In 1940, for instance, of the 438 registered voters at the Lydia Mills Precinct in Laurens County, 336 or 76.71 percent were millworkers. In the Clinton Mills Precinct, also in Laurens County, 69.01 percent of registered voters were millworkers. And in 1938, 52.84 percent of voters in the Bath Mills Precinct in Aiken County were millworkers. In each of these mill precincts, the second largest occupational group listed was housewife.

Meanwhile, in the Laurens City Precinct in 1938, a little more than one-half of one percent of all voters were millworkers. This precinct had an extremely diversified electorate that included farmers, housewives, carpenters, salesmen, doctors, teachers, nurses, bookkeepers, butchers, beauticians, and automobile dealers.

Finally, in largely rural Clarendon County, in 1932, the Doctor Swamp Precinct had 62 registered voters. Forty-one of these Democrats were farmers. In the nearby Panola Precinct in 1932, half of all voters were farmers. Again, the next largest group was housewives, which numbered 28. The third largest profession was merchant; three merchants were registered to vote in Panola in 1932.

The Democratic Party Club lists can be found in the archives by county. However, they are not cataloged by specific club. Therefore the records must be ordered by county. For instance, in order to get the Democractic club list for the Laurens Cotton Mills, you have to order all the records for the county. The outside of each book usually lists the precinct name, but again these names are not in the catalog.

Table A.1. Percentage of Vote for Coleman L. Blease versus James F. Byrnes, U.S. Senate Runoff, 1924

Percentage of Vote for Blease	
Statewide	50.56
County averages	
Low country	45.23
Upcountry	56.23
Upcountry precinct averages	
Town	32.89 (n = 19)
Mill	71.57 (n = 46)

Table A.2. Percentage of Vote for Coleman L. Blease versus James F. Byrnes, U.S. Senate Runoff, 1930

Percentage of Vote for Blease	
Statewide	49.05
County averages	
Low country	51.63
Upcountry	44.60
Upcountry precinct averages	
Town	36.64 (n = 44)
Mill	61.38 (n = 52)

Table A.3. Percentage of Vote for Olin D. Johnston versus Ibra C. Blackwood, Gubernatorial Runoff, 1930

Percentage of Vote for Johnston	
Statewide	49.98
County averages	
Low country	32.54
Upcountry	59.53
Upcountry precinct averages	
Town	37.50 (n = 16)
Mill	76.57 (n = 52)

Table A.4. Percentage of Vote for Olin D. Johnston
versus Coleman L. Blease, Gubernatorial Runoff, 1934

Percentage of Vote for Johnston	
Statewide	56.20
County averages	
Low country	58.33
Upcountry	57.59
Upcountry precinct averages	
Town	48.31 (n = 36)
Mill	68.59 (n = 46)
Rural precinct averages	
Districts with 76–150 voters	50.38 (n = 60)
Districts with less than 75 voters	40.64 (n = 80)

Table A.5. Percentage of Vote for Olin D. Johnston
versus Ellison D. Smith, U.S. Senate Runoff, 1938

Percentage of Vote for Johnston	
Statewide	44.60
County averages	
Low country	37.37
Upcountry	47.68
Upcountry precinct averages	
Town	37.97 (n = 50)
Mill	70.68 (n = 38)
Rural precinct averages	
Districts with 76–150 voters	53.18 (n = 55)
Districts with less than 75 voters	38.53 (n = 71)

Table A.6. Annual Earnings of South Carolina Textile Workers, 1909-1937

Year	Annual Average Wage Index (1909 = 100)	Year	Annual Average Wage Index (1909 = 100)
1909	100.0	1924	229.0
1910	95.8	1925	234.7
1911	97.9	1926	236.9
1912	107.9	1927	246.7
1913	112.0	1928	235.0
1914	116.2	1929	270.9
1916	124.1	1930	226.4
1917	154.7	1931	232.4
1918	221.5	1932	186.7
1919	352.8	1933	200.0
1920	268.5	1934	236.2
1921	238.4	1935	235.0
1922	220.3	1936	249.2
1923	232.4	1937	285.2

Source: Olin D. Johnston Papers, box 39—Departmental Commissions, South Carolina Department of Archives and History, Columbia.

Abbreviations

AI	*Anderson Independent*
BP	Blease Papers, SCDAH
CAB	Conciliation and Arbitration Board
CLB	Coleman Livingston Blease
CN&C	*Charleston News and Courier*
CO	*Charlotte Observer*
CU	Clemson University, Clemson
DU	Duke University, Durham
FDR	Franklin D. Roosevelt
FDRL	Franklin D. Roosevelt Library, Hyde Park
FWP	Federal Writers' Project
GI-J	*Greenwood Index-Journal*
GML	George Meany Memorial Library, Silver Spring
GN	*Greenville News*
HCV	Horse Creek Valley
ICB	Ibra C. Blackwood
JGR	John G. Richards
NA	National Archives, Washington, D.C.
NRA	National Recovery Administration
NYA	National Youth Administration
NYT	*New York Times*
ODJ	Olin D. Johnston
RG	Record Group
SCDAH	South Carolina Division of Archives and History, Columbia
SCFL	South Carolina Federation of Labor
SCL	South Caroliniana Library, Columbia
SH	*Spartanburg Herald*
SHC	Southern Historical Collection, University of North Carolina, Chapel Hill
SHSW	State Historical Society of Wisconsin, Madison
SOHP	Southern Oral History Project, SHC
SPC-V	Southern Politics Collection, Heard Library, Vanderbilt University, Nashville
TWUA	Textile Workers Union of America Records, SHSW
WC	Archives, Wofford College, Sandor Teszler Library, Spartanburg
WPA	Work Progress Administration, SCL

Introduction

1. Will Thompson is a character from Caldwell, *God's Little Acre*. See also Simon, "The Novel as Social History."

2. The quotations in this and the next paragraph are from Caldwell, *God's Little Acre*, 100, 196, 214.

3. Natalie Z. Davis, *Fiction in the Archives*, 4–5; Anne Firor Scott, "Women in the South," 22–35. Although talking about film, Robert Rosenstone makes a similar point about history in *Visions of the Past*, 64–72.

4. Allison, *Skin*. See also Allison, *Trash* and *Bastard Out of Carolina*.

5. Nichols, "Does the Mill Village Foster Any Social Types?"

6. For an overview of the field, see Hall et al., *Like a Family*, xi–xx, and Zieger, "Textile Workers and Historians," *Organized Labor*, 35–59. See also Carlton, *Mill and Town*; Flamming, *Creating the Modern South*; Fink, *Fulton Bag*; Hodges, *New Deal Labor Policy*; Newby, *Plain Folk*; and Tullos, *Habits of Industry*.

7. The figure for the earlier period was calculated by dividing the number of adult male workers in 1914 by the approximate number of white men over age 21—in other words, eligible voters—in the state in 1914. The latter figure is an extrapolation. In order to derive this number, I calculated the difference between the number of men over 21 in 1910 and 1920; then I divided this figure by 10 and multiplied it by 4. Finally, I added this number to the census figures from 1910 and came up with an approximation of the number of white men over 21 in the state in 1914. See U.S. Bureau of the Census, *Census of Manufacturers*, 1414. For figures on voting-age males, see *Thirteenth Census, Population: Reports by States*, 635–58, and *Fourteenth Census, Population: Composition and Characteristics*, 23–27. For figures on the number of voters in the mill villages in the later period, see Carlton, "The State and the Worker," 188, 198.

8. Bell, *Out of This Furnace*, 356.

9. My reading of South Carolina workers' sense of politics resembles in some ways Thomas Bender's ("Wholes and Parts"—quotation, p. 126) conception of "public culture." Others who have helped to shape my understanding of the range of political activities include Fox-Genovese and Genovese, "The Political Crisis of Social History"; Gareth S. Jones, *Languages of Class*, 1–21, 101–2; Baker, "The Domestication of Politics"; Leuchtenburg, "The Pertinence of Political History"; and Kelley, "'We Are Not What We Seem.'"

10. See Cash, *Mind of the South*; George M. Frederickson, *The Black Image*; and Gilmore, *Gender and Jim Crow*.

11. See, e.g., Flynt, *Dixie's Forgotten People*.

12. See Woodward, *Tom Watson*.

13. Key, *Southern Politics*. For Key's contribution to southern political history, see Bartley, "In Search of the New South."

14. See, e.g., Dan Carter's most recent book, *Politics of Rage*, 69. Carter describes demagogues as southern politicians "whose harangues against blacks played on the emotions of simple, uneducated white farmers and blue-collar workers." "Most," he observes, "fought their way into public office on a wave of soak-the-rich rhetoric. Once elected, they made their peace with powerful interests groups and offered their working-class supporters little more than a heavy dose of 'nigger'-baiting."

15. For more complicated explorations of white racism and class politics, see, e.g., Kazin, *Barons of Labor*; Roediger, *Wages of Whiteness*; and MacLean, *Behind the Mask*.

16. Hunter, "Household Workers in the Making," 4. For an example of "simultaneity," see Griffin and Korstad, "Class as Race and Gender."

17. *Time*, August 7, 1944, 18.

Chapter One

1. *Gaffney Ledger*, March 29, 1912. The *Ledger* was Blacksburg's "local" paper.

2. For the fullest accounts of what happened in Blacksburg, see N. W. Hardin to CLB, March 29, 1912, and W. W. Thomas to CLB (telegram), March 29, 1912, box 11, file— Cherokee County 1911-13, BP; *Gaffney Ledger*, March 29, April 2, 5, 9, 1912; and *SH*, March 30, 1912.

3. Raper, *Tragedy of Lynching*, 47.

4. *Gaffney Ledger*, April 2, 4, 1912.

5. On ideas about the kinds of groups that lynch, see Raper, *Tragedy of Lynching*; Brundage, *Lynching in the New South*, 17-48; and Finnegan, "'At the Hands of Parties Unknown.'" Some have attributed lynching to social and economic instability. Obviously, industrialization was a forceful engine of change. Nonetheless, evidence from the U.S. census does not suggest other dramatic changes in Blacksburg and Cherokee County in the first decades of the twentieth century. For instance, population in the area climbed steadily, but not remarkably, in the years leading up to the murders. But between 1900 and 1910 the population of Blacksburg declined by almost 13 percent. In addition, there does not seem to have been a sudden shift in the overall structure of the rural economy of the county. In 1900, 61.1 percent of the county's residents, white and black, were tenant farmers. The relative percentage of white and African American tenants also remained about the same. By 1920 there was, it is worth noting, a slight increase in the number of African American land-owners in Cherokee County. For population changes, see U.S. Bureau of the Census, *Thirteenth Census, Population: Reports by States*, 643, and *Fourteenth Census, Population: Numbers and Distribution*, 603. For the economic structure of the county, see *Twelfth Census, Agriculture*, 118-19; *Thirteenth Census, Agriculture*, 508-15; and *Fourteenth Census, Agriculture*, 276-77.

6. N. W. Hardin to CLB, March 29, 1912; *Gaffney Ledger*, April 2, 1912.

7. This is how rape is seen in most of the most recent scholarship. See, e.g., Hall, "'The Mind That Burns in Each Body,'" and *Revolt against Chivalry*; Bederman, "'Civilization'"; MacLean, "The Leo Frank Case Reconsidered"; and Laura F. Edwards, "Sexual Violence."

8. The growing divide between millworkers and the town classes has been explored by Carlton, *Mill and Town*. Many middle-class South Carolinians equated Bleasism with anarchy and lawlessness. See, e.g., Joel F. Dowling to CLB, March 23, 1912 (box 17, file— Greenville County 1911-13), M. A. Moseley to CLB, March 15, 1912 (box 34, file—Spartanburg County 1912-13), and W. P. Caukey to CLB, March 23, 1912 (box 21, file—Lancaster County 1912), BP.

9. For the crisis of masculinity in the South, see Joel Williamson, *The Crucible of Race*, and Ted Ownby, *Subduing Satan*. See also Kimmel, "Contemporary 'Crisis' of Masculinity," and Stearns, *Be a Man!*

10. For figures on mill building, see Lander, *History of South Carolina*, 83. See also Stephen L. Shapiro, "The Growth," 13-28. For the number of male workers in the factories from 1850 to 1890, see U.S. Bureau of the Census, *Report on Manufacturing Industries*, 188-89; for figures on male workers in 1900, see *Occupations at the Twelfth Census*, 385; and

for the percentage of men in the textile mill workforce in 1910, see *Thirteenth Census, Population, 1910*, 516-17.

11. For South Carolina's geography, see Edgar, *WPA Guide*, 8-14, and Schaper, *Sectionalism*, 17-22.

12. On the economy of the upcountry, see Lacy K. Ford, *Origins of Southern Radicalism*. For the low country, see Coclanis, *Shadow of a Dream*, and McCurry, *Masters of Small Worlds*.

13. Carlton, *Mill and Town*, 40-42; Stephen L. Shapiro, "The Growth," 7-70; Lander, *History of South Carolina*, 82-84.

14. Carlton, "Unbalanced Growth," "Revolution from Above," 448-49, and "The Piedmont and Waccamaw Regions." See also Coclanis and Ford, "The South Carolina Economy," 102-3.

15. For the white supremacy campaign in South Carolina, see Tindall, "Campaign for . . . Disfranchisement"; Key, *Southern Politics*, 548; Kousser, *Shaping of Southern Politics*, 50, 84-91; and Ayers, *Promise of the New South*, 285-87. For the debates on disfranchisement in the South, see Woodward, *Strange Career*. See also Rabinowitz, "More Than the Woodward Thesis," and Woodward, "*Strange Career* Critics."

16. On apportionment, see Simon, "Devaluation of the Vote."

17. See n. 7 in the Introduction.

18. George M. Frederickson, *The Black Image*, 60-61; Van den Berghe, *Race and Racism*.

19. Simkins, *Pitchfork Ben Tillman*, 485 (quotation).

20. A careful study of Blease's correspondence suggests that he either belonged to or had close ties to the Independent Order of Odd Fellows, Improved Order of Red Men, Loyal Order of Moose, Knights of Pythias, Protective Order of Elks, Woodmen of the World, and possibly even the Ku Klux Klan. On Blease and his extensive contacts, see Potwin, *Cotton Mill People*, 32, 45, 98.

21. For election returns, see Jordan, *The Primary State*, 25-30. See also *The State*, August 30, 1906, August 29, 1908, August 31, 1912, August 27, 1914, and September 13, 1916. David Carlton's (*Mill and Town*, 215-20, 273-75) sophisticated quantitative research suggests a strong correlation between the number of millworkers in a district and the Blease vote. My own quantitative evidence also suggests a strong correlation between the Blease vote and the number of millworkers in a county. Qualitative evidence points to a similar relationship. See, e.g., S. M. Smith to CLB, n.d. (box 14, file—Edgefield County 1911-13), J. L. Harris to CLB, May 14, 1912 (box 36, file—Union County 1911-13), and Joshua W. Ansley to CLB, February 28, 1911 (box 4, file—Anderson County 1911-13), BP.

22. Carlton, *Mill and Town*, 2; Newby, *Plain Folk*, 269; Wallace, *South Carolina*, 656 (quotations of textile workers); Warr, "Mr. Blease," 29. The doggerel was related to me by longtime South Carolina resident and noted genealogist Brent H. Holcomb. For additional verses, see J. A. Wilson to CLB, March 3, 1911 (box 19, file—Greenwood County 1911-13), Hilrey Sanford to CLB, n.d. (box 3, file—Anderson County 1912), and Jim Casey, "He Niver Was a Proletarian" (box 20, file—General Correspondence 1913-14), BP.

23. Cash, *Mind of the South*, 250; Warr, "Mr. Blease," 29; Key, *Southern Politics*, 130, 143-45; Kousser, *Shaping of Southern Politics*, 236. For other views on Blease, see Cash, *Mind of the South*, 250-59; Simkins, *Pitchfork Ben Tillman*, 486-504, 536-49; Stone, "Bleasism"; and Hollis, "Blease and the Senatorial Campaign." To date, no one has written a full-length biography of Blease, perhaps because his personal papers have not been found. Nonetheless, there are two unpublished accounts of Blease's political career. See Burnside, "Governorship of . . . Blease," and Anthony B. Miller, "Blease." The Blease historiography is summarized in Carlton, *Mill and Town*, 221-23.

24. The key book is Carlton's *Mill and Town*.

25. Ibid., 83–84. See also Carlton, "'Builders of a New State.'" For the classic view of mill men as regional saviors, see Broadus Mitchell, *The Rise of Cotton Mills*.

26. Carlton, *Mill and Town*, 132. For additional information and interpretations of progressivism in South Carolina, see Mary K. Cann, "Morning After"; Sandra C. Mitchell, "Conservative Reform"; Boggs, "John Patrick Grace"; Lupold, "South Carolina Progressives"; and Burts, *Richard Irvine Manning*. For a review of southern progressivism, see Tindall, *New South*, 219–84; Grantham, "Contours of Southern Progressivism"; and Link, *Paradox of Southern Progressivism*.

27. Carlton, *Mill and Town*, 224–25.

28. Stephanie McCurry ("The Two Faces of Republicanism") has looked at the intersection between the public and the private in antebellum South Carolina. For other examples of mixing the public and private in an analysis of the South, see Hodes, "Sexualization of Reconstruction Politics," and MacLean, *Behind the Mask*. Joan Wallach Scott ("On Language, Gender, and Working-Class History") has framed this question about links between the public and private quite broadly.

29. For the naturalization of difference, see Bederman, "'Civilization.'"

30. For the larger meaning of suffrage, see Foner, "The Meaning of Freedom," 442–43. On the ideology of race, see Fields, "Ideology and Race." See also recent literature on the construction of "whiteness": Roediger, *Wages of Whiteness*; Allen, *Invention of the White Race*; and Neather, "'Whiteness' and the Politics of Working-Class History." On the fears of white yeomen in South Carolina, see Lacy K. Ford, *Origins of Southern Radicalism*, 138–41. For more on the yeomanry, see also Genovese, "Yeomen Farmers," 331–42; Thornton, *Politics and Power in a Slave Society*; and Harris, *Plain Folk and Gentry*.

31. Lacy K. Ford, *Origins of Southern Radicalism*, 49–51, 99–144. Nancy MacLean (*Behind the Mask*, 23–26) makes a similar argument regarding how the petite bourgeoisie of the South felt about the increased concentration of capital after World War I.

32. See Ben Tillman's attacks on the aristocracy in Simkins, *Pitchfork Ben Tillman*, 70–71.

33. For more on sexual tension and Reconstruction, see Hodes, "Sexualization of Reconstruction Politics," and Laura F. Edwards, "Sexual Violence."

34. On the South Carolina constitution of 1895, see Kousser, *Shaping of Southern Politics*, 50, 84–91; Lander, *History of South Carolina*, 40–41; Tindall, "Campaign for . . . Disfranchisement," 228–29; and Simkins, *Pitchfork Ben Tillman*, 285–309.

35. Lacy K. Ford, "Rednecks and Merchants" and "Yeoman Farmers." See also Hahn, *Roots of Southern Populism*.

36. See Ayers, *Promise of the New South*, 202–7. MacLean (*Behind the Mask*, 36) and Flamming (*Creating the Modern South*, 14–15) also discuss control over the household, the commercial economy, and tenancy.

37. T. V. Blair to CLB, November 30, 1914 (box 5, file—Anderson County 1914), and S. E. Arthur to CLB, January 19, 1914 (box 3, file—Aiken County 1914), BP. See also Eric Foner's discussion of wage slavery in *Politics and Ideology*, 59–63, and Roediger, *Wages of Whiteness*. Nancy MacLean makes a similar point about declining authority in *Behind the Mask*, 24.

38. On wage scales, see Wright, "Cheap Labor," and McHugh, *Mill Family*. On southern mill men and their fears of declining patriarchy, see Hall et al., *Like a Family*, 152–53. On wages and masculinity in other settings and contexts, see Hobbs, "Rethinking Antifeminism."

39. On masculinity and the workplace, see MacLean, "The Leo Frank Case Reconsidered," and Hall, "Private Eyes, Public Women."

40. On sexual harassment on the shop floor, see Newby, *Plain Folk*, 329–30, and Fink,

"Efficiency and Control," 25. For examples, from a later period, of a longtime supervisor who was well known for harassing young female employees, see J. H. Palmer to Kamanow, September 11, 1935, J. L. Harding, "Preliminary Report of the Limestone Mill," June 20, 1935, and Roland Hill et al., to W. C. Hamrick, n.d., NRA Records, RG 9, ser. 402, box 75, file—Limestone Mill, NA.

41. On the disposition of wages and family tensions, see Hall et al., *Like a Family*, 62–63. Douglas Flamming ("Daughters, Dollars, and Domesticity") has argued that southern women millworkers kept more of their wages than northern women millworkers.

42. MacLean, *Behind the Mask*, 31–33; Hall et al., *Like a Family*, 257; Hall, "Disorderly Women" and "O. Delight Smith's Progressive Era." For northern examples, see Meyerowitz, *Women Adrift*, and Peiss, *Cheap Amusements*.

43. In 1890 African Americans owned 11.2 percent of the farms in South Carolina; twenty years later the proportion reached 31.7 percent. Ayers, *Promise of the New South*, 514. Although this figure is significant and dramatic, it should not be exaggerated. During this period the value of land dropped. Still, in his 1913 annual address to the legislature, Blease noted with alarm the growing number of black landowners in the state. Burnside, "Governorship of . . . Blease," 236–37.

44. Finnegan, "'At the Hands of Parties Unknown,'" 301–5. Fifteen years later Green was accused of the same crime. This time he was lynched. Raper, *Tragedy of Lynching*, 263–85.

45. William Beard, the Bleasite editor of the *Abbeville Scimitar*, is quoted in Finnegan, "'At the Hands of Parties Unknown,'" 173.

46. Newby, *Plain Folk*, 130–32; Carlton, *Mill and Town*, 195, 205, 208. Alabama town folks looked at industrial laborers through similar lenses. See Flynt, *Poor but Proud*, 107–9, 233. The same could be said of North Carolina elites. See Holland Thompson, *From the Cotton Field*, 116; Rhyne, *Southern Cotton Mill Workers*, 85; and DeNatale, "Bynum," 325–27.

47. On suffrage restriction, see Carlton, *Mill and Town*, 225–27, 229–31, and Anthony B. Miller, "Blease," 99–100.

48. Rev. John White is quoted in *Golden Age*, January 2, 1913, box 3, file—Anderson County 1913, BP. Blease supporters dutifully reported to the governor what his detractors said about him. W. P. Caskey to CLB, March 23, 1912 (box 21, file—Lancaster County 1912), and Joel F. Dowling to CLB, March 23, 1912 (box 17, file—Greenville 1911–13), BP.

49. Link, *Paradox of Southern Progressivism*, 183; Carlton, *Mill and Town*, 226.

50. For reform and suffrage in South Carolina, see Taylor, "Enfranchisement of Women: The Early Years" and ". . .: The Later Years"; Wheeler, *New Women*, 110; and Link, *Paradox of Southern Progressivism*, 183–98. According to the *NYT* (May 5, 1996), in a speech in South Carolina in 1919, Carrie Chapman Catt said, "White supremacy will be strengthened, not weakened," by woman suffrage. See also Dubbert, "Progressivism."

51. For examples of men who wanted to leave the mill village because of their dwindling control over their families, see Hall et al., *Like a Family*, 152.

52. On drinking in the mill village, see, e.g., B. E. Wilkins to CLB, July 11, 1911 (box 32, file—Spartanburg County 1911), and J. R. Dean to CLB, November 11, 1911 (box 33, file—Spartanburg County 1911), BP. On desertion as well as drinking, see Hall et al., *Like a Family*, 165–68.

53. Domestic violence, as Christine Stansell has pointed out in another context, was not simply a reaction against dwindling status in the workplace but also a brutal "attempt to recapture and enforce . . . masculine authority." Stansell, *City Of Women*, 76–83. For stories of violence, see Brice, "The Use of Executive Clemency," 12, and Hall et al., *Like a Family*, 162, 166–67.

54. For accounts of lynching during these years, see Mullins, "Lynching in South Caro-

lina"; Garris, "The Decline of Lynching"; and Finnegan, "'At the Hands of Parties Unknown.'"

55. For workers' views on wages, hours, and unions, see J. T. Blassingame to CLB, June 19, 1914 (box 19, file—Greenville County 1914), and C. P. Lackey to CLB, December 29, 1913 (box 34, file—Spartanburg County 1913), BP. See also Newby, *Plain Folk*, 542-46, and McLaurin, "Early Labor Union Organizational Efforts."

56. For overviews of these primaries, see Jordan, *The Primary State*, 25-26. See also *The State*, August 30, 1906, and August 29, 1908. For quantitative analysis of Blease's support on the mill hills, see Carlton, *Mill and Town*, 215-21, 273-75.

57. Cash, *Mind of the South*, 258; Derieux, "Crawling toward the Promised Land," 178.

58. For an excellent report on the stump meeting, see *Newsweek*, August 12, 1938, 12. Although this is from a later period, the stump meeting seems to have remained pretty much the same from the time Ben Tillman started the ritual in 1892 until the 1940s.

59. Anthony B. Miller, "Blease," 65, 136; W. H. Newbold to CLB, June 6, 1912 (box 11, file—Chester County 1911-12), and CLB to William Woodward Dixon, May 24, 1912 (box 15, file—Fairfield County 1911-12), BP; House Journal, 1913, 158, SCL. On Blease's drinking, see CLB to J. W. Ashely, April 21, 1913, box 4, file—Anderson County 1913, BP. For his response to law-and-order advocates, see Carlton, *Mill and Town*, 248-49.

60. Burnside, "Governorship of . . . Blease," 294, 274; Anthony B. Miller, "Blease," 65, 136; A. H. Walker to CLB, February 10, 1912, box 2, file—Anderson County 1912, BP. For other examples of Blease's labels for his opponents, see CLB to J. C. Wilborn, June 6, 1912 (box 11, file—Chester County 1911-12), CLB to Charles H. Henry, November 10, 1911 (box 33, file—Spartanburg County 1911), and CLB to W. P. Beard, June 1, 1914 (box 1, file—Abbeville County 1914), BP; Wallace, *South Carolina*, 656; and Carlton, *Mill and Town*, 1-4.

61. Carlton, *Mill and Town*, 238-39 (quotations); Link, *Paradox of Southern Progressivism*, 189; Burnside, "Governorship of . . . Blease," 99-100; Anthony B. Miller, "Blease," 36; Wheeler, *New Women*, 25-37; MacLean, *Behind the Mask*, 30-31; Dubbert, "Progressivism."

62. Anthony B. Miller, "Blease," 61, 113, 135-36; clipping, *Seneca Tri-County Harpoon*, ca. 1913, box 4, file—Anderson County 1913, BP.

63. CLB to W. P. Beard, June 1, 1914, box 1, file—Abbeville County 1914, BP. For other examples of the language of aristocracy and the vocabulary of South Carolina politics, see Lacy K. Ford, *Origins of Southern Radicalism*, 109. Antiaristocratic attacks were part and parcel of Tillmanism. See Simkins, *Pitchfork Ben Tillman*, 70-71. For more on the laborite perception of aristocrats and their sexuality, see Gantt, *Breaking the Chains*, 27-133.

64. Blease's gubernatorial inaugural address, January 22, 1913, House Journal, 158; Anthony B. Miller, "Blease," 43, 113. For more on the mythology of Reconstruction in the twentieth-century South, see Goodman, *Stories of Scottsboro*, 52, 114.

65. For some of the measures supporting white supremacy that Blease endorsed, see Carlton, *Mill and Town*, 243-44, 258; CLB to J. W. D. Bolin, May 9, 1912 (box 11, file—Cherokee County 1911-13), and J. A. McGill to CLB, February 25, 1911 (box 17, file—Greenville County 1911), BP; and J. L. Woodward to CLB, February 11, 1914, and CLB to All County Board of Registers, attached to a letter to W. D. Grist, July 7, 1913, box 39, file—Spartanburg County 1913-14, BP. On the firing of the black notaries public, see Milton B. McCuen to CLB, January 20, 1912, box 22, file—Laurens County 1911-13, BP.

66. Burnside, "Governorship of . . . Blease," 255, 18, 38 (first, fourth, fifth quotations); Sandra C. Mitchell, "Conservative Reform," 213 (second quotation); Warr, "Mr. Blease," 31 (third quotation). See also Anthony B. Miller, "Blease," 37, 88-89, and Blease's inaugural address, January 22, 1913, House Journal, 1913, 158.

67. Carlton, *Mill and Town*, 236; Newby, *Plain Folk*, 383.

68. On the medical inspection bill, see Newby, *Plain Folk*, 381–84 (first quotation, p. 383); Anthony B. Miller, "Blease," 37, 88–89; Carlton, *Mill and Town*, 236–39 (third quotation, "third parties," and the "unmetionable crime," p. 237); J. J. Contey to CLB, March 5, 1914, box 12, file—Clarendon County 1914, BP (second quotation); Wallace, *South Carolina*, 660 (Blease on the campaign trail); Burnside, "Governorship of . . . Blease," 216–17 ("negro janitors"). See also J. L Darlington to CLB, n.d., box 18, file—Greenville County 1911–13, BP. For a regional perspective on working-class resistance to medical inspections, see Link, *Paradox of Southern Progressivism*, 208–11.

69. Carlton, *Mill and Town*, 245. See also CLB to C. W. Templeton, January 12, 1914, box 19, file—Greenville County 1914, BP.

70. Brice, "The Use of Executive Clemency," 37; Burnside, "Governorship of . . . Blease," 39, 74–91 (second quotation, p. 75); *CN&C*, August 16, 1910. See also CLB to J. W. D. Bolin, May 9, 1912 (box 11, file—Cherokee County 1911–13), and W. L. Abernathy to CLB, February 12, 1914 (box 12, file—Chester County 1914), BP. For more on Blease's racial ideology from a later period, see *Blease's Weekly*, May 27, 1926. For the wider context, see Newby, *Jim Crow's Defense*.

71. Burnside, "Governorship of . . . Blease," 39, 74–91 (first quotation, p. 75); Carlton, *Mill and Town*, 246–49 (second quotation, p. 246). See also Warr, "Mr. Blease," 25–26. Blease elaborated on his view of lynching in the *Los Angeles Sunday Times*, a clipping of which is attached to a letter from W. O. Grist to CLB, January 1, 1913, file—York County 1913–14, box 38, BP. Blease was not alone in taking this position. See Fitz McMaster, a newspaperman, to H. Brown of New York, June 18, 1930, McMaster Papers, SCDAH.

72. Anthony B. Miller, "Blease," 38, 43 (second quotation), 57, 59–60 (first quotation); *NYT*, August 27, 1915 (third quotation). After Blease made his declaration at the governors' conference, the national press picked up the story and editorial pages buzzed with his words. On his celebratory dances, see Eliot Janeway, "Jimmy Byrnes," *Life*, January 4, 1943, 65.

73. Bederman, "'Civilization,'" 13 (Bederman's paraphrase of Hall). On the broader meaning of lynching in the twentieth-century South, see Joel Williamson, *The Crucible of Race*, 183–89; Hall, "'The Mind That Burns in Each Body'" and *Revolt against Chivalry*; MacLean, "The Leo Frank Case Reconsidered"; and Laura F. Edwards, "Sexual Violence."

74. John M. Cannon to CLB, August 12, 1913, CLB to Cannon, August 13, 1913, and CLB to W. T. Crews, August 18, 1913, box 22, file—Laurens County 1913, BP; Carlton, *Mill and Town*, 247–48. In an interesting side note, it appears that several of the workers who participated in the murder were fired and replaced by African Americans, and they protested to Blease. See Albert E. Sloan et al. to CLB, August 21, 1913, box 22, file—Laurens County 1913, BP.

75. Derieux, "Crawling toward the Promised Land," 178; Warr, "Mr. Blease," 29.

Chapter Two

1. Ayers, *Vengeance and Justice*, 231–33; Finnegan, "'At the Hands of Parties Unknown,'" 213.

2. Raper, *Tragedy of Lynching*, 286–92; *Union Daily Times*, June 23, 1930.

3. Raper, *Tragedy of Lynching*, 293. On Blease's wild movements, see Eliot Janeway, "Jimmy Byrnes," *Life*, January 4, 1943, 65.

4. Janeway, "Jimmy Byrnes," 67; *Union Daily Times*, July 7, 1930. For more on the 1930 campaign, see *GI-J*, July 2–11 1930; *The State*, 20–28 August 1930; *NYT*, August 30, 1930;

Winfred B. Moore, "New South Statesman," 84–93; Anthony B. Miller, "Blease," 166–67; David Robertson, *Sly and Able*, 113–18.

5. *GN* and *GI-J*, September 10, 1930. Blease failed to win a majority of the vote in the mill districts (44.6 percent) of Union or in the county at large (46.04 percent). See *Union Daily Times*, September 10–11, 1930, and Heard, *Southern Primaries and Elections*, 109–10.

6. Hall et al., *Like a Family*, 183; Mary K. Cann, "Morning After," 95; Tindall, *New South*, 57; Dunn and Hardy, *Labor and Textiles*, 56; "South Carolina Textile Industry Grows," 14.

7. The Winnsboro Cotton Mill, for example, doubled its capacity in 1918. W. W. Dixon, "Fairfield County—the Winnsboro Mill—Winnsboro, S.C.," November 17, 1938, A-3-21, WPA. For more wartime changes in the mills, see Hall et al., *Like a Family*, 183–85; Stephen L. Shapiro, "The Growth," 30–32; Wright, *Old South, New South*, 144; and interview with Elam Geddes Dodson, by Allen Tullos, Greenville, S.C., May 26, 1980, SOHP.

8. Stephen L. Shapiro, "The Growth," 34–39; Mary K. Cann, "Morning After," 93–95.

9. Lofton, "Social and Economic History," 12.

10. Mary K. Cann, "Morning After," 90–93; Stephen L. Shapiro, "The Growth," 86–87.

11. Wright, *Old South, New South*, 155.

12. Interview with G. Dodson, by Tullos, SOHP; Hall et al., *Like a Family*, 184–85; Rhyne, *Southern Cotton Mill Workers*, 65–78; Boyte, "The Textile Industry"; "The Labor Situation," *Southern Textile Bulletin*, May 16, 1918, 12. For the labor supply in a Georgia mill community, see Flamming, *Creating the Modern South*, 97–119. There are no exact figures for turnover rates or absenteeism in South Carolina, but for some indication of the scope of this problem, see "Lost Time and Labor Turnover." According to this study, turnover rates in the South varied from mill to mill, ranging from 48.9 percent to 377.3 percent, with 189.5 percent being the regional average. Moreover, turnover rates were twice as high in mills that operated fifty-five hours per week, as opposed to those that ran forty-eight hours. (To calculate turnover rates, I divided the number of separations that occurred during the year by the average number of full-time workers.)

13. About 15 percent of the total mill workforce were African American. Most of these women and men worked outside of the factory or in the initial stages of production. Attempts to use black labor inside the mills usually triggered white resistance. Stokes, "Black and White Labor," 196–212. On the affordability of white labor, see Wright, *Political Economy of the Cotton South*, and Terrill, " 'Eager Hands,' " 89, 94. On the ideology of the mill owners, see Janiewski, "Southern Honor, Southern Dishonor."

14. Carlton, *Mill and Town*, 245. On white resistance to the introduction of African American labor, see Newby, *Plain Folk*, 464–92

15. Newby, *Plain Folk*, 173; Rhyne, *Southern Cotton Mill Workers*, 105–21.

16. Hall et al., *Like a Family*, 183–84.

17. *GI-J*, June 4, 1933; "South Carolina Textile Industry Grows," 18; Miles, "Economic Survey," 69–70; interview with Jamie Adams, by Allen Tullos, Burlington, N.C., May 11, 1979, SOHP. On April 21, 1991, the *Raleigh News and Observer* featured a story that described how much things had changed in Ware Shoals.

18. Tindall, *New South*, 57–58; Herring, *Welfare Work in Mill Villages*. On South Carolina, see "South Carolina Textile Industry Grows," 18; Pettus, "Elliot White Springs"; Potwin, *Cotton Mill People*; and Simpson, *Life in Mill Communities*. For connections between the labor supply and welfare work, see Reid, "Industrial Paternalism." For a similar observation about South Carolina, see Barbare, "Community Welfare Work," 14, 72. On welfare capitalism generally, see Brandes, *American Welfare Capitalism*; Brody, "Rise and

Decline of Welfare Capitalism"; and esp. Cohen, *Making a New Deal*, 159–211, and Zahavi, *Workers, Managers, and Welfare Capitalism*.

19. On wages, see Wright, *Old South, New South*, 148–52.

20. For implementation of the bonus system, see "Lost Time and Labor Turnover," 289; Hall et al., *Like a Family*, 204; and interview with Lacy Wright, by Bill Finger and Chip Hughes, Greensboro, N.C., March 10, 1975, SOHP.

21. On the strikes in South Carolina, see Hall et al., *Like a Family*, 187, 195; George S. Mitchell, *Textile Unionism*, 42–49; *Co*, August, 7–8, 1919; and Proceedings of the SCFL, 1916–17, SCL. While Rock Hill millhands were on strike, streetcar workers in Anderson and Greenville walked off their jobs as well. These events fueled fears of widespread working-class unrest. On the 1919 strike wave generally, see Montgomery, *Fall of the House of Labor*, 388–89; Cronin, "Labor Insurgency"; Brody, *Steelworkers in America*, 180–262; and Goldberg, *A Tale of Three Cities*.

22. See Flamming, *Creating the Modern South*, 112–13, and Wright, *Old South, New South*, 148–52.

23. See Flamming, *Creating the Modern South*, 112–13. For male wages, see Wright, *Old South, New South*, 141–45, and interview with Lora Wright [and Edward], by Allen Tullos, Greenville, S.C., June 7, 1979, SOHP.

24. Interview with Susie Simmons, January 1, 1938, A-3-19-3, WPA; interview with Lora Wright, SOHP; Hall et al., *Like a Family*, 237–88; Morland, *Millways of Kent*, 45–48, 164–65; Flamming, *Creating the Modern South*, 161. According to Marjorie Potwin (*Cotton Mill People*, 41–42), more than a quarter of all Saxon millworkers had cars in 1926 and a significant minority had pianos and Victrolas. Some analysts have maintained that mass consumption was a homogenizing, deradicalizing force, but Cohen, *Making a New Deal*, and Rosenzweig, *"Eight Hours,"* have argued otherwise.

25. Parrish, *Anxious Decades*, xi.

26. Stephen L. Shapiro, "The Growth," 87–102.

27. Irving Bernstein, *Lean Years*, 3.

28. Gerstle, *Working-Class Americanism*, 31–33; Galambos, *Competition*; Irving Bernstein, *Lean Years*, 2–4; Tindall, *New South*, 360–62; McIssac, "Cotton Textile Industry."

29. On the products of South Carolina mills, see Stephen L. Shapiro, "The Growth," 82–87, and NYA, "The Textile Industry in South Carolina" (Columbia, 1938), 86, SCL. The Pacific Mills of West Columbia was an exception to this rule. See Tindall, *New South*, 362, and Byars, *Olympia Pacific*.

30. Irving Bernstein, *Lean Years*, 3.

31. Galambos, *Competition*, 3–112; Hodges, *New Deal Labor Policy*, 47–48.

32. Flamming, *Creating the Modern South*, 172–77.

33. *Southern Textile Bulletin*, November 7, 1925, 7.

34. For the timing and dates of managerial moves, see "Report on the Stretch-Out System for [the South Carolina] Board of Health," Senate Journal, 1933, 70–71, SCL. See also Hall et al., *Like a Family*, 198–99, and Phillip J. Wood, *Southern Capitalism*, 59–93.

35. On the industrial engineers, see Terrill and Hirsch, *Such as Us*, 182–83; Hall et al., *Like a Family*, 209–12; Montgomery, *Fall of the House of Labor*, 221; Rodgers, *Work Ethic*, 166–68; Dunn and Hardy, *Labor and Textiles*, 121–27; "Report on the Stretch-Out System," Senate Journal, 1933, 64; and *GI-J*, March 18, 1929.

36. According to the U.S. Bureau of Labor Statistics, in 1928 the average weekly wage in South Carolina's textile mills was $9.56. In the South loom fixers earned $18.38 per week, male weavers $13.57, and female weavers $12.05. See Berglund, Starnes, and DeVyver, *Labor*

in the Industrial South, 88–90. Weaving is one of the few industrial jobs that is not gender specific.

37. For changes in the weave room, see Hall et al., *Like a Family*, 206–9; Terrill and Hirsch, *Such as Us*, 182–83; Braverman, *Labor and Monopoly Capital*; and Daniel Nelson, *Managers and Workers*. One study indicated that the number of weavers who lost their jobs as a result of the stretchout ranged from 28 to 60 percent depending on the mill. NYA, "The Textile Industry in South Carolina," 66–67, SCL.

38. Hall et al., *Like a Family*, 210–11.

39. This and the next two paragraphs are drawn from Putnam's testimony before the Stretchout Committee Hearings, Spartanburg, July 13, 1933, Byrnes Papers, box—Misc. 1931–33, CU. To fill out this portrait, I have relied on several other sources. For a description of the prestretchout regimen, see interview with Jessie Lee Carter, by Allen Tullos, May 5, 1980, Greenville, S.C., SOHP; The Honest Card and Spinning Workers of the Watts Mill to General Hugh Johnson, February 24, 1934, NRA Records, RG 9, ser. 398, box 33, file—Watts Mills, Laurens, S.C., NA; and DeNatale, "Bynum," 380–86. On fines and docking, see *SH*, February 24, 1933.

40. Thomas Dublin (*Women at Work*, 109) defines the stretchout as the "assignment of additional pieces of machinery to each operative." For a broader definition, see Hall et al., *Like a Family*, 211–12. South Carolina mill owners generally did not use the word "stretchout," preferring such positivist phrases as separation system, extended labor system, and multiple-loom system. Begrudgingly, some spoke of the "so-called efficiency system." Hodges, *New Deal Labor Policy*, 65. During the spring of 1929, the Cotton Manufacturers Association of South Carolina ran a series of advertisements in defense of the stretchout. See *GI-J*, September 24, 1929, and *The State*, May 21, 1929. Most of these advertisements can be found in William Plumber Jacobs, "The Truth about the Cotton Mills" (ca. 1927), SCL.

41. On the stretchout and slavery, see Paul Eli Clark to ICB, n.d. [ca. 1931], ICB Papers, box—Current Subjects 1931, SCDAH; interview with "The Edward Fulmers," by G. L. Summer, Newberry, December 28, 1938, A-3-7-9, WPA; Hall et al., *Like a Family*, 221, 296–97; Markowitz and Rosen, *Slaves of the Depression*, 76; unsigned letter, Langley, to Frances Perkins, Washington, D.C. November 12, 1933, NRA Records, RG 9, ser. 398, box 19, file—Horse Creek Valley, NA; *Rock Hill Evening News*, September 20, 1934; *Textile Worker* 17 (September 1929): 331–35; A Mill Worker to JGR, January 1, 1930, JGR Papers, box 56, SCDAH; and interview with Edward and Lora Wright, by Allen Tullos, Greenville, S.C., June 7, 1979, SOHP.

42. Interestingly enough, unlike workers, national union leaders did occasionally fashion an analogy between white workers and African American slaves. "We do not believe that any man who has sworn to support the Constitution of the United States," wrote John Peel, "can honestly and sincerely say that such action upon the part of any employer is less than slavery, for the abolition of which a war was fought more than sixty years ago." *Textile Worker* 20 (March 1932): 243–44.

43. Slavery, of course, had long served as a powerful image of debilitation and dependence for white South Carolinians. See Lacy K. Ford, *Origins of Southern Radicalism*. On the resonance of the metaphor of slavery for industrial workers, see Cunliffe, *Chattel Slavery*; Foner, *Politics and Ideology*, 59–63; and Roediger, *Wages of Whiteness*.

44. Annual Reports of the South Carolina Department of Agriculture, Commerce, and Industry, 1920-21, SCL; Lander, *History of South Carolina*, 117–21; Mary K. Cann, "Morning After," 17, 20; Terrill and Hirsch, *Such as Us*, 75. For an overview of rural life during this period, see Daniel, *Breaking the Land*, 82–87.

45. Lucille Clark Ford, "An Evening in the Smith House," Winnsboro Mills, Winnsboro, S.C., February 14, 1939, A-3-19-1, WPA. Gavin Wright (*Old South, New South*, 147–55) discusses the motivations behind the movement of rural residents. Confirmation of this trend comes from a variety of sources. In his classic book, *Red Hills and Cotton*, Ben Robertson recalled the movement of people away from the countryside to the mill gates (pp. 278–81). The mill was seen by Jeeter Lester's children as the only escape from the poverty and depravity of the countryside as well. Caldwell, *Tobacco Road*. On the boll weevil, see T. J. Helms, "Insects," in *Encyclopedia of Southern Culture*, edited by Wilson and Ferris, 341–42; Vietmeyer, "Our 90-Year War"; and Jack T. Kirby, *Rural Worlds Lost*, 53–54, 316.

46. DeNatale, "Bynum," 191–92.

47. For statistics on roads in South Carolina, see John H. Moore, *South Carolina Highway Department*, 48–73. Moore also supplies motor vehicle registration figures. In 1917 there were 38,332 registered vehicles in the state, or one vehicle for every forty-two people. Three years later the state had 94,751 registered vehicles, or one for every seventeen people. (These percentages are based on the population of the state in 1910 and 1920; figures for 1917 were adjusted assuming even growth over the period. See U.S. Bureau of the Census, *Sixteenth Census, Population*, 375.)

48. For the move from farm to factory during this period, see Wright, *Old South, New South*, 148–50. On spare hands in South Carolina, see NYA, "The Textile Industry in South Carolina," 86, SCL.

49. For theories on permanent workers and strikes, see Geary, *European Labour Protest*, 75, and Thernstrom, *Poverty and Progress*. A promanagement newspaper also noticed this tendency. See *Greenville Observer*, August 11, 1933.

50. For the strikes of 1929, see Tippett, *When Southern Labor Stirs*; Beal, *Proletarian Journey*; Pope, *Millhands And Preachers*; Irving Bernstein, *Lean Years*, 1–43; Hodges, "Challenge to the New South"; Hall, "Disorderly Women"; and Salmond, *Gastonia, 1929*. At the time of the conflict, the national press paid a great deal of attention to the Gastonia strike. See, e.g., Mary Heaton Vorse, "Gastonia," *Harpers*, November 1929, 700–710.

51. U.S. Department of Labor, *Strikes in the United States*, 117. On the South Carolina strikes, see Paul Blanshard, "Americans on Strike," 552; George Googe, "Textile Workers Organize," *American Federationist*, July 1929, 793–99; Tippett, *When Southern Labor Stirs*, 184–89; and George S. Mitchell, *Textile Unionism*, 78–81.

52. *The State*, April 4, 1929.

53. Tindall, *New South*, 350. The Committee to Investigate the Stretchout, Department of Agriculture, Commerce, and Industry of the South Carolina House of Representatives, headed by Dowell Patterson, the president of the state Federation of Labor, concluded that the strikes were caused in part by the lax enforcement of state labor laws. House Journal, 1930; Proceedings of the SCFL, 1929, GML; *The State*, April 18, 1929. See also *NYT*, April 11, 1929.

54. See Hall et al., *Like a Family*, 222, 225. For the impact of generational change on labor organizing in a later era, see Schatz, *Electrical Workers*.

55. "Report on the Stretch-Out System," Senate Journal, 1933, 59, 77. For more on millhands' sense of a fair workload, see "Gaffney Manufacturing Co., Local Union 1804," April 1935, NRA Records, RG 9, ser. 402, box 52, file—Gaffney Mfg. Co., NA; and FWP, "Old Man Dobbin and His Crowd," *These Are Our Lives*, 209–10. For another perspective, listen to the ballad "Winnsboro Cotton Mill Blues," on Pete Seeger, *American Industrial Ballads* (1992).

56. Barrington Moore Jr. (*Injustice*) has argued that ordinary people's vision of a better society is often either a backward-looking picture or a model of the present stripped of its

most oppressive features. This seems to capture the outlook of many South Carolina textile workers in 1929.

57. Strikers at the Isaqueena Mills of Central and the Woodruff Mills of Spartanburg also called for a return to the "old" system. *GI-J*, March 31, April 1-2, 1929; *The State*, April 2, 1929.

58. *GI-J*, April 1, 1929.

59. *The State*, March 29, 31, April 2, May 9, 1929; *GI-J*, April 15, 1929; Paul Blanshard's testimony is included in the U.S. Senate, *Working Conditions*, 140-43, and Blanshard, "Americans on Strike," 552.

60. On these "leaderless strikes," see Blanshard, "Americans on Strike," 552; Irving Bernstein, *Lean Years*, 32-33; and Hall et al., *Like a Family*, 218-20. A member of the Communist Party's National Union of Textile Workers—"He gave his name as Schultze"—was reportedly sent away by millhands from York as well. *The State*, September 19, 1929. Workers elsewhere also boasted that they did not need the help of national unions. *GI-J*, March 31, May 1, 1929.

61. On the idea that South Carolina workers were exceptional, and how this uniqueness reflected working-class consciousness in the state, see Tindall, *New South*, 350; George S. Mitchell, *Textile Unionism*, 78-83; and Bernstein, *Lean Years*, 32-33. Even the iconoclastic Hall et al., *Like a Family* (218-19), seems to accept prevailing notions of the South Carolina strikes.

62. *SH*, July 21, 1929; *GI-J*, November 11, October 17, 23, 1929. The latter featured reprints of antiunion editorials from the *Anderson Daily Mail* and *Laurens Advertiser*.

63. Janet Irons ("Testing the New Deal") sees the struggle between the goal of southern workers to abolish the stretchout and the business union agenda of the UTW leadership as a major impediment to the emergence of textile trade unionism in the South. The industrial engineer hired by the UTW was Geoffery Brown, who expressed his notion of trade unionism in his article, "The New Unionism," *American Federationist*, May 1930, 542-43. See also Tippett, *When Southern Labor Stirs*, 182.

64. *The State*, May 5, 1929.

65. *GI-J*, April 8, 1929. See also Mary K. Cann, "Morning After," 140-41. The American Spinning Co. was founded in 1895. In 1929 it was capitalized at $525,000, less than one-third of that of the Ware Shoals Manufacturing Co. and about half of the approximate state average. For this information and averages, see *Davison's Textile Blue Book*, July 1929, 376-96.

66. *The State*, April 4, 5 (quotation), May 17, 1929.

67. *GI-J*, April 1-2, 3 (quotations), 16, 1929. See also William Gaston, "Report on Union Buffalo," November 15, 1934, NRA Records, RG 9, ser. 402, box 134, file—Union Buffalo, NA.

68. *The State*, June 14, 1929 (Whitmire); *The State*, July 3, 1929 (Mills Mill); *GI-J*, April 4-8, June 6, 1929 (Anderson).

69. President of Brandon Mills to "The Committee of Former Workers of Brandon Mills," *GI-J*, March 30, 1929. See also *The State*, May 7, 1929, and Mary K. Cann, "Morning After," 154. These strikes fit in a broader context of "control strikes"; see Montgomery, "The 'New Unionism' and the Transformation of Workers' Consciousness in America, 1909-1922," *Workers' Control in America*, 90-112.

70. The AFL called this the Southern Organizing Campaign. See Tippett, *When Southern Labor Stirs*, 194-95, and *Textile Worker* 18 (May 1930): 73-74. On South Carolina, see *The State*, May 10, 19, 25, September 3, 9, 20, 28-29, 1929.

71. Proceedings of the SCFL, 1928-30, GML.

72. See undated clippings that appear to be from the Charleston *News and Courier*

(ca. 1929), Watson Papers, box 6, Labor File, SCL, and Mary K. Cann, "Morning After," 152–53.

73. For general information on conditions in Ware Shoals, see *GI-J*, June 4, 1933; Miles, "Economic Survey," 69–70; and interview with Harry and Janie Adams, by Allen Tullos, Burlington, N.C., May 11, 1979, SOHP. For a more recent account, see *Raleigh News and Observer*, April 21, 1991.

74. *GI-J*, June 3–4, 1929. The two men were fired for ripping down notices from mill bulletins boards. Some said the fliers erroneously broadcast the cancellation of a union meeting. Others claimed that the announcements deliberately distorted an agreement between management and workers regarding wage rates and work assignments.

75. For biographical information on Richards, see *The National Cyclopaedia of American Biography*, vol. 45 (New York: J. T. White, 1962), 64–64, and McClure, "Public Career." Ware Shoals was the first time that Richards intervened in a labor dispute. But when Greenville's Sheriff Smith refused to deputize several company officials earlier in the year, Richards did the job himself. U.S. Senate, *Working Conditions*, 118.

76. H. E. "Smoke" Thompson and W. H. McNary served with Self on the mediation board. Its proceedings were covered by *The State*, June 10–14, 1929.

77. Ibid., June 21, 1929. It was a common practice during strikes for overseers and second hands to be appointed "constables without pay." That way they would have the legal authority to arrest people. Moreover, the number of constables without pay always increased during labor disputes. Ware Shoals's Brent Holmes, for instance, was so appointed "at the time of the strike as an emergency measure." He continued in this capacity until 1931 and perhaps longer. Holmes Report, February 4, 1931, ICB Papers, Constabulary Reports 1931–34, file—Greenwood County, SCDAH.

78. *GI-J*, June 19–20, 1929. According to the author of the labor section of the Works Projects Administration Guide to South Carolina, "When dissatisfaction with living conditions . . . arose among the workers, those who lived in the mill village itself voted to strike. The farm-raised population of millworkers, however, placed a higher value on the cash dollar. They resolved to continue work under existing conditions rather than run the risk of losing their jobs." "Labor in South Carolina," C-1-10, WPA. See also Edgar, *WPA Guide*, 80–81. The place of residence and mind-set of strikebreakers will be taken up in greater detail in Chapter 5.

79. *The State*, July 26, 1929. See also *GI-J*, July 25, 27, 1929; George S. Mitchell, *Textile Unionism*, 80. The *NYT* (July 13–17, 1929) also covered the Ware Shoals strike.

80. W. H. Riddle, Ware Shoals, to JGR, January 15, 1930 (box 14, file R), and E. L. Hayes, Ware Shoals, to JGR, September 12, 1929 (box 23), JGR Papers, SCDAH.

81. Clipping, *Greenville Observer*, August 3, 1929, forwarded by Greenville Trades and Labor Council to JGR (box 23—Alphabetical Files), and W. H. Riddle, Ware Shoals, to JGR, January 15, 1930 (box 14, file R), JGR Papers, SCDAH. See also Brinkley, *Voices of Protest*, 153–54, and Proceedings of the SCFL, 1929–30, GML.

82. *GI-J*, June 29, 1929. See also Mary K. Cann, "Morning After," 152.

83. Ibid. During the 1930 U.S. Senate race, Blease was also heckled in Langley and Spartanburg. See *GI-J*, July 29, August 7, 1930.

84. *GI-J*, July 2, 5, 1929; *The State*, June 25, 1929. The *Southern Textile Bulletin* praised Blease's speech, but the South Carolina Federation of Labor rebuked the senator at its 1929 annual meeting. The UTW also opposed Blease and celebrated his defeat in 1930. *Textile Worker* 18 (September 1930): 375–76. See the reprint of a letter to CLB from Vernon B. Allen, Proceedings of the SCFL, 1929, GML; J. F. Bishop, Union, to James F.

Byrnes, August 25, 1930 ("To hell with Blease" quotation), and Alton Bryant, Graniteville, to Byrnes, November 11, [1929], Byrnes Papers, box—1930 and Prior, CU.

85. In 1932 Blease lost to the incumbent, Sen. Ellison D. Smith. Afterward, the press talked about the "decline of Bleasism." See *GN*, September 15, 1932, and *Greenville Observer*, June 24, 1932. See also Tables A.1, A.2.

86. *The State*, January 11, 26, 30, February 15, March 8, 1929; Carpenter, "Olin D. Johnston," 64. Despite Johnston's efforts, the sewage bill that finally passed the Senate was so weak that it amounted to little more than a suggestion that mill managers should build sewers in their villages sometime in the future. The only other legislation Johnston was able to get through the general assembly removed the tax on tickets to mill baseball games.

87. Carpenter, "Olin D. Johnston," 66–70 (quotations, pp. 67–68). See also Anthony B. Miller, "Palmetto Politician," 59, 68; *GI-J*, August 15, September 1, 1930.

88. For state and county returns, see Jordan, *The Primary State*, 39. Only in 1938, when Burnett Maybank, then the mayor of Charleston, ran for governor did anyone in the first half of the twentieth century receive a higher percentage of votes in Charleston County than Blackwood. See also Table A.3.

Chapter Three

1. Blumer Hendrix to ODJ, November 26, 1937, ODJ Papers, box 13, SCDAH.

2. G. L. Ridger of Bennettsville to JGR, June 14, 1930, JGR Papers, box 14, file R, SCDAH. Statisticians have uncovered a near-perfect correlation between income and pellagra. The pattern seemed true in South Carolina in 1930s. During the decade pellagra cases nearly tripled. See Wallace, *South Carolina*, 685. See also Goldberger et al., *Study of Endemic Pellagra*; Beardsley, *A History of Neglect*; Flynt, *Poor but Proud*, 174–78; and Oshinsky, *"Worse Than Slavery,"* 190–93.

3. W. H. Riddle, Ware Shoals, to JGR, January 15, 1930, JGR Papers, box 14, file R, SCDAH.

4. Edgar Gaddis to ODJ, March 12, 1938, ODJ Papers, box 7—General Correspondence, SCDAH. Apparently Johnston was moved by this appeal. He wrote across the top of the letter, "Have this typed." Across the nation people postponed marriage and the birth rate dropped. For a national perspective, see Badger, *New Deal*, 32–38; Bodnar, *Immigration and Industrialization*, 142–44; and Irving Bernstein, *A Caring Society*, 278–79. For some of the strategies employed in South Carolina, see *Greenville Observer*, July 22, August 19, 1932.

5. See, e.g., interview with Lucy Price, December 14, 1938, A-3-13-3, WPA; Mrs. E. M. Hogan to ICB, February 24, 1930, JGR Papers, box 56—General Correspondence, SCDAH. For more stories about mutuality, see Hall et al., *Like a Family*, 102, 151–52, and Robinson, *Living Hard*, 177–200.

6. Lizabeth Cohen makes a similar point in her book, *Making a New Deal*, 2–3.

7. On this point, see Montgomery, "Labor and the Political Leadership."

8. See Cohen, *Making a New Deal*, and Gerstle, *Working-Class Americanism*.

9. Badger, *New Deal*, 18–22. On the Midwest, see Green, *World of the Worker*, 135, and Biles, *New Deal*, 11. On larger issues of the depression, see Chandler, *America's Greatest Depression*.

10. *The State*, October 25, 1929.

11. On the relative advantages of the textile industry, see Tindall, *New South*, 360–61, and Lofton, "Social and Economic History," v–vii.

12. In 1928 there were 79,170 textile workers in South Carolina. Just two years later, this number dropped to 67,036. See Stephen L. Shapiro, "The Growth," 40. For additional information on unemployment, see U.S. Bureau of the Census, *Fifteenth Census, Population: Numbers and Distribution*, 899, and *Manufacturers*, 2:49. For anecdotal evidence about layoffs and shift cancellations, see E. Hill to JGR, June 13, 1930, JGR Papers, box 65, file—Unemployment, SCDAH, and McCravey, *Memories*, 302-3.

13. For the number of textile workers in Columbia, see U.S. Bureau of the Census, *Fifteenth Census, Occupations by State*, 1478-79, and *Population: Numbers and Distribution*, 902-7. See also Moore, *Columbia and Richland County*, 338, 340, and Lofton, "Social and Economic History," 33, 50-61, 67, 219.

14. *GI-J*, June 28, July 3, 1929; *Textile Worker* 18 (May 1930): 61-63, 19 (June 1931): 118-19, 19 (October 1931): 301-3; *Greenville Observer*, February 29, 1932; *NYT*, September 22, 1932.

15. See, e.g., Rinnie Bishop to JGR, January 22, 1930, JGR Papers, box—Misc. Correspondence, file B, SCDAH. On seniority and the depression, see Schatz, *Electrical Workers*, 105-32.

16. A variety of sources detail the deterioration of conditions in South Carolina's mill villages—e.g., see Proceedings of the SCFL, 1928, GML; *NYT*, August 13, November 2, 1930, August 14, September 15, 1932; Anne Belle Pittman of Rock Hill to Wil Lou Gray, April 19, 1928, Gray Papers, SCL; F. E. Whitman, Treasurer of the Union-Buffalo Mills Co., to Manning, January 1, 1928, Manning Papers, box 4, file 354, SCL.

17. Badger, *New Deal*, 46-54.

18. *SH*, January 2, 4, 6, 1932. This was part of a national program, and it was, as Broadus Mitchell (*Depression Decade*, 102) notes, a very primitive form of relief.

19. Bradley to Eleanor Roosevelt, November 6, 1933, Eleanor Roosevelt Papers, box 1256, FDRL; Tindall, *New South*, 370-71. In 1931, with the aid of the Red Cross, forty-one mill families were relocated to farms in Greenville County. There they were taught about diversified farming and encouraged to buy a small parcel of land and settle down. *SH*, September 3, 1932. The *Union Daily Times* (May 13, August 29, 1930) also favored the return to the countryside.

20. Mr. D. Euta Calvin to ICB, September 21, 1931, ICB Papers, box—Current Subjects 1931, SCDAH; *Union Daily Times*, August 2, September 9-10, 1930. For a similar suggestion from Gov. Blackwood, see *SH*, February 23, 1932.

21. Lofton, "Social and Economic History," 36-40.

22. *NYT*, September 15, 1932. In some cases, mill owners tried to keep charities away from the villages. They wanted workers to remain dependent on their largess. See the comment of local Red Cross chair, McCravey, *Memories*, 302-3. On details about relief in one mill community, see Boyette, "General Textile Strike," 1987, 20-22.

23. Carpenter, "Olin Johnston," 66; Hayes, "South Carolina and the New Deal," 176-78.

24. M. E. Underwood to JGR, November 11, 1930 (box 65, file—Unemployment 1930), and Y. P. Harrison to JGR, August 16, 1927 (box 3—Alphabetical Correspondence 1927), JGR Papers, SCDAH. See also A Mill Worker to JGR, January 1, 1930 (box 56—General Correspondence), ibid.

25. Hendrix to JGR, November 19, 1930, JGR Papers, box 14, file H, SCDAH.

26. J. M. Fletcher to JGR, January 19, 1930, ICB Papers, box—State Agencies, CAB Files, SCDAH. This letter must have arrived during the transition between governors.

27. Ibid. Chicago workers developed a similar view of government and politicians. See Cohen, *Making a New Deal*, 258.

28. The South Carolina General Assembly passed a bill barring African American from the mills, but this was already the unspoken rule in the state. *SH*, January 15, 1932. Two

years earlier unemployed workers had demanded jobs ahead of African Americans on the sanitation crew. *Textile Worker* 18 (December 1930): 543. According to the U.S. Bureau of the Census (*Fifteenth Census, Manufacturers*, 3:775), in 1930 there were 5,358 foreign-born residents of South Carolina or 0.3 percent of the state's total population. On calls for immigration restrictions, see *Labor*, July 19, 1932, and *Winnsboro News and Herald*, September 9, 1932, clippings in Scrapbooks 10 and 12 respectively, E. D. Smith Papers, SCL.

29. Paul Eli Clark to ICB, n.d. [ca. 1931], ICB Papers, box—Current Subjects 1931, SCDAH. See also Address by state AFL president Brookshire, Proceedings of the SCFL, 1931, GML.

30. "Report on the Stretch-Out System," Senate Journal, 1933, 60, SCL; J. L. Sowers, President of the Greenville Trades and Labor Council, to ICB (telegram), November 7, 1931, ICB Papers, box—Current Subjects 1931, SCDAH. For additional and similar views of the stretchout, see J. M. Fletcher to JGR, January 19, 1930 (box—State Agencies, CAB Files), C. M. Bissel (Saxon Mills) to ICB, January 26, 1931 (box—General Correspondence, Appointments, Petitions, file—General Correspondence), and Paul Eli Clark to ICB, n.d. [ca. 1931] (box—Current Subjects 1931), ICB Papers, SCDAH. See also Anonymous to Huge [*sic*] Johnson, August 9, 1933 (box 33, file—Wallace Mfg. Co.), and P. M. Mooney to Dear Sir, July 14, 1933 (box 24, file—Olympia Mills), NRA Records, RG 9, ser. 398, NA; Proceedings of the SCFL, 1929, GML; and *SH*, May 21, 1933.

31. *GI-J*, March 30, 1929; *The State*, May 7, 1929.

32. A. P. Dewitt to JGR, March 10, 1927, box 16—Misc., JGR Papers, SCDAH. On earlier legislative efforts concerning hours, see Cowan, "Labor Regulation," 8–12; and Y. P. Harrison to JGR, August 16, 1927, box 3—Alphabetical Correspondence 1927, JGR Papers, SCDAH.

33. "An Appeal to the Honorable General Assembly of South Carolina," signed by "Textile Workers," January 21, 1930, JGR Papers, box 56—General Correspondence, SCDAH.

34. Paul Eli Clark, to ICB, n.d. [ca. 1931], ICB Papers, box—Current Subjects 1931, SCDAH. See also *Textile Worker* 19 (April 1931): 6–7, and *SH*, February 5, 1932, January 22, February 29, 1933. The reduction of hours was a popular program both within the state and national labor movements as well. See Proceedings of the SCFL, 1931–33, GML, and Irving Bernstein, *Lean Years*, 224–25.

35. On women in the labor force during the depression, see Chafe, *American Woman*, 103; Milkman, "Women's Work"; Scharf, *To Work and Wed*, 157–80; Wandersee, *Women's Work*, 84, 101–2; Kessler-Harris, *Out to Work*, 257–61; and Ware, *Holding Their Own*, 21–50.

36. Public opinion polls, which first appeared in the 1930s, asked Americans whether married women should be permitted to work as long as their husbands had jobs. In a 1936 Gallop Poll, the response of 82 percent was no. Irving Bernstein, *A Caring Society*, 291.

37. Robert K. Booth Jr. to JGR, July 18, 1927, JGR Papers, box 16—Misc., file—Unemployment 1930, SCDAH. See also J. F. Chapman to FDR, August 24, 1933, NRA Records, RG 9, ser. 398, box 26, file—Poe Mills, NA; *Union Daily Times*, August 14, 1930.

38. Mrs. I. Campbell to ICB, June 20, 1932, ICB Papers, box—General Subjects 1931–35, file—General Correspondence—C, SCDAH. See also Hall et al., *Like a Family*, 310–12, and interview with Letha Ann Sloan Osteen, June 8, 1979, by Allen Tullos, Greenville, S.C., SOHP. Weathering public scorn, most women stayed on the job. Even if they had wanted to quit, practically none could have managed it financially. In fact, from 1925 to 1937 the percentage of women working in South Carolina textile mills actually rose slightly. See Seventeenth Annual Report of the Commissioner of Agriculture, Commerce, and Industries of the State of South Carolina—Labor Division (Columbia, 1925), 34, SCL, and "Comparison of Textile Statistics," South Carolina Department of Labor, ODJ Papers, box 39, SCDAH.

39. Kessler-Harris, "Gender Ideology"; Hobbs, "Rethinking Antifeminism."

40. House Journal, 1929-33, Senate Journal, 1932-33, SCL.

41. Letter to the editor, *GN*, n.d., NRA Records, RG 9, box 12, file—Dunean Mill, NA.

42. On the 1932 campaign, see *SH*, August 14-30, 1932, esp. August 14. The headline that day read, "Legislation for Labor Is Pledged." See returns, *SH*, August 30, 1932. Similar discussions took place in Union County. See *Union Daily Times*, July 5, 1930.

43. Senate Journal, 1929-33; House Journal, 1929-32; *SH*, March 23, 1932; *NYT*, August 14, 1932.

44. SCFL, Annual Reports, 1930-34, GML; *SH*, February 24, 1933.

45. *SH*, February 3 ("inviting Communism"), 24 ("Roman slavery"), 28, March 13, April 13 ("industrial slavery"), May 12, 1933. For a sense of the importance of this law to millhands, see "An Appeal to the Honorable General Assembly of South Carolina," signed by "Textile Workers" on January 21, 1930 (JGR Papers, box 56—General Correspondence, SCDAH), which reportedly appeared on a desk in the general assembly. No one was sure who had placed it there.

46. House Journal, 1929-33; Senate Journal, 1932-33; *Greenville Observer*, February 3, 1932; *SH*, February 7, 1932, February 29, April 13, 1933.

47. Bunche, *Political Status*, 130. On the lack of home rule, see Burton et al., "South Carolina," 202, and Graham, "South Carolina Counties."

48. This section is drawn from Simon, "Devaluation of the Vote."

49. These figures are drawn from U.S. Bureau of the Census, *Twelfth Census, Population*, liii; *Thirteenth Census, Population: Reports by States*, 659-67; *Fourteenth Census, Population: General Report*, 1360; and *Fifteenth Census, Unemployment*, 784-87.

50. On Edgar Brown, see Workman, *The Bishop from Barnwell*; Key, *Southern Politics*, 152-55. See also Carlton, "Unbalanced Growth," 125.

51. U.S. Bureau of the Census, *Sixteenth Census, Population*, 375. Because disfranchised African Americans were more likely to live in rural areas than in cities, the proportion of voters living in rural areas was probably smaller than the statewide average.

52. Caldwell, *Trouble in July*, 51.

53. Newby, *The South*, 423.

54. On government alternatives, see Parrish, *Anxious Decades*, 81-88.

55. *The State*, August 2, 1932.

56. The term "business progressives" was coined by Tindall in *New South*, 219-84, esp. 224-25. On South Carolina progressives, see Mary K. Cann, "Morning After"; Sandra C. Mitchell, "Conservative Reform"; Boggs, "John Patrick Grace"; and Lupold, "The Nature of South Carolina Progressives." For southern progressivism, see Grantham, "Contours of Southern Progressivism," 1035-59, and Link, *Paradox of Southern Progressivism*.

57. Mary K. Cann, "Morning After," 290; Sandra C. Mitchell, "Conservative Reform," 128; Lander, *History of South Carolina*, 127, 129-30; Wallace, *South Carolina*, 691-92.

58. John H. Moore, *South Carolina Highway Department*, 138-39; Lander, *History of South Carolina*, 103-5.

59. Barnes, "Economics of Tax Reform," 1-8. On the national scene, see Patterson, *New Deal*, 3-49, and Beito, *Taxpayers in Revolt*, 1-22.

60. Barnes, "Economics of Tax Reform," 26-31, 41-51, 71-78, 103-19; *GI-J*, April 4, 15, 1930.

61. Mary K. Cann, "Morning After," 284. According to *The State* (February 11, 1926), between 1915 and 1925 revenues from the property tax dropped 13 percent. Over roughly the same period, however, the number of farms in South Carolina fell by 18 percent. Barnes, "Economics of Tax Reform," 5.

62. J. J. Fretwell to ICB, September 20, 1932, ICB Papers, box—General Subjects 1931-, file—General Correspondence, SCDAH; Barnes, "Economics of Tax Reform," 4-5; McClure, "Public Career," 25-46; Beito, *Taxpayers In Revolt*, 9; Mary K. Cann, "Morning After," 276-85.

63. Letter to the editor, *SH*, March 14, 1933.

64. On the vision of the economists, see a flier attached to a letter from John K. Breedin to Elliot Springs, n.d. [ca. 1933], Springs Papers, box 37, file 58, SCL. On tax payers versus tax spenders, see Beito, *Taxpayers in Revolt*, 18-21.

65. For more on Christensen, a onetime state senator from low-country Beaufort County, see Reynolds and Faust, *Biographical Dictionary*, 197. On the league, see *GI-J*, April 15, May 28, 1930; Anthony B. Miller, "Palmetto Politician," 56-57; and "Manifesto of the Farmers and Taxpayers League," April 16, 1930, Frank A. Lever Papers, CU.

66. Sol Blatt was at the march. Soon to become speaker of the house, Blatt was an important player in state politics. Like Edgar Brown, he hailed from Barnwell County. He and Brown were close allies, which suggests that the state's probusiness conservatives backed the sales tax. See Cauthen, *Speaker Blatt*, 78-80.

67. The positions of the FTL are made clear in two platforms sent to Blackwood: Farmers and Taxpayers League to ICB, February 24, 1931, and "A Memorial from the Farmers and Taxpayers League of South Carolina to the Governor and the General Assembly," March 25, 1931, ICB Papers, box—Current Federal-State Subjects 1931-35, file—Farmers and Taxpayers League, SCDAH. See also *SH*, February 24, 1932, and *Co*, August 30, 1934.

68. For evidence of the league's support, see identical petitions from FTL backers in St. Matthews, Holly Hill, Dalzell, Union, and Columbia, ICB Papers, box—Current Federal-State Subjects 1931-35, file—Farmers and Taxpayers League, SCDAH. For the mill owners' attacks against the tax codes, see William Plumber Jacobs, "Problems of the Cotton Manufacturer in South Carolina" (1932), 84-128, SCL, and *SH*, September 11, 1932. Lancaster mill owner Elliot Springs regularly contributed to the FTL; J. K. Breedin to Springs, February 10, 1932, and Springs to A. B. Langley, May 4, 1934, Springs Papers, box 37, file 58, SCL.

69. League was killed in a car crash before the election. For his story, see Tullos, *Habits of Industry*, 191-92.

70. See, e.g., H. A. Hendrix to JGR, n.d., JGR Papers, box 56—General Correspondence, SCDAH.

71. Blackwood's Annual Message, 1932, SCL.

72. Only 31 of the 124 members of the 1933 general assembly had been there the year before. *SH*, September 15, 1932.

73. Patterson, *New Deal*, 46-47; *CN&C*, January 8, May 15, 1933; *NYT*, January 29, 1933; *SH*, January 11, 20, May 18, 21, 1933.

74. Proceedings of the SCFL, 1929-30, GML; *SH*, February 2, March 1, April 26, 1933; *GI-J*, November 5, 1930. In 1947 Earle Britton, then president of the South Carolina Federation of Labor, listed the sales tax protest among the highlights of the federation's history. See Britton, "Progress in the Palmetto State," 32. Chester's Charles Darby also thought that the sales tax would hurt the laborers. Darby to JGR, March 28, 1927, JGR Papers, box 16—Misc., SCDAH.

75. *SH*, August 10, September 11, 1932. By 1935 the FTL was on hard times, and officials were constantly asking for money. Rowlette to Leroy Springs, May 17, 1935, and Breedin to E. Springs, November 4, 1935, Springs Papers, box 37, file 58, SCL.

Chapter Four

1. Martha Gellhorn, a New Deal reporter, noticed the pictures of FDR. For her impressions, see "Report to Mr. Hopkins," November 11, 1934, Hopkins Papers, box 66, file—Gellhorn, Martha, FDRL.

2. Laura and W. P. Stringfield to Robert Wagner, January 10, 1934, NRA Records, ser. 398, box 19—HCV, NA.

3. Hall et al., *Like a Family*, 304; Hayes "South Carolina and the New Deal," 355; Mrs. Era B. Duncan to FDR, November 1, 1934, NRA Records, RG 9, ser. 398, box 19, file—Adjustment Horse Creek Valley, NA; *Co*, September 8, 1934; *NYT* and *Anderson Independence*, September 9, 1934.

4. Lillian Davis to FDR, January 8, 1934, NRA Records, RG 9, ser. 398, box 19, file—Adjustment Horse Creek Valley, NA.

5. Not surprisingly, there are dozens of New Deal studies. But whether scholars characterize the New Deal as the "Third American Revolution," "a halfway revolution," or "the conservative achievement of liberal reform," they invariably view the Roosevelt era from the top down through the eyes of politicians and policy makers. For a notable exception that views the New Deal from the bottom up, see Cohen, *Making a New Deal*. For informative historiographical essays on the New Deal, see, e.g., Kirkendall, "New Deal as Watershed"; Auerbach, "New Deal, Old Deal, or Raw Deal"; Braeman, "New Deal and the 'Broker State'"; Sternsher, "Great Depression Labor Historiography"; and Peeler, "Again, the Thirties."

6. Bowers, *Tragic Era*, 423-56. For the most bombastic account of Reconstruction in South Carolina, see Pike, *Prostrate State*.

7. Fleming, *Sequel to Appomattox*, 225, 234.

8. Pike, *Prostrate State*, 12. Thomas Nast's famous cartoon, entitled "Colored Rule in a Reconstructed State," appeared in *Harper's Weekly*, March 14, 1875.

9. Huss, *Senator for the South*, 125. Gov. Johnston made this remark during his post–New Deal incarnation.

10. Bowers quoted by Foner, *Reconstruction*, 609-10. See also Avery, *Dixie after the War*, 377.

11. On the mythology of Reconstruction, see Sullivan, *Days of Hope*, 13, 163; Foner, *Reconstruction*, xix-xx, 609-12; Goodman, *Stories of Scottsboro*, 114; and Weisberger, "Dark and Bloody Ground." White Mississippians also could not talk about politics without alluding to sex. See Lemann, *Promised Land*, 26-27.

12. Simkins quoted by Foner, *Reconstruction*, 610.

13. On southern fears of federalism, see Sullivan, *Days of Hope*, 3. The noted journalist and upcountry resident, Ben Robertson, observed that South Carolinians tended to personalize issues. This might be one of the reasons why people thought of FDR and the New Deal in the very same breath. See Robertson, *Red Hills and Cotton*, 40-41.

14. On the images of Roosevelt, see Daniel, "New Deal," 40-41; McElvaine, *The Great Depression*, 112-18; Hall et al., *Like a Family*, 323-25; Bruce Nelson, "Give Us Roosevelt"; and Egerton, *Speak Now*, 83-84.

15. Schlesinger, *Coming of the New Deal*, 571-73; Lorena Hickok to Hopkins, February 8, 1934, Hopkins Papers, box 58, file—Hickok Report, FDRL; and Annie Sloan to W. E. Gonzales, November 10, 1933, Gonzales Papers, SCL.

16. Quoted in Badger, *New Deal*, 251. See also *Carolina Free Press*, August 21, 1936.

17. Quoted in Egerton, *Speak Now*, 142.

18. Lorena Hickok to Hopkins, February 8, 1934, Hopkins Papers, box 58, file—Hickok

Report, FDRL; FWP, "Old Man Dobbin and His Crowd," *These Are Our Lives*, 210-11. See also Schlesinger, *Coming of the New Deal*, 571-73.

19. Gerstle, *Working-Class Americanism*, 1-15.

20. Ibid. See also the CIO's "culture of unity" in Cohen, *Making a New Deal*, 333-49. See, in addition, the experiences of three generations of eastern European immigrations to the steel town of Braddock, Pa., in Bell, *Out of This Furnace*. For the transformation of ethnic communities into working-class American communities, see Oestreicher, "Urban Working-Class Political Behavior"; Barrett, "Americanization from the Bottom Up"; and Corbin, *Life, Work*, 237-52.

21. Apparently people in the Great Plains defined the role of the federal government in a similar way. See Worster, *Dust Bowl*, 154.

22. McElvaine, *The Great Depression*, 123-25, 138-39; Schlesinger, *Coming of the New Deal*, 1-2; Leuchtenburg, *Franklin D. Roosevelt*, 7-11, 41-42.

23. The Black bill passed in the Senate by a 53 to 30 margin. Both South Carolina senators, Byrnes and Smith, voted for the measure. On the bill itself, see Levine, *Class Struggle*, 69-71, 74; Hodges, *New Deal Labor Policy*, 43-44; and Leuchtenburg, *Franklin D. Roosevelt*, 55-56.

24. The quotations are from Hodges, *New Deal Labor Policy*, 44, and Leuchtenburg, *Franklin D. Roosevelt*, 57.

25. On the NRA, see Gordon, *New Deals*, 97-100, 166-203; Levine, *Class Struggle*, 64-91; Himmelberg, *Origins of the National Recovery Administration*; and Hawley, *New Deal*, 18-33, 211-29.

26. Tomlins, *The State and the Unions*, 106 (Green); Steve Fraser, "'Labor Question,'" 68-69 (Lewis).

27. Thorton Oakley, "NRA," *Textile Worker* 23 (April 1934): 1.

28. On the failure of self-regulation in the textile industry, see Galambos, *Competition*, 3-112, and Hodges, *New Deal Labor Policy*, 47-48.

29. On the drafting of the code, see Galambos, *Competition*, 209-26; Hodges, *New Deal Labor Policy*, 47-55; and Hall et al., *Like a Family*, 289-92. Transcripts of the code hearings can be found in NRA Records, RG 9, ser. 44, boxes 72-73, NA.

30. For descriptions of the code, see *NYT*, July 18, 1933; Hodges, *New Deal Labor Policy*, 52-54; and Hall et al., *Like a Family*, 290.

31. For testimony from the stretchout hearings, see Byrnes Papers, CU, and *The State*, June 30, 1933. It was later reported that D. C. Bush was fired because of his testimony before the Stretch-Out Committee. E. B. Smith to James F. Byrnes, August 1, 1933, NRA Records, RG 9, ser. 398, box 26, file—Pointsett Mill, West Greenville, NA. For more on Byrnes's role, see Robertson, *Sly and Able*, 164-65.

32. Hodges, *New Deal Labor Policy*, 53.

33. For the workers' view of the NRA, see, e.g., F. B. Rodger to Hugh Johnson, November 15, 1933 (ser. 398, box 1, file—AFL), Randall Smith to Johnson, July 2, 1934 (ser. 398, box 12, file—General Correspondence—S, 1934), and Cloyd L. Gibson to Johnson, May 17, 1934 (ser. 397, box 9, file—General Correspondence—G, 1934), NRA Records, RG 9, NA.

34. Roberston, *Sly and Able*, 165.

35. *GI-J*, July 18, 1933.

36. Hayes, "South Carolina and the New Deal," 314, 333-34; *GI-J*, July 18, 1933; *The State*, July 19, 1933.

37. *Textile Worker* 22 (December 1933), 349-51; Hayes, "South Carolina and the New Deal," 334-35.

38. Quoted in Janet Irons, "Testing the New Deal," 170.

39. Perkins quoted by Steve Fraser, "'Labor Question,'" 68–69, and in a letter from E. Springs to Merchant, May 29, 1933, Springs Papers, box 32, file 138, SCL.

40. Leuchtenburg, "New Deal."

41. On Johnson's campaign, see Hall et al., *Like a Family*, 290–91; and Schlesinger, *Coming of the New Deal*, 114 (first and fourth quotations). See also Biles, *New Deal*, 84–85. For the NRA's propaganda efforts in South Carolina, see Hayes, "South Carolina and the New Deal," 312–15.

42. E. F. Rice to Mr. President, November 8, 1935, Clergy File, folder—South Carolina, FDRL. For other examples of FDR seen as a "god-sent man," see Ruth Raticher to W. R. Gilbert, n.d. [ca. February 1934] (ser. 398, box 32, file—Victor Mill, Greer, S.C.), and J. A. Strickland, Ware Shoals, to Robert Bruere, November 11, 1933 (ser. 397, box 12, file—General Correspondence—S), NRA Records, RG 9, NA; and *Carolina Free Press*, September 7, 1934.

43. Calling it "optimism" rather than faith, Worster makes a similar point about workers on the Great Plains. See Worster, *Dust Bowl*, 26.

Chapter Five

1. Anderson quoted in Hodges, *New Deal Labor Policy*, 55. For management's initial response to the NRA, see Lofton, "Social and Economic History," 105–9; George A. Sloan, telephone call to the office of Hugh Johnson, July 9, 1933, President's Official File, OF 238, Cotton, box 1, file—March–August 1933, FDRL; and A. F. McKissick to W. W. Ball, September 25, 1933, Ball Papers, DU.

2. Huff, *Greenville*, 349; *GN*, August 2, 1933; *GI-J*, July 18, 1933; *The State*, July 19, 1933.

3. Hodges, *New Deal Labor Policy*, 56; Hall et al., *Like a Family*, 292–93. For South Carolina, see Hayes, "South Carolina and the New Deal," 332, and "Report of the Committee on the Textile Industry," Table—Earnings per Hour, 1907–34, President's Official File, OF 355, file—Textiles 1936–39, FDRL. For the number of workers, see Seventeenth Annual Report of the Commissioner of Agriculture, Commerce, and Industry of the State of South Carolina—Labor Division (Columbia, 1925), 1934, SCL.

4. Starr to R. L. Gilbert, October 10, 20, 1933, November 6, 1933, NRA Records, RG 9, ser. 397, box 1, file—AFL, NA; Hall et al., *Like a Family*, 293–95.

5. E. W. Hilley to FDR, December 12, 1933, NRA Records, RG 9, ser. 398, box 3, file—Appleton Mills, NA.

6. W. E. McCoy to Hugh Johnson, January 14, 1935 (box 33, file—Ware Shoals Manufacturing Co.), NRA Records, R69, ser. 398, NA. Numerous scholars have used these letters. See, e.g., Sussman, *Dear FDR*; McElvaine, *Down and Out*; and Markowitz and Rosner, *Slaves of the Depression*. On the cotton mill world, see Hall et al., *Like a Family*, and Janet Irons, "Testing the New Deal."

7. For an example of the spinners' letters, see an anonymous complainant from Rock Hill, February 14, 1934, NRA Records, RG 9, ser. 398, box 32, file—Victor Mills, NA.

8. G. E. Adams of the Chiquola Manufacturing Co. earned only nine dollars a week. See Adams to Hugh Johnson, February 14, 1934, NRA Records, RG 9, ser. 398, box 9, file—Chiquola Mfg. Co., NA. Sweepers—mostly young men—also were frequently paid below the code minimum. See, e.g., L. B. Killey to Johnson, April 19, 1934 (box 9, file—Chiquola Mfg. Co.), and Claude Sexton to Mr. Johnston [*sic*], December 5, 1933 (box 24, file—Norris Cotton Mill, Cateechee, S.C.), NRA Records, RG 9, ser. 398, NA.

9. Hall et al., *Like a Family*, 295–96 (first and last quotations); Unnamed Lancaster

worker to *Greenville Observer*, n.d., Elliot Springs Scrapbook 1931–38, Springs Papers, SCL; Mrs. A. T. Watt to Hugh Johnson, September 23, 1933, NRA Records, RG 9, ser. 398, box 33, file—Watts Mills, Greenwood. See also Mrs. Emma Templeton to ICB, September 10, 1933 (ser. 398, box 29, file—Santee Mills, Denmark, S.C.), and Mrs. Annie L. West to FDR, September 18, 1934 (ser. 402, box 117, file—Saxon Mills), NRA Records, RG 9, NA.

10. Unsigned letter from Langley to Frances Perkins, Washington, D.C., November 12, 1933 (box 19, file—Horse Creek Valley), Anonymous to Hugh Johnson, August 15 [no year] (box 23, file—Mollihon Mfg. Co.), and Your Friend to FDR, March 1, 1934 (box 23, file—Monarch Mills), NRA Records, RG 9, ser. 398, NA; Hall et al., *Like a Family*, 295–96.

11. Roy Adams to James F. Burns [*sic*], March 25, 1934 (box 24, file—Orr Mills), C. H. Whitmire, President of UTW Local 1946, to William Green, November 16, 1933 (box 9, file—Chiquola Mfg. Co.), H. S. Holder to Hugh Johnson, January 1, 1934 (box 25, file—Panola Cotton Mills), and The Honest Card and Spinning Workers of the Watts Mill to Hugh Johnson, February 24, 1934 (box 33, file—Watts Mills), NRA Records, RG 9, ser. 398, NA.

12. Anonymous to William Green, n.d. [February 1934] (box 32, file—Victor Monhagan Mills) [note: the author of this letter worked in Rock Hill, so perhaps this was misfiled], Clyde Rodgers to Hugh Johnson, August 9, 1933 (box 29, file—Saxon Mills), T. M. Copeland to FDR, August 21, 1933 (box 12, file—Dunean Mill), and Anonymous to Sir, November 10, 1933 (box 12, file—Drayton Mill), NRA Records, RG 9, ser. 398, NA.

13. For an overview of the growth of unions after the adoption of the NRA, see Zieger, *American Workers*, 26–33. For the growth of the UTW nationally, see Hodges, *New Deal Labor Policy*, 61, and Hall et al., *Like a Family*, 304.

14. On the Palmetto State, see *AI*, June 3, 1934; *Greenville Observer*, July 14, 1934; *Augusta Labor Review*, November 10, 1933; "Union Membership Report," January 1934, NRA Records, RG 9, ser. 398, box 5, file—Curtailment, NA; and Proceedings of the SCFL, 1933–34, GML.

15. Zieger, *American Workers*, 29. More than any other labor leader, John L. Lewis translated the NRA into a prolabor message. "The President wants you to join a union," he told miners, and they did. See Dubofsky and Van Tine, *John L. Lewis*.

16. Hayes, "South Carolina and the New Deal," 334–35; Boyette, "General Textile Strike," 1987, 38–39; E. W. Hilley to FDR, December 12, 1933, NRA Records, RG 9, ser. 397, box 3, file—Appleton Mills, NA; Hall et al., *Like a Family*, 304; and Ruth, Clint, and Clarence DeVore to FDR, January 1, 1934, NRA Records, RG 9, ser. 398, box 19, file—Horse Creek Valley, NA. Behind the UTW's growth, see L. James Johnston to Frances Perkins, July 31, 1933, NRA Records, RG 9, ser. 397, box 1, file—AFL, NA; *Augusta Labor Review*, November 27, December 15, 1933, February 9, 1934; *Greenville Observer*, December 15, 1933; and Janet Irons, "Testing the New Deal," 240.

17. Complaint 197-R, January 19, 1934, NRA Records, RG 9, ser. 398, box 29, file—Saxon Mill, NA; *American Federationist*, May 1934, 546. Elliot Springs, "True Picture of Workers' Place in Resisting Outside Agitators," n.d. [ca. 1933–34], Springs Scrapbook 1931–38, Springs Papers, SCL.

18. Hodges, *New Deal Labor Policy*, 62 (Law); Schlesinger, *Coming of the New Deal*, 144–46; Mrs. B. S. Pettit to FDR, July 20, 1934, NRA Records, RG 9, ser. 398, box 24, file—Orr Mills, NA.

19. Hodges, *New Deal Labor Policy*, 72.

20. Hall et al., *Like a Family*, 306–7; Laura McGhee affidavit, August 10, 1933, and G. H. Leitner, Graniteville, to Unnamed, October 10, 1933, NRA Records, RG 9, ser. 398, box 19, file—HCV, NA. In the above letter, Leitner, vice president of the Graniteville Manu-

facturing Co., admitted that McGhee was fired but claimed that her union affiliation had nothing to do with her dismissal.

21. Hall et al., *Like a Family*, 305, 308. On the Duke incident, see also "Analysis" July 3, 1934, NRA Records, RG 9, ser. 398, box 19, file—HCV, NA.

22. D. H. Powers to Hugh Johnson, September 6, 1933 (box 16, file—Gaffney Mfg. Co.), Bessie Cooly to Johnson, July 24, 1933 (box 32, file—Virginia Mfg. Co.), Mrs. Dora Adams to Dear Sir, August 1, 1933 (box 24, file—Newry Mills), and Minnie Stowe to Johnson, February 1, 1934 (box 12, file—Dunean Mill), NRA Records, RG 9, ser. 398, NA; Needham Harris to FDR, June 6, 1934 (box 11, file—General Correspondence—H), ser. 397, ibid.

23. *Textile Worker* 22 (January 1934): 3–4; W. H. Fowler to Hugh Johnson, July 26, 1933 (box 3, file—Appalache Mill), D. H. Powers to Johnson, September 6, 1933 (box 16, file—Gaffney Mfg. Co.), and A Woman from Laurens, S.C., c/o Lavis Howe to FDR, February 13, 1934 (box 33, file—Watts Mills), NRA Records, RG 9, ser. 398, NA; Hall et al., *Like a Family*, 325 ("A Little Woman"). See also Roy Adams to James F. Burns [*sic*], March 25, 1934 (ser. 398, box 24, file—Orr Mills), Claude Sexton to Hugh Johnston [*sic*], December 5, 1933 (ser. 398, box 24, file—Norris Cotton Mill), Hamrick to H. H. Willis, July 10, 1934 (ser. 397, box 11, file—NRLB 1934), and Affidavit of Edwards, Littlejohn, Baily, and Brown, November 20, 1934 (ser. 402, box 75, file—Limestone Mills), NRA Records, RG 9, NA.

24. Claude Parris to Hugh Johnson, February 18, 1934, NRA Records, RG 9, ser. 397, box 12, file—General Correspondence—P, 1934, NA.

25. On code investigators, see Clement Winston, "Preliminary Abstract of Work on Labor Compliance of the Cotton Textile Industry Code Authority," NRA Records, RG 9, ser. 295, box 1, NA.

26. Complaint B60, Examined by R. F. Howell, July 25, 1935, NRA Records, RG 9, ser. 399, box 3, file—Appleton Mills, NA. For more examples of how complaints were handled, see Investigations by R. F. Howell, September 15, November 8, 1933 (box 6, file—Brandon Mills, and box 12, file—Dunean Mills), and Investigation by E. O. Fitzsimmons, December 12, 1933 (box 6, file—Chesnee Cotton Mills), NRA Records, RG 9, ser. 398, NA. See also *Textile Worker* 21 (December 1933): 349–50; Hall et al., *Like a Family*, 325; and Hodges, *New Deal Labor Policy*, 90–95.

27. Lawrence Boyette ("General Textile Strike," 1987, 48) makes a similar point about the resemblance between the general strike and the civil rights movement.

28. Seventeenth Annual Report of the Commissioner of Agriculture, Commerce, and Industries, 25. Fifteen years later Aiken County had 4,260 textile operatives. U.S. Bureau of the Census, *Sixteenth Census, Population*, 389. On Gregg's enterprises, see Broadus Mitchell, *William Gregg*, and Lander, *Textile Industry*, 50–62, 93–98.

29. Burton, *In My Father's House*, 31.

30. McLaurin, "Early Labor Union Organizational Efforts."

31. Hall et al., *Like a Family*, 187–95; George S. Mitchell, *Textile Unionism*, 42–46.

32. For these strikes, see Janet Irons, "Testing the New Deal," 202–3, 210, 243; *Textile Worker* 20 (May 1932): 53–55, 20 (August 1932): 207–8; M. P. Chavis to FDR, April 6, 1934, NRA Records, RG 9, ser. 398, Aiken Mills, NA; Proceedings of the SCFL, 1932, GML; and B. E. Brookshire to ICB, April 28, 1932, and Melton Report, May 16, 1932, ICB Papers, box—CAB Files, SCDAH. No single factor can explain the valley's militant history. Perhaps its prolonged experience, at least in southern terms, with industrialization led workers to acknowledge their position as permanent wage laborers more readily than others. Then, too, location may have accounted for the pattern of trade union action. The valley fanned out north from Augusta, a city that by the second decade of the century had its own labor newspaper (the *Augusta Labor Review*), a labor church (which preached the

virtues of industrial organization), and a cadre of trade unionists committed to organizing the unorganized millhands.

33. For biographic information on Fuller, see Janet Irons, "Testing the New Deal," 144–45; *Textile Worker* 20 (April 1931): 13; and *Aiken Evening Standard*, June 1, 1934. For more on religious labor radicals in the South, see Dodge, *Southern Rebel in Reverse*, and Simon, " 'I Believed in the Strongest Kind of Religion.' " It is worth noting that the activist tradition within white southern culture shares a great deal in common with African American religious traditions. See, e.g., Genovese, *Roll, Jordon, Roll*, 209–45.

34. For accounts of the strike, see Hayes, "South Carolina and the New Deal," 340–44, and Janet Irons, "Testing the New Deal," 235–52. Interestingly, AFL president William Green seems to have questioned the wisdom of the strike. See "Conference with William Green," November 10, 1933, NRA Records, RG 9, ser. 397, box 1, file—AFL, NA.

35. *Augusta Labor Review*, October 27, 1933 (Fuller); *Augusta Chronicle*, October 26, 1933; E. Duncan to FDR, Graniteville, January 24, 1934, NRA Records, RG 9, ser. 398, box 19, file—HCV, NA; *The State*, October 28, 1933; Mr. and Mrs. Odell Leopard, Warrenville, to FDR, January 3, 1934, NRA Records, RG 9, ser. 398, box 19, file—HCV, NA. See also Janet Irons, "Testing the New Deal," 340–42, and *The State*, October 29, 1933.

36. For the valley's tradition of violence, see Butterfield, *All God's Children*, 3–18, and Terrill, "Murder in Graniteville," 193. For descriptions of these "wild" villages, see John Romaine, Gloverville, to JGR, February 13, 1929, JGR Papers, box 10, file R, SCDAH, and unsigned letter from a Bath resident to ICB, April 2, 1934, ICB Papers, box—Constabulary Reports 1932, file—Aiken, SCDAH. For a description of "Bloody Edgefield"—only a dozen or so miles from the valley—see Simkins, *Pitchfork Ben Tillman*, 23–25.

37. For strike-related violence, see Hearing at Langley-Bath Mills: The Cases of Jesse Walker and Turner Walker, March 2, 1934, NRA Records, RG 9, ser. 398, box 19, file—HCV, NA; Hayes, "South Carolina and the New Deal," 341–42; and *The State*, October 22, 25, 28, 1933.

38. *Augusta Chronicle*, October 31, November 1, 1933; *The State*, October 29, November 1, 1933; L. E. Brookshire to ICB, October 27, 1933, ICB Papers, box—CAB Files, SCDAH.

39. *The State*, October 29, November 1–2, 1933; Report from Mr. Richardson, October 27, 1933, NRA Records, RG 9, ser. 397, box 1, file—Augusta Adjustment, NA. On Blackwood's view of organized labor, see Carlton, "The State and the Worker," 189.

40. On the Bruere Board's history, see Hodges, *New Deal Labor Policy*, 62–72.

41. *The State*, October 31, 1933.

42. Only Bruere and Geer went to the valley. According to press reports, Berry, the labor official, "had pressing duties elsewhere." Janet Irons, "Testing the New Deal," 244–45.

43. *The State*, November 4, 1933; "Decision of the Bruere Board," November 3, 1933, NRA Records, RG 9, ser. 398, box 17, NA. The Willis Board—the statewide equivalent of the Bruere Board—included chair H. H. Willis, J. B. Harris, and Earle R. Britton. Under the code, every state was supposed to form a similar board. Yet James Hodges (*New Deal Labor Policy*, 70) points out that the South Carolina board was the only state board to be actively engaged in the administration of the textile code.

44. Janet Irons, "Testing the New Deal," 246; Mrs. Leila Fulmer, Graniteville, to Sen. Ellison D. Smith, January 1, 1934, and Mrs. Bessie Wilson, Warrenville, to Frances Perkins, Washington, D.C., November 11, 1933, NRA Records, RG 9, ser. 398, box 19, file—HCV, NA.

45. *The State*, November 11, 1933.

46. *Aiken Evening Standard*, December 5, 1933; *The State*, December 3, 1933; "Transcript of Hearing of Horse Creek Valley Workers before the Bruere Board," December 2, 1933,

NRA Records, RG 9, ser. 398, box 19, file—HCV. Apparently one of the obstacles in the union's path was Geer's disdain for Fuller. The mill official regarded the labor leader as a rabble-rouser. Geer to Bruere, January 4, 8, 10, 1934, NRA Records, RG 9, ser. 397, box 10, file—B. E. Geer, NA.

47. Janet Irons, "Testing the New Deal," 246; *Aiken Evening Standard*, February 16, 1934; Viola Smith to Sen. Robert Wagner, January 11, 1934, NRA Records, RG 9, ser. 398, box 19, file—HCV, NA. See also the use of replacements in *The State*, February 15, 1934, and J. Henry Layton et al., January 10, 1934, and Mrs. J. W. Hallman to Mrs. Roosevelt, January 29, 1934, NRA Records, RG 9, ser. 398, box 19, file—HCV, NA.

48. Carlton, "The State and the Worker," 189; Hall et al., *Like a Family*, 308-9. See also *Aiken Evening Standard*, February 16, 1934; *The State*, February 15, 1934; Paul Fuller to ICB, September 11, 1934, and Charles H. Gerald (Blackwood's aide) to Carroll W. Thompson, February 15, 1934, ICB Papers, box—CAB Files, 1933-34, SCDAH.

49. Hall et al., *Like a Family*, 308.

50. For union membership, see table 671, "United States Union Membership in Manufacturing by State, 1984 to 1989," U.S. Department of Commerce, *Statistical Abstract*, 421.

51. Describing this posture of individualism often ascribed to southern workers, Doug Flamming ("Paradox of Community," 4) came up with this brilliant phrase. In recent years, southern labor historians have explored the possibility of biracial unionism in the South. See Arnesen, *Waterfront Workers*, and Letwin, "Interracial Unionism."

52. On the importance of industrial structures, see Marshall, *Labor in the South*, 314-18. See also Galambos, *Competition*; Gerstle, *Working-Class Americanism*, 32-33; Fink, *Fulton Bag*, 144-45; and esp. Carlton, "The State and the Worker," 192. For additional, and wide-ranging, discussions of the failure of southern textile unionism, see Montgomery, "The Violence and the Struggle"; Newman, "Labor Struggles"; Carlton, "The State and the Worker"; and Terrill, "No Union for Me." See also Wyche, "Southern Industrialists."

53. On successful unions in competitive industries, see, on coal mining, Corbin, *Life, Work*; on New England textiles, Gerstle, *Working-Class Americanism*; and on the garment industry, Fraser, "Dress Rehearsal for a New Deal."

54. For contrasts between strikebreakers in the cotton mill world and other places, see Tuttle, "Labor Conflict," and Whatley, "African American Strikebreaking."

55. Flamming, *Creating the Modern South*, 218-19; DeNatale, "Bynum," 214; Rinnie Bishop to JGR, January 22, 1930, JGR Papers, box—Misc. Correspondence, file B, SCDAH. On the importance of seniority to union contracts, see Schatz, *Electrical Workers*, 105-32.

56. On religion and antiunionism, see Corbin, *Life, Work*, 151, and Pope, "Mill Village Churches," 17-20. For management's influence on villages churches, see the life history of Rev. David Brown, "There's Always a Judas," in *Such as Us*, 157-69.

57. David Carlton ("The State and the Worker," 196-97) has stressed the individualism of workers to explain their rejection of trade unionism.

58. Hall et al., *Like a Family*, 307; Mrs. J. W. Hallman to Mrs. Roosevelt, January 29, 1934, NRA Records, RG 9, ser. 398, box 19, file—HCV, NA. For more on trade unionists as longtime residents of their communities, see Ruby Williams to FDR, February 8, 1934, and Hearing at Langley-Bath Mills: The Cases of Jesse Walker and Turner Walker, March 2, 1934, NRA Records, RG 9, ser. 398, box 19, file—HCV, NA; *The State*, October 22, 25, 28, 1933. Leona Hickok, one of the WPA investigators who visited the South, also noted this split between what she labeled old and new hands. Hickok to Harry Hopkins, February 7, 1934, Hopkins Papers, box 56, FDRL. In earlier strikes in the valley, newer workers and rural residents seem to have been disproportionately strikebreakers.

See *Textile Worker* 21 (March 1931): 742; Janet Irons, "Testing the New Deal," 237–38; and Broadus Williams to ICB, May 8, 1932, ICB Papers, box—CAB Files, SCDAH.

Where strikebreakers came from is important to southern labor historians. The *Like a Family* collective has suggested, based on impressionistic evidence, that strikebreakers typically came from outside of the mill villages. My attempts to test this hypothesis have not succeeded. Though I have uncovered lists of pro- and antiunion workers from the Horse Creek Valley (as well as Pelzer), I have been unable to find company records or directories for these areas to determine the place of residence of strikers and loyalists. Alternatively, Doug Flamming directly addressed the question of length of residence and the propensity to strike. When considering the three mills of Dalton, Ga., during a 1939 strike, Flamming discovered, contrary to the impressionistic evidence available from the valley, that length of residence did not seem to be a significant variable in an individual worker's decision to strike or not. But his evidence also suggests a strong correlation between community stability and support for the union. See Flamming, *Creating the Modern South*, 209–29, esp. 220–23.

59. Greenville millhand Letha Ann Sloan Osteen distinguished between her relatives who lived in the country and those who lived in the mill village. In her mind, these were two different groups. Interview with Osteen, by Allen Tullos, Greenville, S.C., June 8, 1979, SOHP.

60. *Union Daily Times*, August 25, 1930. Wilburn made this pledge in a campaign advertisement.

61. For a good account of the attitudes of these "rural" workers, see Shoffer, "The New South." For a later period Kenneth Morland (*Millways of Kent*, 178–80) estimated that 10 percent of the permanent workforce in Kent lived on farms outside the village. For more on the rural labor force, see Rhyne, *Southern Cotton Mill Workers*, 65–78; Hall et al., *Like a Family*, 44–113; and Terrill, "No Union for Me," 209–10. One of the families interviewed by the WPA recounted what he disliked about the mills. See FWP, *These Are Our Lives*, 93. This is not to suggest that a preindustrial outlook stifled all forms of industrial militancy. The point is that rural folk and mill folk viewed the world differently. On the potential militancy of first-generation workers, see Herbert Gutman's seminal essay, "Work, Culture, and Society in Industrializing America, 1815–1919," *Work, Culture*, 3–78.

62. *Augusta Chronicle*, October 31, November 1, 1933; Byars, *Lintheads* and *Olympia Pacific*.

63. As evidence of this disdain, Miss Lucille Knox, of Union, who wrote Eleanor Roosevelt in 1934 asking for money, assured the first lady that she did not live in the mill village, as if this would be evidence of her unworthiness of charity. See Knox to Roosevelt, September 8, 1934, Eleanor Roosevelt Papers, box 2196, FDRL. In addition, see Doug DeNatale ("Bynum," 191–92), who argues that nineteenth-century yeomen did not have a "low opinion" of the mills, but by the twentieth century rural families viewed the "textile mill and village" as "clearly a last resort." See also Morland, *Millways of Kent*, 178, 180, and Rhyne, *Southern Cotton Mill Workers*, 85, 195, 197. On women in public, see Hall, "Disorderly Women," and MacLean, "The Leo Frank Case Reconsidered."

64. Letha Ann Sloan Osteen told Allen Tullos that if you wanted to starve to death, the country was the place to go. Interview with Osteen, by Tullos, SOHP.

65. According to Albert Sanders of Greenville, the "kids who were coming of age" in the 1920s "had grown up in the mills and they preferred the urban life to the rural." Interview with Sanders, by Allen Tullos, Greenville, S.C., May 30, 1980, SOHP. See also Ella Ford, "We Are Mill People," 264–65.

66. On mill folk and the countryside, see Kohn, *Cotton Mills*, 27–28, 69–73; Morland, *Millways of Kent*, 219–20; The Life Story of Elvira Hawkins of Brandon Mills as recounted by Ida L. Moore, April 12, 1939, FWP, file 277, SHC. On the "rough" life of the village, see

Hall et al., *Like a Family*, 250–54; John Romaine to JGR, February 13, 1929, JGR Papers, box 10, file R; and an unsigned letter from a Bath resident to ICB, April 2, 1934, ICB Papers, box—Constabulary Reports 1932, file—Aiken, SCDAH.

67. For Caldwell's background, see Devlin, *Caldwell*, 1–22, and Miller, *Caldwell*, 3–119.

68. Caldwell, *Tobacco Road*, 22–23, 68 (second quotation), 168 (first quotation).

69. Caldwell, *God's Little Acre*, 143–44, 190–201.

70. On rural residents as strikebreakers in the valley around the time of the publication of *God's Little Acre*, see *Augusta Chronicle*, October 31, November 1, 1933; *The State*, November 1, 22, 25, 1933; L. E. Brookshire to ICB, October 27, 1933, ICB Papers, box—CAB Files, 1933–34, SCDAH; and *AI*, July 28, September 7, 1935.

71. Cash, *Mind of the South*, 358; *AI*, July 28, September 7, 1935; DeNatale, "Bynum," 191–92. For cultural hostilities, see the works of Morland, *Millways of Kent*, 178, 180, and Rhyne, *Southern Cotton Mill Workers*, 85, 195, 197.

72. Hayes, "South Carolina and the New Deal," 344–49; Janet Irons, "Testing the New Deal," 339–51; Hamrick to H. H. Willis, July 10, 1934 (box 11, file—NRLB 1934), and Moore to Lawrence Pickney, July 13, 1934 (box 13, file—General Correspondence—T 1934), NRA Records, RG 9, ser. 397, NA.

73. DeVore to FDR, n.d., NRA Records, RG 9, ser. 398, box 19, file—Horse Creek Valley, NA. John Peele, the Greenville union leader, also reported on conditions. See Hayes, "The New Deal and South Carolina," 349–50.

74. Janet Irons, "Testing the New Deal," 347; James Starr to L. J. Gilbert, November 27, 1933, NRA Records, RG 9, ser. 395, box 1, NA.

75. *GI-J*, July 21, 1935.

Chapter Six

1. Hayes, "South Carolina and the New Deal," 350–52; Hall et al., *Like a Family*, 328; Hodges, *New Deal Labor Policy*, 86–90.

2. Resolution of the Cherokee County Textile Council, May 26, 1934, and similar resolutions from UTW Locals in Greenville, Gaffney, Tucapau, Blacksburg, Beaumont, Spartanburg, Cowpens, Piedmont, and Lyman, NRA Records, RG 9, ser. 398, box 5, file—Curtailment, NA.

3. *Aiken Evening Standard*, May 18, 1934; *AI*, May 16, June 1, 1934; *Greenville Observer*, May 26, 1934; *SH*, May 24, 29–31, 1934.

4. *AI*, June 21–22, 1934.

5. *GI-J*, July 15–17, 21, 1934; Boyette, "General Textile Strike," 1987.

6. *Aiken Evening Standard*, June 1, 1934; *NYT*, June 3, 1934. See also Hall et al., *Like a Family*, 328; Hodges, *New Deal Labor Policy*, 86–90; and Janet Irons, "Testing the New Deal," 337–39.

7. For the Alabama uprising, see *NYT*, July 18–22, 1934; James L. Hoffman, "Study of the United Textile Workers"; Taft, *Organizing Dixie*, 76–79; and Alexander Kendrick, "Alabama Goes on Strike," *Nation*, August 29, 1934, 233.

8. *Co*, August 29–30, 1934; Brecher, *Strike!*, 169; Hodges, *New Deal Labor Policy*, 89–95.

9. *Newsweek*, August 25, 1934; Hodges, *New Deal Labor Policy*, 99.

10. *AI*, August 17–18, 1934; Hodges, *New Deal Labor Policy*, 98–99.

11. *Newsweek*, August 25, 1934; Bass to Perkins, July 11, 1934 (ser. 398, box 26, file—Piedmont Mills), and Guy W. Bradley to FDR, August 31, 1934 (box 1, file B), NRA Records,

RG 9, ser. 397, NA; Janet Irons, "Testing the New Deal," 399-400. Roosevelt's advisers, meanwhile, instructed him to stay out of the fracas. Perkins to McIntyre, August 17, 1934, President's Official File, OF 407b, Cotton Textile Strikes 1934-35, FDRL.

12. Douglas G. Woolf, "United Textile Workers vs. Textile Workers," *Textile World* [ca. September 1934], Winant Papers, box 137, file—Textile Bulletins, FDRL; Hayes, "South Carolina and the New Deal," 355; Hodges, *New Deal Labor Policy*, 105; UTW Press Release, September 4, 1934, box 1, file 7A, TWUA. On Gorman's background and leadership, see Jonathan Mitchell, "Here Comes Gorman!" *New Republic*, October 3, 1934, 204, and Hodges, *New Deal Labor Policy*, 104-6. Hodges is critical of the union leader. For a more positive view, see Boyette, "General Textile Strike," 1987, 48-49.

13. *NYT*, September 3, 1934 (Lawrence and Peele); Janet Irons, "Testing the New Deal," 409-10 (Link and Lawrence). On prestrike preparations and rallies in just one town, see *Rock Hill Evening Herald*, August 16, 24, 28, 31, 1934. See also *NYT*, September 1, 1934. For another example of this type of religious imagery, see *Carolina Free Press*, September 7, 1934.

14. UTW Press Release, August 25, 1934, box 1, file 7A, TWUA; *Rock Hill Evening Herald*, August 24, 1934.

15. Irving Bernstein, *Turbulent Years*, 305-6. For AP reports, see *CO*, September 3-26, 1934. See also Brecher, *Strike!*, 168-71; *AI*, September, 5, 1934; *NYT*, September 1-8, 1934; and *Newsweek*, September 22, 1934.

16. Questions about the depth of support for the strike were raised by S. Pemberton Hutchinson in a letter to John G. Winant, September 14, 1934, Winant Papers, box 138, file—Textile Strike, FDRL. The point about distinguishing between lockouts and strikes is made by Hodges, *New Deal Labor Policy*, 108-9.

17. *Co*, September 10, 13, 1934.

18. The editors of the *Laurens Advertiser* (September 6, 1934) commented about all of the "flags waving and pledges of allegiance" evidenced during the strike.

19. Hayes, "South Carolina and the New Deal," 355; Boyette, "General Textile Strike," 1990, 13-15; Flier, n.d., NRA Records, ser. 401, box 1, file—Complaints of Workers (Individual), NA. See also *AI*, September 4, 1934.

20. Haskett, "Ideological Radicals," 8-9 n. 12; Boyette, "General Textile Strike," 1990, 9. For more on the links between civil rights and the textile strike, see Boyette, "General Textile Strike," 1987, 48, and Janet Irons, "Textile Labor Protest."

21. Brecher, *Strike!*, 169; *CO*, September 8, 1934; Woolf, "United Textile Workers vs. Textile Workers." Additional reports on flying squadrons, mostly from alarmed middle-class citizens, can be found in NRA Records, RG 9, ser. 402, box 103, file—Powell Knitting Mills, and ser. 401, box 1, file—Complaints of Workers (Individual), NA; telegram from A. G. Furman Jr. to FDR, September 5, 1934, and E. E. Epting, Commander of Anderson Post, American Legion, to FDR, September 5, 1934, NRA Records, RG 9, ser. 401, box 1, file—Referred from White House, NA; telegram from Greenwood Sheriff E. M. White to ICB, September 6, 1934, ICB Papers, box—CAB Files, 1934, SCDAH. For several newspaper accounts, see *Rock Hill Evening News*, September 5-6, 1934; *GN*, September 4-9, 1934.

22. *NYT*, September 6, 1934; Carpenter, "Olin D. Johnston," 222. See also Hayes, "South Carolina and the New Deal," 357; *The State*, September 5, 1934.

23. *Co* and *GN*, September 4, 1934; Untitled and undated report, NRA Records, RG 9, ser. 402, box 103, file—Powell Knitting Mills, NA. See also Mary E. Frederickson, "Heroines and Girl Strikers."

24. Obviously this is difficult to document, but the argument about sexual harassment and trade unionism is woven through the award-winning film, *Uprising of '34*.

25. *SH*, September 4–9, 1934; *AI*, September 6, 1934.

26. *Abbeville Press and Banner*, September 3, 1934; Janet Irons, "Testing the New Deal," 422.

27. *Aiken Evening Standard*, September 8, 1934; *Co*, September 6, 1934; Janet Irons, "Testing the New Deal," 430–33; T. M. Marchant to Elliot Springs, September 10, 1934, Springs Papers, box 32, file—138, SCL; "War Ace Keeps Mills Running," *New York World Telegram*, September 6, 1934, in Elliot Springs Scrapbook 1931–38, Springs Papers, SCL.

28. UTW 1881, Spartanburg, to FDR, September 7, 1934, NRA Records, RG 9, ser. 401, box 2, NA.

29. Peele quoted by Janet Irons, "Testing the New Deal," 198–99. On tensions in Greenville, see ibid., 433–36; Huff, *Greenville*, 350–55; Woolf, "United Textile Workers vs. Textile Workers"; *GN*, September 4–11, 1934; *Rock Hill Evening Herald*, July 14, 1934; *AI*, May 29, July 14, 17–18, September 3–6, 17, 19, 1934; *Co*, August 14, September 17, 1934; Willis, "A Mill Town in 1934." None of these accounts deal specifically with the question, why didn't Greenville workers join the strike? Some analysts have suggested that Greenville had a particularly antiunion culture. Others have argued that local workers tended to be less politically active than their neighbors. Still others have pointed to the conservative antiunion influence of evangelicalism in the area, noting that these same sources helped to launch Bob Jones University after World War II. In the end, the best evidence points in other directions. In the late 1920s and early 1930s, Greenville workers repeatedly went on strike and each time they lost. By 1934, they may have been exhausted and bereft of key local leadership. At the same time, owners may have honed their antiunion skills. For a discussion of the differences between Greenville and Spartanburg, see Key, *Southern Politics*, 139 n. 5.

30. Hall et al., *Like a Family*, 338–40; *AI*, September 7, 1934; Kennedy, "General Strike," 63–66.

31. *The State, AI, NYT*, and *Co*, September 7, 1934; *Newsweek*, September 15, 1934, 9; Kennedy, "General Strike," 63–66; Janet Irons, "Testing the New Deal," 446–51; DuPlessis, "Massacre in Honea Path," 60–63. A seventh striker died in the hospital several days later. An inquest conducted after the strike confirmed that the slain workers had been shot in the back. *The State*, February 21, 1935. The documentary *Uprising of '34*, which contains some startling footage from Honea Path, has sparked renewed interest in the strike. See, e.g., Applebome, *Dixie Rising*, 182–209.

32. For accounts of the funeral, see Kennedy, "General Strike," 63–66; *AI* and *NYT*, September 9, 1934; *Co*, September 10, 1934; AFL Weekly News Service, Special Supplement, September 10, 1934, box 1, file 7A, TWUA (Gorman's letter).

33. A. G. Furman Jr. to FDR (telegram), September 5, 1934, NRA Records, RG 9, ser. 401, box 1, file—Referral from White House, NA; *Florence News*, n.d., Elliot Springs Scrapbook 1931–38, Springs Papers, SCL; *Easley Progress*, September 6, 1934; *Greenville Observer*, September 7, 1934; *SH*, September 8, 1934; *Lee County Messenger*, September 20, 1934; *AI*, September 8–9, 1934.

34. *Co*, September 2–4, 1934; W. C. Bolick to Frances Perkins, September 8, 1934 (RG 174, box 40, file—Misc. Strikes 1934), and Lawrence G. Robbins to FDR, September 8, 1934 (RG 9, ser. 401, box 1, file—Complaints of Workers [Individual]), NRA Records, NA. For more information, see ICB Papers, SCDAH. For the names and occupations of the constables without pay, by county, see ICB Papers, box—Constabulary Appointments 1931–34, Strike Constables, SCDAH.

35. As a result of the textile strike, the profits of tear gas companies jumped by more then 10 percent in the first nine months of 1934. *Newsweek*, September 29, 1934, 9. Between 1933 and 1936, according to the La Follette Committee investigating antilabor tactics, tear

gas and sickening gas valued at $3,616 had been shipped to South Carolina, "mostly to the mills in the Piedmont section." [Una] News Review, November 2, 1936.

36. Hayes, "South Carolina and the New Deal," 357.

37. ICB to E. W. Dorn, September 6, 1934, and ICB to J. C. Self, November 11, 1934, ICB Papers, box—CAB Files, 1934, SCDAH; Boyette, "General Textile Strike," 1987, 53–54; NYT and Co, September 6, 1934.

38. Co, September 8–9, 1934; "Declaration of State of Insurrection," September 9, 1934, ICB Papers, box—General Subjects 1932–34, file—Proclamations, Celebrations, SCDAH.

39. The State and NYT, September 11, 1934.

40. For more on strike violence and other strike-related events around the country, see Simon, "Textile Strike of 1934," 531–32; Irving Bernstein, Turbulent Years, 308–10; and James E. Allen, "Eugene Talmadge and the Great Textile Strike."

41. Telegrams from Gorman to FDR, September 7, 12, 1934, and from C. B. Huggins, Secretary of Local 1912, UTW, to FDR, September 15, 1934, President's Official File, OF 407b, file—Cotton Textile Strikes, FDRL; NYT, September 10, 1934. FDR's secretary, Marvin McIntyre, wrote in a memo attached to Gorman's telegram: "Quite obviously no action has been taken on this and no reply sent."

42. NYT, September 11–12, 1934; Gorman to Winant, September 9, 1934, NRA Records, RG 9, ser. 401, box 1, NA; Janet Irons, "Testing the New Deal," 451.

43. Brecher, Strike!, 175; Co, September 11, 1934.

44. Janet Irons, "Testing the New Deal," 460.

45. NYT, September 17, 1934; Co, September 14, 21, 1934; L. D. Tindall to Frances Perkins, September 6, 1934, and telegrams from UTW locals at Powell Mills, Spartan Mills, and Saxon Mills and workers in Spartanburg, Inman, Converse, Valley Falls, and Wellford, NRA Records, RG 174, box 40, file—Textile Strikes, NA.

46. Jack Long to A. L. Fletcher, n.d., Ehringhaus Papers, box 103, file—Strike Situation Correspondence, North Carolina Dept. of Archives and History, Raleigh.

47. Mrs. J. W. Hallman to Mrs. Roosevelt, Graniteville, January 29, 1934, and J. W. Williams to FDR, Langley, January 19, 1934 (RG 9, ser. 398, box 19, file—Horse Creek Valley), and Confidential Memo, Furman Battle to Perkins, September 9, 1934 (RG 174, box 40, file—Textile Strikes), NRA Records, NA; NYT, September 17, 1934; Hall et al., Like a Family, 308; Badger, New Deal, 195–96.

48. Gorman to FDR (telegram), September 8, 1934, President's Official File, OF 407b, file—Cotton Textile Strikes, FDRL.

49. Statement by FDR, September, 20, 1934, John G. Winant Papers, box 138, file—Textile Strike, and Gorman to FDR, September 22, 1934, President's Official File, OF 407b, file—Cotton Textile Strikes, FDRL. On FDR's attitude toward strikes, see Leuchtenburg, Franklin D. Roosevelt, 107–8.

50. NYT, September 20–24, 1934.

51. Textile Worker 21 (September 1934): 432; NYT, September 24, 1934. In Union, S.C., thirteen women and children were injured, three critically, when a truck full of strikers was sideswiped. Co, September 23–24, 1934; AI, September 23–25, 1934.

52. On immediate poststrike discrimination, see Confidential Report Issued by South Carolina Manufacturers Association, November 17, 1934 (box 30/31, file 438), and Statement Given by Jacobs to SH, September 25, 1934 (box 37, file 12B), Springs Papers, SCL; AI, November 10, 1934; NYT, September 22–26, 1934; [Una] News Review, September 24, 1937; and Textile Worker 21 (November 1934): 124–25. Charges of discrimination continued into the next year and are listed by mill in NRA Records, RG 9, ser. 402, NA. Yet the best single source on discrimination comes from Minutes of the "Greenville Meeting," Novem-

ber 20, 1934, box 1, file 7A, TWUA; see also Boyette, "General Textile Strike," 1987, 59-60.

53. Janet Irons, "Testing the New Deal," 507. On Gorman's support for a national labor party, see Co, November 21, 1935.

54. For the assessment of Blackwood, see Lawrence G. Robbins to FDR, September 8, 1934, NRA Records, RG 9, ser. 401, box 1, file—Complaints of Workers (Individual), NA. On "yellow scabs," see Co, September 9, 1934, and Boyette, "General Textile Strike," 1987 56.

55. "Report to Mr. Hopkins," November 11, 1934, Hopkins Papers, box 66, file—Gellhorn, Martha, FDRL; Bauman and Coode, *In the Eye of the Great Depression*, 27-29. In 1940 Gellhorn married Ernest Hemingway, and additional biographical information can be found in Kent, *The Hemingway Women*, 286-90.

Chapter Seven

1. David R. Coker to R. Beverly Herbert, August 29, 1934, Coker Papers, SCL. For the choices of the townspeople, see "Working Women" to Byrnes, May 16, 1934, Byrnes Papers, file 17(2), CU; *Beaufort Gazette*, September 9, 1934; *Charleston Evening Post*, September 7, 1934; Co, August 31, 1934; *Greenville Observer*, August 10, 17, 1934; and *NYT*, September 9, 1934.

2. Henry C. Davis, a University of South Carolina English professor, talked about the cynicism of voting for Blease in a letter to his wife. See Davis to Eva Davis, August 29, 1934, Davis Papers, SCL.

3. For the centrality of labor to the election of 1934, see, e.g., *AI*, August 5, 1934, and Walter Stewart to J. J. McSwain, September 5, 1934, McSwain Papers, box 10, SCL.

4. Letter to the editor, *CO*, September 17, 1934.

5. Jason Hoyt to Harry Watson, September 12, 1934, Watson Papers, box 2, file—Hoyt, SCL; *SH*, September 8, 1934; Hall et al., *Like a Family*, 332. For more evidence of the dislocation caused by the strike, see *AI*, September 8-9, 1934. In discussing nineteenth-century British industrial novels, Robyn Penrose noted: "Any kind of working-class militancy tends to be presented in the fiction as a threat to the social order." Lodge, *Nice Work*, 46. A southern example of this can be found in Hamilton Basso's novel—*In Their Image*—set against the backdrop of the General Textile Strike. Basso depicts a group of Aiken socialites made so skittish by the strike that they remained barricaded behind iron gates throughout the conflict. The mere sight of a worker made them cringe.

6. Co and GN, September 4, 1934; Untitled and undated report, NRA Records, RG 9, ser. 402, box 103, file—Powell Knitting Mills, NA; *Abbeville Press and Banner*, September 6, 1934; *AI*, September 2, 1934 (editor of the *Textile Bulletin*).

7. *Greenville Observer*, September 7, 1934.

8. On Manning's father's regime, see Burts, *Richard Irvine Manning*, and Carlton, *Mill and Town*, 267-69. On support for Manning, see N. B. Barnwell, August 18, 1934, Ball Papers, DU; interview with Jimmy Caldwell, January 23, 1948, and Notes on an Interview with Col. Wyndham Manning, January 29, 1948, box 2, One-Party System: South Carolina Piedmont vs. Low Country, Used Material, SPC-V.

9. *Lee County Messenger*, August 22, 1934. On Manning's background, see *Who's Who in South Carolina, 1934-35* (Columbia, 1935), 295. See also Carpenter, "Olin D. Johnston," 88-94; Manning to Coker, July 23, 1934, Coker Papers, SCL; W. W. Ball to Roger Peace [a candidate himself], August 20, 1934, Ball Papers, DU.

10. *CN&C*, August 25, 1934.

11. For a particularly bland speech by Manning, see *AI*, August 21, 1934.

12. Ibid., August 31, 1934; Jordan, *The Primary State*, 40–41.

13. Carpenter, "Olin D. Johnston," 93–94. See also Heyward Gibbes to Manning, August 31, 1934, Manning Papers, SCL.

14. *NYT*, September 2, 1934.

15. David R. Coker to R. Beverly Herbert, August 29, 1934, Coker Papers, SCL. For the choices of the townspeople, see also "Working Women" to Byrnes, May 16, 1934, Byrnes Papers, file 17(2), CU; *Charleston Evening Post*, September 7, 1934; *Co*, August 31, 1934; and *Greenville Observer*, August 10, 17, 1934.

16. *AI*, September 10, 1934; W. W. Ball to James Hagood, September 6, 1934, and R. B. Herbert to Ball, September 1, 1934, Ball Papers, box 25, DU; Anthony B. Miller, "Palmetto Politician," 64, 96.

17. *AI*, August 22, 1934; clipping, *Charleston Evening Post*, n.d. [ca. September 2, 1934], Gonzales Papers, SCL; Ball to R. Charleston Wright, September 14, 1934, Ball Papers, DU. For more, see *AI*, September 10, 1934; Charles M. Griffin to W. W. Smoak, July 18, 1934, Smoak Papers, box 1, file 54, SCL; George R. Koester to Manning, September 5, 1934, Manning Papers, SCL; and R. Beverly Herbert to Ball, September 3, 1934, Ball Papers, DU.

18. Carpenter, "Olin D. Johnston," 95; Ball to Clem, September 14, 1934, box 25, Ball Papers, DU. See also *Aiken Evening Standard*, August 31, 1934; and R. Beverly to Ball, June 27, 1934, and Ball to W. Manning, September 4, 1934, Ball Papers, DU.

19. Carlton, *Mill and Town*, 2; Carpenter, "Olin D. Johnston," 94–95; Ball to Clem, September 14, 1934, box 25, Ball Papers, DU. See also *Aiken Evening Standard*, August 31, 1934; R. Beverly to Ball, June 27, 1934, and Ball to W. Manning, September 4, 1934, box 25, Ball Papers, DU.

20. George R. Koester to Wyndham Manning, September 15, 1934, Manning Papers, SCL.

21. Cash, *Mind of the South*, 258–59.

22. The *Greenville Observer* (September 12, 1934) noted that Blease had "lost the fire."

23. Campaign advertisement, "Olin D. Johnston—the True Friend of Labor," ODJ Papers, Scrapbook 1934, SCL; *Greenville Observer*, August 17, 1934; *AI*, August 8, 1934.

24. Anthony B. Miller, "Palmetto Politician," 102.

25. For county-by-county election returns, see Jordan, *The Primary State*, 40–41, 74–75.

26. *AI*, September August 24, 1934. For other examples, see *AI*, August 7–8, September 22, 1934; *GN*, September 4, 1934; and *Greenville Observer*, September 7, 1934. The editors of the *Aiken Evening Standard* (September 4, 1934) dubbed these commentaries Johnston's "little school boy speeches."

27. *Carolina Free Press*, September 7, 1934; *GI-J*, September 9, 1934; *Co*, September 8, 1934. On Johnston's "quiet" prolabor speeches, see Anthony B. Miller, "Palmetto Politician," 95–96. The *Greenville Observer*, a promanagement paper, regularly commented on Johnston's evening speeches to millworkers. See, e.g., *Greenville Observer*, August 31, September 5, 1934.

28. For descriptions of Johnston on the stump, see *SH*, June 29, August 3, 1934, and *AI*, September 4, 1934.

29. Often county leaders sought out convicts to finish road projects. See, e.g., J. B. McCombs to CLB, February 12, 1914 (box 20, file—Greenwood 1913-14), and J. M. King to CLB, September 25, 1914 (box 5, file—Anderson County 1914), BP. For a breakdown of mileage per county before 1929, see John H. Moore, *South Carolina Highway Department*, 83.

30. Carlton, "Unbalanced Growth." W. W. Smoak was one of those who backed road building as a spur to growth. See a speech he delivered in 1931 [no exact date] in Smoak Papers, file 45, SCL, and *SH*, August 24, 1930.

31. John H. Moore, *South Carolina Highway Department*, 48–73; Suttles, "The Struggle," chap. 4.

32. The phrase "build-now-pay-later" comes from Lander, *History of South Carolina*, 104. Unless otherwise noted, my discussion of the "big bond fight" has relied on Mary K. Cann, "Morning After," 328–32; John H. Moore, *South Carolina Highway Department*, 74–100; and Suttles, "The Struggle," 87–114.

33. Suttles, "The Struggle," 104–5; *The State*, March 2, 1929.

34. House Journal, 1929, 861–62, SCL.

35. Carpenter, "Olin D. Johnston," 68.

36. See Johnston's references to the 1930 campaign in *Carolina Free Press*, October 26, November 16, 1934, and Commager, "South Carolina Dictator," 572.

37. *AI*, June 10, 1934. Johnston summarized these themes in the "Inaugural Address of Olin D. Johnston to the General Assembly of South Carolina," January 15, 1934, SCL.

38. *GI-J*, September 9, 1934. Johnston's economy program is outlined in *Carolina Free Press*, September 7, 1934; *AI*, June 6, July 11, 18, August 8, 21, 1934; and John H. Moore, *South Carolina Highway Department*, 103–5.

39. Campaign advertisement, "Olin D. Johnston—the True Friend of Labor," Scrapbook 1934, ODJ Papers, SCL.

40. Daniel Rodgers talks about the language of the people in his book, *Contested Truths*, 13–14, 80–111.

41. *Co*, September 10–12, 1934.

42. For turnout, see Jordan, *The Primary State*, 107. On enrollment, see *Abbeville Press and Standard*, September 1, 1938.

43. *Abbeville Press and Banner*, September 13, 1934; *Easley Progress*, September 14, 1934.

44. Heard, *Southern Primaries and Elections*, 107. For precinct-level returns, see *AI*, September 12, 1934; *Gaffney Ledger*, *GN*, and *Easley Progress*, September 13, 1934; and *Orangeburg Times and Democrat*, *SH*, and *Rock Hill Evening Herald*, September 12, 1934. See Table A.4.

45. *Newberry Observer*, September 14, 1934.

46. *GN*, September 12, 1934.

47. Johnston won 56.20 percent of the vote statewide, 58.33 percent in the low country, and 61.1 percent in Charleston County. Jordan, *The Primary State*, 107.

48. S. C. Wiggins to W. E. Gonzales, September 7, 1934, Gonzales Papers, SCL.

49. *Charleston Evening Post*, n.d. [ca. September 1934], Gonzales Papers, SCL.

50. Ball to Clem, September 9, 1934, and J. O. Norton to Ball, September 15, 1934, Ball Papers, box 24, DU. Ball himself had little patience with voters who supported Blease simply because they wanted to protect their own economic self-interests. He urged several of his friends to steer clear of this defensive course. After the election Johnston thanked Ball for his efforts. ODJ to Ball, October 3, 1934, ibid.; Anthony B. Miller, "Palmetto Politician," 108–9.

51. R. B. Herbert to Ball, September 1, 1934, Ball Papers, box 25, DU; Anthony B. Miller, "Palmetto Politician," 109. See also Ball to James M. Hagood, September 6, 1934, Ball Papers, box 24, DU; *AI*, August 26, September 11, 1934; and unidentified clipping, n.d., Scrapbook 1938, p. 194, ODJ Papers, SCL.

52. *Carolina Free Press*, September 7, 1934; *AI*, August 31, 1934.

53. Before taking office, Johnston attended a barbecue hosted by FTL leader J. K. Breedin. This joint appearance along with the candidate's commitment to retrenchment led some to wonder if Johnston and the Farmers and Taxpayers League had joined forces in a shaky pro-economy partnership. Johnston did little to muffle these rumors, but given the rest of his platform, it is clear that the FTL was not dictating policy to him. *Greenville Observer*, January 11, 1935.

54. On Talmadge and his campaign against the highway department, see Anderson, *Wild Man*, 16, 66–73.

55. On farmers and Johnston, see *NYT*, July 28, 1930, and an editorial from the *Calhoun Times*, reprinted in *Greenville Observer*, July 20, 1934. This assessment of Johnston's performance in the farm districts is supported by James C. Derieux, "The Julep Era Wanes," *Today*, November 24, 1934, clipping, Scrapbook 1935, p. 10, ODJ Papers, SCL, and *AI*, July 2, 15, 1934.

56. Irving Geisburg to ODJ, January 25, 1935, ODJ Papers, box—Misc. Governor's Papers 1935, SCDAH; A. M. McWhiter to W. E. Gonzales, August 25, 1934, Gonalzes Papers, SCL; Derieux, "The Julep Era Wanes." See also *NYT*, September 2, 1934; *Co*, September 13, 1934; and *Carolina Free Press*, November 26, 1934.

Chapter Eight

1. *Carolina Free Press*, September 21, 1934; John Pollard to ODJ, April 4, 1935, ODJ Papers, box 20, SCDAH. See also *Greenville Observer*, March 22, 1934; and Ellie Smith to ODJ, August 26, 1935 (box 37, file—CAB Files), C. B. Hancock to ODJ and ODJ to Hancock, February 18, 1935 (box—Misc. Governor's Papers 1935), and A. B. Henry, Greenville, to ODJ, March 20, 1935 (box—Misc. Governor's Papers 1935), ODJ Papers, SCDAH.

2. Proceedings of the SCFL, 1934, GML; C. Forster Smith to ODJ, January 31, 1935, ODJ Papers, box—Misc. Governor's Papers 1935, SCDAH. See also *Carolina Free Press*, October 26, November 16, 1934, and Anthony B. Miller, "Palmetto Politician," 114-15.

3. For descriptions of the scene that day, see *The State*, and *SH*, January 16, 1935; *Rock Hill Evening Herald*, January 17, 1935; and *Georgetown Times*, January 16, 1935, clipping, Scrapbook 1935, p. 16, ODJ Papers, SCL; and "Inaugural Address of Olin D. Johnston to the General Assembly of South Carolina," January 15, 1935, SCL.

4. Claude Graves to ODJ, September 5, 1935, ODJ Papers, box—Misc. Governor's Papers 1935, SCDAH. On the mill men, see T. M. Marchant of the South Carolina Manufacturers Association to Elliot Springs, February 18, 1935, and to J. C. Self et al., March 13, 1935, Springs Papers, box 32, file 138, SCL.

5. J. D. Derby to ODJ, September 1, 1935, ODJ Papers, box—Misc. Governor's Papers 1935, SCDAH.

6. *Carolina Free Press*, March 8, 1935.

7. C. B. Hancock to ODJ, February 18, 1935, and ODJ to Hancock, February 21, 1935, ODJ Papers, box—Misc. Governor's Papers 1935, SCDAH.

8. *AI*, April 10, 18, 1935; John Pollard to ODJ, April 4, 1935 (box 20), and Ellie Smith to ODJ, August 26, 1935 (box 37—CAB Files), ODJ Papers, SCDAH.

9. *The State*, May 22, 1935; Anthony B. Miller, "Palmetto Politician," 147-48. For more on labor legislation, see "Proceedings of the Third Southern Regional Labor Conference," 1936, ODJ Papers, box 41, file—Labor Convention, SCDAH; *Charlotte Labor Journal*, May 23, November 10, 24, 1935; *Textile Labor Banner*, July 27, September 21, 1935, and *Knox-*

ville Labor News, April 11, 1935, clippings, Mitchell Papers, box 2, file—Labor—North and South Carolina, DU, and L. James Johnson to Byrnes, April 2, 1935, Byrnes Papers, box—Misc. 1935 G–Z, file J, CU.

10. For studies of workers' compensation elsewhere, especially the business origins of this legislation, see Weinstein, "Big Business," and Lubove, "Workmen's Compensation," esp. 262.

11. Florida, in fact, passed a workers' compensation act in the spring of 1935, several months before Johnston signed South Carolina's bill into law. Arkansas and Mississippi adopted such acts in 1940 and 1948 respectively. See "Transcripts of the Proceedings of the Commemoration Day Program of the Thirtieth Anniversary of the South Carolina Workman's Compensation Law," p. 8, SCL.

12. Simpson, *Workman's Compensation*, 29–30; Dudley, "Workmen's Compensation Legislation," 20–26; Weinstein, "Big Business," 158; "South Carolina Should Adopt Accident Compensation," a handbill produced by the American Association for Labor Legislation attached to a letter from John B. Andrews to ODJ, March 30, 1935, ODJ Papers, box 62, SCDAH.

13. C. C. Johnson to CLB, November 16, 1912 (box 36, file—Union 1911–13), and John Brown to CLB, March 3, 1913 (box 34, file—Spartanburg 1913), BP.

14. *AI*, November 11, 1934.

15. Anthony B. Miller, "Palmetto Politician," 147; Simpson, *Workman's Compensation*, 23–25.

16. Mrs. M. D. Lee to FDR, June 22, 1934, NRA Records, RG 9, ser. 398, box 33, file—Ware Shoals, NA. For another "lucky" example, see *The State*, April 3, 1929.

17. Mr. Z to ICB, n.d., ICB Papers, box—Legislative Matters 1931–35, file—Misc. Matters, SCDAH.

18. For early attempts to pass workers' compensation legislation in South Carolina, see Proceedings of the SCFL, 1915, SCL; Britton, "Progress in the Palmetto State"; Simpson, *Workman's Compensation*, 28–37; Carlton, *Mill and Town*, 241; Burts, *Richard Irvine Manning*, 116; and Sandra C. Mitchell, "Conservative Reform," 70–71.

19. Sen. R. M. Jeffries outlined labor's view in his article, "Workman's Compensation: A Prerequisite to Sound Industrial Development," n.d., JGR Papers, box 10, file—American Association for Labor Legislation 1929, SCDAH. See also Dudley, "Workmen's Compensation Legislation," 16–20; Proceedings of the SCFL, 1916–17, GML; *SH*, August 14–30, 1930; and *Union Daily Times*, July 5, 1930.

20. *The State*, December 6–21, 1929. See also *Greenwood Index-Journal*, September 21, 1929. Early on, the publisher of the *Anderson Daily Mail*, G. P. Browne, also backed workers' compensation. See Browne to JGR, November 22, 1927, JGR Papers, box 16—Misc., SCDAH.

21. For business support, see Dudley, "Workmen's Compensation Legislation," i–xi. Harold A. Hatch, vice president of Deering, Milliken, and Co., voiced his support for workers' compensation in the *Textile Worker* 19 (April 1930): 34–35. See also *CN&C*, June 14, July 16, 1934; Sen. R. M. Jeffries, "Workman's Compensation," SCDAH; Carlton, "Unbalanced Growth"; and "New Plants and Additions to Old Plants, 1930–1937," ODJ Papers, box 39, file—Labor Department, SCDAH.

22. Pace to Coker, July 25, 1934, Coker Papers, box 15, SCL.

23. Dudley, "Workmen's Compensation Legislation," i–ix.

24. *SH*, January 7, 1932.

25. Dudley, "Workmen's Compensation Legislation," 9–12; Cowan, "Labor Regulation," 43–44.

26. After the workers' compensation law passed in 1935, the *Charleston Evening Post* (February 5, 1935, clipping, Scrapbook 1935, p. 108, ODJ Papers, SCL) reflected on Perkins's role in getting the measure through the legislature. See also V. A. Zimmer to Perkins, July 23, 1935, NRA Records, RG 174, box 108, file—Workers' Compensation, NA.

27. "Inaugural Address of Olin D. Johnston to the General Assembly of South Carolina," SCL. On the debate in the house, see unidentified clipping, February 15, 1935, and *Yorkville Enquirer*, April 11, 1935, Scrapbook 1935, pp. 108, 110, ODJ Papers, SCL; *AI*, April 18, 1935, and ODJ to John B. Andrews, April 16, 1935, ODJ Papers, box 44—Departmental Commissions 1935-39, file—Workman's Compensation, SCDAH.

28. Anthony B. Miller, "Palmetto Politician," 147-48; *The State*, May 23, 25, 1935; *SH*, May 17-19, 22-23, 1935; *AI*, May 11-12, 1935.

29. V. A. Zimmer of the Department of Labor described the law that passed as "weak." Zimmer to Frances Perkins, July 23, 1935, NRA Records, RG 174, box 108, file—Workers' Compensation, NA.

30. South Carolina Acts of 1936, 1231-68, SCL.

31. People would later call this illness "brown lung disease" or byssinosis. On early indications of millhands choking on the lint, see Caldwell, *God's Little Acre*. See also Hall et al., *Like a Family*, 81-82, 358, and Tullos, *Habits of Industry*, 276-78, 281-82. On millworkers' long fight to gain compensation for industrial diseases, see Botsch, *Organizing the Breathless*.

32. In 1935 Wisconsin had the highest rates of compensation in the country, paying injured workers 70 percent of their average weekly wages ranging from $8 to $21 a week. Alabama had the lowest rates in the South; injured workers there received between 20 and 60 percent of wages, which ranged between $5 and $15 per week. See "Comparative Benefits Costs of Various Workman's Compensation Acts," May 1, 1935, ODJ Papers, box 42, file—Industrial Commission,SCDAH.

33. *SH*, May 22, 1935.

34. R. P. Burgress to ODJ, May 24, 1935, Dr. Henry N. Synder to ODJ, May 25, 1935, M. H. Thorin to ODJ, June 5, 1935, and L. D. Pitts to ODJ, May 22, 1935, ODJ Papers, box 44—Departmental Commissions 1935-39, file—Workman's Compensation, SCDAH.

35. J. B. Connally to ODJ, May 31, 1935, J. T. Barfield to ODJ, June 27, 1935, Sonto Sottile to ODJ, July 19, 1935, C. W. Legerton to ODJ, July 17, 1935, E. W. Caper to ODJ, July 24, 1935, C. D. Boette to ODJ, July 18, 1935, and Charleston Central Labor Union to ODJ, June 10, 1935, ODJ Papers, box 44—Departmental Commissions 1935-39, file—Workman's Compensation, SCDAH. See also *Charleston Evening Post*, February 9, 1935, clipping, Scrapbook 1935, p. 108, ODJ Papers, SCL, and J. Ross Hanahan to David Coker, July 3, 1935, Coker Papers, box 16, SCL.

36. R. W. Gossett to ODJ, May 17, 1935, ODJ Papers, box 44—Departmental Commissions 1935-39, file—Workman's Compensation, SCDAH; Anthony B. Miller, "Palmetto Politician," 149. (Not surprisingly, a few plaintiff lawyers like Gossett jumped into the fray advocating workers' right to a trial.) See also *The State*, May 19, 23, 1935; *SH*, May 23, 1935; and *AI*, April 10, August 6, 1935.

37. W. H. Hayes to ODJ, May 24, 1935, Clarence Brown to ODJ, May 20, 1935, and P. D. & P of America, Charleston Local 704, to ODJ, May 21, 1935, ODJ Papers, box 44—Departmental Commissions 1935-39, file—Workman's Compensation, SCDAH (first, second, and fourth quotations); *Yorkville Enquirer*, April 11, 1935 (third quotation). See also Simpson, *Workman's Compensation*, 38-39; *The State*, May 18-19, 23, 1935; and *SH*, May 23, 1935.

38. Clifton (Local 1834) to ODJ, May 29, 1935, L. D. Tindall (Pres., Local 1834) to ODJ,

May 21, 1935, Newberry (Local 2118) to ODJ, n.d., and Glendale (Local 2189) to ODJ, September 29, 1935, ODJ Papers, box 44, file—Workman's Compensation, SCDAH.

39. J. B. Rhinhart to ODJ, May 29, 1935, ODJ Papers, box 44, file—Workman's Compensation, SCDAH. See also E. M. Easterlin to ODJ, May 25, 1935, ibid.; *Charlotte Labor Journal*, June 27, 1935. The editor of *The State* (July 19, 1935) echoed this view. "It is much to get the principle adopted," he wrote, "defects can be cured on the basis of information gained by trial and error."

40. Anthony B. Miller, "Palmetto Politician," 149; *The State*, July 18, 1935. For examples from Johnston's mailbag, see ODJ Papers, box 43—Departmental Commissions 1936-39, file—Industrial Commission, and W. A. Marshall to ODJ, February 22, 1935, ODJ Papers, box 22—General Correspondence, SCDAH. The members of the first commission were John Dukes, Coleman C. Martin, I. L. Hyatt, John W. Duncan, and P. M. Camak. The first two represented business interests, the second two labor, and the last the insurance industry. It was later alleged that Martin, the head of the Charleston Chamber of Commerce, had a drinking problem. G. L. B. Rivers to ODJ, April 25, 1936, and Lionel K. Legge to ODJ, April 27, 1936, ODJ Papers, box 43—Departmental Commissions 1936-39, file—Industrial Commission, SCDAH.

41. *The State* and *SH*, July 18, 1935. Nates was elected head of the SCFL after textile workers mobilized within the federation. *Carolina Free Press*, June 27, 1935.

42. *Carolina Free Press*, July 19, 1935; *The State*, July 18, 1935. U.S. Secretary of Labor Frances Perkins sent the governor a congratulatory letter after he signed the bill into law. Perkins to ODJ, July 28, 1935, NRA Records, RG 174, box 108, file—Workman's Compensation, NA.

43. Paul Murdaugh v. Robert Lee Construction Co., Case No. 1428, December 12, 1937, ODJ Papers, box 42, file—Industrial Commission, SCDAH.

44. Mrs. G. S. Price to ODJ, March 10, 1937, box 12, ibid. See also Price to ODJ, September 14, December 28, 1936, box 43, ibid.

45. A. B. Styles to ODJ, December 29, 1937, box 12, ibid.

46. Statement by ODJ, n.d., box 10, and "The Governor's Annual Message, 1936," n.d., box 44, file—Workman's Compensation, ibid.; Proceedings of the SCFL, 1936, GML.

47. "Transcripts of the Proceedings of the Commemoration Day Program of the Thirtieth Anniversary of the South Carolina Workman's Compensation Law," p. 18, SCL; *GN*, January 14-15, June 26, 1937; *Carolina Free Press*, March 19, 1937; *CN&C*, May 22, 1937. Ten years later Earle R. Britton ("Progress in the Palmetto State") accused "reactionaries" of fighting for repeal of the law, but he was wrong. This statement misrepresented the forces behind the repeal movement.

48. In 1936 the commission issued awards to workers in only 11 percent of the cases it heard. The next year this number rose to 18 percent, and in 1938 the figure reached 20 percent. Often, these matters were decided by a 3-2 margin with the business and public representatives voting against the labor spokesmen. See annual reports of the South Carolina Industrial Commission, 1936-39, SCDAH. See also *Carolina Free Press*, November 10, 1935.

49. *Carolina Free Press*, January 1, 1936, March 19, 1937; Proceedings of the SCFL, 1936, 1938, GML.

50. *AI*, February 18, 1937. See also *The State*, February 19, 1938; *Charleston Post*, February 25, 1937, clipping, Scrapbook 1937, p. 5, ODJ Papers, SCL.

51. Letter to the editor, *[Una] News Review*, January 28, 1938. Some charged that plaintiff lawyers were behind the fight for repeal. See *[Una] News Review*, January 21, 1938, and Spartanburg's Sam Orr Black to ODJ, January 18, 1938, ODJ Papers, box 42—Departmental Commissions 1935-39, file—Industrial Commission, SCDAH. See also *CN&C*,

March 22, 1937, and *AI*, January 12, 1938. Even the conservative Barnwell lawmaker, Sol Blatt, voted to retain the law. See untitled speech, n.d. [ca. 1937], Blatt Papers, box 18, file — Speeches, SCL. For more on the legislative moves, see House Journal, 1937, 509, 598, SCL.

52. F. E. Baughman to ODJ, September 9, 1938 (box 7), and Marvin R. Reese to ODJ, December 17, 1937 (box 12), ODJ Papers, SCDAH.

Chapter Nine

1. Between September 1934 and January 1935 the TLRB received 1,600 discrimination complaints involving 579 mills, and charges were filed against 61 separate South Carolina textile factories. There were so many reports of discrimination that B. M. Squires, the national board's executive director, sent almost every mill in the country a form letter warning them against the practice. Hodges, *New Deal Labor Policy*, 124–25 (TLRB figures). On the South Carolina mills, see *Textile Worker* 22 (November 1934): 485–87. Examples of workers' complaints are interspersed throughout the NRA Records, RG 9, ser. 402, NA. See, e.g., Mrs. Ray Maynard to FDR, December 11, 1934, RG 9, ser. 402, box 52, file — Gaffney Mfg. Co. See also Minnie B. King to James F. Byrnes, March 25, 1935, Byrnes Papers, box — Misc. 1935 G–Z, file — Stretch-out System, CU; Report from the "Greenville Meetings," box 1, file 7A, TWUA; and *Textile Worker* 23 (November 1935): 13–15.

2. Gellhorn to Hopkins, November 9, 30, 1934, Hopkins Papers, box 66, file — Gellhorn, FDRL.

3. Brecher, *Strike!*, 176–77; Hall et al., *Like a Family*, 354. For similar views emphasizing the strike's bitter legacy, see Marshall, *Labor in the South*, 332–33; Tindall, *New South*, 512; and Hodges, *New Deal Labor Policy*, 119–40. For another voice of bitterness, this one from the grass roots, see Local 1760 to FDR, November 11, 1934, NRA Records, RG 9, ser. 402, box 79, file — Lonsdale, NA.

4. Hayes, "South Carolina and the New Deal," 165–66; Janet Irons, "Testing the New Deal," 492–93. On the continued existence, but diminished membership, of the UTW in the state, see Hodges, *New Deal Labor Policy*, 130, and interview with D. M. Williams of the TLRB, n.d. [1935], NRA Records, RG 174, box 40, file — Textile Worker Strikes, NA.

5. *Textile Labor Banner*, December 21, 1934.

6. *AI*, June 16, 1935; *Charlotte Labor Journal*, February 21, March 13, 1935; *GN*, July 28, 1935; *The State*, August 5, 1935; Proceedings of the SCFL, 1935, GML; Janet Irons, "Testing the New Deal," 492–93.

7. "What Labor Wants," n.d. [September 20, 1934], NRA Records, RG 9, ser. 401, box 1, file — Unanswered, NA; *Gaffney Ledger*, May 14, 1936. See also Proceedings of the SCFL, 1934–37, GML; E. J. Hughes to William Green, February 26, 1935, NRA Records, RG 9, ser. 397, box 11, NA; Beaumont Local 1705, "What Labor Stands For," *[Una] New Review*, June 12, 1937; and Statement by Cloyd Gibson in unidentified clipping, June 8, 1935, Scrapbook 1935, p. 355, ODJ Papers, SCL.

8. On labor's poststrike agenda, see Anonymous to John Winnat, September 5, 1934, NRA Records, RG 9, ser. 401, box 1, file — Complaints of Workers (Individual), NA; *Co*, January 12, 1935; Resolution of the Newberry County Textile Council, n.d., ODJ Papers, box 12 — General Correspondence, 1937, SCDAH; *Carolina Free Press*, April 10, 1936; Proceedings of the SCFL, 1935, GML; and *Gaffney Ledger*, May 14–15, 1936.

9. *Charlotte Labor Journal*, December 5, 1935; Anthony B. Miller, "Palmetto Politician," 165–66. See also *Co*, November 25, 1935; *The State*, June 23, 1935; and *Greenville Observer*, June 24, 1935, clipping, Scrapbook 1935, p. 350, ODJ Papers, SCL. Throughout his admin-

istration Johnston would continue to affirm labor's right to organize and strike. *[Una] News Review*, January 18, 1936, February 19, 1937; *Charlotte Labor Journal*, January 21, 28, 1937; Resolution of the Newberry County Textile Council, n.d., ODJ Papers, box 12—General Correspondence 1937, SCDAH; Proceedings of the SCFL, 1934, GML. On the 1936 strikes in Gaffney, see NRA Records, RG 9, ser. 402, boxes 52 and 75, files—Gaffney Mfg. Co. and Limestone Mills, respectively, NA; LeRoy Guinn, Secretary of UTW Local 2474, to Byrnes, June 17, 1936, and John Peel to Byrnes, June 19, 1936, Byrnes Papers, box—Misc. 1936 L-W, file—P, CU.

10. Halsey, "Year Finds Sharp South Carolina Labor Fights," unidentified clipping, December 26, 1935, Scrapbook 1935, p. 346, ODJ Papers, SCL. In addition to the walkouts discussed below, there were strikes at the Saxon and Fairmont Mills in Spartanburg County, the Broad River Mills in Gaffney, and the Monarch Mills in Union.

11. For events at the Lydia and Clinton Mills, see Hayes, "South Carolina and the New Deal," 367-68, 385-87, and Carpenter, "Olin D. Johnston," 226-28.

12. On the general strike and poststrike discrimination in Clinton, see "Notes from Lydia Mills," Case XIV, "In the Matter of Lydia Cotton Mills and Employees of Lydia Cotton Mills," January 24, 1935, NA; Francis Gorman to TLRB, November 19, 1935 (box 78, file—Lydia Mills), and Mr. L. J. Mathers to FDR, December 26, 1934 (box 28, file—Clinton Cotton Mills), NRA Records, RG 9, ser. 402, NA.

13. McCroskey to FDR, December 14, 1935, NRA Records, RG 9, ser. 402, box 28, file—Clinton Cotton Mills, NA.

14. Although the TLRB reached its decision in December, a printed copy of its report was not published until January. *Raleigh News and Observer*, January 26, 1935. On the blue eagle's flight, see *Textile Labor Banner*, January 19, February 23, 1935.

15. Mrs. Paul Maudlin to Walter P. Stacey, January 8, 1935, NRA Records, RG 9, ser. 402, box 78, file—Lydia Mills, NA. On the goodwill association," see "Constitution and By-Laws of Clinton Friendship Association," ibid., and *Textile Labor Banner*, May 18, 1935. The Wagner Act of 1935 guaranteed labor's right to organize and clearly spelled out a host of antilabor practices.

16. Wooten's story is told by J. L. Bernard to Samuel R. McClurd, April 1, 1935, NRA Records, RG 9, ser. 402, box 28, file—Clinton Cotton Mills No. 2, NA.

17. *Co*, August 27, October 30, November 1, 1935; Press Release, NLRB, November 1, 1935, and Memorandum from Mr. Cunningham to Mr. McClurd, January 30, 1936, NRA Records, RG 9, ser. 402, box 28, file—Clinton Cotton Mills No. 2, NA; Paul Dean to ODJ, n.d. (box 37—Departmental Commissions 1935-39, CAB Files—Clinton), and Mrs. Lesie Harrison to ODJ, November 19, 1935 (box—Misc. Governor's Papers 1935), ODJ Papers, SCDAH.

18. Gedeist to ODJ, August 31, 1935, ODJ Papers, box 38—Departmental Commissions 1935-39, CAB Files—Clinton, SCDAH.

19. On Johnston's efforts to secure relief supplies for strikers, see ODJ to James B. Brickett, Federal Surplus Commodities Corporation, April 10, 12, 1936, and Johns Nates to Frances Perkins, June 11, 1936, ODJ Papers, box 23—General Correspondence 1936, SCDAH. The federal labor conciliator issued a report on conditions in the tent city. Kamenow to McClurd, November 23, 1936, NRA Records, RG 9, ser. 402, box 28, file—Clinton Cotton Mills No. 2, NA.

20. "Report of the Cotton Textile Work Assignment Board," February 28, 1935, NRA Records, RG 9, ser. 402, box 133, file—Tucapau Mills, NA. See also *SH*, January 29, 1935; Carpenter, "Olin D. Johnston," 248-50; Complaint dated December 8, 1934, T. W. Smith

to Francis Gorman, January 28, 1935, and J. L Bernard to Samuel McClurd, January 29, 1935, NRA Records, RG 9, ser. 402, box 133, file—Tucapau Mills.

21. Bernard to McClurd, February 23, 1935, and John Peel to McClurd, February 26, March 20, 1935, NRA Records, RG 9, ser. 402, box 133, file—Tucapau Mills, NA.

22. *AI*, June 5, 7, 1935; *Textile Labor Banner*, June 22, 1935; *SH*, June 19–22, 1935; *Yorkville Enquirer*, June 21, 1935, clipping, Scrapbook 1935, p. 352, ODJ Papers, SCL.

23. Carpenter, "Olin D. Johnston," 250–51.

24. Ibid.; Bernard to McClurd, May 15, 21, June 2, 6, 10, NRA Records, RG 9, ser. 402, box 133, file—Tucapau Mills, NA.

25. *Textile Worker* 23 (June 1935): 187; ODJ to Alan McNab, June 7, 1935, ODJ Papers, box 38, CAB Files—Tucapau Mills, SCDAH.

26. Carpenter, "Olin D. Johnston," 253.

27. *Textile Labor Banner*, June 29, 1935.

28. On the settlement, see *SH* and *Co*, July 16, 1935; *Textile Labor Banner*, July 27, 1935; Bernard to McClurd, June 23, 1935; McClurd to Bernard, July 8, 1935, and ODJ to McClurd, July 12, 1935, NRA Records, RG 9, ser. 402, box 133, file—Tucapau Mills, NA.

29. *AI*, March 5, 1937. Despite its larger importance, the Hicks controversy did not receive front-page press coverage, although it did make it to the back pages. *Carolina Free Press*, July 12, 1935, February 19, 1937; *SH*, December 18, 1936; *Anderson Daily Mail*, December 21, 1935; *The State*, March 8, 1937; *[Una] News Review*, December 22, 1936, March 12, 1937. Some magistrates did not serve only the interests of the mill owners. George W. Freeman of Bennettsville and D. T. Gossett of Pacolet, for example, both honored requests from Johnston to delay eviction proceedings in order to allow one of the various labor boards to rule. Freeman to ODJ, December 16, 1935 (box 37, CAB files—Tucapau), and Gossett to ODJ, May 26, 1937 (box 29), ODJ Papers, SCDAH.

30. On the early years at Pelzer, see Kohn, *Cotton Mills*, 53, 55, 133; Lander, *South Carolina*, 60; Anthony B. Miller, "Palmetto Politician," 169–70; and interview with James and Dovie Gambrell, by Allen Tullos, Greenville, S.C., May 4, 1980, SOHP. On previous strikes, see *GI-J*, March 25–27, April 2, 1929. Interestingly, Alan McNab, the president of the Tucapau Mills during 1935, apparently held a similar position at Pelzer in 1929.

31. Twenty-one Pelzer workers complained to the Cotton Textile Code Authority between July 1933 and September 1934. Ten charged the mill owners with antiunion discrimination and six others accused them of violating the stretchout; others complained about hours and wages. See NRA Records, RG 9, ser. 398, box 25, file—Pelzer, NA.

32. On the strike and its aftermath, see "Report on Pelzer," February 6, 1935, NRA Records, RG 9, ser. 402, box 98, file—Pelzer, NA. See also "Arbitration Award," April 15, 1936, ibid., and Carlton's excellent article, "The State and the Worker," 193. Southern millworkers did not greet the enactment of the Wagner Act with the same optimism as they had the NRA. There were no wild street dances or emancipation proclamations to mark the occasion. A few, however, sent respectful letters of thanks to Sen. Robert F. Wagner and others. See, e.g., S. O. Neal, Blacksburg, to Sen. Wagner, November 17, 1934, Labor box 2, file 11, Wagner Papers, Georgetown University Archives, Washington, D.C.; Minnie B. King to James F. Byrnes, March 25, 1935, Byrnes Papers, box—Misc. 1935 G–Z, file—Stretch-Out System, CU; *Charlotte Labor Journal*, November 10, 1935; and Hodges, *New Deal Labor Policy*, 145–48.

33. *Yorkville Enquirer*, August 1, 1935.

34. "Constitution and By-Laws of the Goodwill Association of Pelzer, South Carolina," n.d., ODJ Papers, box—Governor's Misc. Papers 1935, SCDAH. Obviously this was a

company union, but management and members of the association vehemently denied the charge. W. H. Taylor and T. C Roche to ODJ, June 21, 1935, box 37—Departmental Commissions, CAB Files—Pelzer, ibid.

35. J. L. Bernard to McClurd, June 1, 1935, Mildred Smith and Annie Garrett to FDR, June 13, 1935, and Peel to McClurd, July 3, 1935, NRA Records, RG 9, ser. 402, box 98, file—Pelzer, NA; Lula Dill to ODJ, August 19, 1935, ODJ Papers, box—Misc. Governor's Papers 1935, SCDAH.

36. The best accounts of the Pelzer strike can be found in *AI*, July 17–September 5, 1935. and Carlton, "The State and the Worker," 193–97. See also Carpenter, "Olin D. Johnston," 235–43; Hayes, "South Carolina and the New Deal," 369–74; and Anthony B. Miller, "Palmetto Politician," 169–81.

37. *AI*, July 17–20, 1935; J. M. Fortner to ODJ, July 17, 1935, ODJ Papers, box—Misc. Papers 1935, SCDAH; Carlton, "The State and the Worker," 194–95.

38. ODJ to Rosa L. Vollroth, July 26, 1935, ODJ Papers, box 37—Department Commissions 1935–39, CAB Files, SCDAH. See also ODJ to C. C. Garrett, September 2, 1935, box—Governor's Misc. Papers, 1935, ibid.

39. Carlton, "The State and the Worker," 194 (second quotation); W. A. L. Sibley to ODJ, July 20, 1935, S. V. Rackley to ODJ, July 24, 1935, H. W. Copeland to ODJ, July 25, 1935, Resolution of the Greenville Trades and Labor Council, July 23, 1935 (all in box 37—Departmental Commissions, CAB Files—Pelzer), and ODJ to J. C. Ingle, August 30, 1935 (box 35—Departmental Commissions 1935–39, CAB Files—Pelzer), ODJ Papers, SCDAH; *Greenville Observer*, July 26, 1935; *GN*, July 17, 1935.

40. On where replacement workers came from, see *AI*, July 28, 1935; *GN*, September 1, 1935; and H. W. Copeland to ODJ, July 25, 1935 (box 37—Departmental Commission 1935–39, CAB Files—Pelzer), and Miss Annie L. Garrison to ODJ, August 6, 1935, and C. B. Brown, August 26, 1935 (both in box—Misc. Governor's Papers 1935), ODJ Papers, SCDAH.

41. J. L. Bernard to Samuel McClurd, July 25, 31, 1935, NRA Records, RG 9, ser. 402, box 98, file—Pelzer, NA.

42. *AI*, July 26–28, 1935; *GN*, July 26–27, 1935; Carlton, "The State and the Worker," 195.

43. *AI*, July 28, 1935. On the strike at Saxon, see ibid., August 1, 3, 1935.

44. Ibid., August 3–6, 1935; *GN*, August 5, 1935. The text of Johnston's declaration of martial law was reprinted in the August 4 edition of the *AI*. For responses to this order, see J. F. Campbell to ODJ, August 1, 1935, ODJ Papers, box 37—Departmental Commissions 1935–39, CAB Files—Pelzer, SCDAH; unidentified clipping, n.d. [August 3, 1935], Scrapbook 1935, p. 361, ODJ Papers, SCL; and Bernard to McClurd, August 17, 25, 31, 1935, RG 9, ser. 402, box 98, file—Pelzer, NA.

45. Anthony B. Miller, "Palmetto Politician," 176–77; Bernard to McClurd, August 7, 1935, NRA Records, RG 9, ser. 402, box 98, file—Pelzer, NA. UTW locals across the state petitioned the governor to close down the mills. See, e.g., telegrams from J. L. Sowers, President of the Greenville Trades and Labor Council, Local 2191 of Lyman, and L. D. Tindall of Clinton's Local 1834 to ODJ, all dated September 2, 1935, ODJ Papers, box 37—Departmental Commissions 1935–39, CAB Files—Pelzer, SCDAH.

46. Unidentified clipping, August 5, 1934, Scrapbook 1935, p. 366, ODJ Papers; *AI* and *GN*, August 6, 1935.

47. Carpenter, "Olin D. Johnston," 239–40; Hayes, "South Carolina and the New Deal," 371–72.

48. This account of the Labor Day shooting is drawn from *AI*, September 3–4, 1935;

GN, *NYT*, and *The State*, September 3, 1935; and Anthony B. Miller, "Palmetto Politician," 177-78.

49. Carlton, "The State and the Worker," 196. For more on the strike ending agreement, see *Carolina Free Press*, September 12, 1935.

50. *AI*, November 9, 1935; *Co*, October 17, 1935; Raymond Farmer to ODJ, October 8, 1935, and O. W. Stewart to ODJ, October 18, 1936, ODJ Papers, box 37—Departmental Commissions, CAB Files—Pelzer, SCDAH; Hayes, "South Carolina and the New Deal," 371-73; List of New Employees, attached to letter from George Kamenow to McClurd, November 6, 1935, and John Peel to Kamenow, June 13, 1936, NRA Records, RG 9, ser. 402, box 98, file—Pelzer, NA.

51. Rosa L. Vollroth to ODJ, July 22, 1935 (box 37—Departmental Commissions 1935-39, CAB Files—Pelzer), W. E. Broderick to ODJ, September 14, 1935 (box—Misc. Papers 1935), and Violet Martin to ODJ, June 6, 1936 (box 23—General Correspondence 1936), ODJ Papers, SCDAH; Anthony B. Miller, "Palmetto Politician," 179-81.

52. "Another Textile Worker," *GN*, August 26, 1935; Mrs. Bessie Bishop to ODJ, August 26, 1935, and Mrs. Mary Guest to ODJ, November 2, 1935, ODJ Papers, box 37—Departmental Commissions 1935-39, CAB Files—Pelzer, SCDAH.

53. W. A. L. Sibley to ODJ, July 20, 1935, Raymond Kirby to ODJ, July 24, 1935, H. W. Copeland to ODJ, July 25, 1935, and Resolution of Greenville Trades and Labor Council, July 23, 1935, box 37, ODJ Papers, SCDAH; ODJ to J. C. Ingle, August 30, 1935, box 35, Departmental Commissions 1935-39, CAB Files—Pelzer, ibid.

54. The Pelzer strike also became an issue in the 1938 election. See Carlton, "The State and the Worker," 196. See also editorial, "An Unlearned Lesson," unidentified clipping, n.d., Scrapbook 1937—Labor Section, ODJ Papers, SCL, and *AI*, August 6, 1938. In his 1934 race against Blease, Johnston had garnered more than 40 percent of the vote in all of the uptown wards in Anderson County, even carrying one. Four years later against Smith, he topped the 40 percent mark in only one city ward. In other areas of the city, he received less than a quarter of the vote. *AI*, September 12, 1934, August 31, 1938.

Chapter Ten

1. The quotations in this and the next paragraph are from John H. Moore, *South Carolina Highway Department*, 110-11, and "Declaration of Martial Law," ODJ Papers, box 20, file—Suppression of the Highway Board, SCDAH. For a description of the scene that day, see *The State*, and *Co*, October 28-29, 1935, as well as *Anderson Daily Mail* and *Atlanta Constitution*, October 28, 1935.

2. *GN*, October 28, 1935.

3. On the highway fight, see Lander, *History of South Carolina*, 69-72; Jay Bender, "Olin D. Johnston," 39-54; John H. Moore, *South Carolina Highway Department*, 101-26; and Anthony B. Miller, "Palmetto Politician," 182-224.

4. *NYT*, October 30, 1935.

5. Commager, "South Carolina Dictator," 568-72.

6. V. O. Key (*Southern Politics in State and Nation*, 154) also saw the highway fight as a struggle over patronage. See interviews—conducted for Key's book by his assistant, Alexander Heard—with George A. Buchanan Jr., editor of the *Columbia Record* (January 26, 1948), Edgar A. Brown (February 7, 1948), and Rep. Thomas Pope (February 12, 1948),

Southern Politics Collection, box 2—One-Party System: S.C. Legislative Organization of Interest, file—Used Materials Notes, Heard Library, Vanderbilt University, Nashville.

7. Commager, "South Carolina Dictator," 572.

8. *Newberry Herald and News*, n.d., clipping, Scrapbook 1935, p. 429, ODJ Papers, SCL.

9. Endorsements of the governor's actions can be found in box 10 of the ODJ Papers, but most are located in boxes 70 and 71, SCDAH. This correspondence is filed by the county from which it came. Newspapers also commented on Johnston's mail. See *AI*, October 29, November 2–3, December 17, 1935.

10. *CN&C*, May 10, 1935.

11. Anthony B. Miller, "Palmetto Politician," 195; Citizens of Greenville to ODJ, December 6, 1936 (box 70, file—Greenville County), and York Resident to ODJ, n.d. (box 71, file—York County), ODJ Papers, SCDAH.

12. Unsigned telegram to ODJ, December 9, 1935 (file—Spartanburg County) (first quotation), UTW to ODJ, November 12, 1935 (file—Richland County), UTW Local 2452 to ODJ, November 12, 1935 (file—Lexington County), and West Greenville Citizens to ODJ, n.d. (file—Greenville County), ODJ Papers, box 70, SCDAH; Mary Biddex, Gaffney, to ODJ, January 1, 1935, ODJ Papers, box 10, SCDAH (second quotation). For more evidence of support, see, e.g., *AI*, October 29, November 11, 1935; *Carolina Free Press*, April 12, 1935; John Nates, head of the SCFL, to ODJ, November 4, 1935 (box 63), and Drayton Local 1835 to ODJ, December 9, 1935, and Saxon Local 1882 to ODJ, November 9, 1935, ODJ Papers (box 70, file—Spartanburg County), ODJ Papers, SCDAH.

13. Local 2014—Oakland Mill to ODJ, October 29, 1935, ODJ Papers, box 70, file—Newberry County, SCDAH; John H. Moore, *South Carolina Highway Department*, 113–14; "Citizens of York County" to ODJ, n.d. (file—York County), and Lt. Col. James A. Hall to ODJ, December 14, 1935 (file—Greenwood County), ODJ Papers, box 70, SCDAH.

14. J. C. Vaughn expressed this view in a letter to the editor, *GN*, December 22, 1935. So did 441 Members of UTW Local 2013 to ODJ, November 11, 1935 (file—Newberry County), and, from the low country, George Terrell to ODJ, November 29, 1935 (file—Marion County), ODJ Papers, box 70, SCDAH. See also John Nates, *GN* [ca. 1935], ODJ Papers, box 70—State Highway Controversy, file—Pickens County, SCDAH; *Carolina Free Press*, August 24, 1934 (last quotation).

15. For some examples of how laborers saw the highway department, see Wilton Hall to ODJ, October 10, 1935, ODJ Papers, box 319, file—Highway 1935, SCL; Jeff D. Parris to ODJ, December 12, 1935, ODJ Papers, box 22—General Correspondence 1935, SCDAH; James Evans Quick to Wil L. Gray, Gray Papers, SCL; and *GN*, December 12, 1935.

16. R. Carl Griffith to ODJ, October 5, 1936 (box 23, General Correspondence—1936), and Claude Graves to ODJ, September 5, 1935 (box—Misc. Governor's Papers 1935), ODJ Papers, SCDAH. See also R. B. Dinkins to ODJ, March 12, 1935, ODJ Papers, box—Misc. Governor's Papers 1935, SCDAH.

17. Claude Graves to ODJ, September 5, 1935, ODJ Papers, box—Misc. Governor's Papers 1935, SCDAH. See also Fred Stevenson to ODJ, January 22, 1936, box 11—General Subjects 1936, ibid., and *AI*, December 16, 1936.

18. Unidentified paper, December 12, 1935, Scrapbook 1935, p. 428, ODJ Papers, SCL.

19. *Greenville Piedmont*, November 8, 1935, clipping, Scrapbook 1935, p. 433, ibid.

20. *Textile Banner*, April 6, 1935.

21. *Anderson Daily Mail*, December 10, 1935, clipping, Scrapbook 1935, p. 435, ODJ Papers, SCL; *AI*, December 11, 1935; *Co*, December 11–12, 1935; W. D. Chenshaw to ODJ, December 14, 1935, ODJ Papers, box 71, file—Charleston County, SCDAH.

22. On the resentments between mill and town, see Caldwell, *God's Little Acre*; Rhyne,

Southern Cotton Mill Workers, 193–99; Pope, *Millhands and Preachers*, 68–69; and Flamming, *Creating the Modern South*, 164–65. See also the discussion with longtime millhand Earl Jeffcoat in *Newsweek*, May 3, 1965.

23. For a contemporary parallel, see the use of "nigger" by African American rappers. *NYT*, January 24, 1993. "Queer" has been similarly used by the gay community.

24. Moody, "To a Cotton Mill Worker," *Wofford College Journal*, April 1936, clipping, Moody Files, WC. (The original version of the poem included several pictures at the top captioned: youth, play, union, and age.) The poem can also be found in Byars, *Lintheads*, 54–55.

25. The poem was also reprinted in *The State*, April 23, 1936, and *Horry Herald*, n.d., ODJ Papers, box 42, SCDAH. The man choking back tears was probably Rep. H. C. Godfrey, of Spartanburg, who is quoted by Wallace, *Wofford College*, 231. For other comments, see Byars, *Lintheads*, 54–55.

26. Byars, *Lintheads*, 54–55. Petition from Laurens Cotton Millhands, n.d., ODJ Papers, box 11—Misc. Papers 1936, SCDAH. The last quotation is from an editorial on Moody's poem, "A Slander," *Textile Tribune*, April 17, 1936, clipping, Moody Files, WC.

27. *AI*, May 27, 1935. It is worth noting that Ponder was a student at Wofford at the same time as Moody. Given the size of the school, they must have known each other, but Ponder never mentioned this in public. Ponder went on to serve as the state's labor commissioner for twenty-three years. Ponder Files, WC.

28. House Journal 1936, 1515–16, SCL. See also *The State*, April 23, 1936; Wallace, *Wofford College*, 231–32; Byars, *Lintheads*, 54–55.

29. *The State*, April 23, 29, 1936. House Journal 1936, 1515–16, SCL. For his part, Moody graduated from Wofford the next year and began a rather remarkable career. He earned degrees from the U.S. Military Academy, Duke University, and finally a Ph.D. in English from Cambridge University. After serving with distinction in World War II, he became a professor of English at the U.S. Military Academy and later chair of the department and vice dean of the faculty. He retired in 1967, a brigadier general. See, "Information on Peter Richard Moody" and "Citations—Alumni Member, Peter Richard Moody," Moody Files, WC.

30. For some thoughts on how nonelite groups challenge authority, in this case African Americans, see Kelley, "Kickin Reality, Kickin Ballistics: 'Gangsta Rap' and Postindustrial Los Angeles," *Race Rebels*, 209–14.

31. Wallace, *Wofford College*, 232. For the persistence of negative images of millhands, see e.g., Morland, *Millways of Kent*; the recollections of Aliene Welser in Byerly, *Hard Times Cotton Mill Girls*, 83; interview with John Bolt Culberton, Labor Lawyer, February 5, 1947, box 1—Party System: S.C. Legislative Organization of Interest, file—Used Materials, SPC-V; and the comments of Charleston's Ravin I. McDavid at the home of Dr. Kimmarle, Boulder, Colo., July 18, 1950, Benjamin A. Botkin Collection, LWO 6080, reel 1, side B, Division of Folk Culture, Library of Congress.

32. *Carolina Free Press*, December 6, 1935.

33. *The State*, December 6–10, 1935; *NYT*, December 8, 1935; *Carolina Free Press*, December 6, 1935.

34. On the Charleston incident, see John H. Moore, *South Carolina Highway Department*, 116, and unidentified Greenville paper, December 7, 1935, clipping, Scrapbook 1935, p. 398, ODJ Papers, SCL.

35. *Carolina Free Press*, December 13, 1935; *The State*, December 12–13, 15, 1935; *Anderson Daily Mail*, December 11–12, 1935, clipping, Scrapbook 1935, p. 415, and ODJ speech, "Fellow Citizens of South Carolina," December 14, 1935, file—Speeches, 1935–36, ODJ Papers, SCL.

36. Anthony B. Miller, "Palmetto Politician," 209-10; *Anderson Daily Mail*, December 21, 1935, clipping, Scrapbook 1935, p. 425, ODJ Papers, SCL.

37. *Anderson Daily Mail*, December 21, 1935, clipping, Scrapbook 1935, p. 425, ODJ Papers, SCL; *The State*, December 20-22, 1935.

38. *AI*, December 22, 1935.

39. *Anderson Daily Mail*, June 2, 1936, clipping, Scrapbook 1936, p. 63, ODJ Papers, SCL.

40. Carpenter, "Olin D. Johnston," 117-19.

41. Johnston delivered dozens of speeches in the weeks leading up to the election. He had planned to start even earlier and talk to even more people, but he was sidetracked by a minor automobile accident. *Co*, August 13, 15, 23, 1936.

42. *Yorkville Enquirer*, July 6, 1936; *GN*, September 7, 1936, clipping, Scrapbook 1936, pp. 156, 160, and "Radio Address Delivered over Station WBT by Governor Olin D. Johnston," September 5, 1936 (file—Speeches 1935-36), ODJ Papers, SCL; Statements by ODJ for the Press, June 6, 1936 (box 19), and July 3, 1936 (box 25), ODJ Papers, SCDAH.

43. "Radio Address . . . by Governor Olin D. Johnston," September 5, 1936.

44. W. Kay Proctor, letter to the editor, *CN&C*, June 14, 1936.

45. Y. A. Edwards to ODJ, August 13, 1936, Babb Smith to ODJ, August 18, 1936, and H. C. Bond to ODJ, August 4, 1936, ODJ Papers, box 5—General Subjects, file—Greenville, SCDAH.

46. All of these letters, filed by county, are from box 5, ODJ Papers, SCDAH. See, e.g., M. E. Alverson of Clifton to ODJ, August 17, 1936, Spartanburg County; T. C. Sisk to ODJ, July 11, 1936, Spartanburg County; and J. G. Breazeals to ODJ, July 27, 1936, Oconee County.

47. *Carolina Free Press*, June 19, July 31, 1936.

48. Ralph L. Sullivan to ODJ, July 8, 1936 (box 11—General Subjects 1936), A. Kinard to ODJ, June 12, 1936 (box 5—General Subjects, file—Newberry), and James McDonald to ODJ, July 21, 1936 (box 11—Misc. Papers 1936), ODJ Papers, SCDAH. For more letters from workers volunteering to run for office, see ODJ Papers, box 5, file—Listed by County, SCDAH.

49. In particular, Spartanburg workers wanted to get rid of Sheriff S. M. Henry, who had deputized hundreds of mill employees during the General Textile Strike and subsequent walkouts.

50. *[Una] New Review*, July 24, 1936.

51. Ibid., June 5, 1936. Fragmentary evidence, recollections, and throwaway lines here and there do suggest that mill women tended to vote less than mill men. Some women maintained that politics was male and thus dirty and corrupt. It is unlikely that middle-class women saw things the same way. Though they divided the world into spheres, many nonetheless saw a role for themselves in electoral politics. On mill women, see, e.g., interview with Delma Todd Cuclasure, December 16, 1938, A-3-4-13, WPA.

52. *SH*, September 11-12, 1936.

53. *Newberry Herald and News*, n.d., clipping, Scrapbook 1935, p. 429, ODJ Papers, SCL.

54. The fears of middle-class citizens were expressed in letters to the governor. See, e.g., David D. Wallace to ODJ, September 12, 1935, box 10, ODJ Papers, SCDAH.

55. *The State* and *AI*, September 9, 1936; *Carolina Free Press*, September 12, 1936.

56. According to John Hammond Moore (*South Carolina Highway Department*, 126), anti-Semitism accounted for some of these defections. In the days leading up to the election, newspaper editor Wilton Hall, a Johnston supporter, referred to Blatt as that "anti-Johnston Barnwell Jew." "Reaction," wrote Moore, "was shift and negative."

57. On the election and Blatt, see *Yorkville Enquirer*, January 15, 1937. See also *Carolina*

Free Press, January 1, 1937; *The State*, January 12, 15, 1937; *Greenville Piedmont*, n.d., and "Speaker's Race Reviewed," n.d., unidentified clippings, Scrapbook 1937, ODJ Papers, SCL.

58. *AI*, November 10, 1935 (editorial comments); John H. Moore, *South Carolina Highway Department*, 114 (responses from other newspapers).

59. On Edgar Brown and state politics, see Workman, *Bishop from Barnwell*, 39–41, and Key, *Southern Politics*, 152–55. Many people whom Alexander Heard talked to in South Carolina mentioned Brown's power and position in the state. Among them were Dr. Carl Epps, February 11, 1948; G. M. Howe Jr., February 14, 1948; and Brown himself, February 7, 1948, box 2—One-Party System: S.C. Legislative Organization of Interest, file—Used Materials Notes, SPC-V.

60. Workman, *Bishop from Barnwell*, 41. On attacks on the governor's power, see *Carolina Free Press*, February 27, 1936, and unidentified clippings, January 22, May 21, 1936, Scrapbook 1936, pp. 31, 63, ODJ Papers, SCL. See also W. W. Ball to McMaster, May 24, 1938, McMaster Papers, box 7, file 112, SCL.

61. E. J. Craig to ODJ, January 9, 1936 (box 71—State Highway Department, file—Aiken County), and William McKay to ODJ, December 16, 1935 (box 70, file—Florence County), ODJ Papers, SCDAH; J. C. Vaughn, letter to the editor, *Greenville News*, December 22, 1935.

62. *AI*, May 16, 1935. See also Hall's afternoon paper, the *Anderson Daily Mail*, May 26, 1935.

63. G. W. Anderson to ODJ, July 29, 1936, ODJ Papers, box 60—Job Applications, Sympathy and Thank You, SCDAH.

64. For views on the senate, see letter to the editor, *CN&C*, May 26, 1935, clipping, Scrapbook 1935, p. 56, ODJ Papers, SCL; *Carolina Free Press*, September 21, 1934; and Broadus O. Simpson to ODJ, December 9, 1935, ODJ Papers, box 70—State Highway Controversy, file—Florence County, SCDAH. For a similar view, see Isaac B. Henderson to ODJ (telegram), December 11, 1935, ODJ Papers, box 71, file—Chester County, SCDAH.

65. The millhand was R. C. Davis. He sent a telegram to ODJ on December 18, 1935, ODJ Papers, box 70—State Highway Controversy, file—Spartanburg County, SCDAH. The lawmaker was John P. Grace. He expressed his views in unidentified, undated clippings, Scrapbook 1935, p. 489, and [May 13], 1936, Scrapbook 1936, p. 321, ODJ Papers, SCL. Although he did not endorse Grace's proposal, Wilton Hall at least thought that the abolition of the Senate was an idea worth considering. *Anderson Daily Mail*, n.d [May 1936], clipping, Scrapbook 1936, p. 68, ODJ Papers, SCL. See also E. J. Craig to ODJ, January 9, 1936, ODJ Papers, box 71, file—Aiken County, SCDAH.

66. Hayes, "South Carolina and the New Deal," 334–35.

67. The "death of the NRA" is discussed by Schlesinger, *Politics of Upheaval*, 263–90, and Leuchtenburg, *Franklin D. Roosevelt*, 145–46. See also Leuchtenburg, *Supreme Court Reborn*.

68. Letter to the editor, *CN&C*, n.d., clipping, Scrapbook 1935, p. 34, ODJ Papers, SCL. The UTW also reacted angrily to the court ruling. *Textile Worker* 23 (June 1935): 168–71.

69. According to a Gallup Poll, South Carolinians were firmly behind the president's plan to change the Court. Results of one such poll conducted in June 1937 can be found in Hopkins Papers, box 55, file—Results of Various Polls, FDRL. On the views of workers, see *[Una] News Review*, February 19, March 5, June 19, July 3, 1937. According to a clipping from the *Spartanburg Herald* attached to a letter from Tuck Stephens to Johnston, Mary Lousie Mill Workers voted 63 to 0 in favor of the president's Court plans; n.d., ODJ Papers, box 12, General Correspondence 1937, SCDAH. Finally, on March 27, 1937 Johnston delivered a speech over a regional radio network in favor of the plan. ODJ Papers,

file—Speeches, 1935–36, SCL. With strong support from upcountry members, the South Carolina House of Representatives passed a motion in favor of the president's Court plan. *The State*, March 6, 1937.

70. Unidentified clipping, n.d., Scrapbook 1935, p. 429, ODJ Papers, SCL.

71. Commager, "South Carolina Dictator," 572.

72. Citizens of McColl to ODJ, December 19, 1935, ODJ Papers, box 70—State Highway Controversy, file—Marlboro County, SCDAH. For other opinions, see the remedies proposed by 182 people from York County through a petition dated December 17, 1935, ODJ Papers (box 71, file—York County), and M. L. Rice to ODJ, February 8, 1936, ODJ Papers (box 24—General Correspondence 1936), SCDAH. See also three unidentified, undated newspaper clippings, Scrapbook 1935, p. 411, and Scrapbook 1936, p. 7, ODJ Papers, SCL.

Chapter Eleven

1. *CN&C*, June 28, 1938. See also *Greenville Observer*, July 26, 1937; *Carolina Free Press*, November 11, 1936.

2. *CN&C*, June 28, 1938; *Beaufort Gazette*, August 11, September 1, 1938, clippings, Scrapbook 17, E. D. Smith Papers, SCL. See also *CN&C*, July 20, 1938. The fear of the carpetbagger was a common theme in the South in 1938. See Biles, *The South and the New Deal*, 147.

3. On the 1936 election, see Sullivan, *Days of Hope*, 59–60, and Leuchtenburg, *The FDR Years*, 101–58.

4. South Carolina proved to be the most Democratic state in the country. Before the election, the lieutenant governor bet his Mississippi counterpart that South Carolina would deliver a higher percentage of the vote to the president than the Magnolia State. He won a mule. *Charleston Evening Post*, n.d., clipping, Scrapbook 1937, ODJ Papers, SCL. In one-party states such as South Carolina, turnout for a general election was usually quite low. FDR, for instance, defeated Alf Landon 83,987 to 1,346. *NYT*, November 11, 1936.

5. *Time*, August 7, 1944, 18.

6. On the emergence of the conservative coalition, see Leuchtenburg, *Franklin D. Roosevelt*, 252–74, and Patterson, *Congressional Conservatism*.

7. On Smith's career, see Rice, *I Came Out of the Eighteenth Century*, 1–40; "Profile of Smith," *NYT*, August 21, 1938; and Bouknight, "Senatorial Campaigns," 3–7.

8. For Smith's message, see, e.g., Hollis, " 'Cotton Ed' Smith," 235–56; Bouknight, "Senatorial Campaigns," 93; *AI*, July 29, 1932; *Charleston Evening Post*, July 14, 1932, clipping, Scrapbook 10, and *Winnsboro News and Herald*, September 9, 1932, clipping, Scrapbook 12, E. D. Smith Papers, SCL.

9. The "born-aginner" line comes from Dan T. Carter's (*Politics of Rage*, 51) description of Chauncey Sparks. See also Egerton, *Speak Now*, 104.

10. On the cotton crisis, see Tindall, *New South*, 112–13, 354–55. On one family's struggles, see Mr. Lessie Wesley to ICB, June 10, 1931, ICB Papers, box—Current Subjects 1931, no file, SCDAH.

11. *Winnsboro News and Herald*, September 9, 1932, clipping, Scrapbook 12, E. D. Smith Papers, SCL.

12. Sullivan, *Days of Hope*, 56–57.

13. Hollis, " 'Cotton Ed' Smith," 248; Sullivan, *Days of Hope*, 56–57.

14. On the AAA and New Deal farm policy in general, see Badger, *New Deal*, 149–63; Kirkendall, "The New Deal and Agriculture"; Tindall, *New South*, 392–405; and Schlesinger, *Coming of the New Deal*, 27–84.

15. The two other most prominent brain trusters were Raymond Moley and Adolf Berle Jr. See Rosen, *Hoover, Roosevelt*, 115-211; Moley, *After Seven Years*, 1-162; and Peter H. Irons, *New Deal Lawyers*.

16. Hollis, "'Cotton Ed' Smith," 249; Sternsher, *Rexford Tugwell*, 251-61; *NYT*, June 12-15, 1934. On Tugwell's view of resettling African Americans, see Egerton, *Speak Now*, 10. My sense of Smith's indictment of Tugwell and New Dealers is drawn in part from the literature on the anti-New Deal character of McCarthyism. For a summary, see Latham, "The Meaning of McCarthyism," and Hofstadter, *Anti-Intellectualism* and *The Paranoid Style*.

17. On African Americans and the New Deal, see Sitkoff, *New Deal for Blacks*, and John B. Kirby, *Black Americans*.

18. According to one Gallup Poll, 65 percent of southerners favored the enactment of a law to make lynching a federal crime. National support for the measure was only five percentage points higher. "January 31—Anti-Lynching Laws," *Gallup Poll*, 48.

19. *CN&C*, April 10, 17, 1937. See also Senator Smith, "The Anti-Lynching Bill," *Congressional Record*, January 1, 1938, SCL. On the antilynching campaign, see Tindall, *New South*, 551-54; Huthmacher, *Senator Robert F. Wagner*, 171-74, 239-43; Zangrando, *NAACP Crusade*, 122-65; and Sitkoff, *New Deal for Blacks*, 280-94.

20. *GN*, April 30, May 1, 1935; *CN&C*, June 6, 1935; "An Address Delivered on July 31, 1935 by United States Senator Ellison D. Smith before the Annual Reunion of Confederate Veterans of South Carolina," Drayton Hall, University of South Carolina, SCL. For Smith's attacks against subsequent antilynching bills, see *Yorkville Enquirer*, January 11, 1938, clipping, Scrapbook 1938, p. 351, E. D. Smith Papers, SCL, and *NYT*, July 31, November 11, 1937.

21. Michie and Ryhlick, *Dixie Demagogues*, 266.

22. *NYT*, June 25-26, 1936. See also *Washington Evening Star*, June 25, 1936, clipping, Scrapbook 13, E. D. Smith Papers, SCL. For reactions in South Carolina, see *The State*, June 25, 1936; *SH*, June 29, 1936; and *GN*, July 10, 1936. For an overview of the convention itself, see Leuchtenburg, *Franklin D. Roosevelt*, 183-84.

23. For Smith's response to the court packing plan, see *GN*, February 9, 1937; *NYT*, July 16, 1937; and *Clinton Chronicle*, February 18, 1937, clippings, Scrapbook 14, E. D. Smith Papers, SCL. On the court as the last bastion of white supremacy, see Leuchtenburg, *Supreme Court Reborn*, 139.

24. *NYT*, July 31, 1937; *[Una] News Review*, July 12, December 21, 1937; *GI-J*, May 10, 19, August 14, 1938; *AI*, June 7, 9, 13, 28, 1938; Leuchtenburg, *Franklin D. Roosevelt*, 261-63. To the surprise of many, Sen. James F. Byrnes also opposed the measure.

25. On the Boardwalk brawl, see *NYT*, October 20, 1935. On the differences between the AFL and the CIO, see Zieger, *CIO*, 22-41, and Fraser, *Labor Will Rule*, 289-348.

26. For this older tradition, see Gutman, "The Negro and the United Mine Workers of America: The Career and Letters of Richard L. Davis and Something of Their Meaning: 1890-1900," *Work, Culture, and Society*, 121-208, and Arnesen, *Waterfront Workers*. On ties between the civil rights movement and the CIO, see Korstad and Lichtenstein, "Opportunities Found and Lost," 787; Kelley, *Hammer and Hoe*; and Honey, *Southern Labor and Black Civil Rights*.

27. Zieger, *CIO*, 2.

28. *Time*, March 29, 1937, 11. On the sit-down strikes, see Brecher, *Strike!*, 177-216; Fine, *Sit-Down*; and Zieger, *CIO*, 42-54, and *American Workers*, 46-51.

29. Zieger, *CIO*, 39-40; Fraser, *Labor Will Rule*, 374-78. The AFL's commitment to voluntarism, however, has probably been exaggerated. For a reexamination of AFL politics, see Julia Greene, "'The Strike at the Ballot Box.'"

30. Fraser, *Labor Will Rule*, 373, 387; Carlton and Coclanis, *Confronting Southern Poverty*, 9; Sullivan, *Days of Hope*, 94-97. For a local comment on the CIO's plans, see *CN&C*, June 28, 1938.

31. On the formation of the TWOC, see Kennedy, "History," 70-84; Walter Galenson, *CIO Challenge*, 329-43; Irving Bernstein, *Turbulent Years*, 616-23; Hodges, *New Deal Labor Policy*, 148-53; Paul D. Richards, "History of the Textile Workers Union," 36-91; and Zieger, *CIO*, 74-78.

32. On CIO messengers, see Dodge, *Southern Rebel in Reverse*; Garrison, "Paul Revere Christopher"; and Salmond, *Miss Lucy of the CIO*.

33. *[Una] News Review*, March 5, April 9, 1937; Hodges, *New Deal Labor Policy*. 153-54.

34. On the connections between communism and racial liberalism in the South, see Goodman, *Stories of Scottsboro*, 114, and Egerton, *Speak Now*, 171.

35. *GI-J*, July 27, 1938.

36. On the anti-TWOC campaign in South Carolina, see Carpenter, "Olin D. Johnston," 280-90; Hayes, "South Carolina and the New Deal," 389-401; and Ellenberg, "Congress of Industrial Organizations," 40-43.

37. For attacks against the CIO, see *CN&C*, June 21, 1938; *NYT*, August 23, 1938; and *Beaufort Gazette*, July 21, 1938, clippings, Scrapbook 1938, pp. 374, 400-401, E. D. Smith Papers, SCL; and Hodges, *New Deal Labor Policy*, 157-68.

38. "Olin D. Johnston; Labor's Governor," n.d., ODJ Papers, box 25—General Correspondence 1936, SCDAH; Address by ODJ, Convention of the South Carolina Federation of Labor, Charleston, June 25, 1937, ODJ Papers, box—Speeches 1935-46, SCL.

39. *AI*, March 6, 28, 1937; ODJ to FDR, March 5, 1937, ODJ Papers, box 41—Departmental Commissions 1935-39, file—Washington, Pres. and Officials, SCDAH. TWOC representative Furman Garrett applauded Johnston's position on the Supreme Court. See Garrett to ODJ, April 14, 1937, box 39—Departmental Commissions 1935-39, file—Roosevelt, Supreme Court 1937, ibid.

40. *GN*, April 18, 1936; *CN&C*, February 2, 1937; ODJ radio address, April 18, 1938, ODJ Papers, box—Speeches 1934-40, SCL.

41. ODJ speech, "Roosevelt the Man," June 1, 1936, ODJ Papers, box—Speeches 1935-46, SCL. The Liberty League was a conservative anti-New Deal organization formed by leading businessmen during FDR's first term.

42. Johnston laid out his views of the economy in several speeches: "South Carolina and Democracy," May 21, 1935, "Roosevelt the Man," June 1, 1936, and "The Pathway Ahead," versions of the speech delivered at the John De La Howe School, June 1, 1936, and at Indiantown High School, May 27, 1937, ODJ Papers, box—Speeches 1935-46, SCL; *[Una] News Review*, August 13, 1937.

43. *Co*, November 20, 1937; *CN&C*, December 17, 1937; "Olin D. Johnston on the Hour and Wage Bill and Regional Differentials," n.d., ODJ Papers, box 28—General Correspondence 1936, SCDAH. Millworkers seemed to have backed the FLSA as well. For examples of this support, see Columbia Millhand to FDR, November 11, 1937 (box 29—General Correspondence), and Walter E. Baker, Langley, to ODJ, January 11, 1938 (box 7—General Correspondence 1938-39), ODJ Papers, SCDAH; T. W. Cooper, Recording Secretary of the Spartanburg Central Labor Union, to James F. Byrnes, April 4, 1938, Byrnes Papers, box—Misc. Correspondence 1938 A-O, file C, CU.

44. *CN&C*, December 12, 1937. On Johnston's support for South Carolina's forty-hour law, see House and Senate Journals, 1936-38, SCL; *The State*, May 22, 1936; *AI*, April 10, 1936, March 11, May 7, 1937, May 8, 1938; and *Columbia Record*, February 1, 1937, clipping, Scrapbook 1937—Legislation, ODJ Papers, SCL.

45. For a similar view, see the definition of "moral capitalism" in Cohen, *Making a New Deal*, 252-53.

46. For Johnston's relationship with the CIO, see Carpenter, "Olin D. Johnston," 280-90; Ellenberg, "Congress of Industrial Organizations," 40-43; *Union Daily Times*, December 3, 1937, and unidentified clipping, November 15, 1937, Scrapbook 1937—Labor, ODJ Papers, SCL. On the Marlboro Mills, see Tindall, *New South*, 518.

47. On the impact of the Roosevelt recession on the TWOC, see Fraser, *Labor Will Rule*, 401-2. Hundreds of workers wrote to Johnston documenting their hardships during this period. See, e.g., J. W. Watts to ODJ, May 24, 1938, and W. W. Roberts to ODJ, July 27, 1938, ODJ Papers, box 48—Welfare Correspondence 1935-39, SCDAH.

48. Ellenberg, "Congress of Industrial Organizations," 40-43; Carpenter, "Olin D. Johnston," 280-90.

49. On events in Gaffney, see Witherspoon Dodge to ODJ, June 8, 1938, ODJ Papers, box 37, SCDAH; Dodge, *Southern Rebel in Reverse*, 105-11; *Co*, June 2, 23, 1938; *AI*, June 2, 1938; *CN&C*, June 2, 10, 1938; and Hodges, *New Deal Labor Policy*, 165-68. Smith, moreover, had an article clipped that headlined "TWOC Official Thanks Johnston" (newspaper unidentified), June 6, 1938, Scrapbook 17, E. D. Smith Papers, SCL. Apparently, he was collecting ammunition for the upcoming campaign.

50. *[Una] News Review*, September 24, 1937; Ray Galloway to FDR, June 28, 1937, NRA Records, RG 9, ser. 402, box 18, file—Brandon Mills Corporation, NA; Janet Irons, "Testing the New Deal," 198-99.

51. Fred Johnson to ODJ, November 11, 1937 and ODJ to Johnson, November 27, 1937, ODJ Papers, box 37—Application Commissions 1935-39, file—KKK, SCDAH; *Columbia Record*, November 30, 1937, clipping, Scrapbook 1937, ODJ Papers, SCL.

52. On Brown's announcement, see *NYT*, May 9, 1938, and Workman, *Bishop From Barnwell*, 233-36. See also Brown campaign leaflet, "This Man Brown," SCL.

53. *GI-J* and *SH*, May 16, 1938; *NYT*, May 17-18, 1938. For hostile reports on Johnston's entrance into the race, see *GN*, May 19, 1938, and esp. *CN&C*, May 19-20, 23, 1938.

54. *GI-J*, May 27, 1938.

55. *Aiken Evening Standard*, July 29, 1938; *AI*, June 16, 19, 24, 29, August 28, 1938; *CN&C*, May 15, 1938; *The State*, June 6, 15, 1938; *Chester Reporter*, reprinted in *GI-J*, June 1, 1938. The *News and Courier* had raised questions about Johnston's "one-hundred percent" support for the president a year before the election. *CN&C*, September 1, 1937.

56. *GI-J*, July 20, 27-28, 1938; *Rock Hill Evening Herald*, July 18, 1938; *GN*, July 31, August 3, 1938.

57. Quoted from Ashmore, *An Epitaph for Dixie*, 100-101. For other versions of Smith's Philadelphia story, see Michie and Ryhlick, *Dixie Demagogues*, 266, and Robertson, *Sly and Able*, 193-94. There is no significant difference between these accounts. On the crowd, see "Carolina Jubilee," *Newsweek*, August 22, 1938, 12. Joseph Alsop and Robert Kintner wrote a particularly good account of Smith on the stump in their column, "The Capital Parade," August 8-9, 1938, clipping, Scrapbook 16, Smith Papers, SCL.

58. Ben Robertson, a noted war correspondent and the author of *Red Hills and Cotton*, made this observation about South Carolina politicians. Robertson to Turner, March 1, 1938, Robertson Papers, CU. See a similar assessment in *Newsweek*, "Carolina Jubilee," August 22, 1938, 12. For more on Johnston, see *AI*, July 16, 1938.

59. Text of ODJ radio addresses, August 26, September 13, 1938, ODJ Papers, box 292, file—Speeches August-September 1938, SCL; *The State*, June 15, 23, 1938.

60. Anthony B. Miller, "Palmetto Politician," 302-3. Edgar Brown made a similar argument throughout the campaign. On one occasion, he said: "We are all anti-nigger. . . . This

thing of the administration rubbing out states' rights and white supremacy is all talk. It is unworthy of you to use such talk in a public campaign." *AI*, June 18, 26, July 28, 1938.

61. Text of ODJ radio address, August 26, 1938, ODJ Papers, box 292, file—Speeches August-September 1938, SCL; *AI* and *GN*, July 28, 1938; Bouknight, "Senatorial Campaigns," 140. Like a good historian, Johnston cited another historian to underscore his point about Smith. Several times during the campaign, he read from Francis Butler Simkins's *The Tillman Movement in South Carolina* to show that Cotton Ed opposed Pitchfork Ben.

62. Text of radio address, August 26, 1938, and speech, August 1938, ODJ Papers, box 292, file, Speeches—August-September 1938, SCL; *AI*, August 25, 30, 1938; *GI-J*, June 22, 1938.

63. *AI*, August 27, 1938; *Florence Morning News*, June 23, 1938; *CN&C*, June 21, 1938, clipping, Scrapbook 16, E. D. Smith Papers, SCL; Bouknight, "Senatorial Campaigns," 140.

64. *NYT*, June 26–27, 1938; *The State*, June 25–26, 1938. On the purge campaign in general, see Badger, *New Deal*, 260–71; Patterson, *Congressional Conservatism*, 250–87; Hopper, "The Purge," 2–6; and Porter, "'Purge' of 1938." On the results of the purge, see Shannon, "Presidential Politics," and Patterson, "Failure of Party Realignment."

65. For early speculation on FDR's role, see *Washington Evening Star*, July 13, 21, 1938; Drew Pearson and Robert S. Allen, "Washington Merry Go Around," *Louisville Courier-Journal*, August 19, 1938, clipping, Scrapbook 16, E. D. Smith Papers, SCL; *Horry Herald*, April 4, 1938; and *GI-J*, July 8, 1938. South Carolinians also weighed in with their opinions. F. K. Bull of the Sumter VFW advised FDR against intervening, whereas P. J. O'Connell and C. E. Leophart thought he should come out against Smith. Bull to FDR, May 18, 1938; O'Connell to FDR, August 23, 1938; Leophart to FDR, August 23, 1938, President's Official File, OF 300, box 30, file—South Carolina, FDRL.

66. Marvin H. McIntyre to Steven Early, July 30, Early to McIntyre, July 30, 1938, Democratic National Committee Papers (box 61), and Byrnes to Hopkins (telegram), n.d. (box 85, file—Byrnes, 1933–40), Hopkins Papers, FDRL; Winfred B. Moore, "New South Statesman," 278–80; Robertson, *Sly and Able*, 267–75.

67. As in South Carolina, the Georgia race also featured a third player—Eugene Talmadge. Talmadge, however, was more of a factor in the contest than was Brown. Anderson, *Wild Man*, 171–82.

68. *Atlanta Constitution*, August 11–12, 1938; *NYT*, August 11, 16, 19, 1938; *The State*, August 11, 1938; Hopper, "The Purge," 157–78, 186. FDR was determined to get involved in the Georgia primary. In his autobiography, James Farley (*Jim Farley's Story*, 134) reported that the president said, "I'm going to endorse someone, if I have to pick my tenant farmer."

69. *GI-J*, August 12, 1938.

70. *The State*, August 12, 1938. So loud was the train when FDR made his final remarks that different reporters heard different messages, although they all agreed on the substance of the president's last line. The Associated Press recorded the line as follows: "I don't believe any man can live on fifty cents a day." *Co*, August 12, 1938. A reporter from the *Greenwood Index-Journal* (August 12, 1938) heard FDR say, "I don't believe any family or man can live on fifty cents a day." See Robertson, *Sly and Able*, 274.

71. *Co*, August 12, 28, 1938; *AI*, August 14, 1938; *GI-J*, August 28, 1938. Ben Robertson wrote the later article. Robertson's brilliant coverage of the 1938 campaign captured the excitement and humor of the stump meetings.

72. *Co*, August 13, 18, 1938. Echoing this portrait of the ill effects of FDR's endorsement were the *Columbia Record*, August 17, 1938, and *GI-J*, August 26, 1938.

73. *AI*, August 14, 1938; *Co*, August 21, 24, 1938; *Winnsboro News and Herald*, August 18, September 1, 1938; Bouknight, "Senatorial Campaigns," 156–57.

74. *AI*, August 10, 22, 1938. See also *AI*, August 18, 1938; *Charlotte Labor Journal*, August 4, 1938; and *GI-J*, August 26-27, 1938.

75. *Co*, August 16, 21, 1938; *GI-J*, August 19, 1938; *NYT*, August 23, 1938.

76. *NYT* and *The State*, August 27-29, 1938. Several of Brown's supporters lamented his withdrawal—see, e.g., H. L. Seay, to Brown, August 30, 1938, and Edward Ninestein to Brown, August 29, 1938, Brown Papers, file L840, CU. Some South Carolina political insiders believed that Smith retired Brown's campaign debt to get him out of the race. Notes from Evening with James Brufus Griffin, Billy McGarity, and Johnny Horne, February 8, 1948, box 2—Latent Bipartisanism, Used Materials, SPC-V.

77. *GI-J*, July 28, August 1, 1938.

78. *AI*, August 29, 1938; *GI-J*, August 18, 25, 28, 1938.

79. *AI* (quotations) and *The State*, September 2, 1938. See also Hamby to FDR, August 21, 1938, President's Official File, OF 300, box 30, file—South Carolina, FDRL. For more on the campaign, see *Twin City News*, September 7, 1938, clipping, Scrapbook 1938, p. 462, ODJ Papers, SCL; *NYT*, September 1, 1938; *AI*, September 7, 1938; Ball to McMaster, McMaster Papers, November 11, 1938, box 7, file—115, SCL; Carpenter, "Olin D. Johnston," 395-97; and Hayes, "South Carolina and the New Deal," 520-22.

80. On the political outlook of black belt whites, see Key, *Southern Politics*, 3-12. Joel Williamson discusses the links between racial control, sexual control, and conservatism in *The Crucible of Race*, 24-35. On South Carolina in 1938, see *CN&C*, June 6, August 9, 1937; *GI-J*, June 26, August 14, 24, 1938; *Laurens Advertiser*, July 28, 1938; *Myrtle Beach News*, June 30, 1938, clipping, Scrapbook 1938, p. 377, ODJ Papers, SCL; and *NYT*, August 22, 1938. See also handbill dated August 1936, unsigned and distributed through Charleston, Byrnes Papers (box—Misc. 1936 L-W, file—Press), and C. L. Cobb to Byrnes, n.d. [August 1938] (box—Misc. 1938 A-O, file C), Byrnes Papers, CU.

81. Byrnes probably was correct when he predicted that Smith would pick up the votes of highway supporters. Byrnes to James Farley, August 22, 1938, Byrnes Papers, box—Misc. 1938 A-O, file F, CU. Walter Brown agreed. Brown to Byrnes, n.d. [ca. September 1938], box—Personal 1936-40, file A-G, ibid.

82. *CN&C*, June 19, 1938.

83. Robertson, *Sly and Able*, 267-87; Winfred B. Moore, "New South Statesman," 217-51. Byrnes's support for the Court plan brought him some angry letters. See, e.g., H. W. Ambrose, Secretary-Treasurer, Conway Lumber Co., to Byrnes, February 19, 1937, Byrnes Papers, box—Misc. 1937 SPE-Z, file—Supreme Court A-Z, CU. Byrnes introduced a bill to outlaw sit-down strikes. *GN*, April 3-4, 1937; M. E. Alverson to Byrnes, April 15, 1937, Byrnes Papers, box—Misc. 1938, A-O, file 3, CU. The line "negroes control the Democratic Party" appeared in *CN&C*, July 19, 1937, and June 19, 1938. The junior senator also opposed the FLSA. See Fraser, *Labor Will Rule*, 401.

84. See Marvin Cann, "Maybank and the New Deal." On Maybank's position on labor, see *Carolina Free Press*, April 8, 1938, and *GI-J*, January 16, 1938.

85. Ball to Hoyt, September 19, 1938, Ball Papers, DU. In his autobiography (*All in One Lifetime*, 101-2), Byrnes denied any involvement in this scheme. Nevertheless, the evidence suggests otherwise. See Byrnes to B. M. Baruch, August 16, 1938, Byrnes Papers, box—Misc. 1938, file—Baruch, CU; interview with George A. Buchanan, January 28, 1948, box 2—Latent Bipartisanism, Used Materials, SPC-V; Hayes, "South Carolina and the New Deal," 515-16; and Winfred B. Moore, "New South Statesman," 274-80.

86. The accusation that Smith received financial support from manufacturers was made some years later by Michie and Rhlick, *Dixie Demagogues*, 277-78, and Bouknight, "Senato-

rial Campaigns," 141–42. On a related question of campaign costs, Smith reportedly spent $15,037 as compared to Johnston's $5,124 and Brown's $12,000. See Shannon, "Presidential Politics in the South," 300.

87. The *New York World Telegraph* (June 30, 1938) pointed out that Smith usually ran well with "townspeople and businessmen." As early as 1936 Ben T. Leppard, head of the state Democratic Party, noticed a slip in support for the New Deal among "commercial, industrial, and business fields—that is the heads of such enterprises." Leppard to James A. Farley, July 21, 1936, President's Official File, OF 300, box 30, file—South Carolina, FDRL. See also a speech by manufacturer William Jacobs against the FLSA and for Smith, *GI-J*, May 27, 1938, and J. F. Blackmon, Superintendent of the Pelzer Mills, to Byrnes, July 15, 1937, Byrnes Papers, box—Misc. 1937 H-SPA, file—Majority Leader, CU, and W. W. Ball to Fitzhugh McMaster, November 10, 1938, McMaster Papers, box 7, file 115, SCL.

88. For complaints against FDR's advisers, see *GI-J*, August 21–22, 1938; A. J. Geer to Byrnes, March 6, 1935 (box—Misc. 1935 A-Greenville, file—Geer), Jack Card, "Madness in Mill Town," *Textile World* (1938) (box—Misc. 1938 A-O, file—C), and P. B. McElhanie to Byrnes, January 30, 1938 (box—Misc. 1938 A-O, file—Mac), Byrnes Papers, CU. Assaults on academic advisers and "infantile professors," as one voter called them, occasionally shaded into anti-Semitic and xenophobic attacks on the New Deal.

89. *GI-J*, August 22, September 7, 1938. Republican rhetoric during the 1936 presidential campaign was aimed at middle-class Americans. See vertical files of the Division of Political History, files 1936, Museum of American History, Smithsonian Institution, Washington, D.C. Here is one example.

> Moses said to the Chosen People
>> Pack your camels and load your asses
>> for we leave for the Promised Land.
> Roosevelt says to the People
>> Sit on your asses and smoke your camels,
>> for we are in the Promised Land

90. John D. Tukinson, "Why For Smith" (letter to the editor), *CN&C*, May 15, 1938.

91. *AI*, August 10, 22, 1938; *Charlotte Labor Journal*, August 4, 1938; *GI-J*, July 27, August 11, 26–27, 1938; *Newberry Observer*, June 25, 1937, June 29, 1938, clippings, Scrapbook 1938, Smith Papers, SCL. For national opposition, see Leuchtenburg, *Franklin D. Roosevelt*, 239–44, and Doyle, "Out of Step," 654–55.

92. *AI*, July 28, 1938; S. T. Hubbard to David Coker, June 30, 1937, Coker Papers, box 17, SCL; *[Una] News Review*, July 29, 1938; Tukinson, "Why For Smith," *CN&C*, May 15, 1938; *GN*, July 17, 1938. Law and order was also a central theme in the 1938 governor's race. All seven candidates in the first primary supported a proposed state law that would have outlawed sit-down strikes. *AI*, June 15, 30, 1938. For more on this campaign, see Marvin Cann, "End of a Political Myth," 139–49. On the threat of strikes, see *GI-J*, July 11, 1938.

93. The question asked was, "Do you think this state should pass legislation making sit-down strikes illegal?" For a breakdown of responses, see "Sit-down Strikes," March 21, 1937, *Gallup Poll*, 52.

94. *AI*, July 28, 1938. See also Brinkley, *Voices of Protest*, 199; Jerome Farrell to Farley, December 1, 1938, President's Official File, OF 300, box 42, file—Political Scene before the Election, FDRL; *Anderson Daily Mail*, August 31, 1938; *GI-J*, August 23, 1938.

95. *AI*, June 16, 1938.

96. *AI*, June 11, 1938, *GI-J*, August 21, 24, October 7, 1938; Tukinson, "Why For Smith," *CN&C*, May 15, 1938.

97. Table A.5; *CN&C*, May 15, 1938; *GI-J*, August 21, November 7, 1938; *[Una] News Review*, September 2, 1938. In a letter to Turner ———, Ben Robertson noted that small farmers were Smith's "biggest backers." March 1, 1938, Robertson Papers, CU. See also Byrnes to James Farley, August 22, 1938, Byrnes Papers, box—Misc. 1938 A-O, file—F, CU.

98. *Charlotte Labor Journal*, August 4, 1938; *GI-J*, July 27, August 11, 26-27, 1938. One of the main stages for this fight was over the post of commissioner of the newly formed state Department of Labor. When the general assembly first authorized the formation of this department, it stipulated that the state AFL, then the only labor organization in South Carolina, submit to the governor a list of candidates for the position to choose from. With the split in labor's ranks, this became a contentious issue. The first commissioner, John Nates, had ties to the CIO, and Johnston later refused to remove him as an AFL leader demanded.

99. "We are surprised," wrote the editors of the prolabor *[Una] News Review* (July 2, 1938), "to see the leaders of the AFL steal the communistic club that the manufacturers have used on us up until this split." For the AFL perspective, see *Carolina Free Press*, July 9, 23, 1937; *Charlotte Labor Journal*, November 11, 1937; *GI-J*, May 27, 1938; and Kennedy, "History," 76-77.

100. For similarities between Smith and the AFL, see *Charlotte Labor Journal*, March 24, 1938, February 2, 1939; *CN&C*, March 27, 1938; *AI*, September 7, 1938; and *[Una] News Review*, June 25, July 9, 1937. On the national level, see Leuchtenburg, *Franklin D. Roosevelt*, 262, 279, and Zieger, *American Workers*, 60.

101. *Abbeville Press and Standard* and *GN*, September 1, 1938. See Table A.5.

102. On the outlook of skilled workers in the 1930s, see Brinkley, *Voices of Protest*, 198-203. See also Proceedings of the SCFL, 1937-39, GML.

103. *GI-J*, August 26-27, September 11, 1938. For similar concerns, see *AI*, August 22, 1938.

104. *CN&C*, June 9, 16-17, July 15, 20, August 17, 1938.

105. *[Una] News Review*, August 12, 1938; letter to the editor, *CN&C*, July 20, 1938.

106. *GI-J* and *AI*, August 31, 1938.

107. *Beaufort Gazette*, September 1, 1938; *CN&C*, August 31, 1938; *Co*, August 31, 1938; *The State*, September 3, 1938.

108. William Leuchtenburg (*Franklin D. Roosevelt*, 268), for instance, writes that Smith split the mill vote. See also Brinkley, "The New Deal and Southern Politics," 108-9.

Chapter Twelve

1. The best source of wartime rumors is Odum, *Race*. See also Miles S. Richards, "Osceola E. McKaine," 117-19, and Anthony B. Miller, "Palmetto Politician," 396-98. Others mention race rumors more generally—see, e.g., Tindall, *New South*, 717-18; Daniel, *Standing at the Crossroads*, 141-42; and Goodwin, *No Ordinary Time*, 370-71.

2. Increasingly historians are recognizing that the civil rights movement began before the 1950s. See, e.g., Kuhn, "Two Small Windows of Opportunity." See also Egerton, *Speak Now*, and Sullivan, *Days of Hope*.

3. For broader discussions on the meaning of rumors, see White, "Between Gluckman and Foucault"; Turner, *I Heard It through the Grapevine*; and Allport and Postman, *The Psychology of Rumor*.

4. This is a paraphrase of Eldridge Cleaver's famous remark about Rosa Parks. Cleaver is quoted by Sitkoff, *Struggle for Black Equality*, 42.

5. On the highest estimates of NAACP membership, see interview with James Hinton, January 20, 1948, box 2—Latent Bipartisanism, file—The Negro, Used Material, SPC-V.

More modest estimates come from Zangrando, *NAACP Crusade*, 171; Miles S. Richards, "Osceola E. McKaine," 107–9; and Sullivan, *Days of Hope*, 142. See also Edwin D. Hoffman, "Genesis of the Modern Movement."

6. Sullivan, *Days of Hope*, 143. See also Egerton, *Speak Now*, 428; Sosna, *In Search of the Silent South*.

7. From South Carolina, see "The Negro Citizens Convention of South Carolina to the South Carolina State Convention of the Democratic Party," May 19, 1942, and A Flier for a NAACP Meeting, March 15, 1942, Voting Rights Campaign, part 4, reel 10, NAACP Papers, microfilm collection, University Publications of America, Frederick, MD. On the national campaign for Double V, see Blum, *V Was for Victory*, 207–20.

8. On eligible voters in Beaufort and Greenville, see Sullivan, *Days of Hope*, 144; Bunche, *Political Status*, 242–45, 421–24; and U.S. Bureau of the Census, *Fifteenth Census, Unemployment*, 784–87.

9. Mrs. Lottie P. Gaffney to NAACP, August 25, November 7, 1940, Voting Rights Campaign, part 4, reel 10, NAACP Papers.

10. NAACP press release, May 29, 1941, Voting Rights Campaign, ibid;. Bunche, *Political Status*, 238–47, 425–27.

11. Brinkley, *End of Reform*, 10.

12. Ibid.; Zieger, *CIO*, 186; Bartley, *New South*, 70–73; Gerstle, *Working-Class Americanism*, 289–302, 317–18.

13. On the trends in Washington, see Sullivan, *Days of Hope*, 133–68; Reed, *Seedtime*; Blum, *V Was for Victory*, 196–98, 212–15; and *NYT*, September 6, November 6, 14, 1942.

14. Sullivan, *Days of Hope*, 144–49, 169–70, 189–91; Egerton, *Speak Now*, 227–28; Miles S. Richards, "Osceola E. McKaine," 174–85.

15. On the alleged increase in African American crime, see *The State*, September 6, 1941.

16. Odum, *Race*, 22, 57 (quotation), 62–64, 115, 117, 122. More generally, see Sancton, "Trouble in Dixie."

17. Bertie Mae Loner to Eleanor Roosevelt, March 3, 1994, Eleanor Roosevelt Papers, box 2962, FDRL.

18. Miles S. Richards, "Osceola E. McKaine," 119–20.

19. Egerton, *Speak Now*, 362. See also Burran, "Racial Violence."

20. Edwin D. Hoffman, "Genesis of the Modern Movement," 205–6, 211; Sullivan, *Days of Hope*, 144–45; Bunche, *Political Status*, 422–23.

21. *The State*, July 24, 30, August 22, 1941.

22. See Lawson, *Black Ballots*, 53–54; Burran, "Racial Violence," 259; and Sitkoff, "Racial Militancy."

23. "Survey of Racial Conditions in the United States," p. 256, President's Official File, FDRL.

24. On the war-ending celebrations, see Huff, *Greenville*, 384.

25. Egerton, *Speak Now*, 362–63, 365; Kari Frederickson, "'The Slowest State,'" 180–83. On the rash of killings of African Americans who had voted or participated in early civil rights events in Georgia, Texas, and South Carolina, see Bartley, *New South*, 76.

26. West, "Opera in Greenville," 34.

27. The most revealing account of the events surrounding the murder and trial comes from West, "Opera in Greenville." See also *Life*, June 2, 1947, 27–29; Huff, *Greenville*, 399–400; Egerton, *Speak Now*, 371–73; and Kari Frederickson, "'The Slowest State,'" 188–98.

28. *The State*, August 13, 1941.

29. *NYT*, April 1, May 21, June 21, 1944.

30. *The State*, August 17, 1941.

31. Anthony B. Miller, "Palmetto Politician," 159-60; Miles S. Richards, "Osceola E. McKaine," 159; Bartley, *New South*, 12.

32. *NYT*, March 1, 2, 1944.

33. Miles S. Richards, "Osceola E. McKaine," 164.

34. For hints of white liberalism in South Carolina, see Press Release, May 5, 1942, Voting Rights Campaign, part 4, reel 10, NAACP Papers, and Miles S. Richards, "Osceola E. McKaine," 160-61.

35. West, "Opera in Greenville," 46.

36. Bunche, *Political Status*, 424-25. See also M. L. Woode, President of the Labor Democratic Club of South Carolina, January 21, 1948, Southern Politics Collection (box 2, file—One-Party System: South Carolina Piedmont vs. Low Country, Used Material), and interview with James Hinton, January 20, 1948 (box 2—Latent Bipartisanism, file—The Negro, Used Material), SPC-V.

37. Egerton, *Speak Now*, 484.

38. Anthony B. Miller, "Palmetto Politician," 344; ODJ Speeches, August 15, September 1, ODJ Papers, box 292, file—Speeches, August-September 1941, SCL; *Co*, August 15, 17, 19-20, 29, September 3, 1941; *The State*, September 2, 11, 1941; *NYT*, September 17-18, 1941.

39. Anthony B. Miller, "Palmetto Politician," 341-43, 359-62, 364; *NYT*, August 26-27, 1942.

40. Huss, *Senator for the South*, 115; Anthony B. Miller, "Palmetto Politician," 397-99; *The State*, July 17, 1943.

41. For reactions to the Court ruling, see Huss, *Senator for the South*, 124; *AI*, April 12, 1944; *CN&C*, April 4, 14, 18, 1944; *The State*, April 4, 6-7, 1944.

42. Huss, *Senator for the South*, 125.

43. "Killbillies," *Newsweek*, May 1, 1944, 33; *The State*, April 15-21, 1944; *NYT*, April 16, 18, 1944; Lawson, *Black Ballots*, 49-50. On Waring, see Edgar, *South Carolina*, 86.

44. For the contest, see *The State*, July 18, 20-22, August 3, 1944, and Leemhuis, "Johnston Runs for the Senate," 60-62.

45. Cohodas, *Strom Thurmond*, 210-11. See also "Olin D. Johnston to Fellow South Carolinians," June 26, 1950, ODJ Papers, box 304, file—Campaign 1950, SCL; and Leemhuis, "Johnston Runs for the Senate," 62-65. Ironically, some political observers suggested that African American voters, enfranchised by the *Smith* decision, provided Johnston with his thin margin of victory.

46. Egerton, *Speak Now*, 400. In 1962 Johnston did have an opponent, Fritz Hollings. Hollings, however, did not attack Johnston's record on race but tried to suggest that he was in the pocket of the big-city bosses of organized labor. The strategy did not work. In addition, in the fall of 1962 Johnston faced the first serious Republican challenge in South Carolina since Reconstruction. The candidate was the journalist W. D. Workman, who courted the votes of "country club" Republicans alienated by Johnston's lingering labor ties along with working-class people fearful of the national Democratic Party's ties to civil rights.

47. For "sound bites" from Johnston speeches, see Faggart, "Johnston versus Hollings," 14-15, and *Co*, May 3-4, 16 1962.

48. Huss, *Senator for the South*, 140-47.

49. Ibid., 208-9.

50. The continuing resonance of populist language is explored by Kazin, *Populist Persuasion*.

51. Korstad and Lichtenstein ("Opportunities Found and Lost," 786–811) have suggested that "most social movements have a life cycle of about six years." The struggles of South Carolina textile workers, therefore, lasted a little longer than most.

52. Mattie Jones, "You Do What You Want To," Life History of Mrs. Collie Croft, December 1, 1939, and "The Kellys on William Street," Life History of Reverend Charles M. Kelly, January 4, 1939, WPA Life Histories, box 30, file 326, SHC.

53. For more on trade unionism, see *Charlotte Labor Journal*, July 4, December 12, 1940, and *NYT*, March 20, 1942. For evidence of labor's continued role in South Carolina politics, see interview with M. L. Woode, President of the Labor Democratic Club of South Carolina, January 21, 1948, and with Thomas H. Pope, February 12, 1948, box 2, file—One-Party System: South Carolina Piedmont vs. Low Country, Used Material, SPC-V; and "Dedication of AFL-CIO Community Building," September 9, 1962, SCL.

54. *NYT*, August 3, 1941; Lander, *History of South Carolina*, 209–12. The best account of the rise in working-class income comes from Minchin, *What Do We Need a Union For?* For a personal recollection, see the interview in Byerly, *Hard Times Cotton Mill Girls*, 181.

55. Lichtenstein, *Labor's War at Home*, 209–21; Flamming, *Creating the Modern South*, 233–61.

56. Bartley, *New South*, 70–73.

57. Others make a similar point; see Kazin, *Populist Persuasion*, 225–29, and Norrell, "Labor Trouble." White southerners were not the only group of white Americans trying to protect the privileges of race in the postwar period; see Gerstle, "Working-Class Racism," and Sugrue, "Crabgrass-Roots Politics."

58. In her fascinating study of anti-Semitism and race in the postwar South, Melissa Fay Greene (*The Temple Bombing*, 432–33) argues that some poor whites saw democracy in this way.

59. For evidence of this distrust, see "The Race Question," *[Una] News Review*, July 31, 1936.

60. For the long history of this process, see Hale, *Making Whiteness*.

Conclusion

1. *GN*, April 21, 1965; *SH*, April 19, 1965; *NYT*, April 19–21, 1965.

2. *Newsweek*, May 3, 1965. For some similar trends nationally, see Sugrue, *Origins of the Urban Crisis*.

3. O'Neill quoted by Williams, *Modern Tragedy*, 116.

Manuscripts

Chapel Hill, North Carolina
North Carolina Collection, University of North Carolina
   Harriet Laura Herring Clipping File
Southern Historical Collection, University of North Carolina
   Jonathan Daniels Papers
   Federal Writers' Project
   Frank Porter Graham Papers
   Harriet Laura Herring Papers
   Howard Odum Papers
   Southern Oral History Project
   Works Progress Administration, Life Histories

Clemson, South Carolina
Clemson University
   Edgar A. Brown Papers
   James F. Byrnes Papers
   John Dewey Lane Papers
   Frank A. Lever Papers
   Quattlebaum Papers
   Ben Robertson Papers

Columbia, South Carolina
South Carolina Division of Archives and History
   County Precinct Lists and Democratic Club Rolls
   Gubernatorial Papers of Ibra C. Blackwood
   Gubernatorial Papers of Coleman Livingston Blease
   Gubernatorial Papers of Olin D. Johnston
   Gubernatorial Papers of Burnett Maybank
   Gubernatorial Papers of John G. Richards
   South Carolina Industrial Commission Records
South Caroliniana Library, University of South Carolina
   Solmon Blatt Papers
   Henry L. Campbell Papers
   David Coker Papers
   Henry C. Davis Papers
   Louise Jones DuBose Papers

W. E. Gonzales Papers
Wil Lou Gray Papers
James Alfred Hoyt Papers
Richard M. Jeffries Papers
Olin D. Johnston Papers
Fitz Hugh McMaster Papers
J. J. McSwain Papers
Wyndham Meredith Manning Papers
John G. Richards Papers
Ellison D. Smith Papers
Mendel L. Smith Papers
William Wightman Smoak Papers
South Carolina House and Senate Journals
Elliot Springs Papers
Harry L. Watson Papers
William D. Workman Jr. Papers
Works Progress Administration Papers

Durham, North Carolina
Perkins Library, Duke University
   William Watts Ball Papers
   John P. Grace Papers
   John J. McSwain Papers
   George S. Mitchell Papers

Hyde Park, New York
Franklin D. Roosevelt Library
   Democratic National Committee Records
   Harry Hopkins Papers
   President's Official File
   President's Personal File
   Eleanor Roosevelt Papers
   John Winant Papers

Madison, Wisconsin
State Historical Society of Wisconsin, University of Wisconsin
   Textile Workers Union of America Records

Nashville, Tennessee
Alexander Heard Library, Vanderbilt University
   Southern Politics Collection

Raleigh, North Carolina
North Carolina Department of Archives and History
   Gubernatorial Papers of J. C. B. Ehringhaus

                                            Bibliography

Silver Spring, Maryland
George Meany Memorial Archives
   William Green Papers
   Proceedings of the South Carolina Federation of Labor

Spartanburg, South Carolina
Archives, Sandor Teszler Library, Wofford College
   Peter R. Moody Files
   William Fred Ponder Files

Washington, D.C.
Georgetown University Archives
   Robert F. Wagner Papers
Library of Congress
   Division of Motion Pictures and Broadcasting
      God's Little Acre
      Promotion for Tobacco Road
   Division of Recorded Sound
      Bodkin Recordings
      Vertical Files
National Archives
   Department of Labor Records
   National Recovery Administration Records
   Women's Bureau Records
   Works Progress Administration Records
National Museum of American History, Smithsonian Institution
   Division of Political History
      Button Collection
      Poster Collection
      Vertical Files

Newspapers and Periodicals

Abbeville Press and Standard
Aiken Evening Standard
American Federationist
Anderson Daily Mail
Anderson Independent
Atlanta Constitution
Augusta Chronicle
Augusta Herald
Augusta Labor Review
Beaufort Gazette
Blease Weekly
Carolina Free Press
Charleston News and Courier
Charlotte Labor Review

Charlotte Observer
Columbia Record
Columbia State
The Crisis
Davison's Textile Blue Book
Easley Progress
Gaffney Ledger
Greenville News
Greenwood Index-Journal
Hartsville Messenger
Laurens Advertiser
Lee County Messenger
Manning Times
Monthly Labor Review
Nation
Newberry Herald Observer
New Republic
Newsweek
New York Times
Raleigh News and Observer
Rock Hill Evening Herald
Southern Textile Bulletin
Spartanburg Herald
Textile Worker
Time
Una News Review
Union Daily Times

Books, Articles, Dissertations, and Theses

Allen, James E. "Eugene Talmadge and the Great Textile Strike in Georgia, September 1934." In *Essays in Southern Labor History*, edited by Fink and Reed, 31–49.
Allen, Theodore W. *The Invention of the White Race*. Vol. 1 of *Racial Oppression and Social Control*. London: Verso, 1994.
Allison, Dorothy. *Bastard Out of Carolina*. New York: Dutton, 1992.
———. *Skin: Talking about Sex, Class, and Literature*. Ithaca, N.Y.: Firebrand Books, 1994.
———. *Trash*. Ithaca, N.Y.: Firebrand Books, 1988.
Allport, Gordon W., and Leo Postman. *The Psychology of Rumor*. New York: H. Holt, 1947.
Anderson, William. *The Wild Man from Sugar Creek: The Political Career of Eugene Talmadge*. Baton Rouge: Louisiana State University Press, 1975.
Andrews, Mildred Gwin. *The Men and the Mills: A History of the Southern Textile Industry*. Macon, Ga.: Mercer University Press, 1987.
Applebome, Peter. *Dixie Rising: How the South Is Shaping American Values, Politics, and Culture*. New York: Times Books, 1996.
Argersinger, Peter H. "The Value of the Vote: Political Representation in the Gilded Age." In *Structure, Process, and Party: Essays in American Political History*, edited by Peter H. Argersinger, 69–102. Armonk, N.Y.: M. E. Sharpe, 1992.

Arnesen, Eric. *Waterfront Workers of New Orleans: Race, Class, and Politics, 1863–1923*. New York: Oxford University Press, 1991.

Ashmore, Harry S. *An Epitaph for Dixie*. New York: Norton, 1958.

Auerbach, Jerold S. *Labor And Liberty: The La Follette Committee and the New Deal*. Indianapolis: Bobbs-Merrill, 1966.

———. "New Deal, Old Deal, or Raw Deal: Some Thoughts on New Left Historiography." *Journal of Southern History* 35 (February 1969): 18–30.

Avery, Myrta Lockett. *Dixie after the War*. 1906. Reprint, Boston: Houghton Mifflin, 1937.

Ayers, Edward L. *The Promise of the New South: Life after Reconstruction*. New York: Oxford University Press, 1992.

———. *Vengeance and Justice: Crime and Punishment in the Nineteenth Century American South*. New York: Oxford University Press, 1984.

Badger, Anthony J. *The New Deal: The Depression Years, 1933–1940*. New York: Noonday Press, 1989.

———. *North Carolina and the New Deal*. Raleigh: North Carolina Department of Cultural Resources, 1981.

Bailey, N. Louise. *Biographical Directory of the South Carolina Senate, 1776–1985*. Columbia: University of South Carolina Press, 1986.

Baker, Paula, "The Domestication of Politics: Women and American Political Society, 1780–1920." *American Historical Review* 84 (June 1984): 620–47.

Ball, W. W. *The State That Forgot: South Carolina's Surrender to Democracy*. Indianapolis: Bobbs-Merrill, 1932.

Barbare, Ralph Carsbol. "Community Welfare Work in the Mill Villages of Greenville, South Carolina." M.A. thesis, University of South Carolina, 1930.

Barnes, Oliver Lee. "The Economics of Tax Reform in South Carolina during the Decade 1920–1930." M.A. thesis, University of South Carolina, 1948.

Baron, Ava, ed. *Work Engendered: Toward a New History of American Labor*. Ithaca, N.Y.: Cornell University Press, 1991.

Barrett, James R. "Americanization from the Bottom Up: Immigration and the Remaking of the Working Class in the United States, 1880-1930." *Journal of American History* 79 (December 1992): 996–1020.

Bartley, Numan V. *The New South, 1945–1980*. Baton Rouge: Louisiana State University, 1995.

———. *The Rise of Massive Resistance: Race and Politics in the South during the 1950's*. Baton Rouge: Louisiana State University Press, 1969.

———. "In Search of the New South: Southern Politics after Reconstruction." *Reviews in American History* 10 (December 1982): 150–63.

Baskerville, Stephen W., and Ralph Willet, eds. *Nothing Else to Fear: New Perspectives on America in the Thirties*. London: Manchester University Press, 1985.

Bass, Jack, and Walter DeVries. *The Transformation of Southern Politics: Social Change and Political Consequence since 1945*. New York: Basic Books, 1976.

Basso, Hamilton. *In Their Image*. New York: Scribner and Sons, 1935.

Batchelor, Alexander A. "A Textile Community in South Carolina." M.A. thesis, University of South Carolina, 1926.

Bauman, John F., and Thomas H. Coode. *In the Eye of the Great Depression: New Deal Reporters and the Agony of the American People*. De Kalb: Northern Illinois University Press, 1988.

Beal, Fred. *Proletarian Journey: New England, Gastonia, Moscow*. New York: Da Capo Press, 1971.

Beardsley, Edward H. *A History of Neglect: Health Care for Blacks and Mill Workers in the Twentieth-Century South*. Knoxville: University of Tennessee Press, 1987.

Beatty, Bess. "Textile Labor in the North Carolina Piedmont: Mill Owner Images and Worker Responses, 1830–1900." *Labor History* 25 (Fall 1984): 485–503.

Bederman, Gail, "'Civilization,' the Decline of Middle-Class Manliness, and Ida B. Wells's Antilynching Campaign, 1892–1894." *Radical History Review* 52 (Winter 1992): 5–30.

Beito, David T. *Taxpayers in Revolt: Tax Resistance during the Great Depression*. Chapel Hill: University of North Carolina Press, 1989.

Bell, Thomas. *Out of This Furnace: A Novel of Immigrant Labor in America*. Pittsburgh: University of Pittsburgh Press, 1976.

Bender, Jay. "Olin D. Johnston and the Highway Controversy." *Proceedings of the South Carolina Historical Association* (1972): 39–54.

Bender, Thomas. "Wholes and Parts: The Need for Synthesis in American History." *Journal of American History* 73 (June 1986): 120–36.

Berglund, Abraham, Geroge T. Starnes, and Frank T. DeVyver. *Labor in the Industrial South: A Survey of Wages and Living Conditions in Three Major Industries of the New Industrial South*. Charlottesville: Institute for Research in the Social Sciences, 1930.

Bernstein, Barton J., ed. *Towards a New Past: Dissenting Essays in American History*. New York: Pantheon, 1968.

Bernstein, Irving. *A Caring Society: The New Deal, the Worker, and the Great Depression: A History of the American Worker, 1933–1941*. Boston: Houghton Mifflin, 1985.

———. *The Lean Years: A History of the American Worker, 1920–1933*. Boston: Houghton Mifflin, 1960.

———. *The New Deal Collective Bargaining Policy*. Berkeley: University of California Press, 1950.

———. *The Turbulent Years: A History of the American Worker, 1933–1941*. Boston: Houghton Mifflin, 1970.

Biles, Roger. *A New Deal for the American People*. De Kalb: Northern Illinois University Press, 1991.

———. *The South and the New Deal*. Lexington: University Press of Kentucky, 1994.

Billings, Dwight B., Jr. *Planters and the Making of a "New South": Class, Politics, and Development in North Carolina, 1865–1900*. Chapel Hill: University of North Carolina Press, 1979.

Black, Earl, and Merle Black. *Politics and Society in the South*. Cambridge: Harvard University Press, 1987.

Blackwelder, Julia R. "Quiet Suffering: Atlanta Women in the 1930s." *Georgia Historical Quarterly* 61 (Summer 1977): 112–24.

Blanshard, Paul. *Labor in Southern Cotton Mills*. New York: New Republic, Inc., 1927.

———. "One Hundred Percent Americans on Strike." *Nation*, May 8, 1929, 552–56.

Blicksilver, Jack. *Cotton Manufacturing in the Southeast: An Historical Analysis*. Atlanta: Bureau of Business and Economic Research, School of Business Administration, Georgia State University, 1959.

Blum, John Morton. *V Was for Victory: Politics and American Culture during World War II*. New York: Harcourt Brace Jovanovich, 1976.

Bodnar, John E. *Immigration And Industrialization: Ethnicity in an American Mill Town, 1870–1940*. Pittsburgh: University of Pittsburgh Press, 1977.

Boggs, Doyle W. "John Patrick Grace and the Politics of Reform in South Carolina, 1900–1931." Ph.D. diss., University of South Carolina, 1977.

Borsos, John E. "Support for the National Democratic Party in South Carolina during the Dixiecrat Revolt of 1948." M.A. thesis, University of South Carolina, 1987.

Botsch, Robert E. *Organizing the Breathless: Cotton, Dust, Southern Politics, and the Brown Lung Association.* Lexington: University Press of Kentucky, 1993.

Bouknight, Martha Nelle. "The Senatorial Campaigns of Ellison D. (Cotton Ed) Smith of South Carolina." M.A. thesis, Florida State University, 1961.

Bowers, Claude G. *The Tragic Era: The Revolution after Lincoln.* Cambridge, Mass.: Riverside Press, 1929.

Boyette, Lawrence. "The General Textile Strike of 1934 in Greenwood County: In Search of Sadie Harris." Seminar paper, University of North Carolina, Chapel Hill, 1987.

———. "The General Textile Strike of 1934 in Greenwood County, South Carolina." Paper delivered at the Southern Historical Convention, New Orleans, 1990.

Boyte, Harry. "The Textile Industry: Keel of Southern Industrialization." *Radical America* 6 (March–April 1972): 4–49.

Bradford, William Rufus. *Twenty-One Governors of South Carolina: Tillman to Byrnes, Including Both: A Related Tragedy and Other Matters.* Rock Hill: N.p., 1954.

Braeman, John. "The New Deal and the 'Broker State': A Review of the Recent Scholarly Literature." *Business History Review* 46 (Winter 1972): 409–29.

Braeman, John, Robert H. Bremner, and David Brody, eds. *The New Deal: The National Level.* Columbus: Ohio State University Press, 1975.

———. *The New Deal: The State and Local Levels.* Columbus: Ohio State University Press, 1975.

Brandes, Stuart D. *American Welfare Capitalism, 1880–1940.* Chicago: University of Chicago Press, 1976.

Braverman, Harry. *Labor and Monopoly Capital: The Degradation of Work in the Twentieth Century.* New York: Monthly Review Press, 1974.

Brecher, Jeremy. *Strike!* San Francisco: Straight Arrow Books, 1972.

Brice, James Taylor. "The Use of Executive Clemency under Coleman Livingston Blease, Governor of South Carolina, 1911-1915." M.A. thesis, University of South Carolina, 1965.

Brinkley, Alan. *The End of Reform: New Deal Liberalism in Recession and War.* New York: Knopf, 1995.

———. "The New Deal and Southern Politics." In *The New Deal and the South*, edited by Cobb and Namorato, 97-115.

———. *Voices of Protest: Huey Long, Father Coughlin, and the Great Depression.* New York: Knopf, 1982.

Britton, Earle R. "Progress in the Palmetto State." *American Federationist* 54 (October 1947): 30-32

Brody, David. "The Rise and Decline of Welfare Capitalism." In *Workers in Industrial America*, 48-81.

———. *Steelworkers in America: The Nonunion Era.* Cambridge: Harvard University Press, 1960.

———. *Workers in Industrial America: Essays on the Twentieth-Century Struggle.* New York: Oxford University Press, 1980.

———, ed. *The American Labor Movement.* New York: Harper and Row, 1971.

Brooks, Robert R. R. "The United Textile Workers of America." Ph.D. diss., Yale University, 1935.

Brooks, Thomas R. *Picket Lines and Bargaining Tables: Organized Labor Comes of Age, 1933-1935.* New York: Grossett and Dunlop, 1968.

Browning, Wilt. *Linthead: Growing Up in a Carolina Cotton Mill Village*. Asheboro, N.C.: Down Home Press, 1990.

Brundage, W. Fitzhugh. *Lynching in the New South: Georgia and Virginia, 1880–1930*. Urbana: University of Illinois Press, 1993.

Bunche, Ralph J. *The Political Status of the Negro in the Age of FDR*. Chicago: University of Chicago Press, 1973.

Burke, Fielding. *A Stone Came Rolling*. New York: Longmans, Green, 1935.

Burns, James MacGregor. *Roosevelt: The Lion and the Fox*. New York: Harcourt, Brace, 1956.

Burnside, Ronald D. "The Governorship of Coleman Livingston Blease of South Carolina, 1911–15." Ph.D. diss., Indiana University, 1963.

———. "Racism in the Administration of Governor Cole Blease." *Proceedings of the South Carolina Historical Association* (1964): 43–57.

Burran, James Albert. "Racial Violence in the South during World War II." Ph.D. diss., University of Tennessee, 1977.

Burton, Orville Vernon. *In My Father's House Are Many Mansions: Family and Community in Edgefield, South Carolina*. Chapel Hill: University of North Carolina Press, 1985.

Burton, Orville Vernon, Terence R. Finnegan, Peyton McCrary, and James Loewen. "South Carolina." In *Quiet Revolution in the South: The Impact of the Voting Rights Act, 1965–1990*, edited by Chandler Davidson and Bernard Grofman, 126–51. Princeton, N.J.: Princeton University Press, 1994.

Burton, Orville Vernon, and Robert McMath, eds. *Toward a New South?: Studies in Post–Civil War Southern Communities*. Westport, Conn.: Greenwood Press, 1982.

Burts, Robert M. *Richard Irvine Manning and the Progressive Movement in South Carolina*. Columbia: University of South Carolina Press, 1974.

Butterfield, Fox. *All God's Children: The Bosket Family and the American Tradition of Violence*. New York: Knopf, 1995.

Byars, Alvin. *Lintheads*. Caycee, S.C.: Olympia-Pacific, 1983.

———. *Olympia Pacific: The Way It Was, 1895–1970*. West Columbia, S.C.: A. W. Byars, 1981.

Byerly, Victoria. *Hard Times Cotton Mill Girls: Personal Histories of Womanhood and Poverty in the South*. Ithaca, N.Y.: ILR Press, 1986.

Byrnes, James F. *All in One Lifetime*. New York: Harper, 1958.

Caldwell, Erskine. *God's Little Acre*. New York: Modern Library, 1933.

———. *Tobacco Road*. Athens: University of Georgia Press, 1994.

———. *Trouble In July*. Savannah, Ga.: Beehive Press, 1977.

Caldwell, Erskine, and Margaret Bourke-White. *You Have Seen Their Faces*. New York: Viking Press, 1937.

Camak, D. E. *Human Gold from Southern Hills: Not a Novel but a Romance of Facts*. Greer, S.C.: Private press, 1960.

Cann, Marvin. "Burnet Maybank and Charleston Politics in the New Deal Era." *Proceedings of the South Carolina Historical Association* (1970): 39–48.

———. "Burnet Rhett Maybank and the New Deal in South Carolina, 1931–1941." Ph.D. diss., University of North Carolina, Chapel Hill, 1967.

———. "The End of a Political Myth: The South Carolina Gubernatorial Campaign of 1938." *South Carolina Historical Magazine* 72 (July 1971): 139–49.

Cann, Mary Katherine Davis. "The Morning After: South Carolina in the Jazz Age." Ph.D. diss., University of South Carolina, 1984.

Carlton, David L. " 'Builders of a New State'—the Town Classes and Early Industrialization of South Carolina, 1880–1907." In *From the Old South to the New: Essays on the Transitional South*, 43–62.

———. *Mill and Town in South Carolina, 1880–1920*. Baton Rouge: Louisiana State University Press, 1982.

———. "The Piedmont and Waccamaw Regions: An Economic Comparison." *South Carolina Historical Magazine* 88 (April 1987): 83–100.

———. "The Revolution from Above: The National Market and the Beginnings of Industrialization in North Carolina." *Journal of American History* 77 (September 1990): 445–75.

———. "The State and the Worker in the South: A Lesson from South Carolina." In *The Meaning of South Carolina History*, edited by Chesnutt and Wilson, 186–201.

———. "Unbalanced Growth and Industrialization: The Case of South Carolina." In *Developing Dixie*, edited by Moore, Tripp, and Tyler, 111–30.

Carlton, David L., and Peter A. Coclanis. "Capital Mobilization and Southern Industry, 1880–1945: The Case of the Carolina Piedmont." *Journal of Economic History* 64 (March 1989): 73–94.

———. *Confronting Southern Poverty in the Great Depression: The Report on Economic Conditions of the South with Related Documents*. Boston: Bedford Books, 1996.

Carpenter, JoAnn Deakin. "Olin D. Johnston, the New Deal, and the Politics of Class in South Carolina, 1934–1938." Ph.D. diss., Emory University, 1987.

Carter, Dan T. *The Politics of Rage: George Wallace, the Origins of the New Conservatism, and the Transformation of American Politics*. New York: Simon and Schuster, 1995.

Cash, W. J. *The Mind of the South*. New York: Knopf, 1941.

Cauthen, John K. *Speaker Blatt: His Challenges Were Greater*. Columbia: University of South Carolina Press, 1978.

Chafe, William H. *The American Woman: Her Changing Social, Economic, and Political Roles, 1920–1970*. New York: Oxford University Press, 1972.

Chandler, Lester V. *America's Greatest Depression, 1929–1941*. New York: Harper and Row, 1970.

Chesnutt, David R., and Clyde N. Wilson, eds. *The Meaning of South Carolina History: Essays in Honor of George C. Rogers Jr*. Columbia: University of South Carolina Press, 1991.

Cobb, James C. *Industrialization and Southern Society, 1877–1984*. Lexington: University Press of Kentucky, 1984.

———. "Not Gone, but Forgotten: Eugene Talmadge and the 1938 Purge Campaign." *Georgia Historical Quarterly* 59 (Summer 1975): 197–209.

———. *The Selling of the South: The Southern Crusade for Industrial Development, 1936–1980*. Baton Rouge: Louisiana State University Press, 1982.

Cobb, James C., and Michael V. Namorato, eds. *The New Deal and the South*. Jackson: University Press of Mississippi, 1984.

Coclanis, Peter A. *The Shadow of a Dream: Economic Life and Death in the South Carolina Low Country, 1670–1920*. New York: Oxford University Press, 1989.

Coclanis, Peter A., and Lacy K. Ford. "The South Carolina Economy Reconstructed and Reconsidered: Structure, Output, and Performance, 1670–1985." In *Developing Dixie*, edited by Moore, Tripp, and Tyler, 93–110.

Cohen, Lizabeth. *Making a New Deal: Industrial Workers in Chicago, 1919–1939*. New York: Cambridge University Press, 1990.

Cohodas, Nadine. *Strom Thurmond and the Politics of Southern Change*. New York: Simon and Schuster, 1993.

Coleman, James Karl. *State Administration in South Carolina*. New York: Columbia University Press, 1935.

Commager, Henry Steele. "A South Carolina Dictator." *Current History* 43 (March 1936): 568–72.

Conkin, Paul. *The New Deal*. New York: Crowell, 1967.

Conway, Mimi. *Rise Gonna Rise: A Portrait of Southern Textile Workers*. Garden City, N.Y.: Anchor Press, 1979.

Cooper, William J. *The Conservative Regime: South Carolina, 1877–1890*. Baltimore: Johns Hopkins University Press, 1968.

Corbin, David. *Life, Work, and Rebellion in the Coal Fields: The Southern West Virginia Miners, 1880–1922*. Urbana: University of Illinois Press, 1981.

Cowan, Concord Ray. "Labor Regulation and Administration in South Carolina." M.A. thesis, University of South Carolina, 1948.

Cronin, James E. "Labor Insurgency and Class Formation: Comparative Perspectives on the Crisis of 1917–1920." In *Work, Community, and Power: The Experience of Labor in Europe and America, 1900–1925*, edited by Cronin and Carmen Sirianni, 20–28. Philadelphia: Temple University Press, 1983.

Cunliffe, Marcus. *Chattel Slavery and Wage Slavery: The Anglo-American Context, 1830–1860*. Athens: University of Georgia Press, 1979.

Cutler, Addison T. "Labor Legislation in Thirteen Southern States." *Southern Economic Journal* 7 (1941): 297–316.

Daniel, Pete. *Breaking the Land: The Transformation of Cotton, Tobacco, and Rice Cultures since 1880*. Urbana: University of Illinois Press, 1985.

———. "The New Deal, Southern Agriculture, and Economic Change." In *The New Deal and the South*, edited by Cobb and Namorato,

———. *Standing at the Crossroads: Southern Life in the Twentieth Century*. New York: Hill and Wang, 1986.

Davidson, Elizabeth H. *Child Labor Legislation in the Southern Textile States*. Chapel Hill: University of North Carolina Press, 1939.

Davis, Burke. *War Bird: The Life and Times of Elliot White Springs*. Chapel Hill: University of North Carolina Press, 1987.

Davis, Mike. *Prisoners of the American Dream: Politics and Economy in the History of the US Working Class*. London: Verso, 1986.

Davis, Natalie Z. *Fiction in the Archives: Pardon Tales and Their Tellers in Sixteenth-Century France*. Stanford, Calif.: Stanford University Press, 1987.

DeNatale, Douglas Paul. "Bynum: The Coming of Mill Village Life to a North Carolina County." Ph.D. diss., University of Pennsylvania, 1985.

Derber, Milton, and Edwin Young. *Labor and the New Deal*. Madison: University of Wisconsin Press, 1957.

Derieux, J. C. "Crawling toward the Promised Land." *Survey* 48 (April 29, 1922): 175–80.

Devlin, James E. *Erskine Caldwell*. Boston: Twayne, 1984.

Dodge, D. Witherspoon. *Southern Rebel in Reverse: The Autobiography of an Idol-Shaker*. New York: American Press, 1961.

Doyle, Judith Kaaz. "Out of Step: Maury Maverick and the Politics of the Depression and the New Deal." Ph.D. diss., University of Texas at Austin, 1989.

Dubbert, Joe L. "Progressivism and the Masculinity Crisis." In *The American Man*, edited by Elizabeth H. Pleck and Joseph H. Pleck, 303–20. Englewood Cliffs, N.J.: Prentice-Hall, 1980.

Dublin, Thomas. *Women at Work: The Transformation of Work and Community in Lowell, Massachusetts, 1826–1860*. New York: Columbia University Press, 1979.

Dubofsky, Melvyn. "Not So 'Turbulent Years': Another Look at the American 1930s." *Amerikastudien* 24 (1979): 5-20.

———. *The State and Labor in Modern America*. Chapel Hill: University of North Carolina Press, 1994.

Dubofsky, Melvyn, and Warren Van Tine. *John L. Lewis: A Biography*. New York: New York Times Book Co., 1977.

———, eds. *Labor Leaders in America*. Urbana: University of Illinois Press, 1987.

Dudley, Marion. "Workmen's Compensation Legislation for South Carolina." M.A. thesis, University of South Carolina, 1932.

Duffy, John Joseph. "Charleston Politics in the Progressive Era." Ph.D. diss., University of South Carolina, 1963.

Dunn, Robert W., and Jack Hardy. *Labor and Textiles: A Study of Cotton and Wool Manufacturing*. New York: International Publishers, 1931.

DuPlessis, Jim. "Massacre in Honea Path." *Southern Exposure* 17 (Fall 1989): 60-63.

Edgar, Walter B. *South Carolina in the Modern Age*. Columbia: University of South Carolina Press, 1992.

———, ed. *Biographical Directory of the South Carolina House of Representatives*. Columbia: University of South Carolina Press, 1974.

———. *South Carolina: The WPA Guide to the Palmetto State*. Columbia: University of South Carolina Press, 1988.

Edmonds, Richard Woods. *Cotton Mill Labor Conditions in the South and New England*. Baltimore: Manufacturers' Record Publishing Co., 1925.

Edwards, Laura F. "Sexual Violence, Gender, Reconstruction, and the Extension of Patriarchy in Granville County, North Carolina." *North Carolina Historical Review* 68 (July 1991): 237-60.

Edwards, Richard. *Contested Terrain: The Transformation of the Workplace in the Twentieth Century*. New York: Basic Books, 1979.

Egerton, John. *Speak Now Against the Day: The Generation Before the Civil Rights Movement in the South*. Chapel Hill: University of North Carolina Press, 1994.

Ellenberg, Henry Cooper. "The Congress of Industrial Organizations in South Carolina, 1938-1945." M.A. thesis, University of South Carolina, 1951.

Eller, Ronald D. *Miners, Millhands, and Mountaineers: Industrialization of the Appalachian South, 1880–1930*. Knoxville: University of Tennessee Press, 1982.

Faggart, Luther B. "Johnston versus Hollings: The 1962 Democratic Primary for the U.S. Senate in South Carolina." Seminar paper, University of South Carolina, 1992.

Farley, James. *Jim Farley's Story: The Roosevelt Years*. New York: Whittlesey House, 1948.

Farmer, James O. "The End of the White Primary in South Carolina: A Southern State's Fight to Keep Its Politics Whites." M.A. thesis, University of South Carolina, 1969.

Federal Writers' Project (FWP). *These Are Our Lives: As Told by the People and Written by Members of the Federal Writers' Project of the Works Progress Administration in North Carolina, Tennessee, and Georgia*. Chapel Hill: University of North Carolina Press, 1939.

Fields, Barbara J. "Ideology and Race in American History." In *Region, Race, and Reconstruction*, edited by Kousser and McPherson, 143-77.

Fine, Sidney. *Sit-Down: The General Motors Strike of 1936-37*. Ann Arbor: University of Michigan Press, 1969.

Fink, Gary M. "Efficiency and Control: Labor Espionage in Southern Textiles." In *Organized Labor in the Twentieth-Century South*, edited by Zieger, 13-34.

————. *The Fulton Bag and Cotton Mills Strike of 1914–1915: Espionage, Labor Conflict, and New South Industrial Relations*. Ithaca, N.Y.: ILR Press, 1993.

Fink, Gary M., and Merle E. Reed, eds. *Essays in Southern Labor History: Selected Papers, Southern Labor History Conference, 1976*. Westport, Conn.: Greenwood Press, 1977.

————. *Race, Class, and Community in Southern Labor History*. Tuscaloosa: University of Alabama Press, 1994.

Fink, Leon. "Labor, Liberty, and the Law: Trade Unionism and the Problem of the American Constitutional Order." *Journal of American History* 74 (December 1987): 904–25.

————. "The New Labor History and the Powers of Historical Pessimism: Consensus, Hegemony, and the Case of the Knights of Labor." *Journal of American History* 75 (June 1988): 115–36.

————. *Workingmen's Democracy: The Knights of Labor and American Politics*. Urbana: University of Illinois Press, 1983.

Finnegan, Terence R. " 'At the Hands of Parties Unknown': Lynching in Mississippi and South Carolina, 1881–1940." Ph.D. diss., University of Illinois, 1993.

Fite, Gilbert C. *Cotton Fields No More: Southern Agriculture, 1865–1980*. Lexington: University Press of Kentucky, 1984.

Flamming, Douglas. *Creating the Modern South: Millhands and Managers in Dalton, Georgia, 1884–1984*. Chapel Hill: University of North Carolina Press, 1992.

————. "Daughters, Dollars, and Domesticity: Family Wages and Female Autonomy in American Textiles, Evidence from the Federal Survey of 1908." Humanities Working Paper 153, California Institute of Technology, Spring 1992.

————. "The Paradox of Community: Unity and Division among the Millhands of Dalton, Georgia, 1885–1940." Paper presented at the Southern Sociology Society annual meeting, Nashville, Tenn., March 17, 1988.

Fleming, Walter Lynwood. *The Sequel to Appomattox: A Chronicle of Reunion of the States*. New Haven: Yale University Press, 1921.

Flynt, J. Wayne. *Dixie's Forgotten People: The South's Poor Whites*. Bloomington: Indiana University Press, 1979.

————. *Poor but Proud: Alabama's Poor Whites*. Tuscaloosa: University of Alabama Press, 1989.

Foner, Eric. "The Meaning of Freedom in the Age of Emancipation." *Journal of American History* 81 (September 1994): 435–60.

————. *Politics and Ideology in the Age of the Civil War*. New York: Oxford University Press, 1980.

————. *Reconstruction: America's Unfinished Revolution, 1863–1877*. New York: Harper and Row, 1988.

————. "Reconstruction Revisited." *Reviews in American History* 10 (December 1982): 82–100.

————. "Why Is There No Socialism in the United States?" *History Workshop* 17 (Spring 1984): 57–80.

Ford, Ella. "We Are Mill People." In *Writing Red: An Anthology of American Women Writers, 1930–1940*, edited by Charlotte Nekola and Paula Rabinowitz, 264–69. New York: Feminist Press, 1987).

Ford, Lacy K., Jr. "The Affable Journalist as Social Critic: Ben Robertson and the Early Twentieth-Century South." *Southern Cultures* 2 (December 1996): 353–73.

————. *Origins of Southern Radicalism: The South Carolina Upcountry, 1800–1860*. New York: Oxford University Press, 1988.

———. "Rednecks and Merchants: Economic Development and Social Tensions in the South Carolina Upcountry, 1865-1900." *Journal of American History* 71 (September 1984): 294-318.

———. "Yeoman Farmers in the South Carolina Upcountry: Changing Production Patterns in the Late Antebellum Era." *Agricultural History* 60 (Fall 1986): 17-37.

Fox-Genovese, Elizabeth, and Eugene D. Genovese. "The Political Crisis of Social History: A Marxian Perspective." *Journal of Social History* 10 (Winter 1976): 205-20.

Frankel, Linda Jean. "Women, Paternalism, and Protest in a Southern Textile Community, 1900-1960." Ph.D. diss., Harvard University, 1986.

Fraser, Steve. "Dress Rehearsal for a New Deal." In *Working-Class America*, edited by Frisch and Walkowitz, 212-55.

———. " 'Labor Question.' " In *The Rise and Fall of the New Deal Order, 1930-1980*, edited by Fraser and Gerstle, 55-84.

———. *Labor Will Rule: Sidney Hillman and the Rise of American Labor*. New York: Free Press, 1991.

Fraser, Walter J., Jr., and Winfred B. Moore Jr., eds. *From Old South to the New: Essays on the Transitional South*. Westport, Conn.: Greenwood Press, 1981.

Frederickson, George M. *The Black Image in the White Mind: The Debate on Afro-American Character and Destiny, 1817-1914*. New York: Harper and Row, 1971.

Frederickson, Kari. " 'The Slowest State' and 'Most Backward Community': Federal Civil Rights Legislation, 1946-1948." *South Carolina Historical Magazine* 98 (April 1997): 177-202.

Frederickson, Mary E. "Four Decades of Change: Black Workers in Southern Textiles, 1941-1981." *Radical America* 16 (November-December 1982): 27-44.

———. "Heroines and Girl Strikers: Gender Issues and Organized Labor in the Twentieth-Century American South." In *Organized Labor in the Twentieth-Century South*, edited by Zieger, 84-112.

———. "A Place to Speak Our Minds: The Summer School for Women Workers." Ph.D. diss., University of North Carolina, Chapel Hill, 1981.

Freidel, Frank. *F.D.R.: Launching the New Deal*. Boston: Little, Brown, 1973.

———. *FDR and the South*. Baton Rouge: Louisiana University Press, 1965.

Friedlander, Peter. *The Emergence of a UAW Local, 1936-1939: A Study in Class and Culture*. Pittsburgh: University of Pittsburgh Press, 1975.

Frisch, Michael, and Daniel J. Walkowitz, eds. *Working-Class America: Essays on Labor, Community, and American Society*. Urbana: University of Illinois Press, 1983.

Galambos, Louis. *Competition and Cooperation: The Emergence of a National Trade Association*. Baltimore: Johns Hopkins University Press, 1966.

Galenson, Alice. *The Migration of the Cotton Textile Industry from New England to the South, 1880-1930*. New York: Garland Publishing, 1985.

Galenson, Walter. *The CIO Challenge to the AFL: A History of the American Labor Movement, 1935-1941*. Cambridge: Harvard University Press, 1960.

The Gallup Poll: Public Opinion, 1935-1971. Vol. 1, *1935-1948*. New York: Random House, 1972.

Gantt, T. Fulton. *Breaking the Chains: A Story of the Present Industrial Struggle*. In *The Knights in Fiction: Two Labor Novels of the 1880s*, edited by Mary C. Grimes. Urbana: University of Illinois Press, 1986.

Garris, Susan Page. "The Decline of Lynching in South Carolina, 1915-1947." M.A. thesis, University of South Carolina, 1973.

Garrison, Joseph Yates. "Paul Revere Christopher: Southern Labor Leader, 1910–1974." Ph.D. diss., Georgia State University, 1976.

Gaston, Paul M. *The New South Creed: A Study in Southern Mythmaking*. New York: Knopf, 1970.

Geary, Dick. *European Labour Protest, 1848–1939*. New York: St. Martin's Press, 1981.

Genovese, Eugene D. *Roll, Jordon, Roll: The World the Slaves Made*. New York: Vintage, 1974.

———. "Yeoman Farmers in a Slaveholders' Democracy." In *Fruits of Merchant Capital: Slavery and Bourgeois Property in the Rise and Expansion of Capitalism*, edited by Eugene Genovese and Elizabeth-Fox Genovese, 249–64. New York: Oxford University Press, 1983.

Gerstle, Gary. "The Politics of Patriotism: Americanization and the Formation of the CIO." *Dissent* 33 (Winter 1986): 84–92.

———. *Working-Class Americanism: The Politics of Labor in a Textile City, 1914–1960*. New York: Cambridge University Press, 1989.

———. "Working-Class Racism: Broaden the Focus." *International Labor and Working-Class History* 44 (Fall 1993): 33–40.

Gilman, Glenn. *Human Relations in the Industrial Southeast: A Study of the Textile Industry*. Chapel Hill: University of North Carolina Press, 1956.

Gilmore, Glenda Elizabeth. *Gender and Jim Crow: Women and the Politics of White Supremacy in North Carolina, 1896–1920*. Chapel Hill: University of North Carolina Press, 1996.

Goldberg, David J. *A Tale of Three Cities: Labor Organization and Protest in Patterson, Passaic, and Lawrence, 1916–1921*. New Brunswick, N.J.: Rutgers University Press, 1989.

Goldberger, Joseph, G. A. Wheeler, Edgar Sydenstricker, and Wilford I. King. *A Study of Endemic Pellagra in Some Cotton-Mill Villages of South Carolina*. Hygienic Laboratory Report, Bulletin 153. Washington, D.C., 1929.

Goldman, Eric. *Rendezvous with Destiny: A History of Modern American Reform*. New York: Knopf, 1952.

Goodman, James. *Stories of Scottsboro: The Rape Case That Shocked 1930's America and Revived the Struggle for Equality*. New York: Pantheon Books, 1994.

Goodwin, Doris Kearns. *No Ordinary Time: Franklin and Eleanor Roosevelt: The Home Front in World War II*. New York: Simon and Schuster, 1994.

Goodwyn, Lawrence. *The Populist Moment: A Short History of the Agrarian Revolt in America*. New York: Oxford University Press, 1978.

Gordon, Colin. *New Deals: Business, Labor, and Politics in America, 1920–1935*. New York: Cambridge University Press, 1994.

Gordon, David M., Richard Edwards, and Michael Reich. *Segmented Work, Divided Workers: The Historical Transformation of Labor in the United States*. New York: Cambridge University Press, 1982.

Graham, Cole Blease, Jr. "South Carolina Counties." In *Local Government in South Carolina*, edited by Tyer and Graham, 51–72.

Graham, Otis L., Jr. *An Encore for Reform: The Old Progressives and the New Deal*. New York: Oxford University Press, 1967.

———, ed. *The New Deal: The Critical Issues*. Boston: Little, Brown, 1971.

Graham, Otis L., Jr., and Meghan Robinson Wander, eds. *Franklin D. Roosevelt: His Life and Times: An Encyclopedic View*. Boston: G. K. Hall and Co., 1985.

Grantham, Dewey W. "The Contours of Southern Progressivism." *American Historical Association* 86 (December 1981): 1035–59.

———. "Regional Claims and National Purposes: The South and the New Deal." *Atlanta History* 38 (Fall 1994): 5–17.

———. *Southern Progressivism: The Reconciliation of Progress and Tradition.* Knoxville: University of Tennessee Press, 1983.

———. *The South in Modern America: A Region at Odds.* New York: HarperCollins, 1994.

Green, James R. *The World of the Worker: Labor in Twentieth-Century America.* New York: Hill and Wang, 1980.

Greene, Julia. " 'The Strike at the Ballot Box': The American Federation of Labor's Entrance into Electoral Politics, 1906–1909." *Labor History* 32 (Spring 1991): 165–92.

Greene, Melissa Fay. *The Temple Bombing.* Reading, Mass.: Addison-Wesley, 1996.

Griffin, Larry J., and Robert R. Korstad. "Class as Race and Gender: Making and Breaking a Labor Union in the Jim Crow South." *Social Science History* 19 (Winter 1995): 425–54.

Griffith, Barbara S. *The Crisis of American Labor: Operation Dixie and the Defeat of the CIO.* Philadelphia: Temple University Press, 1988.

Gross, James A. *The Making of the National Labor Relations Board: A Study in Economics, Politics, and the Law, 1933–1937.* Albany: State University of New York Press, 1974.

———. *The Reshaping of the National Labor Relations Board: National Labor Policy in Transition, 1937–1947.* Albany: State University of New York Press, 1981.

Grundy, Pamela. "From Il Trovatore to the Crazy Mountaineers: WBT-Charlotte and Changing Musical Culture in the Carolina Piedmont, 1922–1935." M.A. thesis, University of North Carolina, Chapel Hill, 1991.

Gutman, Herbert G. *Work, Culture, and Society in Industrializing America: Essays in American Working-Class and Social History.* New York: Vintage Books, 1977.

Hagood, Margaret Jarman. *Mothers of the South: Portraiture of the White Tenant Farm Woman.* Chapel Hill: University of North Carolina Press, 1939.

Hahn, Steven. *The Roots of Southern Populism: Yeoman Farmers and the Transformation of the Georgia Upcountry, 1850–1890.* New York: Oxford University Press, 1983.

Hahn, Steven, and Jonathan Prude, eds. *The Countryside in the Age of Capitalist Transformation: Essays in the Social History of Rural America.* Chapel Hill: University of North Carolina Press, 1985.

Hale, Grace Elizabeth. *Making Whiteness: The Culture of Segregation in the South, 1890–1940.* New York, forthcoming.

Hall, Jacquelyn Dowd. "Disorderly Women: Gender and Labor Militancy in the Appalachian South." *Journal of American History* 73 (September 1986): 354–82.

———. " 'The Mind That Burns in Each Body': Women, Rape, and Racial Violence." In *Powers of Desire: The Politics of Sexuality,* edited by Ann Snitow, Christine Stansell, and Sharon Thompson, 328–49. New York: Monthly Review Press, 1983.

———. "O. Delight Smith's Progressive Era: Labor, Feminism, and Reform in the Urban South—Atlanta, Georgia, 1907–1915." In *Visible Women,* edited by Hewitt and Lebsock, 166–98.

———. "Private Eyes, Public Women: Images of Class and Sex in the Urban South, Atlanta, 1913–1915." In *Work Engendered,* edited by Baron, 243–72.

———. *Revolt against Chivalry: Jessie Daniel Ames and the Women's Campaign against Lynching.* New York: Columbia University Press, 1979.

Hall, Jacquelyn Dowd, Robert Korstad, and James Leloudis. "Cotton Mill People: Work, Community and Protest in the Textile South, 1880–1940." *American Historical Review* 91 (April 1986): 245–86.

Hall, Jacquelyn Dowd, James Leloudis, Robert Korstad, Mary Murphy, Lu Ann Jones, and Christopher B. Daly. *Like a Family: The Making of a Southern Cotton Mill World.* Chapel Hill: University of North Carolina Press, 1987.

Hamby, Alonzo L. *The New Deal: Analysis and Interpretation.* New York: Longmans, 1981.

Hareven, Tamara K. *Family Time and Industrial Time: The Relationship between the Family and Work in a New England Industrial Community.* New York: Cambridge University Press, 1982.

Hareven, Tamara K., and Randolp Langenbach, eds. *Amoskeag: Life and Work in an American Factory City.* New York: Pantheon Books, 1978.

Harris, J. William. *Plain Folk and Gentry in a Slave Society: White Liberty and Black Slavery in Augusta's Hinterlands.* Middletown, Conn.: Wesleyan University Press, 1985.

Haskett, William. "Ideological Radicals: The American Federation of Labor and Federal Labor Policy in the Strikes of 1934." Ph.D. diss., University of California at Los Angeles, 1958.

Hawley, Ellis W. *The New Deal and the Problem of Monopoly: A Study in Economic Ambivalence.* Princeton, N.J.: Princeton University Press, 1966.

Haws, Robert, ed. *The Age of Segregation: Race Relations in the South, 1890–1945.* Jackson: University Press of Mississippi, 1978.

Hayes, Jack Irby, Jr. "South Carolina and the New Deal, 1932-1938." Ph.D. diss., University of South Carolina, 1972.

Heard, Alexander. *Southern Primaries and Elections, 1920–1949.* Tuscaloosa: University of Alabama Press, 1950.

———. *A Two-Party System?* Chapel Hill: University of North Carolina Press, 1952.

Heer, Clarence. *Income and Wages in the South.* Chapel Hill: University of North Carolina Press, 1930.

Herd, E. Don. *The South Carolina Upcountry: Historical and Biographical Sketches, 1540–1980.* Greenwood, S.C.: Attic Press, 1981.

Herring, Harriet. *Passing of the Mill Village: Revolution in a Southern Institution.* Chapel Hill: University of North Carolina Press, 1949.

———. *Welfare Work in Mill Villages: The Story of Extra-Mill Activities in North Carolina.* Chapel Hill: University of North Carolina Press, 1929.

Hewitt, Nancy A., and Suzanne Lebsock, eds. *Visible Women: New Essays on American Activism.* Urbana: University of Illinois Press, 1993.

Hill, Herbert. "Myth-Making as Labor History: Herbert Gutman and the United Mine Workers of America." *International Journal of Politics, Culture, and Society* 2 (Winter 1988): 132-200.

———. "The Problem of Race in American Labor History." *Reviews in American History* 24 (1996): 189-208.

Himmelberg, Robert. *The Origins of the National Recovery Administration: Business, Government, and the Trade Association Issue, 1921-1933.* New York: Fordham University Press, 1976.

Hobbs, Margaret. "Rethinking Antifeminism in the 1930s: Gender Crisis or Workplace Justice? A Response to Alice Kessler-Harris." *Gender and History* 5 (Spring 1993): 4-15.

Hodes, Martha. "The Sexualization of Reconstruction Politics: White Women and Black Men in the South after the Civil War." *Journal of the History of Sexuality* 3 (January 1993): 402-17.

Hodges, James A. "Challenge to the New South: The Great Textile Strike in Elizabethton, Tennessee, 1929." *Tennessee Historical Quarterly* 23 (December 1964): 343-57.

———. *The New Deal Labor Policy and the Southern Cotton Textile Industry, 1933-1941.* Knoxville: University of Tennessee Press, 1986.

Hoffman, Edwin D. "The Genesis of the Modern Movement for Civil Rights in South Carolina." In *The Negro in Depression and War: Prelude to Revolution, 1930–1945,* edited by Bernard Strensher, 193–214. Chicago: Quadrangle Books, 1969.

Hoffman, James L. "A Study of the United Textile Workers of America in a Cotton Mill in a Medium-Sized Southern Industrial City: Labor Revolt in Alabama, 1934." Ph.D. diss., University of Alabama, 1986.

Hofstadter, Richard. *The Age of Reform: From Bryan to F.D.R..* New York: Vintage, 1955.

———. *The American Political Tradition and the Men Who Made It.* New York: Vintage, 1974.

———. *Anti-Intellectualism in America.* New York: Knopf, 1963.

———. *The Paranoid Style in American Politics.* New York: Knopf, 1965.

Hollis, Daniel. "Cole L. Blease and the Senatorial Campaign of 1924." *Proceedings of the South Carolina Historical Association* (1978): 53–68.

———. " 'Cotton Ed' Smith—Showman or Statesman?" *South Carolina Historical Magazine* 71 (October 1970): 235–56.

Honey, Michael. *Southern Labor and Black Civil Rights: Organizing Memphis Workers.* Urbana: University of Illinois Press, 1993.

Hood, Robin. "A Bibliography on Southern Labor." *Social Forces* 13 (October 1943): 133–37.

Hopper, John Edward. "The Purge: Franklin D. Roosevelt and the 1938 Democratic Nominations." Ph.D. diss., University of Chicago, 1966.

Horowitz, Ruth L. *Political Ideologies of Organized Labor: The New Deal Era.* New Brunswick, N.J.: Transaction Books, 1978.

Huff, Archie Vernon, Jr. *Greenville: The History of the City and County in the South Carolina Piedmont.* Columbia: University of South Carolina Press, 1995.

Hunter, Tera. "Household Workers in the Making: Afro-American Women in Atlanta and the New South, 1861 to 1920." Ph.D. diss., Yale University, 1990.

Hurt, Rick. "New Deal Labor Policy and the Containment of Radical Union Activity." *Review of Radical Political Economy* 8 (1976): 32–43.

Huss, John E. *Senator for the South: A Biography of Olin D. Johnston.* Garden City, N.Y.: Doubleday, 1961.

Huthmacher, J. Joseph. *Senator Robert F. Wagner and the Rise of Urban Liberalism.* New York: Atheneum, 1968.

Hutton, Sybil V. Wilson. "Social Participation of Married Women in a South Carolina Mill Village." M.A. thesis, University of Kentucky, 1948.

Irons, Janet. "Testing the New Deal: The General Textile Strike of 1934." Ph.D. diss., Duke University, 1988.

———. "Textile Labor Protest during the 1930s: A Civil Rights Movement?" Paper presented at Southern Labor Studies Conference, 1997, in author's possession.

Irons, Peter H. *The New Deal Lawyers.* Princeton, N.J.: Princeton University Press, 1982.

Jacoby, Sanford M. *Employing Bureaucracy: Managers, Unions, and the Transformation of Work in American Industry, 1900–1945.* New York: Columbia University Press, 1985.

Janiewski, Dolores E. *Sisterhood Denied: Race, Gender, and Class in a New South Community.* Philadelphia: Temple University Press, 1985.

———. "Southern Honor, Southern Dishonor: Managerial Ideology and the Construction of Gender, Race, and Class Relations in Southern Industry." In *Work Engendered,* edited by Baron, 70–91.

Jarrell, Hampton M. *Wade Hampton and the Negro: The Road Not Taken.* Columbia: University of South Carolina Press, 1949.

Johnson, Elmer D. *South Carolina: A Documentary Profile of the Palmetto State*. Columbia: University of South Carolina Press, 1971.

Johnson, Gerald W. *South-Watching: Selected Essays*. Chapel Hill: University of North Carolina Press, 1983.

Johnson, Kirk Lee. "The Institutionalization of the South Carolina Senate." M.A. thesis, University of South Carolina, 1972.

Jones, Gareth Stedman. *Languages of Class: Studies in English Working History Class, 1832–1982*. Cambridge: Cambridge University Press, 1983.

Jones, Lewis P. *South Carolina: A Synoptic History for Laymen*. Columbia: Sandlapper Press, 1971.

Jordan, Frank E. *The Primary State: A History of the Democratic Party in South Carolina, 1876–1962*. Columbia: Democratic Party of South Carolina, n.d.

Joyce, Patrick. *Work, Society, and Politics: The Culture of the Factory in Later Victorian England*. New Brunswick, N.J.: Rutgers University Press, 1980.

Judt, Tony. "The Clown in Regal Purple: Social History and Historians." *History Workshop* 7 (Spring 1979): 66–94.

Kazin, Michael J. *Barons of Labor: The San Francisco Building Trades and Union Power in the Progressive Era*. Urbana: University of Illinois Press, 1987.

———. *The Populist Persuasion: An American History*. New York: Basic Books, 1995.

———. "Struggling with Class Struggle: Marxism and the Search for a Synthesis in United States Labor History." *Labor History* 28 (Fall 1987): 497–514.

Kelley, Robin D. G. *Hammer and Hoe: Alabama Communists during the Great Depression*. Chapel Hill: University of North Carolina Press, 1990.

———. *Race Rebels: Culture, Politics, and the Black Working-Class*. New York: Free Press, 1994.

———. " 'We Are Not What We Seem': Rethinking Black Working-Class Opposition in the Jim Crow South." *Journal of American History* 80 (June 1993): 75–112.

Kelly, Richard. *Nine Lives for Labor*. New York: Praeger, 1956.

Kennedy, John W. "The General Strike in the Textile Industry, September 1934." M.A. thesis, Duke University, 1947.

———. "A History of the Textile Workers' Union of America, CIO." Ph.D. diss., University of North Carolina, Chapel Hill, 1950.

Kent, Bernice. *The Hemingway Women*. New York: Norton, 1983.

Kessler-Harris, Alice. "Gender Ideology in Historical Reconstruction: A Case Study from the 1930s." *Gender and History* 1 (Spring 1989): 31–49.

———. *Out to Work: A History of Wage-Earning Women in the United States*. New York: Oxford University Press, 1982.

Key, V. O. *Southern Politics in State and Nation*. New York: Knopf, 1949.

Kimmel, Michael. "The Contemporary 'Crisis' of Masculinity in Historical Perspective." In *The Making of Masculinities: The New Men's Studies*, edited by Harry Brod, 121–53. Boston: Allen and Unwin, 1987.

Kirby, Jack Temple. *Rural Worlds Lost: The American South, 1920–1960*. Baton Rouge: Louisiana State University Press, 1987.

Kirby, John B. *Black Americans in the Roosevelt Era: Liberalism and Race*. Knoxville: University of Tennessee Press, 1980.

Kirkendall, Richard S. "The New Deal and Agriculture." In *The New Deal: The National Level*, edited by Braeman, Bremner, and Brody, 83–109.

———. "The New Deal as Watershed: The Recent Literature." *Journal of American History* 54 (March 1968): 839–52.

Kohn, August. *The Cotton Mills of South Carolina*. Columbia: South Carolina Department of Agriculture, Commerce, and Immigration, 1907.

Korstad, Robert, and Nelson Lichtenstein. "Opportunities Found and Lost: Labor, Radicals, and the Early Civil Rights Movement." *Journal of American History* 75 (December 1988): 786–811.

Kousser, J. Morgan. *The Shaping of Southern Politics: Suffrage Restriction and the Establishment of the One-Party South, 1880–1910*. New Haven: Yale University Press, 1974.

Kousser, J. Morgan, and James M. McPherson, eds. *Region, Race, and Reconstruction: Essays in Honor of C. Vann Woodward*. New York: Oxford University Press, 1982.

Kuhn, Clifford M. "Two Small Windows of Opportunity: Black Politics in Georgia during the 1940s and the Pertinent Oral History Sources." Paper in author's possession, 1992.

Lahne, Herbert J. *The Cotton Mill Worker in the Twentieth Century*. New York: Farrar and Rinehart, 1944.

Lander, Ernest McPherson, Jr. *A History of South Carolina, 1865–1960*. Chapel Hill: University of North Carolina Press, 1960.

———. *South Carolina: An Illustrated History of the Palmetto State*. Northridge, Calif.: Windsor Publications, 1988.

———. *The Textile Industry in Antebellum South Carolina*. Baton Rouge: Louisiana State University Press, 1969.

Latham, Earl. "The Meaning of McCarthyism." In *Conflict and Consensus in Modern American History*, edited by Allen F. Davis and Harold D. Woodman, 369–80. Lexington, Mass.: D. C. Heath, 1988.

Lawson, Steven F. *Black Ballots: Voting Rights in the South, 1944–1969*. New York: Columbia University Press, 1976.

Lears, T. J. Jackson. "The Concept of Cultural Hegemony: Problems And Possibilities." *American Historical Review* 90 (June 1985): 567–93.

Leary, Marty. "'The Power of Public Opinion': The Commercial-Civic Elite and the Textile Question in Greensboro, North Carolina, 1870–1934." Honors thesis, University of North Carolina, Chapel Hill, 1987.

Leemhuis, Roger P. "Olin D. Johnston Runs for the Senate, 1938 to 1962." *Proceedings of the South Carolina Historical Association* (1986): 57–69.

Leiter, Jeffrey, Michael D. Schulman, and Rhonda Zingraff, eds. *Hanging by a Thread: Social Change in Southern Textiles*. Ithaca, N.Y.: ILR Press, 1991.

Lemann, Nicholas. *The Promised Land: The Great Migration and How It Changed America*. New York: Vintage Books, 1992.

Lemert, Ben F. *The Cotton Textile Industry of the Southern Appalachian Piedmont*. Chapel Hill: University of North Carolina Press, 1933.

Letwin, Daniel. "Interracial Unionism, Gender, and 'Social Equality' in the Alabama Coalfields, 1878–1908." *Journal of Southern History* 61 (August 1995): 519–54.

Leuchtenburg, William E. *The FDR Years: On Roosevelt and His Legacy*. New York: Columbia University Press, 1995.

———. *Franklin D. Roosevelt and the New Deal, 1932–1940*. New York: Harper and Row, 1963.

———. "Franklin D. Roosevelt's Supreme Court 'Packing' Plan." In *Essays on the New Deal*, edited by Harold M. Hollingsworth, 69–115. Austin: University of Texas Press, 1969.

———. "The New Deal and the Analogue of War." In *Change and Continuity in Twentieth-*

Century America, edited by John Breaman, Robert Bremner, and Everett Walters, 81-143. Columbus: Ohio State University Press, 1964.

———. *The Perils of Prosperity, 1914–1932*. Chicago: University of Chicago Press, 1958.

———. "The Pertinence of Political History: Reflections on the Significance of the State." *Journal of American History* 76 (December 1986): 585-600.

———. *The Supreme Court Reborn: The Constitutional Revolution in the Age of Roosevelt.* New York: Oxford University Press, 1995.

Levine, Rhonda F. *Class Struggle and the New Deal: Industrial Labor, Industrial Capital, and the State*. Lawrence: University Press of Kansas, 1988.

Lewis, Sinclair. *Cheap and Contented Labor: The Picture of a Southern Mill Town in 1929.* New York: United Features Syndicate, 1929.

Lichtenstein, Nelson. *Labor's War at Home: The CIO in World War II*. New York: Cambridge University Press, 1982.

Link, William A. *The Paradox of Southern Progressivism, 1880–1930*. Chapel Hill: University of North Carolina Press, 1992.

Lodge, David. *Nice Work*. London: Secker and Warburg, 1988.

Lofton, Paul S. "A Social and Economic History of Columbia, South Carolina, during the Great Depression, 1929-1940." Ph.D. diss., University of Texas, 1977.

"Lost Time and Labor Turnover among Women Workers in Cotton Mills in 1922." *Monthly Labor Review* 24 (February 1927): 287-89.

Lubove, Roy. "Workmen's Compensation and the Prerogatives of Voluntarism." *Labor History* 8 (Fall 1967): 245-277.

Lupold, John Samuel. "The Nature of South Carolina Progressives, 1914-1916." M.A. thesis, University of South Carolina, 1968.

McClure, Charles F., Jr. "The Public Career of John G. Richards." M.A. thesis, University of South Carolina, 1972.

McCravey, Edwin Parker. *Memories*. Easley, S.C.: Edwin Parker McCravey, 1941.

McCurry, Stephanie. *Masters of Small Worlds: Yeoman Households, Gender Relations, and the Political Culture of the Antebellum South Carolina Low Country*. New York: Oxford University Press, 1995.

———. "Piedmont Mill Workers and the Politics of History." *Labour/Le Travail* 29 (Spring 1992): 229-37.

———. "The Two Faces of Republicanism: Gender and Proslavery Politics in Antebellum South Carolina." *Journal of American History* 78 (March 1992): 1245-64.

MacDonald, Lois. *Southern Mill Hills: A Study of Social and Economic Forces in Certain Textile Mill Villages*. New York: Alexander L. Hillman, 1928.

McElvaine, Robert S. *Down and Out in the Great Depression: Letters from the "Forgotten Man."* Chapel Hill: University of North Carolina Press, 1983.

———. *The Great Depression: America, 1929–1941*. New York: New York Times Books, 1984.

McHugh, Cathy L. *Mill Family: The Labor System in the Southern Cotton Textile Industry, 1880–1915*. New York: Oxford University Press, 1988.

McIssac, A. M. "The Cotton Textile Industry." In *The Structure of American Industry*, edited by Walter Adams, 1-28. New York: Macmillan, 1954.

McLaurin, Melton A. "Early Labor Union Organizational Efforts in South Carolina Cotton Mills, 1880-1905." *South Carolina Historical Magazine* 72 (January 1971): 44-59.

———. *The Knights of Labor in the South*. Westport, Conn.: Greenwood Press, 1978.

———. *Paternalism and Protest: Southern Cotton Mill Workers and Organized Labor, 1875–1905*. Westport, Conn.: Greenwood Press, 1971.

MacLean, Nancy. *Behind the Mask of Chivalry: The Making of the Second Ku Klux Klan.* New York: Oxford University Press, 1994.

———. "The Leo Frank Case Reconsidered: Gender and Sexual Politics in the Making of Reactionary Populism." *Journal of American History* 78 (December 1991): 917–48.

Markowitz, Gerald, and David Rosner. *Slaves of the Depression: Workers' Letters about Life on the Job.* Ithaca, N.Y.: Cornell University Press, 1987.

Marshall, F. Ray. *Labor in the South.* Cambridge: Harvard University Press, 1967.

———. "Southern Unions: History and Prospects." In *Perspectives on the American South: An Annual Review of Society, Politics, and Culture*, vol. 3, edited by James Cobb and Charles Wilson, 163–78. New York: Gordon and Breach Science Publishers, 1983.

Martin, Charles H. "Southern Labor Relations in Transition: Gadsden, Alabama, 1930–1943." *Journal of Southern History* 47 (November 1981): 545–68.

Mason, Lucy Randolph. *To Win These Rights: A Personal Story of the CIO in the South.* New York: Harper, 1952.

Matthews, Donald R., and James W. Prothro. *Negroes and the New Southern Politics.* New York: Harcourt, Brace and World, 1966.

Mertz, Paul. *New Deal Policy and Southern Rural Poverty.* Baton Rouge: Louisiana State University Press, 1978.

Meyerowitz, Joanne J. *Women Adrift: Independent Wage Earners in Chicago, 1880–1930.* Chicago: University of Chicago Press, 1988.

Michie, Allan, and Frank Ryhlick. *Dixie Demagogues.* New York: Vanguard Press, 1939.

Miles, James Franklin. "Economic Survey of the South Carolina Textiles." M.A. thesis, University of South Carolina, 1939.

Milkman, Ruth. *Gender at Work: The Dynamics of Job Segregation by Sex during World War II.* Urbana: University of Illinois Press, 1987.

———. "Organizing the Sexual Division of Labor: Historical Perspectives on 'Women's Work' and the American Labor Movement." *Socialist Review* 49 (January–February 1980): 95–150.

———. "Women's Work and the Economic Crisis: Some Lessons from the Great Depression." *Review of Radical Political Economics* 8 (Spring 1976): 73–97.

Miller, Anthony B. "Coleman Livingston Blease: South Carolina Politician." M.A. thesis, University of North Carolina, Greensboro, 1971.

———. "Palmetto Politician: The Early Career of Olin D. Johnston, 1896–1945." Ph.D. diss., University of North Carolina, Chapel Hill, 1976.

Miller, Dan B. *Erskine Caldwell: The Journey from Tobacco Road.* New York: Knopf, 1994.

Miller, Marc, ed. *Working Lives: Southern Exposure History of Labor in the South.* New York: Pantheon Books, 1980.

Minchin, Timothy J. *What Do We Need a Union For?: The TWUA in the South, 1945–1955.* Chapel Hill: University of North Carolina Press, 1997.

Mitchell, Broadus. *Depression Decade: From New Era through New Deal, 1929–1941.* New York: Rinehart, 1947.

———. *The Rise of Cotton Mills in the South.* Baltimore: Johns Hopkins University Press, 1921.

———. *William Gregg: Factory Master of the Old South.* Chapel Hill: University of North Carolina Press, 1928.

Mitchell, George Sinclair. *Textile Unionism and the South.* Chapel Hill: University of North Carolina Press, 1931.

Mitchell, George Sinclair, and Broadus Mitchell. *The Industrial Revolution in the South.* Baltimore: Johns Hopkins University Press, 1930.

Mitchell, Sandra Corley. "Conservative Reform: South Carolina's Progressive Movement, 1915–1929." M.A. thesis, University of South Carolina, 1979.

Moley, Raymond. *After Seven Years*. New York: Harper and Brothers, 1939.

Montgomery, David. *The Fall of the House of Labor: The Workplace, the State, and American Labor Activism, 1865–1925*. Cambridge: Cambridge University Press, 1987.

———. "Labor and the Political Leadership of New Deal America." *International Review of Social History* 39 (December 1994): 335–60.

———. "Violence and the Struggle for Unions in the South, 1880–1930." In *Perspectives on the American South: An Annual Review of Society, Politics, and Culture*, vol. 1, edited by John Shelton Reed and Merle Black, 35–47. New York: Gordon and Breach Science Publishers, 1981.

———. *Workers' Control in America: Studies in the History of Work, Technology, and Labor Struggles*. New York: Cambridge University Press, 1979.

Moore, Barrington, Jr. *Injustice: The Social Bases of Obedience and Revolt*. White Plains, N.Y.: M. E. Sharpe, 1978.

Moore, John Hammond. *Columbia and Richland County: A South Carolina Community, 1740–1990*. Columbia: University of South Carolina Press, 1993.

———. *The South Carolina Highway Department, 1917–1987*. Columbia: University of South Carolina Press, 1987.

Moore, Winfred B., Jr. "New South Statesman: The Political Career of James Francis Byrnes, 1911–1941." Ph.D. diss., Duke University, 1976.

———. "The 'Unrewarding Stone': James F. Byrnes and the Burden of Race, 1908–1944." In *The South Is Another Land: Essays in the Twentieth-Century South*, edited by Bruce Clayton and John Salmond, 3–28. Westport, Conn.: Greenwood Press, 1987.

Moore, Winfred B., Jr., Joseph F. Tripp, and Lyon G. Tyler Jr., eds. *Developing Dixie: Modernization in a Traditional Society*. Westport, Conn.: Greenwood Press, 1988.

Morgan, Ted. *FDR: A Biography*. New York: Simon and Schuster, 1985.

Morgan, Thomas S. "James F. Byrnes and the Politics of Segregation." *The Historian* 56 (Summer 1994): 654–54.

Morland, John Kenneth. *Millways of Kent*. Chapel Hill: University of North Carolina Press, 1958.

Mullins, Jack Simpson. "Lynching in South Carolina, 1900–1914." M.A. thesis, University of South Carolina, 1961.

Murchison, Claudius T. *King Cotton Is Sick*. Chapel Hill: University of North Carolina Press, 1930.

Neather, Andrew. " 'Whiteness' and the Politics of Working-Class History." *Radical History Review* 61 (Winter 1995): 190–96.

Nelson, Bruce. "Give Us Roosevelt: Workers and the New Deal Coalition." *History Today* 40 (January 1990): 40–48.

Nelson, Daniel. *Managers And Workers: Origins of the New Factory System in the United States, 1880–1920*. Madison: University Wisconsin Press, 1975.

Newby, I. A. *Black Carolinians: A History of Blacks in South Carolina from 1865 to 1968*. Columbia: University of South Carolina, 1973.

———. *Jim Crow's Defense: Anti-Negro Thought in America, 1900–1930*. Baton Rouge: Louisiana State University Press, 1965.

———. *Plain Folk in the New South: Social Change and Cultural Persistence, 1880–1915*. Baton Rouge: Louisiana State University Press, 1989.

———. *The South: A History*. New York: Holt, Rinehart and Winston, 1978.

Newman, Dale. "Labor Struggles in the American South." *International Labor and Working-Class History* 14-15 (Spring 1979): 42-47.

———. "The Myth of the 'Contented' Southern Mill Worker." In *Perspectives on the American South: Annual Review of Society and Politics and Culture*, vol. 1, edited by John Shelton Reed and Merle Black, 187-204. New York: Gordon and Breach Science Publishers, 1981.

———. "Textile Workers in a Tobacco County: A Comparison between Yarn and Weave Mill Villages." In *The Common People of the South*, edited by Edward Magdol and Jon L. Wakelyn, 345-68. Westport, Conn.: Greenwood Press, 1980.

———. "Work and Community Life in a Southern Textile Town." *Labor History* 19 (Spring 1978): 204-25.

Nichols, Jeannette P. "Does the Mill Village Foster Any Social Types?" *Journal of Social Forces* 2 (March 1924): 350-57.

Norrell, Robert J. "Labor at the Ballot Box: Alabama Politics from the New Deal to the Dixiecrat Movement." *Journal of Southern History* 57 (May 1991): 201-34.

———. "Labor Trouble: George Wallace and Union Politics in Alabama." In *Organized Labor in the Twentieth-Century South*, edited by Zieger, 250-72.

Odum, Howard W. *Race and Rumors of Race: Challenge to American Crisis*. Chapel Hill: University of North Carolina Press, 1943.

Oestreicher, Richard. "Urban Working-Class Political Behavior and Theories of American Electoral Politics, 1870-1940." *Journal of American History* 74 (March 1988): 1257-86.

Osborne, Anne. *The South Carolina Story*. Orangeburg, S.C.: Sandlapper Publications, 1988.

Oshinsky, David M. *Worse Than Slavery: Parchman Farm and the Ordeal of Jim Crow Justice*. New York: Free Press, 1996.

Ownby, Ted. *Subduing Satan: Religion, Recreation, and Manhood in the Rural South, 1865-1920*. Chapel Hill: University of North Carolina Press, 1990.

Page, Dorothy Myra. *Southern Cotton Mills and Labor*. New York: Workers Library Publishers, 1929.

Parrish, Michael E. *Anxious Decades: America in Prosperity and Depression, 1920-1941*. New York: Norton, 1992.

Patterson, James T. *Congressional Conservatism and the New Deal: The Growth of the Conservative Coalition in Congress, 1933-1939*. Lexington: University of Kentucky Press, 1967.

———. "The Failure of Party Realignment in the South." *Journal of Politics* 27 (August 1965): 602-17.

———. *The New Deal and the States: Federalism In Transition*. Princeton, N.J.: Princeton University Press, 1969.

Peeler, David P. "Again, the Thirties." *American Quarterly* 46 (March 1994): 107-13.

———. *Hope Among Us Yet: Social Criticism and Social Solace in Depression America*. Athens: University of Georgia Press, 1987.

Peiss, Kathy L. *Cheap Amusements: Working Women and Leisure in Turn-of-the Century New York*. Philadelphia: Temple University Press, 1986.

Perkins, Frances. *The Roosevelt I Knew*. New York: Viking Press, 1946.

Pettus, Louise. "Elliot White Springs: Master of the Mills and Many Other Things." *Proceedings of the University of South Caroliniana Society* (1988): 3-11.

———. *The Palmetto State: Stories from the Making of South Carolina*. Winston-Salem, N.C.: Sandlapper Publications, 1991.

Pike, James S. *The Prostrate State*. New York: D. Appleton, 1874.

Polenberg, Richard. *Reorganizing Roosevelt's Government: The Controversy over Executive Reorganization, 1936–1939*. Cambridge: Harvard University Press, 1966.

Pope, Liston. *Millhands and Preachers: A Study of Gastonia*. New Haven: Yale University Press, 1942.

———. "Mill Village Churches." *Social Forces* 11 (September 1941): 1–37.

Porter, Davie L. " 'Purge' of 1938." In *Franklin D. Roosevelt*, edited by Graham and Wander, 338–39.

Potwin, Marjorie A. *Cotton Mill People of the Piedmont: A Study in Social Change*. New York: Columbia University Press, 1927.

Preston, Howard. *Dirt Roads to Dixie: Accessibility and Modernization in the South, 1885–1935*. Knoxville: University of Tennessee Press, 1991.

Prior, John P. "From Community to National Unionism: North Carolina Textile Labor Organizations, July 1932–September 1934." M.A. thesis, University of North Carolina, Chapel Hill, 1972.

Rabinowitz, Howard N. "More Than the Woodward Thesis: Assessing *The Strange Career of Jim Crow*." *Journal of American History* 75 (December 1988): 842–56.

Raper, Arthur F. *The Tragedy of Lynching*. Chapel Hill: University of North Carolina Press, 1933.

Rauch, Basil. *The History of the New Deal, 1933–1938*. New York: Creative Age Press, 1944.

Regensburger, William Edward. "Ground into Our Blood: The Origins of Working-Class Consciousness and Organization in Durably Unionized Southern Industries, 1930–1946." Ph.D. diss., University of California at Los Angeles, 1987.

Reed, Merl E. *Seedtime for the Modern Civil Rights Movement: The President's Committee of Fair Employment Practice, 1941–1946*. Baton Rouge: Louisiana State University Press, 1991.

Reid, Donald. "Industrial Paternalism: Discourse and Practice in Nineteenth-Century French Mining and Metallurgy." *Comparative Studies in Society and History* 27 (October 1985): 579–607.

Reynolds, Emily Bellinger, and Joan Reynolds Faust, eds. *Biographical Dictionary of the Senate of the State of South Carolina, 1776–1964*. Columbia: Archives Department, 1964.

Rhyne, Jennings J. *Some Southern Cotton Mill Workers and Their Villages*. Chapel Hill: University of North Carolina Press, 1930.

Rice, John Andrew. *I Came Out of the Eighteenth Century*. New York: Harper, 1942.

Richards, Miles S. "Osceola E. McKaine and the Struggle for Black Civil Rights, 1917–1946." Ph.D. diss., University of South Carolina, 1994.

Richards, Paul David. "The History of the Textile Workers Union of America, CIO, in the South, 1937 to 1945." Ph.D. diss., University of Wisconsin-Madison, 1978.

Robertson, Ben. *Red Hills and Cotton: An Upcountry Memory*. New York: Knopf, 1942.

Robertson, David. *Sly and Able: A Political Biography of James F. Byrnes*. New York: Norton, 1994.

Robinson, John L., ed. *Living Hard: Southern Americans in the Great Depression*. Washington, D.C.: University Press of America, 1981.

Rodgers, Daniel T. *Contested Truths: Keywords in American Politics since Independence*. New York: Basic Books, 1987.

———. *The Work Ethic in Industrial America, 1850–1920*. Chicago: University of Chicago Press, 1978.

Roediger, David R. *The Wages of Whiteness: Race and the Making of the American Working Class*. London: Verso, 1991.

Rosen, Elliot. *Hoover, Roosevelt, and the Brains Trust: From Depression to New Deal.* New York: Columbia University Press, 1977.

Rosenstone, Robert. *Visions of the Past: The Challenge of Film to Our Idea of History.* Cambridge: Harvard University Press, 1995.

Rosenzweig, Roy. *"Eight Hours for What We Will": Workers and Leisure in an Industrial City, 1870–1920.* New York: Cambridge University Press, 1983.

Rosner, David, and Gerald Markowitz, eds. *Dying for Work: Workers' Safety and Health in Twentieth-Century America.* Bloomington: Indiana University Press, 1987.

Salmond, John A. *Gastonia 1929: The Story of the Loray Mill Strike.* Chapel Hill: University of North Carolina Press, 1995.

———. *Miss Lucy of the CIO: The Life and Times of Lucy Randolph Mason, 1882–1959.* Athens: University of Georgia Press, 1988.

Sancton, Thomas. "Trouble in Dixie: The Returning Tragic Era." *New Republic,* January 4, 1943, 11–14.

Schaper, William. *Sectionalism and Representation in South Carolina.* 1901. Reprint, New York: Da Capo Press, 1968.

Scharf, Lois. *To Work and Wed: Female Employment, Feminism, and the Great Depression.* Westport, Conn.: Greenwood Press, 1980.

Schatz, Ronald. *The Electrical Workers: A History of Labor at General Electric and Westinghouse, 1923–1960.* Urbana: University of Illinois Press, 1983.

Schlesinger, Arthur M., Jr. *The Coming of the New Deal.* Vol. 2 of *The Age of Roosevelt.* Boston: Houghton Mifflin, 1959.

———. *The Crisis of the Old Order, 1919–1933.* Vol. 1 of *The Age of Roosevelt.* Boston: Houghton Mifflin, 1957.

———. *The Politics of Upheaval.* Vol. 3 of *The Age of Roosevelt.* Boston: Houghton Mifflin, 1960.

Schulman, Bruce J. *From Cotton Belt to Sunbelt: Federal Policy, Economic Development, and the Transformation of the South, 1938–1980.* New York: Oxford University Press, 1991.

Schwenning, G. T. "Prospects of Southern Textile Unionism." *Journal of Political Economy* 39 (December 1931): 783–810.

Scott, Anne Firor. "Women in the South: History as Fiction, Fiction as History." In *Rewriting the South: History and Fiction,* edited by Lothar Hönnighausen and Valeria Gennaro Lerda, 22–34. Tübingen, Germany: A. Francke Verlag, 1993.

Scott, James. *Domination and the Arts of Resistance: Hidden Transcripts.* New Haven: Yale University Press, 1990.

———. *Weapons of the Weak: Everyday Forms of Peasant Resistance.* New Haven: Yale University Press. 1985.

Scott, Joan W. "Gender: A Useful Category of Historical Analysis." *American Historical Review* 91 (December 1986): 1053–75.

———. "On Language, Gender, and Working-Class History." *International Labor and Working-Class History* 31 (Spring 1987): 1–13.

Selby, John G. " 'Better to Starve in the Shade Than in the Factory': Labor Protest in High Point, North Carolina, in the Early 1930s." *North Carolina Historical Review* 65 (January 1987): 43–64.

Sewell, William H. *Work and Revolution in France: The Language of Labor from the Old Regime to 1848.* Cambridge: Cambridge University Press, 1980.

Shannon, Jasper Berry. "Presidential Politics in the South, 1938, Part II." *Journal of Politics* 2 (1939): 278–300.

———. *Toward a New Politics in the South.* Knoxville: University of Tennessee Press, 1949.

Shapiro, Herbert. *White Violence and Black Response: From Reconstruction to Montgomery*. Amherst: University of Massachusetts Press, 1988.

Shapiro, Stephen L. "The Growth of the Cotton Textile Industry in South Carolina, 1919-1930." Ph.D. diss., University of South Carolina, 1971.

Shoffer, E. T. H. "The New South: A Textile Development." *Atlantic Monthly*, October 1922, 562-68.

Simkins, Francis Butler. *Pitchfork Ben Tillman: South Carolinian*. Baton Rouge: Louisiana State University Press, 1944.

———. *The Tillman Movement in South Carolina*. Durham, N.C.: Duke University Press, 1926.

Simkins, Francis Butler, and Robert H. Woody, *South Carolina during Reconstruction*. Chapel Hill: University of North Carolina Press, 1932.

Simon, Bryant. "The Appeal of Cole Blease of South Carolina: Race, Class, and Sex in the New South." *Journal of Southern History* 62 (February 1996): 57-86.

———. "The Devaluation of the Vote: Legislative Apportionment and Inequality in South Carolina, 1890-1962." *South Carolina Historical Magazine* 97 (July 1996): 226-45.

———. " 'I Believed in the Strongest Kind of Religion': James Evans and Working-Class Protest in the New South." *Labor's Heritage* 4 (Fall 1992): 60-77.

———. "The Novel as Social History: Erskine Caldwell's *God's Little Acre* and Industrial Relations in the New South." *Southern Cultures* 2 (December 1996): 375-92.

———. "Textile Strike of 1934." In *Labor Conflict in the United States: An Encyclopedia*, edited by Ronald L. Filippelli, 528-32. New York: Garland Publishing, Inc., 1990.

———. "When Votes Don't Add Up: Labor Politics and South Carolina's Workman's Compensation Acts, 1934-1938." *Proceedings of the South Carolina Historical Association* (1991): 69-74.

Simpson, William Hays. *Life in Mill Communities*. Clinton, S.C.: Presbyterian College, 1943.

———. *Workman's Compensation in South Carolina*. Durham, N.C.: N.p., 1949.

Sitkoff, Harvard. *A New Deal for Blacks: The Emergence of Civil Rights as a National Issue*. New York: Oxford University Press, 1978.

———. "Racial Militancy and Interracial Violence in the Second World War." *Journal of American History* 58 (December 1971): 661-81.

———. *The Struggle for Black Equality, 1954-1980*. New York: Hill and Wang, 1981.

Skelton, Billy Ray. "Industrialization and Unionization in North Carolina and South Carolina: An Economic Comparison." Ph.D. diss., Duke University, 1964.

Skocpol, Theda. "Political Responses to Capitalist Crisis: Neo-Marxist Theories of the State and the Case of the New Deal." *Politics and Society* 10 (1980): 155-201.

Sloan, Cliff, and Robert Hall. "It's Good to Be Home in Greenville . . . but It's Better if You Hate Unions." *Southern Exposure* 7 (Spring 1979): 83-93.

Smith, Robert Sidney. *Mill on the Dan: A History of the Dan River Mills, 1882-1950*. Durham, N.C.: Duke University Press, 1960.

Smith, Selden K. " 'Cotton Ed' Smith's Response to Economic Adversity." *Proceedings of the South Carolina Historical Association* (1971): 16-23.

———. "Ellison Durant Smith: A Southern Progressive, 1909-1929." Ph.D. diss., University of South Carolina, 1970.

Sosna, Martin. *In Search of the Silent South: Southern Liberals and the Race Issue*. New York: Columbia University Press, 1977.

"South Carolina Textile Industry Grows." *Southern Textile Bulletin*, February 12, 1920.

Spears, R. W. "The Attitude of the Southern Methodists of South Carolina in Regard to the Textile Industry in South Carolina." B.D. thesis, Duke University, 1936.

Stansell, Christine. *City of Women: Sex and Class in New York, 1789–1860*. New York: Knopf, 1986.

Stark, John. *Damned Upcountryman: William Watts Ball: A Study in American Conservatism.* Durham, N.C.: Duke University Press, 1968.

Stearns, Peter N. *Be a Man!: Males in Modern Society*. New York: Holmes and Meier, 1979.

Sternsher, Bernard. "Great Depression Labor Historiography in the 1970s: Middle-Range Questions, Ethnocultures, and Levels of Generalization." *Reviews in American History* 11 (1983): 300–319.

———. *Rexford Tugwell and the New Deal*. New Brunswick, N.J.: Rutgers University Press, 1964.

Stokes, Allen H., Jr. "Black and White Labor and the Development of the Southern Textile Industry, 1880–1920." Ph.D. diss., University of South Carolina, 1977.

Stone, Clarence. "Bleasism and the 1912 Election in South Carolina." *North Carolina Historical Review* (January 1963): 54–74.

Sugrue, Thomas J. "Crabgrass-Roots Politics: Race, Rights, and the Reaction against Liberalism in the Urban North, 1940–1964." *Journal of American History* 82 (September 1995): 551–86.

———. *The Origins of the Urban Crisis: Race and Inequality in Postwar Detroit*. Princeton, N.J.: Princeton University Press, 1996.

Sullivan, Patricia. *Days of Hope: Race and Democracy in the New Deal Era*. Chapel Hill: University of North Carolina Press, 1996.

Sussman, Leila A. *Dear FDR: A Study of Political Letter-Writing*. Totowa, N.J.: Bedminster Press, 1963.

Suttles, William L. "The Struggle for Control of Highways in South Carolina, 1908–1930." M.A. thesis, University of South Carolina, 1971.

Taft, Philip. *Organizing Dixie: Alabama Workers in the Industrial Era*. Revised and edited by Gary M. Fink. Westport, Conn.: Greenwood Press, 1981.

Tannenbaum, Frank. *Darker Phases of the South*. New York: Putnam, 1924.

Tate, Rodger D., Jr. "Easing the Burden: The Era of Depression and New Deal in Mississippi." Ph.D. diss., University of Tennessee, 1978.

Taylor, Antoinette Elizabeth. "South Carolina and the Enfranchisement of Women: The Early Years." *South Carolina Historical Magazine* 78 (April 1976): 115–26.

———. "South Carolina and the Enfranchisement of Women: The Later Years." *South Carolina Historical Magazine* 80 (October 1979): 298–310.

Tentler, Leslie Woodcock. *Wage-Earning Women: Industrial Work and Family Life in the United States, 1900–1930*. New York: Oxford University Press, 1979.

Terkel, Studs. *Hard Times: An Oral History of the Great Depression*. New York: Pantheon Books, 1970.

Terrill, Tom E. "Eager Hands: Labor for Southern Textiles, 1850–1860." *Journal of Economic History* 36 (March 1976): 84–101.

———. "Murder in Graniteville." In *Toward a New South?: Studies in Post–Civil War Southern Communities*, edited by Orville Vernon Burton and Robert McMath, 193–222. Westport, Conn.: Greenwood Press, 1982.

———. "No Union for Me: Southern Textile Workers and Organized Labor." In *The Meaning of South Carolina History*, edited by Chesnutt and Wilson, 202–13.

———. "Southern Mill Workers." *Reviews in American History* 16 (December 1988): 591–98.

Terrill, Tom E., and Jerrold Hirsch, eds. *Such as Us: Southern Voices of the Thirties*. Chapel
 Hill: University of North Carolina Press, 1978.
Thernstrom, Stephan. *Poverty and Progress: Social Mobility in a Nineteenth-Century City*.
 Cambridge: Harvard University Press, 1964.
Thompson, E. P. "Time, Work-Discipline, and Industrial Capitalism." *Past and Present* 38
 (December 1963): 56–97.
Thompson, Holland. *From Cotton Field to the Cotton Mill: A Study of the Industrial Transition
 in North Carolina*. New York: Macmillan, 1906.
Thompson, William Walker. "A Managerial History of a Cotton Textile Firm: Spartan
 Mills, 1888–1958." Ph.D. diss., University of Alabama, 1960.
Thornton, J. Mills, III. *Politics and Power in a Slave Society: Alabama, 1800–1860*. Baton
 Rouge: Louisiana State University Press, 1978.
Tindall, George Brown. "The Campaign for the Disfranchisement of Negroes in South
 Carolina." *Journal of Southern History* 15 (May 1949): 212–34.
———. *The Emergence of the New South, 1913–1945*. Baton Rouge: Louisiana State
 University Press, 1967.
———. *South Carolina Negroes, 1877–1900*. Columbia: University of South Carolina
 Press, 1952.
Tippett, Tom. *When Southern Labor Stirs*. New York: J. Cape and H. Smith, 1931.
Tomlins, Christopher L. *The State and the Unions: Labor Relations, Law, and the Organized
 Labor Movement in America, 1880–1960*. Cambridge: Cambridge University Press, 1985.
Triplette, Ralph R., Jr. "One-Industry Towns: Their Location, Development, and
 Economic Character." Ph.D. diss., University of North Carolina, Chapel Hill, 1974.
Tullos, Allen. *Habits of Industry: White Culture and the Transformation of the Carolina
 Piedmont*. Chapel Hill: University of North Carolina Press, 1989.
Turner, Patricia A. *I Heard It through the Grapevine: Rumor in African American Culture*.
 Berkeley: University of California Press, 1993.
Tuttle, William. "Labor Conflict and Racial Violence: The Black Worker in Chicago,
 1894–1919." *Labor History* 10 (Summer 1969): 408–32.
Tyer, Charlie B., and Cole Blease Graham Jr. *Local Government in South Carolina: The
 Governmental Landscape*. Vol. 1. Columbia: University of South Carolina, 1984.
U.S. Bureau of the Census. *Census of Manufacturers. Reports by States*, vol. 1. Washington,
 D.C.: Government Printing Office, 1918.
———. *Twelfth Census of the United States, 1900. Population: Part 1*, vol. 1. *Agriculture: Part
 1*, vol. 5. Washington, D.C.: Government Printing Office, 1902.
———. *Thirteenth Census of the United States, 1910. Population: Report by States*, vol. 3.
 Population, 1910: Occupational Statistics, vol. 4. *Agriculture, 1909 and 1910: Reports by
 States, with Statistics for Counties*, vol. 7. Washington, D.C.: Government Printing
 Office, 1913.
———. *Fourteenth Census of the United States, 1920. Population: Numbers and Distribution of
 Inhabitants*, vol. 1. *Population: General Report*, vol. 2. *Population: Composition and Charac-
 teristics of the Population*, vol. 3. *Agriculture: Report for States*, vol. 6. Washington, D.C.:
 Government Printing Office, 1922.
———. *Fifteenth Census of the United States, 1930. Unemployment*, vol. 1. *Manufacturers,
 1929*, vols. 2–3. *Population: Part 2*, vol. 4. *Occupations by State*. Washington, D.C.:
 Government Printing Office, 1932–33.
———. *Sixteenth Census of the United States, 1940. Population: Part 6*, vol. 2. Washington,
 D.C.: Government Printing Office, 1940.

———. *Occupations at the Twelfth Census: Special Reports*. Washington, D.C.: Government Printing Office, 1904.

———. *Report on Manufacturing Industries in the United States at the Eleventh Census, 1890: Part III: Selected Industries*. Washington, D.C.: Government Printing Office, 1895.

U.S. Department of Commerce. *Statistical Abstracts of the United States*. 112th ed. Washington, D.C.: Government Printing Office, 1992.

U.S. Department of Labor. Bureau of Labor Statistics. *Strikes in the United States, 1880–1936*. Washington, D.C.: Government Printing Office, 1958.

U.S. Senate. Committee on Manufacturers. *Working Conditions in the Textile Industry in North Carolina, South Carolina, and Tennessee*. Washington, D.C.: Government Printing Office, 1930.

Van den Berghe, Pierre L. *Race and Racism: A Comparative Perspective*. New York: Wiley, 1967.

Van Osdell, John Garrett, Jr. "Cotton Mills, Labor, and the Southern Mind, 1880–1930." Ph.D. diss., Tulane University, 1966.

Vietmeyer, Noel D. "Our 90-Year War with the Boll Weevil Isn't Over." *Smithsonian*, August 1982, 60–68.

Wallace, David Duncan. *History of Wofford College, 1854–1949*. Chapel Hill: University of North Carolina Press, 1951.

———. *South Carolina: A Short History, 1520–1948*. Columbia: University of South Carolina Press, 1951.

Wandersee, Winifred D. *Women's Work and Family Values, 1920–1940*. Cambridge: Cambridge University Press, 1981.

Ward, David C. "Industrial Workers in the Mid-Nineteenth-Century South: Family and Labor in the Graniteville, South Carolina, Textile Mill, 1845–1880." *Labor History* 28 (Summer 1987): 328–48.

Ware, Susan. *Holding Their Own: American Women in the 1930s*. Boston: Twayne, 1982.

Warr, Osta L. "Mr. Blease of South Carolina." *American Mercury* 16 (January 1929): 25–32.

Weaver, John C. "Lawyers, Lodgers, and Kinfolk: The Workings of a South Carolina Political Organization, 1920–1936." *South Carolina Historical Magazine* 78 (January 1977): 272–85.

Weinstein, James. "Big Business and the Origins of Workman's Compensation." *Labor History* 8 (Spring 1967): 156–74.

———. *The Corporate Ideal in the Liberal State, 1900–1918*. Boston: Beacon Press, 1968.

Weisberger, Bernard A. "The Dark and Bloody Ground of Reconstruction Historiography." *Journal of Southern History* 25 (1957): 427–47.

Wesser, Robert F. "Conflict And Compromise: The Workmen's Compensation Movement in New York, 1890s–1913." *Labor History* 12 (Summer 1971): 345–72.

West, Rebecca. "Opera In Greenville." *New Yorker*, June 14, 1947.

Whatley, Warren C. "African American Strikebreaking from the Civil War to the New Deal." *Social Science History* 17 (Winter 1993): 525–58.

Wheeler, Marjorie Spruill. *New Women of the New South: The Leaders of the Woman Suffrage Movement in the Southern States*. New York: Oxford University Press, 1993.

White, Luise. "Between Gluckman and Foucault: Historicizing Rumor and Gossip." *Social Dynamics* 20 (Winter 1994): 75–92.

Whites, Lee Ann. "The DeGraffenried Controversy: Race, Class, and Gender in the New South." *Journal of Southern History* 54 (August 1988): 449–78.

Wiley, Stephen R. "Songs of the Gastonia Textile Strike of 1929: Models of and for

Southern Working-Class Woman's Militancy." *North Carolina Folklore Journal* 30 (Fall–Winter 1982): 87–98.

Williams, Raymond. *Modern Tragedy*. Stanford, Calif.: Stanford University Press, 1966.

Williamson, Gustavus G., Jr. "South Carolina Cotton Mills and the Tillman Movement." *Proceedings of the South Carolina Historical Association* (1949): 36–49.

Williamson, Joel. *After Slavery: The Negro in South Carolina during Reconstruction, 1861–1877*. Chapel Hill: University of North Carolina Press, 1965.

———. *The Crucible of Race: Black-White Relations in the American South since Emancipation*. New York: Oxford University Press, 1984.

Willis, Susan. "A Mill Town in 1934." Honors thesis, University of South Carolina, 1985.

Wilson, Charles Reagan, and William Ferris, eds. *Encyclopedia of Southern Culture*. Chapel Hill: University of North Carolina Press, 1989.

Wood, Peter. *Black Majority: Negroes in Colonial South Carolina from 1670 through the Stono Rebellion*. New York: Knopf, 1974.

Wood, Phillip J. *Southern Capitalism: The Political Economy of North Carolina, 1880–1980*. Durham, N.C.: Duke University Press, 1986.

Wood, Robert. *To Live and Die in Dixie*. New York: Southern Workers Defense Committee, 1948.

Woodman, Harold D. "Sequel to Slavery: The New History Views Postbellum South." *Journal of Southern History* 43 (November 1977): 523–54.

Woodward, C. Vann. *Origins of the New South, 1877–1913*. Baton Rouge: Louisiana State University Press, 1951.

———. "*Strange Career* Critics: Long May They Persevere." *Journal of American History* 75 (December 1988): 857–68.

———. *The Strange Career of Jim Crow*. New York: Oxford University Press, 1955.

———. *Tom Watson: Agrarian Rebel*. New York: Macmillan, 1938.

Workman, W. O. *The Bishop from Barnwell: The Political Life and Times of Senator Edgar A. Brown*. Columbia, S.C.: R. L. Bryan Co., 1963.

Worster, Donald. *Dust Bowl: The Southern Plains in the 1930s*. New York: Oxford University Press, 1979.

Wright, Gavin. "Cheap Labor and South Textiles, 1880–1930." *Quarterly Journal of Economics* 96 (November 1981): 605–29.

———. *Old South, New South: Revolutions in the Southern Economy since the Civil War*. New York: Basic Books, 1986.

———. *The Political Economy of the Cotton South: Households, Markets, and Wealth in the Nineteenth Century*. New York: Norton, 1978.

Wyche, Billy H. "Southern Industrialists View Organized Labor in the New Deal Years, 1933–1941." *Southern Studies* 19 (Summer 1980): 157–81.

Young, Marjorie W., ed. *Textile Leaders of the South*. Anderson, S.C.: James R. Young, 1963.

Zahavi, Gerald. "Negotiated Loyalty: Welfare Capitalism and the Shoeworkers of Endicott Johnson, 1920–1940." *Journal of American History* 70 (December 1983): 602–20.

———. *Workers, Managers, and Welfare Capitalism: The Shoemakers and Tanners of Endicott Johnson, 1890–1940*. Urbana: University of Illinois Press, 1988.

Zangrando, Robert L. *The NAACP Crusade against Lynching, 1909–1950*. Philadelphia: Temple University Press, 1980.

Zieger, Robert H. *American Workers, American Unions, 1920–1985*. Baltimore: Johns Hopkins University Press, 1986.

————. *The CIO, 1935–1955.* Chapel Hill: University of North Carolina Press, 1995.

————, ed. *Organized Labor in the Twentieth-Century South.* Knoxville: University of Tennessee Press, 1991.

Zinn, Howard, ed. *New Deal Thought.* New York: Bobbs-Merrill, 1966.

Dabbs, James McBride, 229
Democratic National Convention: 1936, 195–96, 204–5, 228–29; 1944, 224, 228. *See also* Smith, Ellison: in 1938 election
Democratic Party, 17, 22, 122, 190, 194–95, 207, 211, 223, 224, 228, 241–42
Disfranchisement, 4, 5, 16, 69, 210–11, 222

Easley, S.C., 181
Economy campaign, 72–78, 135–36
Education, 45, 73, 75–76, 130, 135, 171, 237; compulsory school laws, 29–30; Blease on, 30
Eleanor Clubs, 219, 224, 225
Elections, 17–18, 26; 1908, 25; 1910, 17; 1912, 17; 1924, 38–39, 243; 1930, 38–40, 57–58, 129, 132–33, 143, 150, 243; 1932, 60, 77; 1934, 123–36, 213, 217, 244; 1936, national, 122, 189, 205, 211, 300 (n. 89); 1936, statewide campaigns, 180–83; 1938, governor's race, 212, 300 (n. 92); 1938, in South Carolina, 189–90, 203, 218, 220, 230, 244; in Georgia, 207–8; postwar period, 230–32
Elizabethton, Tenn., 50
Employers' liability, 140–42, 149

Fair Employment Practice Commission (FEPC), 223
Fair Labor Standards Act (FLSA), 189, 196–97, 201, 207, 209, 213, 215, 216
Farmers and Taxpayers League (FTL), 75–78, 135, 143. *See also* Economy campaign
Federal Bureau of Investigation (FBI), 219, 226, 227
Flying squadrons, 113–14, 116, 118, 119, 124, 127. *See also* General Textile Strike
Flynn, Aloysius, 215
Ford, Lacy, 21
Franklin Mills (Greer), 148
Fuller, Paul W., 93, 97–98

Gaffney, S.C., 12, 56, 95, 107–8, 170; General Textile Strike in, 114; 1935 strike in, 152, 153; CIO campaign in, 202

Gaffney Ledger, 12
Gastonia, N.C., 50, 54
Geer, Benjamin, 99
Gellhorn, Martha, 122, 152, 193, 278 (n. 58)
General Textile Strike, 109–22, 154, 155; women and, 113–14, 125; employer counteroffensive against, 119–20; relief and, 119–20; and 1934 election, 123–27, 129–30, 133–34; memories of, 124–25, 152–53, 214. *See also* Gorman, Francis
George, Walter F., 207
Gerstle, Gary, 83
GI Bill, 235
Gloverville, S.C., 97
Gluck Mills (Anderson), 164
Godfrey, H. C., 139, 146, 291 (n. 21)
Gonzales, W. E., 142
Goodwill associations. *See* Company unions
Googe, George, 79, 117
Gorman, Francis, 111, 113, 117, 120–21, 130, 152; background, 111; as leader of General Textile Strike, 111; assessment of strike, 121
Governor's office: power of, 68, 162, 165, 169; and highway fight, 184–85. *See also* Senators; South Carolina Constitution
Graniteville, S.C., 2, 4, 53, 94, 97, 109, 120, 134, 149. *See also* Horse Creek Valley, S.C.
Gray, Wil Lou, 143
Great Depression, 8, 71–72, 192, 201; in mill villages, 59–60, 61–63; and coping strategies, 60, 63–67, 201–2; in South Carolina, 61–63, 72; in country, 71–72, 192, 201; for skilled workers, 215
—analyses of, 64–65; workers', 64–66; rural people's, 74–75; Olin D. Johnston's, 200–201
Green, William, 84, 85, 215–16. *See also* American Federation of Labor
Greenville, S.C., 2, 15, 70–71, 87, 90, 93, 95, 107, 109, 132, 152, 170, 172, 173, 180, 183, 202, 216, 256 (n. 21); 1929 strikes in, 51, 62; Great Depression in, 62; NRA celebration in, 87; 1933–34 strikes in, 107; General Textile Strike in, 114–15, 118, 276 (n. 29); Franklin D.

Roosevelt's 1938 speech in, 208–9; African Americans organizing in, 222

Greenville Independent, 184

Greenville News, 184, 241

Greenville Trades and Labor Council, 55, 161

Greenwood, S.C., 54, 92, 93, 109, 152, 170, 210, 225; Great Depression in, 62; NRA celebration in, 87; support for Johnston in, 134

Greenwood Cotton Mill, 87

Greenwood Index-Journal, 217

Greer, S.C., 121, 148, 149, 181

Gregg, William, 97

Grendel Mill (Greenwood), 40

Griffith, D. W., 231

Hall, Jacquelyn Dowd, 32

Hall, Wilton, 185, 186, 210, 214

Hampton, Wade, 206, 230

Haskell, Alexander, 206

Herronvolk democracy, 17

Hicks, J. D., 158, 165, 187

Highway fight, 167–87, 206, 218; workers' perceptions of, 170–74, 177–78, 181–82; political implications of, 180, 211, 212, 213; impact on 1936 elections, 180–83. *See also* Johnston, Olin D.: and highway fight; Sawyer, Benjamin

Highway patrol, 99, 110, 118

Highway Reorganization Act (1936), 180–81, 184

Hillman, Sidney, 198

Hoerger, E. L., 177

Honea Path, S.C., 40, 57, 92, 129, 181–82; General Textile Strike in, 115–19, 124, 133, 276 (n. 31)

Hopkins, Harry, 152

Horse Creek Valley, S.C., 1–2, 53, 79, 92, 93, 94, 114, 143, 151, 185; traditions of militancy in, 96, 270–71 (n. 32); 1933 strike in, 96–101, 108, 165

Independence: notions of, 19, 20–26, 31, 43

Industrial Commission, 146–48, 149, 284 (n. 48). *See also* Workmen's Compensation Act

Industrial engineers, 45, 46–47, 52

Industrial structures, 44–45, 102–3, 238–39

Inman, S.C., 110, 158, 181; 1935 strike in, 152

Isaqueena Cotton Mill (Central), 52, 134

Iva Cotton Mill (Calhoun Falls), 148

Jasper County, S.C., 230; representation of, 70

Jeffries, Richard M., 131, 143, 228–29

Johnson, Hugh, 87–88, 93, 99, 109

Johnston, Olin D., 9–10, 137–39, 141, 143, 151, 190, 198, 235, 238, 239; support for labor, 9, 129, 151–52, 182, 200, 201–3, 215, 232–33, 261 (n. 86); and politics of race, 9, 205–6, 230–34; 1930 election, 57–58, 129, 132, 243; called a radical, 122–27, 129; 1934 election, 123–36, 153, 164, 244; conservative/business opposition to, 128, 130, 135, 206–7, 213–14; as campaigner, 128–29, 232; as New Dealer, 128–30, 200–201, 206–7; background of, 129, 130, 200, 205; and highway fight, 130–33, 167–74, 178–86; support for economy, 135–36, 281 (n. 55); and millworkers' expectations of, 136, 137–39, 147; and workers' compensation act, 144–50; during Clinton strike, 155–56; during Tucapau strike, 157–58; during Pelzer strike, 159–65; political implications of acts in Pelzer, 164–65; called a dictator, 169, 184; and "us" vs. "them," 173, 179, 233–34; 1938 election, 189–90, 203–18, 220, 244; economic philosophy, 200–201; postwar campaigns, 230–34, 303 (n. 46); opposition to Taft-Hartley Act, 233; funeral, 237

Jones, J. Roy, 144

Key, V. O., 6–7

Knights of Labor, 97

Ku Klux Klan (KKK), 7, 63, 114, 225, 227; as antiunion force, 114, 121, 152, 202–3

Labor legislation, 63–71, 139, 153; anti-stretchout, 64–65, 66–67, 71, 139; hours and wage, 65–66, 71, 201, 206; opposition to from low-country conservatives, 71, 139, 169, 171, 184–86. *See also* Fair

Labor Standards Act; Wagner Act; Workers' compensation

Greenville speech (1938), 208; move away from New Deal liberalism, 233–36. *See also* Whiteness: workers' commitment to

Moody, Peter R., 174–78, 186, 187, 291 (n. 29); "To a Cotton Mill Worker," 175–77

Moore, John Hammond, 13

Musgrove Mill (Gaffney), 107

Nast, Thomas, 80

Nates, John, 147, 301 (n. 98)

National Association for the Advancement of Colored People (NAACP), 52, 195, 221, 228; in South Carolina, 221–22

National Guard: called to stop lynching, 37–38; in strikes, 54–55, 99, 118–20, 124, 133–34, 151, 156, 157; in Pelzer, 160–64; in highway fight, 167–68, 178–80, 183, 213

National Industrial Recovery Act (NIRA), 84–85; section 7(a), 85, 93

National Labor Relations Board (NLRB), 155, 158

National Recovery Administration (NRA), 79, 85–89, 159, 186, 193, 206; enforcement of, 86–88; blue eagle symbol, 88, 91, 154; management's view of, 90–91, 94; workers' views of, 90–91, 94, 120, 186

National Union of Textile Workers, 97

Newberry, S.C., 3, 17, 110, 133, 137, 146, 170, 182

New Deal, 8, 75, 77–78, 79, 81–82, 84, 120–21, 125, 133–34, 136, 170, 174, 177, 187, 189–90, 192–93, 194, 196, 198, 206–7, 216, 222–23, 232, 235, 266 (n. 5); as threat to white supremacy, 199, 210–11, 217; losing steam after 1937, 207, 222–23, 234; as threat to law and order, 213–14. *See also* National Recovery Administration; New Deal Americanism; Roosevelt, Franklin D.; Textile code

New Deal Americanism, 83–89, 91, 95, 98, 99, 101, 116, 117, 121–22, 125, 129, 164; and gender, 114

New Liberalism, 222–23, 235, 239

New Republic, 229

Newsweek, 230

New York Times, 126, 158, 183, 194, 210, 228

Nichols, Jeanette, 3

Ninety-Six, S.C., 3, 224; Great Depression in, 62

North Augusta, S.C., 97

O'Neill, Eugene, 239

Pace, H. C., 142–43

Paternalism, 19, 159

Peele, John, 87, 112, 114–15

Pellagra, 59, 106, 152, 261 (n. 2)

Pelzer, S.C., 3, 23, 40, 51, 53, 79, 108, 140, 152, 173, 289 (n. 54); 1929 strike in, 51, 52–53; General Textile Strike in, 114, 159; 1935 strike in, 158–65

People, the: rhetoric of, 132–33

Perkins, Frances, 88, 111, 144, 155

Politics: defined, 5

Ponder, William Fred, 177, 186, 291 (n. 27)

Potwin, Marjorie, 67

Powell Knitting Mill (Spartanburg), 113

Progressive Democratic Party, 224, 229

Progressivism, 19, 34, 35, 73–74, 141

Prohibition, 24, 38; as political issue, 134–35

Prosperity, S.C., 59, 181

Race: conceptions of, 5–6, 7–8, 24, 138–39, 176–77; and trade unionism, 53–54, 216–17, 229; and politics, 83, 195–96, 205–6, 210–11, 217, 220–21, 227–36, 297–98 (n. 60); rumors, 219, 224, 225. *See also* Reconstruction: political meanings of; Whiteness: workers' commitment to

Racial violence, 26; in 1940s, 225–27. *See also* Lynching

Randolph, A. Philip, 223

Raper, Arthur, 3, 249 (n. 5)

Reconstruction, 15, 21–22, 29, 97, 238; "tragic era" view of, 4, 11, 80–82; political meanings of, 29, 124–25, 149, 187, 188–89, 192, 195, 204, 209, 210, 218, 227, 229

Reconstruction Finance Corporation, 63

Red Cross, 63, 156
Red Shirts, 218, 230
Relief: during 1929 strike, 54–55; during Great Depression, 63–64; during General Textile Strike, 119–20
Religion, 88–89, 94, 103–4, 216; and trade unionism, 97–98, 111–12, 117, 199; and Pelzer strike (1935), 163
Republican Party, 22, 207, 218
Richards, John G., 37, 54, 64, 151
Right to strike, 67, 83, 139, 151–66, 213
Road building, 69, 73, 130–33, 169–70, 211. See also Highway fight
Rock Hill, S.C., 43, 53, 145, 151, 152, 165, 256 (n. 21); General Textile Strike in, 114
Roosevelt, Eleanor, 95, 224–25, 227
Roosevelt, Franklin D., 84–85, 87, 128, 129, 132, 138, 152, 180, 193, 196, 198, 200–201, 203, 206, 211, 213, 222, 234; and 1932 election, 60, 77; workers' expectations of, 79–80, 82–83, 88–89, 93, 97–99, 108, 112–13, 121–22, 208; personification of New Deal, 82; fireside chats, 82, 207; letters to, 91, 96, 109; General Textile Strike performance, 111, 119, 120–22; plan for Supreme Court, 122, 186, 196, 200, 207, 213; and 1936 election, 122, 189; and 1938 "purge" campaigns, 207–10
Roosevelt recession, 202, 215
Rural economy, 21–23, 41, 49–50, 72, 165, 192, 193, 239
Rural people, 197, 201, 214–15, 264 (n. 51); perceptions of mill world, 41, 49, 105, 106–7, 173–74, 273 (nn. 59, 63); in mills, 49, 95, 115, 119, 162, 164; as strikebreakers, 49, 98, 101, 107, 108, 118, 239, 260 (n. 78), 272 (n. 58), 273 (n. 61); as important voting group, 71–72; electoral behavior, 76–77, 136–37, 214–15, 218, 301 (n. 97); importance of cars to, 135–36; Smith's appeal to, 192–93, 214–15; and Agricultural Adjustment Act, 193

Santee, S.C., 40
Sawyer, Benjamin, 130–33, 167–73, 178–87, 211, 233

Saxon Mills (Spartanburg), 46–47, 161–62, 256 (n. 24)
Scientific management, 45–46
Section 7(a). See National Industrial Recovery Act
Self, James C., 54
Senators: power of, 70–71, 131, 139–40, 165, 184–85, 238
Seneca, S.C., 40, 110
Sexual harassment: in mills, 23, 114, 178
Simkins, Francis Butler, 81, 298 (n. 61)
Sit-down strikes, 198–99, 211, 217; in Flint, Mich., 197–98; opposition to, 213–14, 300 (n. 92). See also Byrnes, James F.; Congress of Industrial Organizations
6-0-1 law, 73, 76
Skilled workers, 197; and Great Depression, 64–65; opposition to Johnston in 1938, 203, 215–16; as middle class, 216
Slavery, 15, 21, 28; language of, 8, 9, 47–49, 51, 83, 87, 90, 92, 111–12, 132, 182, 186, 201, 257 (n. 42); before stretchout, 23
Sloan, George, 111
Smith, Ellison ("Cotton Ed"), 9, 189, 190, 227, 228, 229, 231, 238; in 1938 election, 189–90, 203–18, 244, 299 (n. 76); background, 190–92; appeal to rural people, 191–93, 214–15; opposition to New Deal, 192–200, 203–4, 209–10, 218; performance at 1936 Democratic National Convention, 195–96, 204–5, 211; and FLSA, 196–97; AFL support for, 198, 209
Smith v. Allwright (1944), 223–24, 227, 228; and actions of South Carolina General Assembly, 231–32
Soldiers Vote Bill, 223, 224, 227
South Carolina Constitution (1895), 4, 5, 16–17, 22, 69, 157, 169
South Carolina Council on Human Relations, 229
South Carolina Department of Agriculture, 57, 144
South Carolina Federation of Labor (SCFL), 141, 147, 149, 215; opposition to Blease, 56

South Carolina Federation of Textile
Workers (SCFTW), 110, 137, 139, 146
South Carolina General Assembly, 77, 143,
199, 231; getting legislation through, 69,
141–42; during Reconstruction, 80–81
South Carolina Highway Department,
131, 167, 169, 178–87
South Carolina Supreme Court, 178, 186,
228
Southern Conference for Human Welfare,
229, 230
Southern exceptionalism: considered,
101–4
Southern Regional Council, 229, 230
Southern Tenant Farmers Union (STFU),
72
Southern Textile Bulletin, 50, 125
Spartanburg, S.C., 2, 15, 51, 53, 57, 87, 93,
132, 145, 152, 158, 170, 181, 183, 199,
211, 222, 225, 237; stretchout in local
mills, 46–47; working-class politics in,
66–68, 134, 149, 181, 182; stretchout
investigation in, 86; NRA celebration
in, 87; flying squadron in, 113; General
Textile Strike in, 114; 1936 elections in,
182; African Americans organizing in,
222
The State, 142, 210
Stock market crash, 61, 214
Stono Slave Rebellion, 109
Stretchout, 8, 47–49, 50–53, 64–65,
68–69, 90–91, 139, 154, 159, 217, 257
(n. 40); in weave room, 46–47; as cause
of 1929 strikes, 50; cited by workers as
cause of Great Depression, 64–65; in
spinning room, 91–92. *See also* Labor
legislation; Slavery: language of
Strikebreaking, 49–50, 98, 103–7, 108,
115–16, 119, 121, 151, 161–63, 165, 260
(n. 78), 272 (n. 58); race and, 101–2. *See
also* Rural people: in mills; Rural people:
as strikebreakers
Strike-related violence, 98–99, 115–17,
162–63
Strikes, 109, 110, 151, 154; in 1929, 8,
50–56; political implications of, 8,
55–56, 64; in 1919, 42–43, 45, 256
(n. 21); in fall of 1933, 96–97; in Alabama (1934), 110. *See also* Clinton, S.C.;

General Textile Strike; Horse Creek
Valley, S.C.; Pelzer, S.C.; Sit-down
strikes; Tucapau, S.C.
Stump, the, 26–27, 126, 130, 191–92, 253
(n. 58)

Taft-Hartley Act (1947), 233
Talmadge, Eugene, 135, 298 (n. 67)
Taxes, 74–78, 130, 237
Tennessee Valley Authority (TVA), 193,
204
Textile code, 86, 88, 99; Section 15 of, 86,
92, 99; workers' view of, 86–88, 92–94,
95, 97, 113–14; celebrations to mark
enactment of, 87, 108; mill owners'
view of, 90–91, 94, 95; enforcement of,
95–96, 107–8
Textile Labor Relations Board, 154, 156,
158, 163
Textile Workers Organizing Committee
(TWOC), 199–200, 202–3, 214, 215–16
Thompson, Will. *See* Caldwell, Erskine
Thurmond, J. Strom, 232, 239
Tillman, Benjamin ("Pitchfork Ben"), 17,
136, 180–81, 205, 206, 231
Time, 9, 189
Truman, Harry T., 232, 233
Tucapau, S.C., 40, 152; 1935 strike in,
155–58, 165
Tugwell, Rexford, 194, 201, 213

[Una] News Review, 217
Unbalanced growth, 15–16, 130–31
Unemployment, 60–61, 65, 66, 217. *See
also* Labor supply
Union, S.C.; 38–39, 40, 44, 104; 1929
strikes in, 53, 56; General Textile Strike
in, 114, 277 (n. 51); support for John-
ston, 134
Union Daily Times, 202
Unions, 7–8, 166, 217; organizing in
South Carolina, 26, 97; 1929–34, 53–55;
in South, 101; after General Textile
Strike, 152–53, 164; and TWOC,
202–3. *See also* American Federation
of Labor; Congress of Industrial Orga-
nizations; Textile Workers Organizing
Committee; United Textile Workers of
America

United Automobile Workers of America
(UAW), 197, 198
United Textile Workers of America
(UTW), 51–54, 86, 93–94, 135, 146,
147, 173, 182, 199; and General Textile
Strike, 109–22, 124; August 1934 con-
vention of, 110; after General Textile
Strike, 151–66
University of South Carolina, 197, 198,
216
Upcountry vs. low-country tensions,
15–16, 131–32; voting differences
between, 212, 243–44

Wages, 19, 23, 42–43, 45, 47, 62–63,
109–10, 199, 202, 217, 234, 239, 245;
and patriarchy, 22, 23–24, 43–44, 62–63,
66; under textile code, 86, 91–92, 94–95,
96; and regional differences, 86, 212
Wagner Act, 155, 159, 198, 287 (n. 32)
Walhalla, S.C., 24
Wallace, David Duncan, 178
Wallace, George, 239
Wallace, Henry, 193
Wannamaker, L. C., 183
Ware Shoals, S.C., 53, 59, 141, 151, 165;
1929 strike in, 52, 54–55, 59; 1934 strike
in, 109
Waring, J. Waties, 232
Warrenville, S.C., 97
Welfare capitalism, 42, 45, 159
White, Walter, 195, 210
Whiteness: workers' commitment to, 1, 7,
32–33, 51, 60–61, 83, 101, 174, 178,
235–36, 237–38
Whitmire, S.C., 53

Willis Board, 100
Winant, John G., 120
Winant Board, 120, 154
Wofford College, 145, 174, 176–78, 191
Woman suffrage, 25–26
Women, 24, 43–44, 73; in mills, 15, 23–24,
94; in rural households, 22; and rape/
Reconstruction myth, 32, 81, 195, 211;
during Great Depression, 60, 66, 263
(n. 38); as targets of attack during Great
Depression, 66; and voting, 67, 182, 242,
292 (n. 51); and textile code, 73, 87; support for textile code, 87, 114; as spinners, 91–92; as strikers, 113–14, 125
Woodruff, S.C., 53
Woodward, C. Vann, 6
Work Assignment Board, 156
Workers' compensation, 66, 67, 141–50,
171, 233–34; labor's support for, 141;
and lawyers, 141–42, 283 (n. 36); mill
owner's position on, 141–42, 145; labor's
opposition to, 143
Workmen's Compensation Act (1935), 139,
144–50, 158, 284 (n. 47); workers' support for, 145–46; opposition to, 145–46,
147–49; amendments to, 148–49; political implications of, 149–50. See also
Industrial Commission
Works Progress Administration (WPA),
152, 206
World War I, 40–41, 48, 60, 73, 140, 142,
193
World War II, 219, 234, 237

York, S.C.: General Textile Strike in, 114;
support for Johnston in, 134